Psyched Up

The Deep Knowledge that Liberates the Self

Peter Michaelson

© 2017 Peter Michaelson

Also by the Author

Why We Suffer: A Western Way to Understand and Let Go of Unhappiness

Democracy's Little Self-Help Book

The Phantom of the Psyche: Freeing Ourself from Inner Passivity

Freedom from Self-Sabotage: How to Stop Being Our Own Worst Enemy

See Your Way to Self-Esteem: Healing Your Psyche through Depth Psychology

Secret Attachments: Exposing the Roots of Addictions and Compulsions

Books by Sandra Michaelson

The Emotional Catering Service: The Quest for Emotional Independence

Is Anyone Listening: Repairing Broken Lines in Couples Communication

LoveSmart: Transforming the Emotional Patterns that Sabotage Relationships

These paperback and e-books are available at **WhyWeSuffer.com**

Contents

Introduction 8

I – ASPECTS OF DEPTH PSYCHOLOGY 15

    1 . Why Our Emotional Suffering Persists
    2 . Mark Twain's Mysterious Misery-Machine
    3 . Free Yourself from Inner Conflict
    4 . Get to Know Your Psychological Defenses
    5 . Lost in the Fog of Inner Passivity
    6 . Finding Inner Longitude
    7 . A Chaos Theory of the Mind
    8 . Chasing the Shadow

II – FURTHER REACHES OF THE PSYCHE 57

    9 . Escaping the Clutches of Helplessness
    10 . The Addiction behind the Video Games Addiction
    11 . Why We're Quick to "Go Negative"
    12 . The Bittersweet Allure of Feeling Unloved
    13 . Cognitive Therapy's Distorted Thinking
    14 . Three Great Truths from Psychology

III – A VARIETY OF PAINFUL SYMPTOMS 89

    15 . How Worriers Unconsciously Chose to Suffer
    16 . Indecisive No More
    17 . A New Understanding of Bipolar Disorder
    18 . The Futility of Compulsive Approval-Seeking
    19 . The Human Weakness behind Alcoholism
    20 . The Mysterious Allure of Kinky Sex
    21 . A Hidden Reason for Suicidal Thoughts
    22 . Oh Shame, Where is Thy Secret Source?

23. Cultivating a Live of Disappointment
24. Cynicism, the Battle Cry of the Wimp
25. Overcoming Incompetence and Its Miseries
26. When Sexual Desire Covers Up Self-Sabotage
27. Four Favorite Ways to Suffer
28. Get Rid of Guilt with Deeper Insight
29. Understanding Anorexia
30. Hooked on Deprivation
31. The Missing Link in OCD
32. Wallowing in the Lap of Bitterness
33. When You Feel Bad About Yourself
34. Desperately Seeking Validation
35. The Origins of Feeling Overwhelmed
36. Stubbornness: The Guts to Fight Reality
37. The Dire Determinants of Divorce
38. Nagging: Love Destroyer, Marriage Killer
39. The Temptations of the Injustice Collector
40. Deeper Issues that Produce Meanness
41. Panic Attacks Arise from Within Our Psyche
42. The Hidden Cause of Clinical Depression
43. How Inner Fear Becomes Our Worst Nightmare
44. The Dreary Distress of Boredom
45. Problem Gamblers Are Addicted to Losing
46. A Common Ingredient in Human Misery

IV – MORE EXAMPLES OF INSIGHT 243

47. Obesity and the Dopamine Fallacy
48. The Pain We Lock Away
49. The Private Joke behind Our Laughter
50. Why We Fear and Hate the Truth
51. Underlying Dynamics that Breed Bullies
52. The Three Amigos of Woe
53. The Problem with Positive Psychology
54. A Question of Forgiveness
55. Oh, Sweet Narcissism

56. Overcoming Fear of Intimacy
57. Vital Knowledge for Marriage Intimacy
58. When Money Enriches Our Suffering
59. Being Seen in a Negative Light

V – THE PSYCHE'S INFLUENCES ON SOCIETY . . 306

60. How Inner Passivity Robs Men of Power
61. The Psychological Roots of National Disunity
62. Stressed Out in America
63. Lincoln's Integrity, Our Integrity
64. A Participant in National Self-Sabotage
65. A Singular Cause of War
66. The Overlooked Factor in Criminal Behavior
67. Terrorism and the Death Drive
68. The Secret Allures of Pornography
69. Rebutting 9/11 Conspiracy Beliefs
70. Curbing Our Appetite for Brutality
71. The Psychology behind Mass Shootings
72. The Double Barrels of Gun Mania
73. Men's Resistance to Women's Empowerment
74. Aspects of Women's Empowerment
75. Why We Dither on Climate Change
76. Eight Ways We Sabotage Physical Health

VI – STRUGGLES, PROCEDURES & TECHNIQUES . 388

77. Overcoming a Type of Resistance to Studying
78. The Futile Dialogue in Our Head
79. Exterminate Infestations of Negative Thoughts
80. Four Steps to Stifle Our Inner Critic
81. Ease Tension and Stress at Family Gatherings
82. Deliverance from Low-Level Anxiety
83. Hidden Dynamics of Marital Strife

84 . When Eyes Are Blinders of the Soul
85 . Avoidable Miseries of the Workplace
86 . Taming the "Little Monsters" of Insomnia
87 . Deliverance from the Lonesome Blues
88 . The Helplessness Trap in Cravings and Addictions
89 . Prose to Shatter Writer's Block
90 . Stop Smoking through Psychological Insight
91 . A Remedy for Feeling Trapped
92 . Stung by Ingratitude
93 . Does Inner Growth Require Practical Steps?
94 . How to Be Your Own Inner Guide

VII – REFLECTIONS ON CONSCIOUSNESS . . . 479

95 . Achieving Inner Freedom
96 . The Golden Rule Needs Depth Psychology
97 . The Need to Believe in Yourself
98 . Enjoy the Quality of Your Consciousness
99 . Teach Your Children Well
100 . Our Global Strategy for Self-Defeat
101 . Welcome Aboard the Voyage of Self-Discovery

EPILOGUE 513

102 . The Love Song of the Self

Introduction

I have always admired investigative journalists. They dig into the underbelly of political and economic life to dredge up the truth about human affairs. They often uncover gruesome facts about the shady side of human nature.

People and democracy benefit when revelations about wrong-doing are uncovered and put on public display. Truth sets us free because it exposes what's good and what's evil, what benefits us and what hurts us, as we navigate individually and collectively along life's rocky roads.

I was a journalist, though not an investigative one, in my previous career which spanned the years from 1966 to 1984. In my present station as a psychotherapist, author, and blogger, I like to think I operate according to the principles of investigative journalism. I dig up important facts about the shady side of human nature, namely the repressed content of the unconscious mind. I expose humanity's deepest secrets, the ones we keep from ourselves. This knowledge of the dynamics of our inner life empowers our intelligence, frees us from suffering, and raises our consciousness. My "exposés" reveal the extent to which, in our daily affairs, we can be so unwise and self-defeating. As the knowledge is assimilated over time, it sets us free from malaise and misery.

Society's dirty little secrets are very much like the hidden operations and repressed content of the psyche.

In fact, our political, economic, and social life is a creation of both our conscious and unconscious minds. We can clearly see the conscious, mental genius in our marvelous creations and undertakings. For the most part, though, we fail to see, or are reluctant to consider, just exactly how our emotional, unconscious side produces self-defeat and threatens our collective wellbeing and survival. The conflicts and dysfunction that plague the daily life of humanity correlate directly with the inner conflict in our psyche that, in large measure, we have failed to expose and understand. We've got a lot of unfinished business in the realms of inner space.

Our inner world can operate as a closed system, like a sealed-off backward country where civility, rationality, and legal protocols are in short supply. Primitive dynamics rule in our psyche. We can, however, learn the characteristics and features of this inner operating system so as not to be defeated by it.

What is it we're not accessing from these inner realms? In this book, I offer hundreds of valuable insights into our subterranean shenanigans. This writing—my journalistic "scoops"—reveals the shady dealings conducted out of public sight in the backwaters of our mind. I've gleaned this insight about unconscious dynamics and conflicts from my practice as a psychotherapist, from my own inner work, and from the best knowledge produced by classical psychoanalysis. While my interpretations are rooted in classical psychoanalysis, I'm not bound to it. I weave into the discussion many comments on how our authentic self emerges from inner depths, as well as my reflections on personal, social, and cultural matters.

Throughout this book, I take critical looks at mainstream psychology. My comments are intended entirely for constructive purposes. I'm trying to clearly distinguish the methods and solutions of mainstream psychology from what the best of depth psychology has to offer. There's a vast chasm between these two alternatives. I believe that mainstream psychology is offering us, by way of mental-health nutrition, only bland, highly processed, fast food. My readers, in contrast, dine on the organic roots of deep self-knowledge. My food might be too rich for some people. But I want you to understand the choices and to judge for yourself how to proceed as, in reading this, you are introduced to a fascinating new dimension of human nature.

The major ways in which we experience emotional pain are all discussed in these pages. This material explores the unconscious processes by which we produce shame, guilt, anger, depression, loneliness, addiction, conflict, cynicism, worry, anxiety, greed, envy, rejection, fear, failure, passivity, and egotism. Also included in this book are insights into bipolar disorder, obsessive-compulsive disorder, obesity, anorexia, gender issues, racism, suicide, boredom, procrastination, narcissism, insomnia, criminal behavior, and the causes of corruption, violence, and war.

These 102 short articles were originally published on my website, WhyWeSuffer.com, between 2011 and 2014. Some of them make reference to events that were current at the time. In this book, the topics are now organized around seven main categories, and they are all woven around a central theme. This theme addresses the role we play—unconsciously—in producing our suffering and self-defeat. From topic to topic, I often discuss the same principles. This repetition is required to illustrate how it is that the same recurring dynamics in our psyche are able to produce so many varied symptoms and so many different forms of suffering and self-defeat. The repetition is also required because we have significant resistance to assimilating inner truth. The knowledge has to penetrate our thick skulls. I have tried to minimize the repetition so it doesn't feel like I'm pounding nails into your head.

Our psyche has, paradoxically, a wondrous unity and a magnificent chaos. In this inner world, we find the knowledge most worth attending to. I shine a laser beam on an area of inner turbulence—involving conflicts, defenses, and attachments—that generates much of our behavioral and emotional dysfunction. This knowledge gives us the strength and the insight to break free from the clutch of negative emotions.

In this book, you'll learn why it's so hard to shake off painful emotions, even when they're obviously hurting you and holding you back. Readers will acquire insight into how we all tend to remain identified with old hurts and grievances we experienced in childhood. We learn how, in significant measure, we "know" ourselves (we identify with our self) through both inner conflict and its symptoms. As we begin to understand how we gravitate to painful default positions in our psyche, we're able to break free of these old ways of "knowing" ourselves.

We experienced many of these distressful emotions in childhood, even if we had kind and decent parents. I explain in this book precisely how these negative emotions arise within us. These emotions can remain unresolved, largely because we aren't seeing the dynamics that hold them in place or the great extent to which we identify with them. Unwittingly, we recreate and recycle these familiar, painful feelings through the events and situations of our everyday life.

Our psyche operates according to its own rules of logic and procedure. These mental and emotional dynamics operate irrationally and counter-intuitively. They defy the laws of logic and protocols of common sense. Normally, when we learn something—about math or science, for instance—we acquire the knowledge through a straightforward cognitive process. When it comes to acquiring self-knowledge, though, the process is quite different. Now we're required to understand something that, cognitively speaking, defies common sense. For instance, while it does make sense that we want to be happy, we actually, on an inner level, chose to recycle negative emotions, unresolved from childhood, that maintain a state of unhappiness. These include feeling deprived or refused—or helpless, criticized, rejected, betrayed, or abandoned. Because this mysterious impulse to embrace negativity is so contrary to common sense, human intelligence has failed to fathom the paradoxes of unconscious dynamics that govern both our inner world and our experiences of daily life.

I use the term *emotional attachments* to explain this psychological predicament. An emotional attachment can be understood as an unconscious compulsion to continue to experience a particular negative emotion. Behind these attachments is our unconscious willingness, even determination, to hold on to unresolved negative emotions and go looking for ways to relive them. While consciously we very much dislike being unhappy or miserable, *unconsciously* we can be willing and determined to experience the unresolved negative emotions that produce unhappiness. Vast numbers of people have these emotional attachments.

The problem, as mentioned, goes largely untreated because it's not well understood.

Emotional attachments constitute a form of inner conflict. We say we want love, for instance, at the same time that we can be attached to rejection or abandonment. It's important to see the inner conflict clearly, and this book makes that possible. If we're attached to rejection, we understand that we do indeed, at a conscious level, want to experience love in our life, while, unconsciously, we're also prepared to recycle and replay experiences of rejection or abandonment. Often when I'm writing about emotional attachments, I'm simultaneously writing about inner conflict. Our attachment to unresolved negative emotions produces the inner conflict.

In one common conflict, we desire consciously to feel strong, at the same time that we gravitate to a default position within us through which we experience ourselves as weak, helpless, and lacking in resolve. There is, simultaneously, a wish to be strong and a willingness to be weak. This affinity for inner weakness, which I call *inner passivity*, is the result of our lingering identification with (or emotional attachment to) the helplessness of childhood. Inner passivity produces a hit-and-miss struggle to establish a sense of our own authority, and it sabotages our behavioral and emotional regulation. This inner glitch, which I track throughout this book, is a hurdle in the process of our evolvement. It is an instigator of numerous painful symptoms, and it impinges to some degree on the health and happiness of just about everyone.

This book also discusses other deep aspects of our thoughts, feelings, and beliefs. We enhance our mental clarity through self-knowledge. The quality of our thinking and intelligence is enhanced by the success we have in resolving inner conflict. The quality of our consciousness is also explored. Our growing consciousness is conjoined with our emerging self. All this inner work is the nutrition that grows our authentic self. This self, which I discuss in more detail later in the book, emerges as we're in the process of letting go of conscious and unconscious negativity. The self is the essence of each of us. Its emergence gives meaning to our existence.

Our evolving self enhances our ability to monitor and regulate our emotional life. As we grow, we also acquire more self-regulation of thoughts, and we free up for creative purposes the energy that once we used for resistance and denial. Above all, this book reveals a new language of self-understanding. Jargon-free, it makes liberating insight available to all. It helps us to be really smart about what's vitally important to know.

I - ASPECTS OF DEPTH PSYCHOLOGY

1. Why Our Emotional Suffering Persists

Were we born to suffer? William Wordsworth seemed to think so when he wrote: "Suffering is permanent, obscure and dark. And shares the nature of infinity."

Much *physical* suffering has been alleviated by modern medicine, of course. But I'm not so sure that *emotional* suffering is on the wane. I believe we need brighter flares to illuminate those "obscure and dark" recesses of our psyche. Yet our resistance to facing deeper truth pushes the best knowledge to the outskirts of the mind, there to flicker on the periphery of our awareness.

The first principle of this knowledge recognizes that our misery and misfortune are produced from within. We have a tendency to be our own worst enemies, even as we strive to be kind and good. In this book, we begin to see more clearly how our chronic upset, nagging self-doubt, and persistent complaints are symptoms of unresolved negative emotions that we're unwittingly generating from within. This dysfunction is no fault of ours. It's simply the character of human nature. This is where we find ourselves on the spectrum of evolution. We're struggling to become smarter and wiser. In that respect, we can acquire vital self-knowledge that empowers our intelligence and liberates us from emotional and behavioral problems.

Growing awareness of our self-defeating tendencies produces an understanding that a deep negativity—

consisting of an assortment of unresolved emotions—lurks in our psyche. These unresolved emotions have a life of their own. They exist, and therefore they will be felt. They are even *determined* to be felt; in this sense, they can be understood as emotional attachments. We can be burdened by these attachments, even when, much of the time, we remain optimistic, clever, and resourceful.

Deep in our psyche we harbor the unfinished business of humanity, namely our tendency to get "triggered" by life's daily challenges and to stumble back into unresolved negative emotions. These negative emotions—the leftovers of childhood—simmer and stew in our psyche. They include feelings associated with deprivation, loss, helplessness, control, domination, criticism, betrayal, and abandonment.

Usually we're unaware of our tendency to jump unwittingly into these painful emotions. And we don't necessarily experience these underlying emotions directly. Instead, we start to feel the consequences (symptoms) of this self-defeating tendency. These symptoms include anger, depression, hatred, greed, withdrawal, cynicism, envy, jealousy, loneliness, apathy, and a judgmental attitude. Accompanying these emotional symptoms are *behavioral* symptoms such as addictions, compulsions, and other acts of self-defeat or self-sabotage.

Typically, people try to address the painful symptoms without recognizing the source. The true source remains unconscious for most people. Without conscious access to that source, we might not be able to put an end to (or even modify) the suffering and self-defeat.

As a next step, we become aware that we're used to our suffering. It defines us, and we don't know who we are without it. We come to the realization that we're emotionally attached to our suffering. What does it mean to be *attached* in this way? This attachment is the consequence of the fact that, when we remain unaware of deeper dynamics, we have no choice but to experience in a painful way whatever is unresolved in our psyche. As mentioned, these unresolved negative emotions are *determined* to be experienced, and our challenge is to liberate ourselves from them. Through our intelligence, we can break free of them when we expose the dynamics in our psyche that hold the attachments in place.

What are examples of unresolved negative emotions to which we are attached? We want love but, at some deeper level, we're attached to rejection. We want to feel strong, but we are identified with ourselves through weakness. We want to get rewards and benefits from life, but unconsciously we're expecting to be refused or deprived. We're *compelled* to continue experiencing in a painful way, often on a daily basis, the symptoms that arise from these unresolved conflicts.

Here are three more examples to help us understand emotional attachments and their accompanying inner conflicts: 1) Even as we greatly dislike feeling helpless, we're accustomed to the feeling, entangled in it, and compelled to recycle it; 2) we dislike feeling criticized, even as we expect criticism and compulsively behave in ways that make criticism more likely to happen; 3) we don't like feeling lonely, even as we use our loneliness to recycle a sense of being unworthy and abandoned.

Most of us are considerably under the influence of two oppositional positions in our psyche. On one side of this conflict is *inner passivity*. This is an inherent weakness of our psyche that's positioned in what is sometimes called the subordinate ego. Much of our self-doubt, fearfulness, and confusion are experienced through this part of our psyche. The other side of the conflict is experienced by us as *inner aggression*, and this aggression emanates from our inner critic or superego. Inner aggression is a negative drive or energy that comes at us with considerable force and even cruelty. I usually refer to this negative drive simply as the inner critic. We tend to process this harsh energy through our inner passivity, meaning that we process it through inner defensiveness and weakness, which in turn means that we absorb much of the negativity from our inner critic.

Through this inner conflict, we experience aggression in one moment and passivity in the next. Most of us teeter back-and-forth, identifying with the emotional perspective of one or the other of these two polarities. Hence, we're unable to establish wise inner authority. We're not establishing an authentic self through which inner wisdom and the pleasure principle are more readily accessed.

Our consciousness does not see the source of our suffering, our attachment to the variations of deep negativity (again, these variations include emotions associated with deprivation, loss, helplessness, control, domination, criticism, betrayal, and abandonment.) All we usually see are our symptoms or reactions to deep negativity (again, these symptoms include anger, depression, hatred, greed, withdrawal, cynicism, envy, jealousy, loneliness, apathy, and a judgmental attitude.)

We give all the headlines to the symptoms, and we fail to see the root cause of our suffering (emotional attachments) in the small print at the bottom of the page.

We practice self-deception through our psychological defense system. This system is designed to protect our *ego*, the operating system (now outdated software) of our mind. We protect our ego out of unconscious fear: "I will disappear into thin air, or not be who I think I am, if I let go of my ego." Meanwhile, people cover up their emotional attachments to unresolved negative emotions (which can be understood as "deep negativity") by using the symptoms as psychological defenses.

For example, consider the plight of Harry, a fellow who's feeling criticized by his boss. Harry is feeling quite angry at his boss for apparently being critical of him. Harry, however, is easily triggered by criticism, and he often feels angry at his wife when he perceives her to be critical. Harry's anger is a symptom of his emotional attachment to criticism, yet his anger also serves as a defense. Through the defense, Harry makes this (unconscious) claim: "I'm not attached to feeling criticized. Look at how angry I get when so-and-so criticizes me. That proves I don't secretly want to feel criticized." This defense covers up the fact that, through his attachment to what is psychologically unresolved (in this case, criticism), Harry is indeed interested in revisiting the old familiar pain of feeling criticized. Harry displays, through his use of anger as a defense, the tendency we all have to adamantly deny such inner truth.

We use defenses such as anger, blame, jealousy, and feelings of superiority to cover our tracks. When we blame others, we're making them responsible for our suffering and covering up how we produce the misery we feel. Sometimes, as when we're depressed or apathetic, we blame ourselves, though invariably for incorrect reasons that are themselves defenses.

While many people are overwhelmed by their suffering, many others do manage to keep it in check. For those of us who are doing reasonably well in life, smaller deposits of negative emotions can still degrade the quality of our relationships, work, and self-esteem. If we don't uncover them, we're the poorer for it. We'll likely be less intelligent and more prone eventually to stumble into some form of self-defeat. Our lack of self-knowledge produces a dearth of brain power, a gap in our intelligence, which is a major detriment in a highly complex, challenging world.

Through this learning process, we connect with ourselves at a deeper level. We feel our goodness and value ourselves more fully as we expose and then cast out deep negativity. As we make it a daily practice to review and assimilate this knowledge, we liberate the amazing self within us.

2 . **Mark Twain's Mysterious Misery-Machine**

We all like to think we're motivated by self-interest, self-protection, and self-love. Consciously, we may be. Unconsciously, though, we operate a misery-machine inside us that churns up self-defeat, self-damage, and self-rejection.

A reference to a misery-machine is made by Satan, the character in Mark Twain's final novel, *The Mysterious Stranger*. The reference is found in this passage from the book:

> Every man is a suffering-machine and a happiness-machine combined. The two functions work together harmoniously, with a fine and delicate precision, on the give-and-take principle. For every happiness turned out in the one department the other stands ready to modify it with a sorrow or a pain—maybe a dozen. In most cases the man's life is about equally divided between happiness and unhappiness. When this is not the case, the unhappiness predominates—almost never the other. Sometimes a man's make and disposition are such that his misery-machine is able to do nearly all the business. Such a man goes through life almost ignorant of what happiness is.[1]

This short novel, while nihilistic and grim in places, presents many insights into human nature. Twain's savvy on matters of human conduct and motivation is consistent, of course, with his greatness as a writer. He addresses the idea that the truth about human nature is not as pleasant as we would like. That in itself is not a popular notion, which might account, in part, for why the novel is one of his readers' least favorites.

So what is this misery-machine of which he writes? Twain presents only the machine's finished products—ignorance, self-serving hypocrisy, violence, despair,

---

[1] Twain, Mark. *The Mysterious Stranger and Other Stories*. New York: Harper and Row. 77-78.

stupidity, malice, anger, vanity. He didn't get to the nuts and bolts of the machine itself, which in his time the emerging science of psychoanalysis was beginning to do.

Machines create inner friction. The equivalent process in the human psyche is *inner conflict*. This is the inner struggle among competing or incompatible needs, drives, wishes, or demands. There are thousands of examples of inner conflict. It can occur, for instance, in the experience of ambivalence when children both love and reject their mother at the same time. Conflict also occurs when, say, an envious person consciously desires some object, while unconsciously being emotionally attached to the painful, unresolved feeling of being deprived of that object.

In another example, a person wants desperately to be recognized and appreciated, at the same time that he or she keeps returning unconsciously to an old unresolved feeling of being unappreciated and seen as unworthy.

In this example, the misery-machine kicks into high gear when it produces a defense that covers up the individual's temptation to go on feeling unappreciated. That defense might be anger. "Can't you see how angry I am at (whoever) for belittling me! That proves I'm not secretly willing to indulge in feeling unappreciated and ignored." The angrier someone becomes, the more likely the anger is covering up the person's unconscious determination to indulge in an old unresolved hurt that has become an emotional attachment.

In still another example, a person who is failing in his career desperately wants to succeed. Deeper down, however, he can be attached to the painful self-recrimination that comes at him from his inner critic (superego), assailing him for being a loser. He can also be attached to unresolved feelings of being helpless and overwhelmed, because those feelings are a significant part of his identity.

We can turn off our misery-machine when we begin to see clearly (1) how we are unwittingly tempted to recycle and replay unresolved negative emotions from our past, (2) how we use various defenses to cover up our participation in our suffering, and (3) how resistant we are to assimilating this knowledge.

This knowledge enables us to see *correctly* just how our misery-machine works. To acquire accurate self-knowledge, we often have to penetrate into the dark side of our psyche. Let's consider, as another example, a student who eagerly heads off for his freshman year at university. In high school, his scholastic achievement brought him much pleasure. At university, he anticipates the pleasure of learning new knowledge and testing his intellect at a higher level. For the first few months he does well. But then, unexpectedly, he starts to procrastinate on his reading and writing assignments. Soon he's dreading each new day as he falls further behind with his studies. If he had done the work and kept up, he would likely be feeling great. Instead, he's in agony because of his procrastination. His misery-machine is running at full throttle.

What possible self-knowledge applies to his situation? His procrastination may be a symptom of a deeper emotional issue, his unrecognized affinity for the feeling of helplessness. In other words, feeling helpless and overwhelmed—a common infantile impression—can be such a familiar feeling that we don't know how to step outside of it and *stay* outside of it. We do, in fact, free ourselves from this attachment to helplessness when we begin to see it more objectively as, in the clinical sense, an anomaly in our psyche.

Another example involves a student who also is starting university. Though she's always been a bit shy, she's been quite able to enjoy life. But at university she becomes highly anxious, distressed mostly about her disappointing social life. Her misery-machine, too, is revving up for spell of suffering. What self-knowledge applies to her situation? The challenge of university may have triggered an issue that was latent within her psyche, her repressed sense that she is somehow unworthy and lacking in value. She becomes socially inept as that old issue surfaces, producing a painful impression of being unworthy in the eyes of faculty and fellow students. Deepening awareness reveals her emotional attachment to that old feeling. This awareness helps her to step out of her painful emotional conviction that unworthiness represents some actual truth about her. In other words, she can feel better about herself, and likely manage her social life more skillfully, when she penetrates her psyche to expose her emotional attachment to that painful old repressed sense of being unworthy and lacking in value. She's able to take ownership of the fact that, deep down, she's choosing to gravitate to that painful old sense of herself. She sees that she goes in for "a hit" on that feeling. She acknowledge her attachment to the feeling. This insight constitutes self-knowledge, and it produces freedom from the attachment and from painful symptoms as it's assimilated and processed over time.

We can get our misery-machine to rust away by splashing it every day with the cold, clear water of self-knowledge.

3 . **Free Yourself from Inner Conflict**

This is a good time to say more about inner conflict. Such conflict is a private war within oneself. People tend to think of conflict, however, in a superficial way. It's typically perceived as the difficulty we often encounter when making a decision. According to conventional thinking, that decision can range from choosing a style of shoes to more serious considerations such as a career move to another city or the compromise of one's integrity over an ethical issue.

But these examples illustrate only *conscious* inner conflict. Much more significant are the *unconscious* varieties. These deeper conflicts form the roots of our suffering. When we expose the roots, we can resolve the conflict and end the suffering.

One way to expose the roots is get a shovel and start digging. Here we penetrate the ground beneath eight common emotional experiences: *1 – loneliness; 2 – envy; 3 – depression; 4 – greed; 5 – guilt; 6 – sadness; 7 – boredom; and 8 – indecision.* I'm talking here about chronic conditions, meaning, as in this first example, not occasional loneliness but chronic loneliness. My intention is to show how inner conflict is involved in each of these experiences. I'm trying to expose this deeper conflict because it may be the most important single feature in our understanding of depth psychology.

1—*Loneliness,* when chronic, is the result of wanting to be in the friendly or loving company of others *at the same time* that the person is prepared, unconsciously, to experience old unresolved feelings such as separation, rejection, abandonment, or unworthiness. Put succinctly, the conflict is between wanting love yet expecting rejection or abandonment. Typically, the individual is aware of wanting friendly or loving company but is unaware of how prepared or even determined he or she is at that moment to feel unloved and unworthy. As we expose our emotional attachment to feeling unloved or unworthy (a remnant of childhood perceptions and hurt), we become stronger emotionally and capable of moving beyond loneliness. We see that our loneliness is a result of the fact that we're choosing unconsciously to continue to feel rejection, unworthiness, etc. We expose these attachments behind the loneliness, which clears our mind and fortifies our intelligence.

2—Envy comes about when we yearn for something we're usually unlikely to get. We feel a strong desire for a certain object, status, wealth, or person that remains out of reach. We're convinced that we really want what we're yearning for, yet we're also, simultaneously, indulging in the bittersweet feeling of *not having* or *not getting* that alleged benefit. Paradoxically, *we want to get the desired object* and *we want to feel deprived or refused*, all at the same time. The envious person is aware of *wanting* but completely unaware of the appeal of the self-pitying victimhood of *not getting*. This old pain is familiar from the person's past, and it can become a cornerstone of one's identity. Usually envy is dropped when this potent insight is absorbed.

3—Depression feels like getting sucked into a black-hole of daily existence. Here the conflict is between inner aggression, which emanates from the inner critic or superego, and inner passivity, the place in our psyche where self-doubt accumulates (or where consciousness of our goodness and value has not permeated). Our inner critic hammers away at us with all sorts of insinuations, allegations, and outright accusations of our defectiveness and unworthiness. Our inner passivity, on the other side of the conflict, tries to defend us, but it manages to do so mostly with weak and ineffective excuses, denials, and defenses. The more we absorb the inner critic's aggression, the more likely we are to become depressed. As we recognize and resolve this conflict, our true, genuine, or authentic self emerges to become our contact-point with strength, wisdom, and positive emotions. (See "The Hidden Cause of Clinical Depression.")

4—Greed is comparable to envy, and it's also the particularly painful feeling of never being satisfied, never having enough. On the surface, greedy people believe they really do *want* more. But deeper down they're cozying up to the feeling of emptiness or nothingness. That negative association haunts them at their core. They're so disconnected from their essential value that only more and more accumulation of materialistic benefits seems to have any chance of filling the inner void. The inner sense of unworthiness is their default position, and often they compensate with arrogance and narcissism as well as greed. The more desperately they want to accumulate materialistic benefits, the more acute is their impression of lacking within themselves a foundation of goodness, integrity, and value.

5—Guilt is the feeling, arising out of inner conflict, that we have done something bad or wrong. (Guilt is appropriate, of course, if you've cheated on your spouse or betrayed a friend, but most of the suffering associated with guilt arises out of inner conflict.) When our aggressive inner critic accuses us of being flawed or foolish, or of indulging in some unresolved negative emotion, we typically absorb some degree of that aggression. In other words, we "buy into" the accusations coming from our inner critic, which means we take them seriously instead of dismissing them out of hand. It's through our unconscious inner passivity that we allow our inner critic to hold us accountable. Guilt becomes a measure of the degree to which we absorb the inner critic's accusations and aggression and take them to heart instead of being able through inner strength to deflect or neutralize them.

6—*Sadness* can be appropriate much of the time. Yet often it's an inappropriate response to a particular situation. It can also get in the way of being able to offer emotional support or compassion for oneself or others. Chronically sad people can be entangled in self-pity and prone to identify strongly, from a passive victim perspective, with their "plight" and the "plight" of others (often, to deepen the sense of victimhood, the severity of the plight is exaggerated emotionally). Squeezed in the inner conflict between aggression and passivity, they offer themselves up as the defeated underdog. This unconscious strategy attempts to curb the inner critic's bullying through the proposition that you shouldn't kick someone when they're down.

7—*Boredom* is largely a product of a blocked imagination, such that more intense stimulation is required to produce an appetite for life. This can produce hyperactive individuals. The creative blockage is due not to a lack of intelligence, of course, but to inner conflict. A creative imagination uses psychic energy that in turn produces pleasure. But psychic energy can be usurped by the inner critic and turned into a negative force that demeans and belittles the individual, along with his or her creative efforts. Also, the inner critic can oppose "the power" of the creative imagination, and shift the individual over to the passive side. The passive side can also sacrifice pleasure, and adopt various forms of emptiness and suffering, in the hope of deflecting the inner critic's ruthlessness.

8—*Indecision* is sometimes appropriate to particularly challenging situations that call for studied consideration. But often the painful feelings are produced because we have a default position in our psyche that produces an impression of weakness or helplessness (inner passivity). We usually experience this passivity as painful and so we fight against it. But while one part of us hates it, a deeper unconscious part is willing to experience it because, as an unresolved emotion left over from childhood, we still in part identify with ourselves through that weakness and uncertainty.

It's important to understand, as well, that most of the varieties of suffering that arise out of inner conflict are not just symptoms of that conflict but are also employed unconsciously as psychological defenses that block us from awareness of our determination to stay entangled in the conflict. I say more on this in the following discussion.

With unresolved inner conflict, we produce conflict with others. That's why it's so important for each of us to do the inner work that leads to peace and harmony within ourselves and also in our family, community, and country.

4. Get to Know Your Psychological Defenses

We're often the dupes of our defenses. They can render us blind to our emotional life and mislead us about the sources of our suffering. For starters, we don't see that common varieties of suffering are both *symptoms* of mysterious dynamics unfolding in our psyche as well as *defenses* covering up our participation in our suffering.

To understand this, take a look at the following painful experiences and see if you can tell what they have in common:

Anger and rage; sadness, grief, depression; worry, anxiety, guilt, and fear; envy, jealousy, and loneliness; resentment, humiliation, and shame (This is List 1).

These painful experiences are both symptoms and defenses of deeper dynamics in our psyche. Our ability to avoid these unpleasant states is hampered when we fail to understand the deeper processes that instigate these forms of suffering.

What are we defending against? Deeper down, we remain entangled in unresolved negative emotions first experienced in childhood. Through psychological defenses, we cover up our willingness to remain entwined in these painful emotions. They include, as mentioned earlier, the sense of being:

Deprived, refused; helpless, controlled, and dominated; criticized, rejected, and abandoned; unloved, seen as unworthy (This is List 2).

Image yourself as a child and read over again these emotions in List 2. As you do so, you're apt to recognize old (maybe painful) memories associated with them. As adults, these negative emotions can continue to trigger us to the degree that they remain unresolved in our psyche.

In fact, we often make unconscious choices to continue to replay and recycle these painful emotions in List 2. The emotions are still part of our identity. We haven't yet broken free from them. It's as if we know and recognize ourselves through them.

I know, it defies common sense that we would be willing to replay and recycle painful emotions. Who in their right mind would want to suffer like this? But this is how it is. Our emotional side has a logic all its own. It doesn't listen to common sense. This means that our intelligence, rather than relying on common sense, has to become more sophisticated.

When these core emotions (List 2) are triggered by everyday situations, we often suffer more from the symptoms (List 1). Remarkably, the symptoms also serve as psychological defenses. That's right, we use one form of suffering (List 1) as a defense to cover up our deeper suffering (List 2). We're always erecting defenses without even knowing it. Any one of the symptoms listed above can serve as a defense. Take jealousy, for example. The chronically jealous person is likely emotionally attached to feeling rejected, abandoned, or unworthy. His jealousy, when used as a defense, makes this unconscious claim: "I'm not looking for the feeling of rejection (or being abandoned or unworthy). Look at how jealous I am! That proves how much I hate feeling rejected (or abandoned or unworthy)."

All it proves, though, is that this person is being fooled by his defense. Seeing through our defenses is a vitally important step in overcoming the influence of the primary negative emotions (List 2), freeing ourselves from the resulting suffering (List 1), and keeping our evolution on track. More than anything, it's our evolving consciousness that will help each of us and all of humanity safely navigating the world's troubled waters.

Let's look at an example of how our defenses operate. George is angry at his friend Jack. The previous evening Jack had invited him to join a group of friends going to a ball game and said he would pick him up. But Jack never showed up. George is deeply hurt and offended, and he believes his anger at Jack is justified. True, George is entitled to be annoyed, hurt, and even angry. But if he holds on to the anger and allows it to fester, he may be indulging unconsciously in feelings of being rejected and unworthy. At that point, George's real pain (beneath his anger) comes from within his psyche, specifically from his emotional entanglement in feeling rejected and unworthy. He has personalized Jack's behavior and is resonating emotionally with feeling devalued. George now uses his anger at Jack to cover up his readiness to plunge into his own unresolved negative emotions (feeling rejected or seen as unworthy—or even abandoned) from List 2. In his anger, George decides to "unfriend" Jack. Yet he likely would have been wiser to talk to Jack about what happened, with the intention of trying to save the friendship.

A few days later, George is angry at Judy, a coworker. But now George's anger can be traced to a different emotion in List 2. Judy made comments at an office meeting that George interpreted as criticism of him. George is not only attached to feeling devalued (as in his experience with Jack), he's also attached to feeling criticized (as seen in his experience with Judy). He sometimes chooses unconsciously to feel criticized (or devalued) by misinterpreting comments as if criticism (or disrespect) were intended.

George uses his anger as a psychological defense that prevents him from being aware of his unconscious willingness to indulge in the negative emotions that are unresolved in his psyche. In the encounter with Judy, he gets triggered by criticism which is an unresolved hurt (and therefore an attachment or emotional addiction) from his past. Because the hurt is unresolved, George is tempted to feel criticized when opportunities arise for him to adopt or "take on" that emotional interpretation. To protect his ego and self-image, however, he refuses to look deeply enough into himself (or his psyche) to see that he is the one who is choosing unconsciously to feel criticized.

George holds a grudge against Judy and tosses his friend Jack overboard rather than acknowledge how he produces his anger as a cover-up for his willingness to indulge in these negative emotions. (In cases of divorce, husbands and wives are typically tossing each other overboard rather than acknowledging and addressing their own contributions to the disharmony.) So George is using his anger as a defense: "I don't want to feel criticized—Look how angry I get at Judy when she does that to me!" The anger allows him to blame others while covering up his determination to hold on his emotional attachments.

It may appear that George, in getting angry over two days at two different people for two different reasons, is an exceptionally dysfunctional guy. Yet the neurotic behavior he exhibits is no worse than what is acted out by a large percentage of the world's population.

Sometimes people get angry at themselves, and even then they're likely to be using anger as a defense. In another example, Adele is absorbing criticism from her inner critic for making a careless mistake on an important project, and she starts to feel angry at herself. In this process, her unconscious defense claims, "I'm not willing to absorb the negative aggression coming at me from my inner critic for this mistake. Look, I'm mad at myself for getting this wrong. The mistake was very costly. I deserve to be punished for screwing up so badly." Now, the more Adele punishes herself the more she can claim she's not willing to feel criticized but, rather, is deserving of being criticized. Many people do, over time, become clinically depressed because they absorb so much of their inner critic's negative judgments concerning their everyday activities and conduct.

People unwittingly employ thousands of different tricks and defensive maneuvers to cover up their willingness to cozy up to the unresolved negative emotions from List 2. Over time, as we observe ourselves with this understanding, we can break free of these emotional attachments that linger from our past.

5 . Lost in the Fog of Inner Passivity

All of us have in our psyche an aspect or feature that goes by the name of inner passivity. This hindrance to our creativity, self-fulfillment, and humanity may be the most difficult thing for us to see and understand about ourselves. I do talk about it in many contexts throughout this book, as I try to make it as visible as possible.

One of my earlier books, originally published in 2002 (with a 2015 edition), deals with this topic. The title—*The Phantom of the Psyche: Freeing Ourself from Inner Passivity*—attests to the ghostly nature of this inner aspect. In this new book, I try with fresh examples and new wording to bring inner passivity into better focus.

Inner passivity produces a wide range of reactions to situations and events, including the tendency to go through the motions of daily life taking everything for granted and feeling that our options are limited. This negative influence on our state of mind is a huge problem for many of us. It is a deficit of consciousness that can block us from creating a sense of direction for our life and prevent us from achieving fulfillment and happiness.

When inner passivity contaminates our psyche, we can, among other symptoms, feel overwhelmed by events and situations, experience acute self-doubt or become reactive in the face of authority, interpret neutral situations as confrontation or conflict, become easily discouraged, and find that our attempts at logical or rational thinking churn unproductively in loops and circles. We're easily lost in the fog of inner passivity, to the point where we don't even recognize the fog.

Inner passivity is at play in our moods and personality traits. It lurks beneath procrastination, cynicism, apathy, indecision, indifference, hopelessness, and despair. It's a feature of the psyche of codependents, chronic complainers, and pessimists. Paradoxically, optimists do, at times, unconsciously employ their optimism to cover-up their emotional entanglement in inner passivity.

This foggy state of being is an extended coastline shrouding the path of human evolvement. I associate it with, among other things, youngsters addicted to video games, individuals caught in addictive behaviors, people abdicating their citizenship responsibilities, and parents having difficulty practicing wise authority in their supervision and guidance of children. Inner passivity is also associated with our difficulty in feeling pleasure in learning and in our tendency to close our minds and engage in willful ignorance to avoid feeling overwhelmed by reality. We can be significantly impaired by inner passivity, even when we're smart and aggressive enough to be successful in some areas of our life.

Often our dreams reveal our entanglement in inner passivity. People frequently dream of being trapped, constricted, overwhelmed, bullied, or terrorized, or of being unable to perform a task or manage some situation. One client had two such dreams in the same night, one in which he was frustratingly unable to kill a spider that was running around on the floor, and the other in which he was unable to sing a song he had just composed.

People are experiencing themselves in the passive mode when they say, "Oh, I'll get by. I'm a survivor." Sure, you might get by, but that fate expresses the path of least resistance, namely the willingness to endure the pain of shortchanging yourself.

A great deal of modern fiction expresses, through bumbling anti-heroes and weak protagonists, the problem of inner passivity. However, almost never does the writing expose the nature or origins of the condition. Horror stories and movies are pure expressions of this passivity because they present their characters in predicaments of helpless terror. We read these books and go to these movies because, through such fantasy, we can experience a degree of pleasure as we sublimate inner fear into spine-tingling thrills. Mystery or detective books and movies also titillate the reader or viewer with the passive sensations of being overwhelmed by life-or-death predicaments and by the allure of forbidden murder and evil. Our appetite for sensations involving bizarre, forbidden, and violent scenes and images reveals the extent of inner passivity in our psyche.

An article[2] in *The New Yorker* magazine captures the passive nature of the Austrian writer Stefan Zweig, who committed suicide in 1942. The author of the article doesn't directly address Zweig's passivity. Instead, he blames Zweig's "frailties," as he calls them, on the totalitarian culture of the day. He writes—incorrectly, in my view—that Zweig's frailties "emerge as the source of his best work."

2

http://www.newyorker.com/arts/critics/atlarge/2012/08/27/120827crat_atlarge_carey

A passage from one of Zweig's short stories portrays, with literary skill, the painful inner passivity experienced by one of his characters:

> I felt as if I were made of glass, with the world outside shining straight through me and never lingering within, and hard as I attempted on this and many similar occasions to feel something, however much I tried, through reasonable argument, to make myself feel emotion, no response came from my rigid state of mind. People parted from me, women came and went, and I felt much like a man sitting in a room with rain beating on the window panes; there was a kind of sheet of glass between me and my immediate surroundings, and my will was not strong enough to break it.[3]

Zweig expressed, through his characters, his own emotional experience of inner passivity. But he couldn't get beyond a straightforward description of this painful passivity. Writers are limited, of course, by their own range of emotional experiences, and their art is made possible by their mental and emotional resonance with their characters. But the public is shortchanged when writers, unwilling or unable to make any psychological headway in themselves, present characters who fail to acquire insight and achieve growth.

Schools of classical psychoanalysis have different terminology for this problem of the weak self. French psychoanalyst Jacques Lacan raised ideas about the ego as a fortress against inner fragmentation. Melanie Klein, the British psychoanalyst and author, also observed a

---

[3] Ibid.

"disintegrating tendency" in people that produces a chronic state of inner weakness she called the paranoid-schizoid position. The weak ego, as psychologist Stephen Frosh put it, "searches for something rigid to bolster it, to explain the disintegration surrounding it and to oppose that disintegration through absorption in a powerful totality."

That "totality" often turns out, on the political level, to be an authoritarian or totalitarian government that subjugates and tyrannizes its citizens. Political tyranny succeeds when inner passivity enables it. On an inner level, that "totality" is represented by the inner critic, the powerful superego of psychoanalysis, which denies the authority or even the existence of an authentic inner self. Meanwhile, the "disintegration" is facilitated by inner passivity, the weak unconscious ego that serves as a poor stand-in for inner authority and that for many people is their only bulwark against the inner critic. As we escape from our identification with inner passivity, we can establish a legitimate inner authority and wrest power away from the inner critic. At the political level, those of us who are breaking free of inner passivity and becoming anchored in the self are more able to quell any uprisings of the authoritarian or totalitarian mentality.

Inner passivity can be overcome by making conscious its modes of operation in our psyche. The most helpful insight concerning inner passivity is the understanding of our powerful temptation—our unconscious willingness—to experience it repeatedly and to come under its influence in many possible ways in daily life. In fact, we have an emotional attachment to inner passivity. It's a default position in our psyche and a major element in the identity of so many of us.

Here's a practice or technique that addresses our unconscious willingness to experience inner passivity. In this practice, we repeat to ourselves a statement, a kind of mantra that exposes at our deepest core the nature of our entanglement in inner passivity. We can think or say words to this effect, "I'm feeling helpless (or overwhelmed, confused, or defeated) at this moment. This is what I secretly expect and want, to feel this helplessness, as I recycle this unresolved passive feeling from my past. This is how, right now, I'm determined to know myself, through this feeling of being helpless and overwhelmed in the face of . . . (some person, situation, event, or craving)."

The statement defies common sense. Who would want to feel helpless? Our unconscious mind, however, brims with irrationality. As mentioned, it has its own set of rules and procedures, one of which is to remain mired in unresolved negative emotions. Our unconscious mind also prompts us to deny or disprove our inner passivity by reacting to situations with reactive aggression. This phony aggression is usually negative and self-defeating, and I discuss throughout the book many of the ways in which it emerges.

Through the above technique, we can recognize our emotional attachment to inner passivity. We're taking responsibility for our secret willingness to experience life in passive terms. We're plunging consciously into the core of inner weakness, while awakening our intelligence to the psychological dynamics of this limited consciousness and its varieties of self-defeat.

6. Finding Inner Longitude

The marine chronometer invented in the 18th Century made ocean navigation much more precise. The chronometer determined longitude, and it enabled sailors to avoid ramming their ships into unexpected reefs and shorelines.

Emotionally, many millions of us still crash upon life's hard rocks. Often we're not sure why or how it happens, just that we somehow drifted badly off course. Each of us, metaphorically, is captain of a ship that can start to sink when unruly emotions surge against our hull and waves of negativity crash upon our deck.

We have instruments of emotional navigation to keep us afloat and on course. These include the methods, techniques, and knowledge of applied psychology. Unfortunately, experts can't agree on what constitutes the basic axioms, principles, or truth of human nature. Psychological schools of thought clash like factions in a religious war. Scientific studies in psychology and brain research are failing to unlock the mystery[4] of human suffering. Psychologists not only can't discern what's true, they don't even speak the same language.[5] Psychiatrists, as well, have been attacking each other[6] within the profession over what constitutes mental illness.

---

[4] http://www.psychologytoday.com/blog/side-effects/201303/why-dsm-5-concerns-european-psychiatrists
[5] http://www.psychologytoday.com/blog/theory-knowledge/201301/psychologys-tower-babel
[6] http://www.newyorker.com/online/blogs/elements/2013/04/the-dsm-and-the-nature-of-disease.html

A growing number of scientists believe that psychiatry needs an entirely new paradigm for understanding mental and emotional health, though they can't say what that new knowledge and system would look like.

What we require is not necessarily *new* knowledge. Sigmund Freud recognized a vitally important aspect of human nature that has since been overlooked by mainstream psychology. In 1929, when he was 73, he wrote about it in *Civilization and Its Discontents*. (For any readers who are reluctant to take Freud seriously, a cover story[7] in the April, 2014 issue of the science magazine, *Discover*, explains why he's enjoying a resurgence of respect.) Here he describes this aspect as "an unconscious need for punishment." Freud recognized it as nonsexual masochism, and he said that it arises through our unconscious ego as we process the feeling of being harshly judged by our inner critic (superego):

> The fear of this critical agency [superego] . . . the need for punishment, is an instinctual manifestation on the part of the [unconscious] ego, which has become masochistic under the influence of a sadistic super-ego; it is a portion, that is to say, of the instinct toward internal destruction present in the [unconscious] ego, employed for forming an erotic attachment to the super-ego. *(The Freud Reader.* New York: W.W. Norton & Co., 1989, 765).

These words from *Civilization and Its Discontents* may constitute the most significant insight Freud ever produced. Yet any discussion of it has largely gone

[7] http://discovermagazine.com/2014/april/14-the-second-coming-of-sigmund-freud

unheeded in the thousands of books and papers written about psychoanalysis. Freud says in this passage that we absorb the superego's aggression, and then, as our best defense against it, we use libido (the functioning of the pleasure principle) to make the best of a bad situation. We produce a perverse gratification by fusing libido with our passive acceptance of self-aggression. In other words, we defend against the harsh superego by making a third-rate pleasure out of the incoming aggression.

This nonsexual masochism at the heart of human nature is experienced through the clash of inner aggression and inner passivity. The masochistic nature of inner conflict locks people into neurosis, causing us to cling stubbornly to our suffering—experiencing guilt, shame, and inner fear—all the while claiming to be victims of the ignorance and malice of others or the hardships of a "cruel" world. (This conflict, when more severe, can also be a significant feature of mental-health disorders.) Under the influence of this self-defeating aspect, our creative and mental capacities are diminished. It's worth considering, by way of contrast, that love itself can be understood as the "libidinization" of the experience of unity, wholeness, connection, and even reality.

The knowledge of this nonsexual masochism is an instrument by which we can establish inner longitude and navigate our way to the shores of evolved destiny.

This masochistic instinct loiters in the underworld of our psyche, producing a compulsion to turn inner experiences of aggression and passivity into third-rate pleasures of a morbid, perverse, stubborn, and grimly satisfying sort. We tend not to be aware of this perverse gratification because it's registered unconsciously. (To understand how aggression and passivity are transformed into conscious sexual pleasure, read "The Mysterious Allure of Kinky Sex.") Our superego's self-aggression, according to Freud, develops when, as babies, we're unable to expend the overwhelming drive and energy of our biological aggression completely into the environment; consequently, a portion of this aggression turns against us to become insensitive, often cruel self-aggression. Through our inner passivity, we absorb the aggression and become weighed down with self-doubt, self-criticism, self-rejection, and, in some cases, self-condemnation and self-hatred.

As we absorb inner aggression, the accumulation of negativity causes us to become aggressive toward one another and life in general. Humanity's taste for mindless aggression is evidenced in our industrial rape of the earth and our cruelty, violence, and warfare. We take perverse pleasure in exercising wanton destruction because doing so gratifies our ego and serves as an unconscious defense. "I'm not a willing, passive receptacle of my own unregulated aggression," our unconscious defense proclaims, "nor do I feel frightened and helpless to the forces of existence. The fact is, I'm powerful, I enjoy my supremacy, and the world is at my mercy."

The idea that we harbor such a self-defeating tendency is intellectually and emotionally revolting—a narcissistic insult. Just thinking about it, especially as it applies to us personally, can activate a kind of psychological gag-reflex. The danger is that, should this knowledge remain unconscious, it can "lead organic life back into the inanimate state," as Freud said of the death drive. It's urgent that we now seriously consider this possibility and begin to investigate it with determined effort. We don't have to take it personally and feel embarrassed or mortified. Actually, this flaw in human nature is quite fascinating. Only our ego gets all huffy about it.

A complete body of work on unconscious masochism was produced by Edmund Bergler, M.D. (1899-1962), a psychiatric psychoanalyst who lived in New York City.[8] He wrote 27 books on psychoanalysis, many of them printed and distributed by major publishers, and had 273 articles published in leading medical and psychological journals. Many of his books are available from International Universities Press (iup.com). One of my books describes Bergler's work in detail.[9]

For supporting evidence of this theory of unconscious masochism, we only have to glance around at humanity's ineffectiveness related to growing global crises. Recognizing our paralysis and self-defeat, we may be ready at last for this vital knowledge to serve as our chronometer of inner longitude.

7. A Chaos Theory of the Mind

How could we possibly become attached to negative emotions such as passivity and aggression? How could people in their right mind be willing to recycle and replay experiences of refusal, helplessness, control,

---

[8] http://en.wikipedia.org/wiki/Edmund_Bergler
[9] http://www.amazon.com/Why-We-Suffer-Understand-Unhappiness-ebook/dp/B004WOVLR6/ref=sr_1_1?ie=UTF8&qid=1396365870&sr=8-1&keywords=why+we+suffer+michaelson

rejection, criticism, and betrayal? Readers are going to want to know, of course, how this could happen. The previous essay provides some explanation. Here, succinctly outlined, is further elaboration on this theory, as derived from classical psychoanalysis and, in particular, the writings of Edmund Bergler.

As adults, we like to think we've put away most childish things. But infantile and childish ways of experiencing ourselves and life linger in our unconscious mind. That baby in the adult's psyche can be highly mischievous and harmful, producing chaotic reactions.

Early childhood's influences on our adult experiences have parallels to the scientific concept of Chaos theory. This mathematical theory attempts to understand erratic behavior as it occurs in certain nonlinear systems such as weather patterns. The theory proposes, as one example, that small air disturbances in one location can result, days or weeks later, in storms or hurricanes more than a thousand miles away.

Comparatively, the unconscious mind of adults is buffeted by gale-force winds of emotional chaos that originated as an infantile effect decades earlier. Emotional associations from our distant past now impact our life in incredible, mysterious, spectacular, and frequently painful and self-defeating ways.

Emotions percolate and circulate in our unconscious mind with some degree of chaos. We all know what it's like to be happy one moment, sad the next, with no apparent conscious input from us. We also know how hard it can be to regulate our desires, impulses, and emotional reactions. Both neuroscience and psychology have established[10] that our brain struggles mightily and often unsuccessfully to limit the effects of irrationality. Often we try to apply common sense and reason to moderate unpleasant emotions or to curb self-defeating impulses. Yet our emotional side, with a life of its own, is often impervious to rational entreaties. Still, we can bring order to the chaos when we understand just what we're dealing with.

Developmental psychologists observe that the children's first signs of self-awareness show up after twelve months. They detail the emergence of growing rationality in the second year and beyond. Their scientific methods are just beginning to illuminate a parallel development, namely the baby's instinctive *irrational* consciousness and intense entanglement in a false reality driven by acute self-centeredness, primitive wishes, libidinal instincts, inner aggression and fear, and self-defeating compromises.[11] This infantile consciousness continues in various degrees over a lifetime to influence our struggle to distinguish the rational from the irrational and wisdom from folly.[12]

According to psychoanalysis, the irrational consciousness starts with the baby's experiences of the oral stage, when the mouth is the primary zone of pleasure. In the first months of life, the baby experiences feeding as self-given, meaning that the feeding and the food itself are

---

[10] http://www.nytimes.com/2011/11/27/books/review/thinking-fast-and-slow-by-daniel-kahneman-book-review.html?_r=0

[11] Eisenberg, N., Hofer, C., Sulik, M. J., & Spinard, T. L. (2014). Self-regulation, effortful control, and their socioemotional correlates. In J. Gross (Ed.), *Handbook of Emotion Regulation* (pp. 157-172). New York: The Guilford Press.

[12] Rothbart, M. K., Sheese, B. E., & Posner, M. I. (2014). Temperment and emotion regulation. In J. Gross (Ed.), *Handbook of Emotion Regulation* (pp. 305-320). New York: The Guilford Press.

services and substances that are provided through the baby's own powers. What accounts for such irrationality? Babies experience the world through megalomania, or profound self-centeredness, along with a sense of omnipotence or magic power. All the child knows are the physical and emotional sensations of his or her our own little body. In this primitive consciousness, nothing exists except what the child experiences directly. Whatever is given to the child by others is experienced by the child as an act of his or her magic power. An emotional association with having such magic powers still resonates very strongly in adolescents and teenagers, as evidenced in the widely popular Harry Potter series of books and movies.

This infant's profound misreading of reality may be his or her evolutionary compensation, a will-to-live booster-shot for the reality of being so profoundly helpless.

According to Bergler, the psychiatric psychoanalyst and author who studied the oral stage, a complication soon arises. Food is not always available exactly when baby wants it. Mother may be busy with other children or obligations. Baby begins to experience *not getting* the food when the food is desired. The baby can't understand the relativity of time, so a 10-minute wait for food can seem like eternity. This *not getting* is a serious affront to the baby's sense of magic power, and loud wails of protest often result.

How does the baby compensate psychologically? He or she is determined to preserve the magical feeling of being a little wizard at the center of life. The baby "decides," in an instinctive manner of deduction, that *not getting* must be what he or she wants. The baby is able to turn displeasure into pleasure and make the feeling of *not getting* acceptable and gratifying. "It's what I want," the child deduces irrationally, "so it must be good." Note that all of us have the capacity to turn displeasure into pleasure. This occurs unconsciously when we indulge in feelings of loss, rejection, oppression, or other forms of victimization. Spiteful or malicious people, along with those who withhold emotional support and love, are taking perverse satisfaction in their negativity. Perverse gratification is also felt by bullies, domestic abusers, and other kinds of oppressors, and, in an equally or more pronounced way, by sadists, sexual masochists, and pedophiles.

Freud deduced that the ability to eroticize or "sugar-coat" various experiences is attributed to libido or the pleasure principle, which refers to the psychological-biological process whereby both pleasant and unpleasant experiences can be enjoyed or eroticized. As another example, everyday people are quite capable of indulging in an unhealthy yet compulsive way in bittersweet feelings of self-pity. As another example, people can "libidinize" inner fear, enabling them to experience macabre delight reading thrillers, going to horror movies, and speculating incessantly about terrorist threats.

According to this theory, the baby's impression of *not getting*—feeling refused or deprived—is libidinized through his or her profound self-centeredness: "If refusal is what I'm experiencing, it must be what I like." The resulting third-rate pleasure becomes an emotional attachment. The negative feeling becomes a default position in the psyche. Not only is that negative emotion familiar, it easily becomes an indulgence. From an early age we become hooked on the feeling, or attached to it. As I say repeatedly, it can also be understood as an emotional *addiction*. This attachment or addiction tends to become an integral part of our identity, meaning we don't quite know who we are without it.

This theory of Bergler's is an elaboration on the *repetition compulsion*,[13] as Freud called it. According to Freud's meaning, we're creatures who seek consciously or unconsciously to experience situations in ways that replay our unresolved emotions.

What are some repercussions of unresolved oral issues? They include chronic feelings involving dissatisfaction, refusal, and deprival, leading frequently to struggles with self-defeating behaviors. Greed, envy, boredom, anger, and passivity are symptoms of this lingering oral attachment to deprivation and refusal. It's possible our consumer-based economy—with its environmentally degrading, entitlement-inducing, and debt-driven side-effects—is stimulated, in part, by our deep grievances about allegedly having been deprived and refused at this early age.

Of course, other factors such as genetics and individual biology can influence the degree to which individuals are swept up by irrationality, leading sometimes to mental illness. Incompetent child-rearing also tends to make the negative consequences of the inner chaos more problematic. The chaotic irrationality also goes on to influence later stages of child development beyond the oral stage.

Evidence supporting these psychoanalytical ideas concerning the human mind is overwhelming. It abounds in millions of examples of individual and collective

---

[13] http://en.wikipedia.org/wiki/Repetition_compulsion

suffering and self-defeat recorded in mythology, literature, scripture, history, and in the scientific forecasts of a dire climate future for civilization. Growing awareness of this inner chaos and its discontents can speed up our evolution.

8. Chasing the Shadow

Our brightest thinkers struggle to expose the hidden dynamics of the shadow, the dark side of our psyche. Depth psychology can shed light on those repressed regions of the mind. Yet experts are having difficulty understanding the discipline's basic tenets.

By way of illustration, I'd like to recommend a lovely book, with the proviso that one section of it is flawed. The book, written by Ken Wilber and three of his associates, is titled *Integral Life Practice: A 21st Century Blueprint for Physical Health, Emotional Balance, Mental Clarity, and Spiritual Awakening* (Integral Books, Boston & London, 2008).

Based on Wilber's admirable body of work[14] on human consciousness, the book adopts a method of healing that integrates body, mind, spirit, and shadow. It's a fabulous blueprint for expanding our consciousness and getting us beyond our negativity, irrationality, and egotism.

---

[14] http://en.wikipedia.org/wiki/Ken_Wilber

The authors state correctly that the shadow is "the most sorely neglected area" in self-help literature. Even the Eastern spiritual traditions "don't adequately address the psychodynamic shadow," they say, adding that shadow work "*frees up energy* that would otherwise be spent shadowboxing within ourselves." That freed-up energy becomes available for growth, creativity, and wise, healthy pursuits.

Unfortunately, the book's presentation of the shadow is flawed or, at best, incomplete. Employing depth psychology, the authors discuss repression, projections, and disowning of emotions, but they fail to see how these dynamics are linked to psychological defenses and emotional attachments.

Using three examples from their book (in the essay titled "The Shadow Module"), I'll try to show, in the spirit of friendly debate, what I believe the authors both miss and misunderstand.

Example 1 - *the situation*: A little girl becomes angry at her mother and then represses the anger. The child feels scared, sad, and depressed.

Authors' analysis: The child represses her anger rather than risk the bond of love with mother on which the child depends. In repressing the anger, the child might project that anger on to others and begin to see a world full of angry people. The child will be inclined to more fully repress the anger until all she feels are "internal decoys" consisting of sadness, fear, and depression. Anger is "the root cause" of the child's distress, and it's the "primary actual (and thus 'authentic') emotion." Her sadness and fear are "secondary, inauthentic emotions."

My analysis: Anger is sometimes authentic (for instance, getting angry at a man for abusing a child), but often it is not. We have to understand why the child becomes angry at her mother in the first place. The mother might have behaved quite innocently or even kindly, and the child still could have interpreted the mother's action (or inaction) as refusal, control, criticism, or rejection. Or the mother might have refused the child some favor, which triggered the child into becoming angry. In this case, the child's anger is now a reaction to the feeling of being refused. Yet, depending on circumstances, refusal is often a requirement of good parenting. It's typical for young children to become angry when they have misinterpreted the intentions of their parents.

So the child's anger is likely not, despite what the authors say, "an authentic emotion." Instead, it's likely an *inauthentic* emotion, a symptom of a deeper problem and a defense against recognition of that deeper problem. The girl's deeper problem is her unconscious determination to experience refusal in a given situation, whether or not she's actually being refused. This painful feeling often lingers in adults as an unresolved emotional attachment, meaning the individual is unconsciously expecting refusal and is willing to have another "run-in" with that negative experience. Such wayward behavior defies common sense, but irrationality is nonetheless a driving force in human affairs and the "language" of the psyche.

Children (and adults) are unconsciously determined to cover up (defend against realization of) their readiness to feel and recycle an unresolved negative emotion. Emotions involving refusal are orally-based, and they remain unresolved in vast millions of children and adults. When refusal is felt with accompanying anger, the person is likely using the anger as a psychological defense to cover up his or her willingness to absorb a painful experience of that refusal. Anger, as a defense, makes this claim: "I hate feeling refused. Look at how angry I get at mom (or whoever) when she refuses me."

Another way to perceive this dynamic is through an awareness of the inner conflict: The child *consciously* wants to get, *not* to feel refused, yet *unconsciously* the child is expecting to feel refused and is anticipating an angry clash with mother. That anger is a protest to cover up the child's expectation of (or emotional attachment to) feeling refused.

Any therapist who claims that such anger is authentic is only helping to strengthen the defense and to cover up the deeper dynamics. Typically, people are grateful to a therapist who strengthens their defenses. This way they can avoid the consciously and unconsciously feared deeper examination of the shadow side.

Example 2 - *the situation*: Phil is dreading going to visit Joe, his childhood best friend. Phil gets triggered because, as he says, Joe is "such a wimp! His wife runs his life! He's got a super safe, secure, and dead-end job. . . . He's betraying himself. It makes me sick. It drives me nuts to be around him."

Authors' analysis: Phil becomes triggered because "he's disowned his own needs for safety and security so much that he's easily triggered by Joe's qualities." Phil believes in "risk-taking and pushing the envelope and going for the max." Phil has disowned the side of himself that needs "safety, security, predictability . . ." He "can become more whole" when he realized this.

My analysis: Phil sees in Joe what he doesn't want to see in himself. Both men have unresolved inner passivity. Phil's risk-taking lifestyle is likely a potentially self-defeating reaction to his own inner passivity. Macho men and compulsive success hunters, for instance, are usually inwardly weak and unsure of themselves.

Phil sees passivity in Joe, and he (Phil) identifies (resonates emotionally) with that passivity. His discomfort around Joe is a psychological defense that makes this claim: "I don't want to feel passive. I don't want to identify with Joe's passivity. Look, I hate it in him. I can't stand to be around him."

Phil also likely has an aggressive inner critic (inner passivity servers as an enabler of this critical side). Phil's critical feelings toward Joe likely mirror the manner in which Phil is treated by his own inner critic. When Phil learns about the inner conflict in his psyche between aggression and passivity, he can free himself from it.

Example 3 - *the situation*: Harry is procrastinating on doing his taxes, and he later snaps at his wife when she innocently asks, "How are the taxes going?"

Authors' analysis: Harry overlooks his own drive to do the taxes and becomes convinced that his wife is pressuring him "to do the stupid taxes." After projecting this inner drive on to his wife, Harry now experiences the drive as outside pressure, and he objects to feeling pressured. The solution is for Phil to recognize his disowned projections and make them conscious.

My analysis: Harry, through inner passivity, is emotionally attached to the feeling of being pressured.

At his office, he reacts passively-aggressively to that sense of pressure—the obvious need to do the taxes—by procrastinating and failing to do them. The procrastination says, in effect: "I do what I want, not what some responsibility or obligation tells me I need to do."

When Harry gets home, he reacts angrily to his wife's innocent question about the taxes. Because of his attachment to inner passivity, Harry, who's already had a very passive experience at his office, unconsciously jumps at the chance to feel pressure coming from his wife. Instantly, he reacts with inappropriate aggression: "Get off my back." That aggression is a self-defeating reaction to his passivity, and it, too, serves as a defense: "I'm not passive with my wife in feeling that she's pressuring me. Hey, I yell at her which means I'm aggressive." Harry much prefers to feel guilty for his inappropriate aggression than to recognize his inner passivity.

When Harry feels that he's being held accountable by his wife, he's transferring on to her his own sense of being held accountable by his inner critic. He would greatly benefit from this insight.

Depth psychology is a powerful tool for penetrating the shadow and resolving the conflict imbedded there. Hopefully one day soon its essential principles will be integrated into mainstream psychology.

II - FURTHER REACHES OF THE PSYCHE

9. **Escaping the Clutches of Helplessness**

We can all feel fragile at times, fading feebly in and out like a tiny sparkle in the vast firmament. It's easy then to feel helpless, overlooked, insignificant, and unappreciated.

An entanglement in helpless feelings can certainly dampen our light, leaving us afraid to be venturesome. We can feel befuddled, overwhelmed, or exhausted, buffeted about by the winds of misfortune. Disappointment, dissatisfaction, and the sorrow of not living up to our potential are likely to haunt us.

A chronic sense of helplessness keeps us from believing in ourselves, trusting ourselves, and pursuing our destiny. Our self-regulation weakens, and we fall prey to impulses to overeat, overspend, and overindulge. We also lose our ability to regulate our emotional life or maintain physical health, causing us to sink into apathy or become increasingly bitter, depressed, or ill.

We are indeed helpless when it comes to influencing many events and situations. We accept this fact with equanimity when we're emotionally strong. But we can't accept it so easily when plagued by chronic helplessness. Instead, like a turtle on its back, we experience the personal challenges of daily life through a painful sense of being unable to rise to the occasion.

Laid low like this, we also perceive global problems such as war, poverty, and weather changes through the conviction of our inability to influence them positively in a meaningful way. Instinctively, we back away from challenges to reform situations, close our mind to heroic possibilities, and succumb to temptations that adversely affect our health and general wellbeing.

Some of us sense acutely our painful predicament, and we desperately want liberation from it. But we can't see the nature of our problem clearly enough to get any footing. As we struggle to break free of helplessness, we can feel, in a Catch-22 kind of way, helpless to extricate ourselves from overriding impressions of impotence, powerlessness, futility, passivity, and subservience.

If ever there was a quandary—or, more accurately perhaps, an emotional quagmire—it's the helplessness we can feel when we try to figure out how we can possibly unravel our entanglement in passivity. As we thrash about, an inner entrapment seems to close more tightly around us. We need real insight into the nature of this quandary. The best psychological knowledge can help to liberate us.

One person told me he felt helpless in detaching himself from his feelings of helplessness. "I have a tendency to 'overthink' and get myself stuck," he said. He was feeling desperately stuck because his efforts in thinking so hard to figure things out were, in themselves, exercises in helplessness. He ended up spinning his wheels. He was convinced his thinking represented a form of power, yet he was going about it in a way that produced the familiar feeling of more helplessness.

Thinking is important, of course, but it isn't enough in itself to deal with chronic helplessness. We also need the self-knowledge that reveals how our emotions operate. And we don't have to "over-think." Our intelligence works for us behind the scenes as we keep tracking inner truth. One such truth reveals our emotional attachment to our helplessness. The fact that we're emotionally attached to our helplessness is an important concept we need to understand.

How is helplessness an emotional attachment? The negative feeling is integral to our self-concept and entangled in our identity. We don't know who we are without this (conscious or unconscious) sense of chronic weakness. The afflicted individual holds on to the attachment, even when it's painful, because it's the framework, a kind of primitive lean-to, for his or her psychological home in the world.

Feelings of helplessness are as old as the day we're born, and they can linger in our psyche, despite our best efforts to be independent, self-reliant, and successful in the world. As we're growing up, we oscillate emotionally between feeling aggressive and feeling passive. Many of the fears and doubts of childhood and teenage years are associated with the feeling that we won't have the ability, strength, or resolve to meet the challenges of becoming a functional, successful adult.

A temptation to interpret daily challenges through the sense of helplessness is one of the main symptoms of inner passivity. As mentioned, this passive side of our psyche is a limitation or deficit in our consciousness, and it impedes the development of our humanity. Inner passivity, a major player in our psyche and a drag on our evolution, is an enabler of our aggressive inner critic. In our psyche, we can feel helpless and defensive in the face of our authoritarian inner critic that treats us as if we're supposed to be subservient to it. The conflict between our inner aggression and inner passivity, when reverberating in our psyche, can reduce us to the status of a helpless observer of our own life or, even worse, a clueless bystander.

Another person told me, "I haven't been able to believe that I'm not helpless. Even though I know on an intellectual basis that this whole thing [being tangled up in the helpless experience] is irrational, some part of me still believes that I'm helpless. The effects of believing this weigh me down."

I told him, "Believing that you're helpless, or getting hung up on the idea that you're truly helpless, is a defense which goes like this: 'I'm not attached to feeling helpless—Look, the problem is that I really am helpless.' By accentuating your impression of being truly helpless, you create a clever (though self-defeating) defense that enables you to continue to hold on to your attachment to feeling helpless. You have to see through the deceptiveness of your defense."

Freedom from helplessness follows our assimilation of this ultimate insight, that we're emotionally attached to the feeling of helplessness. We have lived so long with the passive feeling—through childhood up to the present—that it's now part of our identity. We must begin to recognize those moments or times when we're choosing unconsciously to experience ourselves in a passive way.

An emotional person who cries a lot can be triggered by helpless feelings. Crying in itself can be appropriate and healthy, especially when it's experienced as a deeper, positive connection with one's self or others. It's also appropriate when experienced as tears of happiness or joy (although at times such tears can be a defense in themselves when they show relief that some expected bad outcome didn't occur). But often people are in tears because they're feeling hopeless or helpless about a situation and don't know what to do. Their tears reflect a sense of being on the receiving end of abuse while not knowing how to protect or take care of themselves. They feel they have no options, and their crying becomes an expression of self-pity. In such cases, they have plunged into inner passivity and are drowning in the feeling of it. Even if some relief is felt at the end of the tears, the sorrow and self-pity constitute a dead-end. The tears are wasted. Nothing is resolved for the long term.

The solution is to become conscious of the nature of one's tears. If in the moment we see our attachment to a negative emotion such as helplessness, the power of that perception is enough to shift us over to a neutral or even a pleasant state of mind. Like children, adults don't always think in terms of having a choice when it comes to inner experiences. But here a choice presents itself. Self-knowledge is empowering. Just be willing to see that your tears are prompted by your attachment to the feeling of helplessness or some other negative emotion. Own the fact that you're making unconscious choices to indulge in the negative emotion. (Read, "How to Be Your Own Inner Guide.") The willingness and determination to expose this inner knowledge is empowering. In that moment, the insight gives you the power to say *No* to the negative experience. You don't necessarily have to choose a positive experience instead. Just decline the negative. Choose to say *No* to the negative experience, and then see what happens.

As we recognize our willingness to continue to experience ourselves and the world through helplessness, we're able to find and cleave the concealed chains of inner bondage.

10. The Addiction behind the Video Games Addiction

Is an unconscious tendency to experience ourselves through helplessness a factor in addictions? It's curious that we humans get addicted to both substances and behaviors. On the substance side, people get hooked on drugs, alcohol, nicotine, sugar, and fat. We can also become addicted without substance abuse, in behaviors involving video games, gambling, shopping, promiscuity, pornography, and even work.

Experts offer a range of theories to explain the causes of addictions, and they often disagree sharply with one another. The causes are attributed variously to neurological disorders, brain chemistry, genetic factors, and low self-esteem. The psychologist and author Stanton Peele has a novel theory. He says we become addicted because the "delivery systems"—hypodermic syringes, nicotine-packed cigarettes, ubiquitous online porn, pocket-sized game consoles, chemically flavored food, seductive marketing messages—have become so effective at breaking down our resistance.[15] Maybe so, yet why aren't we able to protect ourselves more

[15] http://www.psychologytoday.com/blog/addiction-in-society/201204/iphones-games-and-the-addictive-experience

successfully, even when we're up against potent "delivery systems"? What psychological insight explains why our resistance breaks down in the first place?

All the various theories are worthy of consideration, yet I believe we really can't understand addictions fully without understanding deeper elements of human nature. An essential cause of addictions, I believe, derives from our lack of consciousness, particularly concerning the emotional resonance we have with feeling helpless. People who become entangled emotionally in feeling helpless—and who have no awareness of this attachment—can be quite inept at self-regulation. We're reluctant to acknowledge this attachment because its association with unconscious masochism repels us. Our proud, cherished self-image can't bear the thought that we would be so blind and so flawed.

This helplessness factor can be observed in boys who become addicted to playing video games. Often they're drawn to violent games in which they relish the thrill of exercising ruthless killing power. This sensation of power serves as a compensation for (or a defense that covers up) their underlying passivity. This condition in the human psyche—inner passivity—produces the unconscious addiction to the negative emotions of helplessness and powerlessness. Throughout this book, I refer frequently to the existence and influence of inner passivity. It's the hidden saboteur in our struggle to establish a strong sense of self. Inner passivity produces a compulsion to experience oneself in negative ways, particularly through self-doubt and a lack of self-regulation. As mentioned, this passivity has been "libidinized" (activated through the pleasure principle) in such a way as to produce a comfortable familiarity, or a grim satisfaction or bittersweet gratification. In addictions as well as in other self-defeating behaviors, distinguishing between the passivity and the masochism can be difficult. In the throes of helpless feelings, they are often one and the same.

I believe a lot of boys are in danger of delaying the development of their will, integrity, and sense of self as they're captivated emotionally by the technologically and visually stunning allure of video games. (Visual craving and the craving for excitement are also involved in this addiction, and they are powerful drives or instincts that can be regulated with more self-awareness.) Despite the marvel of video-game technology, the essential addictive element is not the "delivery system" but the unconscious passivity in the human psyche. That passivity, because it's unresolved, yearns to be experienced. Again, it can be understood as an adjunct to Freud's *repetition compulsion*, whereby in a kind of naïve innocence we're compelled to repeat actions or behaviors, often inappropriate and self-defeating, which are being instigated by unresolved conflicts and emotions.

In playing video games, young people (and many adults with online games such as poker) easily succumb to the temptation, familiar from the prolonged biological helplessness of early childhood and the dependence of adolescence, to feel "taken over," overwhelmed, or "psychologically possessed" by some force, directive, or influence beyond their capacity to neutralize. It's normal for people to "lose themselves" in some activity such as work or a pleasant or passionate hobby. If we go overboard, though, we "lose ourselves" in a way that becomes self-defeating. Discernment and the ability to monitor one's experience are lost, while pure sensation and automatic processing take over. The activity becomes compulsive and obsessive, and we lose perspective, balance, and self-regulation.

How much easier is it for children, given the deposits of inner passivity in human nature, to be overwhelmed by the brilliant offerings of technological devices? The passivity involved is not so different from being susceptible to inane and violent children's television programming. The visual drive is a powerful emotional stimulant. (So is the death drive which is a powerful influence in alcohol and drug addiction.) In any case, our psychological Achilles' heel—inner passivity—makes it easier for children to become too cozy and familiar with the feeling of being overpowered and overwhelmed. They might become, as possible dangers, weak citizens unable to protect democracy or people unable to muster the emotional strength to deal with climate change.

My theory of addictions helps explain why compulsive video-gamers can be drawn especially to violent games in which they feel a scintillating sensation in being able to shoot and kill the bad guys. As mentioned, this sense of power feels pleasurable because it's a compensation— as well as a psychological defense—for their underlying passivity. The psychological defense produces, as part of its effectiveness, an emotional thrill or pleasure that makes the aggression seem real and appropriate. The defense goes like this: "I'm not passive—look at how much I enjoy having this power." The gaming activity also produces the feeling that one's intelligence, instincts, visual acuity, and motor skills are highly engaged, as indeed they may be. While this activity does display one's skilful and mental abilities, these expressions of inner resources do not compensate (except as a defense) for the totality of one's involvement in a passive experience.

Although psychologist Stanton Peele, the addictions expert quoted earlier, doesn't apparently subscribe to the theory of inner passivity, he does precisely describe in an online post the passive experience of video-game addicts ("iPhones, Games and the Addictive Experience"). He writes: It's the ability of video games "to take us away from what is meaningful that underlies their ability to absorb our attention and to produce the repetitive engagement and escapist gratification that are the essence of powerfully addicting experiences."[16]

Yet, why is escapist gratification so enticing? Why are we so easily taken away "from what is meaningful"? The experience of inner passivity can itself be highly enticing. It represents a return to an infantile state of mind in which we don't have to make any particular effort or deal with reality. "Let grown-ups run things," the feeling goes. "I'll just bury myself in my closed world of sensation and excitement." People who develop mental-health disorders live in closed worlds of sensation, anguish, excitement, and illusions.

In a wide range of addictive behaviors, individuals experience themselves through inner weakness. As I've been saying, the particular substance or behavior to which they're addicted is secondary to their attachment to one or more unresolved negative emotions. Much of the time the primary attachment and the primary craving are to the feeling of helplessness. In other words, they're determined unconsciously to experience

[16] http://www.psychologytoday.com/blog/addiction-in-society/201204/iphones-games-and-the-addictive-experience

this negative emotion in conjunction with their cravings for some substance or behavior. The cravings and the feelings of helplessness are indistinguishable, at the same time that they can both be used as defenses to cover up an underlying attachment. This approach to understanding addictions helps to explain why people become addicted to such a wide range of substances and behaviors, and why they so often continue helplessly down this path despite the obvious self-defeat.

Addictive personalities are tempted or compelled to go looking for some way (with alcohol, drugs, gambling, video games, or whatever) through which to act out their unresolved entanglement in a negative emotion. This pattern of behavior is based on the psychological axiom that we're tempted, if not compelled, to act out whatever is unresolved in our psyche, unwittingly producing suffering and self-defeat. In other words, behind the substance or behavioral addiction is an unconscious compulsion to experience this inner weakness or inner pain. The addiction becomes simply a symptom, albeit a potentially grievous one, of the inner conflict.

As mentioned, the conflict often involves inner passivity. Experts can see the passivity in the *behavior* of addicts, but they can't see the passivity in the *psyche* of addicts. After debating the causes of addiction for more than 100 years, scientists still have no definitive answer. They tend to support remedies involving medical drugs, structured programs, or the expert interventions of others. This approach can reinforce passivity because it makes people beholding to outside sources. Such interventions are often necessary, of course. But, as a vital alternative, it's time to start using our intelligence to unravel the mysterious dynamics of our psyche in order to raise our consciousness and to tap into the power that arises from deeper insight.

11. Why We're Quick to "Go Negative"

Comedian Bill Maher wrote an amusing article[17] asking, "When did we get it in our heads that we have the right to never hear anything we don't like?" In the article, Maher makes the point that we've become too easily offended and too quick to be outraged over nothing. It's as if we're eager to take everything personally.

Well, guess what? Unconsciously, we are indeed eager to take things personally. We jump at the chance to feel insulted, disrespected, or disgusted by what others say, even though their words may be only mildly inappropriate, or even just candid, and have nothing directly to do with us.

Why would we want to feel that aggravation? Obviously, we're the ones who suffer with tension and stress if we get "ticked off" this way. Once triggered, we're stuck with a negative feeling that can last for days.

We all remember that old adage, "Sticks and stones can break my bones, but names can never hurt me." In principle, we certainly want to see a decrease in derogatory language, racial slurs, and displays of

---

[17] http://www.nytimes.com/2012/03/22/opinion/please-stop-apologizing.html?_r=1

ignorance and incivility. Yet, as Maher said, we show a willingness to get upset over nothing. We feel offended when some jerk or loudmouth says something stupid or when some high-profile person (actor Robert De Niro, to use Maher's example) makes an attempt at humor that might be, at worst, a dumb joke.

In a similar vein, we can get irritated and even outraged over trifles involving a friend or spouse. We can easily get ticked off by a spouse's peculiar mannerisms or details of appearance, or by his or her harmless personal idiosyncrasies. Most of us can remember times when we felt such irritation.

Before I get to why we so easily "go negative," I'll review some basic principles. Some of these have been discussed earlier, but they need to be repeated in this new context.

On an inner level, we resonate with the feeling of being mocked, disrespected, and criticized. We're inwardly defensive against allegations of wrongdoing or condemnations of stupidity from our inner critic. This agency in our psyche is a villain in the drama of our life, and its voice may or may not be conscious. Its role is to dominate our inner life, and its primary procedure is to question our judgment and to hold us accountable for being wrong, foolish, stupid, flawed, or worthless. This primitive drive in our psyche is a biological fact of human life. However, it can be tamed and brought to heel by our intelligence and awareness (in other words, the quality of our consciousness).

Often, we find ourselves unable to squirm out from under the thumb of the inner critic. Yet this voice or drive is just one-half of an inner conflict that, for most of us, is so familiar we don't know who we are without it. As mentioned, our defensive unconscious ego (the seat of inner passivity) takes up the other half of the conflict. As we resolve this conflict, our authentic self emerges.

This brings us to the heart of the issue, namely why we're so easily feel offended by the allegedly insensitive remarks of others, even when those remarks don't directly apply to us. There are two main reasons.

First, we're quick to identify with the person or group that we imagine is feeling slighted and disrespected by a seemingly offensive remark. We identify with the other in this way because we ourselves are quick to feel slighted or disrespected, particularly through the dynamic relationship we have with our inner critic. To cover up our resonance with the feeling of being criticized or disrespected, we create a psychological defense. That defense can operate on this basis: "I'm not willing to feel disrespected and indulge in the feeling. Look, I'm angry at the person who made that offensive remark. That person needs to be identified as the problem." So we unconsciously produce the unpleasant sensation of being offended or insulted as a psychological defense. The defense covers up our emotional resonance with feeling criticized, mocked, or belittled.

Second, we often look for a scapegoat so we can minimize our own inner sense of wrongdoing and deflect our inner critic's spotlight away from us. Now the defense reads, "I'm not the one who's guilty of wrongdoing. It's that fool over there. Look at what he just said. He's the one who needs to be condemned." In such cases, the deeper our sense of being offended by the other, the more we're trying to cover up (defend against realization of) our inner conflict and emotional attachments. This defense exacts a heavy price, namely the burden of our ugly outrage. We set off this negative roar inside ourselves in order to cover up our resonance with (attachment to) the feeling of being criticized or belittled.

This dynamic can be observed in the tendency to become irritated or enraged by a spouse's or a friend's trifling idiosyncrasy. We feel this flash of disapproval toward our friend or spouse because we do to others what our inner critic does to us. It pounces on us for alleged wrongdoing, often over minor or even imagined transgressions. Instinctively, as if blowing off steam, we do the same to our loved ones.

When we bring the inner critic's incessant negativity into focus, we can remain free of its influence. Eventually, under the gaze of our awareness, the inner critic's power dissipates and we become much less prone to its negative influences.

Once liberated from the primary conflict between our inner critic (inner aggression) and our unconscious ego (inner passivity), we no longer practice or tolerate inner incivility. Now we're immune to the outer manifestations of it. We no longer "go negative" at the drop of an offhand comment.

12 . **The Bittersweet Allure of Feeling Unloved**

Heartbreak and shattered relationships look tragic on the surface. But the real sad story is the readiness of people to produce these painful outcomes. Though it's mostly unconscious, many people have an affinity for feeling rejected, abandoned, and unloved. Yes, this idea flies in the face of common sense. Who would want to bear the pain of feeling unloved?

Like the mysterious physics that permeate outer space, the inner realm of our psyche doesn't always adhere to the principles of common sense. If we're willing to investigate all the nooks and crannies of our psyche, we come across some startling truths that defy conventional thinking.

Our affinity for feeling *unloved* is one of these truths. Feeling unloved is a familiar hurt for many of us. We can easily get used to that feeling. Sometimes it even defines us. We won't know ourselves or recognize ourselves without this old pain. We often identify with ourselves as the victims of rejection or other kinds of cruelty or unfairness that others are apparently inflicting upon us.

Sometimes the feeling arises in the familiarity of bittersweet self-pity. We can't climb out of the pits of "poor little me." It's as if we're determined to be loyal to our suffering self or to refuse to manifest any other way of being. We drag ourselves down into unhappiness, depression, and ill health when we cling to this false (yet emotionally powerful) impression of who we are.

Such people are convinced that they want to be loved and feel love. Sometimes they feel a desperate longing for love, which further convinces them that love is what they want. This desperate feeling covers up their unconscious willingness to go on living through the feeling of being unloved. If they don't see their attachment to feeling unloved, they'll continue to suffer with feelings of being unloved and to sabotage themselves in the process of trying to establish love in their life.

A needy person who appears to be desperate for love is often entangled in the familiar pain of feeling unloved. Unconsciously, this person often chooses to feel unloved rather than to feel loved. He or she often turns away from love when it's available and runs off in self-pitying agony to where love is unavailable. When that person's attachment to feeling unloved is brought into the light of awareness, the person can usually improve his or her situation dramatically.

Our affinity for rejection, abandonment, and betrayal are emotional attachments. These attachments are like barnacles on the side of a hull that are slowing down, often agonizingly so, our passage through life. They're jelly beans we keep eating even though our teeth are hurting and decaying badly. We first experience these negative emotions in childhood because we're so sensitive to any signs of being refused, controlled, or rejected. These old hurts don't magically go away when we turn twenty-one.

A basic axiom of depth psychology states that we will continue to feel, no matter how painful, whatever is unresolved in our psyche. We just keep tripping over the feeling. Sometimes all it takes is a word or a look from someone else to set off that pain inside us.

When we feel unloved, we usually believe that other people are the cause or the source of our feeling. We perceive that they're rejecting us or being unkind or insensitive to us. But feeling unloved is ultimately the result of an unresolved inner conflict. We want to respect and love ourselves, but something is in the way. Often we're stuck in ambivalence, liking or loving ourselves in one moment, disliking or rejecting ourselves in the next. To make matters even murkier, our self-doubt, self-criticism, and self-rejection can be mostly unconscious.

Let's look at an example. James and Julie, married for ten years, are heading for divorce. They've grown increasingly angry with each other, and that anger now spills out almost every day. They're both convinced their anger is justified by the other's failure to be supportive, attentive, and appreciative. However, those negative impressions are familiar to both of them. They both had parents who they felt had failed, in a variety of ways, to acknowledge their value and appreciate them for their own sake.

James and Julie now have decent relations with their parents. Yet the old hurts, based on both actual and subjective impressions from childhood, are unresolved in their psyche. Their painful memories are also repressed and largely unconscious. But they both remain emotionally attached to that pain. That means the bad feelings can pop up or reoccur at the slightest provocation, often in situations in which one of them is misinterpreting the intentions or words of the other.

Over the years, James and Julie often did express love for one another. Yet the old inner conflict always reasserted itself. Frequently when one of them was being affectionate, the other could easily feel that the effort wasn't good enough, that something was still missing. They each remained emotionally attached to that old painful feeling. Deep down, the feeling of being unworthy or undeserving was part of their identity. They didn't break clear of this emotional attachment because they never became aware of their unconscious willingness or compulsion to continue to experience the old hurt.

Since they can't see their entanglement in these negative emotions, they react by blaming the other for causing the hurt, at the same time that they instinctively deny that they are each party to their own sorrows. The angrier they get at each other, the more emphatically they cover up their own individual determination to replay the old unresolved hurt.

Insight about these unconscious dynamics helps so much to avoid conflict. However, some experts in psychology don't agree with this contention. They believe we can overlook the contents of our unconscious mind in favor of mental strategies and conscious processing. Dr. Richard A. Friedman writes that psychological insight (the truth we recover from our unconscious mind) is overrated.[18] As evidence for his assertion, Friedman mentions the case of a man in his 30s who was sad and anxious after being dumped by his girlfriend for the second time in three years. This fellow had also experienced separation anxiety with earlier girlfriends. Despite his years of psychotherapy, during which he traced the painful feelings back to a separation

---

[18] http://www.nytimes.com/2011/01/18/health/views/18mind.html?_r=3&n=Top%2fNews%2fScience%2fColumns%2fMind&

from his hospitalized mother when he was four, the man was not feeling any better. Friedman asks, "Was this because his self-knowledge was flawed or incomplete? Or is insight itself, no matter how deep, of limited value?" The doctor concludes, "...it seems fair to say that insight is neither necessary nor sufficient to feeling better."

It's apparent to me that the man referred to by Friedman didn't get effective psychotherapy, which means that he didn't get adequate insight. Good therapy would have explored this man's unconscious determination to live through old unresolved feelings of being abandoned and rejected. This is the real insight: The man grows in his awareness when he recognizes his unresolved emotional attachments to feelings of being abandoned and rejected. That means, in this situation, that he would recognize his determination to pursue experiences of abandonment and rejection. He would also learn how he covers up awareness (through various psychological defenses) of how he himself participates in those negative emotional experiences. Once he realizes that he's choosing unconsciously in his relationships to experience these negative emotions, he has a greatly improved chance of avoiding the self-sabotage.

Unconsciously, this fellow is compelled in his relationships with women to go looking for those unresolved negative emotions. He needs insight that exposes his unconscious determination to experience his relationships through abandonment and rejection. Otherwise, he's likely, in self-pity, to go on feeling himself to be a victim. He will then likely continue to be attached to feel rejected and he will repeat his self-defeating behavior with other women. Dysfunction of this kind persists in the human psyche on the basis of this principle: *Whatever is unresolved in our psyche is going to be sought after and experienced by us, no matter how painful.* Unresolved hurts and painful memories are the soul food of our psyche's dark side. This is what it means to become aware of having emotional attachments.

We don't need the presence of others to feel unloved. We can feel it very much within ourselves. Driving this inner pain is our inner critic which can be very harsh and unforgiving. We end up absorbing this negativity and feeling that it somehow represents the truth about us. Our inner critic can feel like a bully who despises us. When we see more clearly into these dynamics in our psyche, we use insight and intelligence to avoid unnecessary suffering.

13 . Cognitive Therapy's Distorted Thinking

Recently I came across a best-selling psychology textbook, and I believe the sections of it dealing with the essentials of self-awareness are not accessing a deep enough level of understanding.

The widely used textbook, written by three Harvard University professors of psychology, is titled simply *Psychology* (Worth Publishers, New York, 2009). Students were paying $162.98 for the latest edition of this textbook.[19] They're not getting their money's worth, and I'll tell you why.

---

[19] http://www.amazon.com/Psychology-Daniel-L-

In this textbook, the authors express their preference for cognitive therapy. (They subtly—and not so subtly—disparage psychodynamic therapy which is based on depth psychology.) Cognitive therapy, they say, "focuses on helping a client identify and correct any distorted thinking about self, others, or the world." The key term here is "distorted thinking." Who decides what constitutes distorted thinking? People who are receptive to being told what to think have a tendency to be passive and to become adherents to fundamentalist dogma or rigid ideologies. Most people who go to psychotherapists don't need someone telling them what or how to think. Rather, they need help in discovering their inner truth and developing their authentic self.

The best psychotherapists don't mess with this notion of distorted thinking. We don't deal in "cognitive restructuring," to use one of the textbook authors' favored terms. Instead, we trace the client's difficulties back to the source, using as clues the content of painful memories, events, and situations associated with the client's anxiety, stress, painful emotions, and self-defeating behaviors. We're guides for the exploration of their unconscious mind. We don't tell them what to believe or what to think, although we do introduce basic principles and knowledge for them to consider.

Let's compare the two approaches, cognitive therapy and psychodynamic therapy, using an example from the textbook. The cognitive approach, excerpted below (on page 551 of the First Edition), is then followed by my analysis.

Schacter/dp/1429237198

[*From the textbook*] For example, a depressed client may believe that she is stupid and will never pass her college courses—all on the basis of one poor grade. In this situation, the therapist would work with the client to examine the validity of this belief. The therapist would consider relevant evidence such as grades on previous exams, performance on other coursework, and examples of intelligence outside of school. It may be that the client has never failed a course before and has achieved good grades in this particular course in the past. In this case, the therapist would encourage the client to consider all this information in determining whether she is truly "stupid." . . . [the therapist may] help the client decide whether doing poorly in one course constitutes being "stupid" and whether there is anything the client can do to better prepare for future exams.

As I see it, this cognitive approach does the woman a disservice. She's indeed feeling stupid, but that painful feeling is likely a symptom of (as well as a defense against recognition of) a deeper problem. As her therapist, I would listen to her to get a sense of what that deeper problem might be, and I would guide her, if she were willing to be guided, towards her own inner truth, whatever that truth might be.

So, what might be that truth? It's possible that she's feeling overwhelmed by college life and the rigors of her academic program. These circumstances aren't necessarily overwhelming in themselves, but she experiences them that way because the challenges of college life have triggered within her an old unresolved emotion from childhood having to do with lingering helplessness and powerlessness. All of us are reluctant to see our lingering entanglements in old unresolved emotions. The entanglements mean that one or more negative emotions (refusal, helplessness, criticism, or rejection, for instance) are still unresolved within us. As a result, we're still unconsciously inclined, even determined or programmed, to experience one or more of those negative emotions, even though it's painful and self-defeating to do so.

This woman hasn't achieved inner freedom. She wants to feel strong and competent, but she still remains an emotional prisoner of lingering helplessness. She has to expose this emotional "default position" and understand that she has been making an unconscious choice to continue to experience it. Such insight produces inner freedom.

This woman is likely using the idea of being stupid as a defense. The unconscious defense makes this claim: "I'm not willing to experience the challenges of college academics through old unresolved feelings of weakness or helplessness. The problem is I'm stupid." This is a defense called "pleading guilty to the lesser crime." According to the irrational terms imposed by our unconscious mind, the lesser crime is being stupid, the more serious crime is being emotionally attached to helplessness and being unconsciously prone to replaying and recycling that unresolved negative emotion.

This analysis of mine might not apply to this particular woman. Her plight could be due to something else, and she and her psychodynamic therapist would pursue other possibilities. She could, for instance, be entangled emotionally in being a disappointment to herself and others. Her father might have felt this way about himself, and then projected this negative expectation on to her. The woman consciously wants to do well, but unconsciously she expects to be a disappointment. She could be exceedingly smart, yet still be determined unconsciously to act out this unresolved conflict. The defense now reads: "I don't want to be a disappointment or to be seen in a negative light. The problem is that I'm stupid." Again, in the unconscious mind's irrational reckoning, being stupid is the lesser crime, being emotionally attached to the feeling of being a disappointment is the more serious crime.

Though the defense "works" in hiding the inner facts, she pays a painful price in feeling herself to be stupid. That painful defense, when not exposed for what it is, would also cause her to lose confidence and could lead to failure in her academic program.

If either of the above analyses were true (ongoing therapy helps determine what is true, and other possibilities can be explored), then obviously that self-knowledge is of much greater value to her than what the cognitive approach offers. (This report in *The Journal of the American Medical Association* comments on the superior effectiveness of psychodynamic therapy.[20]) While the cognitive method does have value in certain situations, its use with this woman is like talking to a university student at a fifth-grader's level. We have to be smarter than that, especially about what really matters.

Knowing her deeper truth, this woman moves vital knowledge from her unconscious mind to her conscious mind and thereby to her intelligence. Knowing what's

---

[20] http://jama.jamanetwork.com/article.aspx?articleid=1028649

true, she's greatly empowered. It's not "cognitive restructuring" that frees her from her plight. Rather, it's her intelligence, now enhanced by vital insight, which does so. This process doesn't require years of therapy. With skilled psychodynamic therapists, some people can begin to assimilate the inner facts and have that knowledge begin quite quickly to benefit them, sometimes within a month or two of beginning weekly therapy. Some people, of course, decline to do the deeper work, yet they should at least be presented with that option.

Cognitive therapists claim that clinical studies have proven the benefits of their method. (Possible flaws in the methodology of psychological studies are noted here,[21] here,[22] and here.[23]) How are these benefits ascertained? Researchers ask the clients how they're feeling and doing after experiencing cognitive therapy. Yes, some clients do feel better and they express satisfaction with the therapy. However, because they consciously want to do well, they can renounce, on a temporary basis, some of the lesser symptoms of their dysfunction. But their inner conflicts remain unresolved, and different symptoms relating to those conflicts can soon emerge in ever more painful and self-defeating ways. Moreover, these individuals are initially grateful to their cognitive therapists and will praise their effectiveness because, through this superficial form of therapy, they (the clients) have avoided the often fear-inducing challenge of deeper introspection and self-examination.

---

[21] http://www.nytimes.com/2008/04/08/science/08tier.html?_r=2&
[22] http://en.wikipedia.org/wiki/Cognitive_therapy#Criticisms
[23] http://gleaner.rutgers.edu/2011/02/esp-and-the-flaws-of-psychological-research/

The textbook's authors say, as a way of explaining their aversion for the psychodynamic approach, that the dark view of human nature emphasizes limitations and problems rather than possibilities and potentials. Yet these "scientists" don't offer any evidence for why this "dark" view is wrong. Truth is what offers the best possibilities and potentials. Human nature—like Nature itself—is what it is, both light and dark, positive and negative. We're magnificent creatures, though we won't fully appreciate that fact when afraid of our deeper dimensions.

When inner truth comes into focus, we're able to use our enhanced intelligence and awareness to overcome inner conflicts and emotional roadblocks. We don't need any brand of "straight thinking." We need inner truth that helps us to discover our authentic self.

Meanwhile, a new interdisciplinary field, known as affective science, is emerging alongside cognitive science.[24] This new field includes the study of emotions, moods, preferences, attitudes, value, and stress. The leaders of this science will need to overcome emotional resistance and blend into their analyses the knowledge of inner conflict, emotional attachments, and unconscious defenses in order to fulfill their highest aspirations.

24

http://www.psychologicalscience.org/index.php/publications/observer/2013/october-13/the-emerging-field-of-affective-science.html

14. Three Great Truths from Psychology

Three of Freud's discoveries deserve to be identified as essential facts or practical truths. I say this especially in light of the evidence emerging from neuroscience in the past decade that Freud was right, in so many ways, about the dynamic forces that operate in our unconscious mind and significantly determine how we experience everyday life.[25]

Freud was himself a pioneering neuroscientist.[26] Now brain scans are showing that he was right that guilt plays a role in depression.[27] New evidence is also emerging that he was right about the extent to which sexual feelings influence our dream life.[28] A report in *Newsweek* says that, despite its flaws, Freud's psychological map "happens to be the most coherent and, from the standpoint of individual experience, meaningful theory of the mind there is."[29]

His discoveries revealed the existence in our psyche of the dynamics of transference, projection, and identification. Although this knowledge has been available for more than 100 years, only a small percentage (I would guess less than five percent) of the world's population understands these concepts as they apply to themselves. Yet it's knowledge that can easily

[25] http://discovermagazine.com/2014/april/14-the-second-coming-of-sigmund-freud
[26] http://www.theguardian.com/science/neurophilosophy/2014/mar/10/neuroscience-history-science
[27] http://www.bmedreport.com/archives/32719
[28] http://aeon.co/magazine/altered-states/was-freud-right-about-dreams-all-along/
[29] http://www.newsweek.com/what-freud-got-right-142575

be learned and that can greatly alleviate human suffering.

Academic psychologists tend to refer to these dynamics or processes as *psychoanalytic concepts*. These processes are, however, much more than concepts. They're actual inner processes that tend to be unconscious, through which people experience unpleasant or painful emotions. The knowledge needs to be taught in our schools so it can begin to benefit individuals and society. I attempt in this essay to present the knowledge with straightforward simplicity, in a way in which it can be easily learned. (Later, in "Vital Knowledge for Marriage Intimacy," I write about these dynamics as they apply to married life.)

Let's start by looking at transference. It is most helpful to understand this process through the idea of *negative* transference, as opposed to *normal* transference, because this is how the suffering is experienced. Negative transference occurs when one individual (Jim) senses or believes that another person (Jane) is expressing negative emotions such as criticism, disapproval, disappointment, or rejection toward him, even when that impression does not correspond with her actual feelings or behaviors. In other words, Jane could be quite neutral in her feelings and thoughts about Jim, yet he still "reads" a negative intention from her words or actions. Jim is transferring on to Jane some unresolved emotions from his own past concerning feelings of being criticized, rejected, and so on. Because these negative emotions are unresolved in Jim, he is interested unconsciously in recreating and recycling them. Hence, he transfers on to others the expectation that they are directing (or will direct) these negative emotions toward him. Convinced that his "readings" of such situations are objective and accurate, Jim consequently regards others with less trust and openness. He also suffers unnecessarily because he is "taking on" negative impressions that are not justified by actual circumstances.

Transference is a common problem in marriages. As the saying goes, men "marry" their mothers, while women "marry" their fathers. This happens, in part, because of this unconscious propensity to repeat with our partners—through transference—the old unresolved emotions that we experienced with our parents (or siblings and caretakers). When Jim realizes that he's experiencing a situation through transference, he's able to begin to observe himself and his emotions with more objectivity. He's no longer going to deceive himself about what's real and true.

While transference is about what we feel coming at us from others, the second process, projection, is about what we feel as we project our own impressions on to others. An individual (Larry) "sees" a defect or weakness in someone else (Judy) that upsets or annoys him. If Larry's negative feelings about Judy's alleged defect are intense enough, he might overlook her good qualities and be cold and distant toward her. Unconsciously, Larry is disapproving or critical of himself for having a similar weakness. (Frequently, this weakness involves a person's emotional entanglement in self-doubt and other variations of passivity.) Larry's defense could be saying, "I'm not the one who is passive—she is!" He is defending against his inner critic's (superego's) disapproval of his inner weakness. As he deflects the inner criticism outwardly toward Judy, he can feel toward her a negative intensity that is the equivalent of the negative aggression coming at him from his inner critic. When he understands this dynamic, he can turn inward with the power of insight, learning to deflect his inner critic's unwarranted harassment and illegitimate authority. Projection, which often leads to personality clashes, has many variations, and the Wikipedia article on the subject is enlightening.

The last process, identification, can be understood as the unconscious tendency or temptation to identify with what another person is feeling (or what we imagine the other person is feeling), regardless of whether that's a positive or negative feeling. Positive identification is usually beneficial, as in the case of someone identifying with an admirable role model. Yet identification can be misleading and negative as when, for instance, a youth identifies with a bully in the neighborhood. Identification can also be troublesome in another way. For instance, a father (Sam), who often golfs with his son (Tom), identifies strongly with Tom when the boy plays badly on the golf course. Both Sam and Tom have unresolved issues with feelings of being seen in a negative light and being a disappointment. These unresolved issues sabotage Tom when he attempts to perform well, and his father unconsciously can't resist getting "hit up" with this negative feeling and resonating with it as he sees his son struggling. If Sam understands his identification with his son, he can refrain from getting triggered, and he can have a better chance of helping Tom settle down emotionally and avoid self-sabotage. Our identifications can occur in so many different ways, including the emotional identifications we can have inside ourselves involving shame and failure.

As we learn about these three dynamics—transference, projection, and identification—we begin to see them operating within us. These dynamics are the psychological means or mechanisms whereby much of our suffering and self-defeat are recycled and replayed in our daily life. Breaking free of our suffering and self-defeat is a learning process. We learn about the unconscious procedures and dynamics in our psyche that can operate "with a mind of their own" in opposition to our best interests.

An understanding of these dynamics reveals that the negativity we're experiencing (worry, anxiety, fear, sense of weakness, and so on) is coming from within us. Other people or difficult circumstances are not *causing* this negativity, only *triggering* it. We understand, of course, that the negativity, including shame and guilt, is not our fault. However, we might be considered to be somewhat at fault, or at least unwise, if we decline to learn about these dynamics when they're presented to us. It's time to fill in the blank spots in our awareness. It's a powerful act of consciousness to take ownership of the negativity that's been circulating inside us while simultaneously bringing into focus the dynamics and aspects of that inner process. This is the means whereby we eliminate negativity, misery, and unhappiness.

III - A VARIETY OF PAINFUL SYMPTOMS

15 . How Worriers Unconsciously Chose to Suffer

People these days are snapping a lot of *selfies,* those close-up self-portraits taken with a cell-phone camera. Could this activity foretell a coming trend in which more of us turn inward to take close-ups of our psychological self? When we penetrate our psyche, new intelligence about the nature of our suffering is disclosed.

Let's take a close-up of the mild-to-serious form of suffering known as worry. Worrywarts abound, and many of them are highly skilled at picturing worst-case scenarios. They're good at taking snapshots of dreadful things that are happening only in their imagination.

Not only do they worry, they worry for nothing much of the time. The things they worry about frequently never happen. So worriers suffer for nothing. That's at least as bad as working for nothing or crying for nothing.

Worriers produce expectations or visualizations of future problems or calamities. They visualize and anticipate being harmed, helpless, defeated, overwhelmed, hurt or disadvantaged in some manner should those problems arise. Some therapists tout as a remedy the benefits of producing "positive visualizations," yet this approach doesn't acknowledge the likelihood that our negative attachments are going to overwhelm our positive intentions. For resolution, we have to empower our intelligence with the reality of inner conflict and the sabotaging effects of emotional attachments.

Worriers also tend to believe that their worry is appropriate because, as we all know, bad things do happen on occasion. Uncertainty is built into the DNA of life. Unpleasant experiences likely do await us. It's also possible some disaster or tragedy will befall us. Yet the healthier we are emotionally, the more we're able to flourish in the present, confident we can handle what life has in store. But some people see the uncertainties of life (or vagaries of fate) as opportunities to suffer right now, in this moment, long before anything bad has happened.

Worriers "play" a game of self-deceit. They think their worries are appropriate, but they have a hidden reason for their worries: They're making an inner choice to entertain or recycle old unresolved negative emotions. Using their imagination, they compulsively peep into the future in order to suffer in the present. (This compulsion is a product of unresolved inner conflict: while we want *consciously* to experience what is pleasant, we chose *unconsciously* to feel negative emotions, unresolved from our past, including feelings of being helpless, defeated, or victimized in the face of difficult situations.)

There're a lot of different things a person can worry about. Let's look at a few examples.

Todd worries that his girlfriend will reject or abandon him. Jealousy often accompanies his worry. He's not aware that he's indulging in the prospect of being rejected or abandoned. Todd admits that he has problems with worry and jealousy, but he doesn't recognize where the worry and jealousy come from.

These painful feelings arise because of his emotional attachment to rejection and abandonment, two negative emotions that are unresolved from his childhood. He's compelled to replay and recycle his emotional associations with rejection and abandonment unless he resolves them through deeper awareness.

Todd is also tempted, through his imagination, to produce visualizations of his girlfriend in the embrace of some fellow. Unwittingly, he produces these fantasies for the purpose of intensifying his bittersweet affinity for (hence, attachment to) rejection and abandonment. And the more acutely he worries, the more he's using worry as a psychological defense to cover up his emotional attachments to rejection and abandonment. "I'm not expecting to be rejected," the unconscious defense reads, "look at how worried I am that it might happen."

Alisa worries that the project she handed in at work won't be well received. Long before she hears from her boss, she's already suffering with the feeling of doing badly. In the present moment, as she speculates about an outcome days away, she dwells in her imagination on how she'll feel when she finds out her work didn't meet company standards. What's going on here? Alisa may be entertaining the feeling of being criticized or condemned for doing badly. She's attached to the feeling of criticism (an unresolved emotion from childhood), and unconsciously she's compelled to continue to feel that emotion in the form of self-criticism. Though her worry is irrational (she's smart and highly capable), her unconscious determination to continue to experience criticism overrides a rational expectation of doing well. By peering into the future and seeing herself fail, she creates the experience of self-criticism in the present moment.

Larry worries he doesn't have enough money saved for his retirement. He makes a good salary, has invested his savings wisely, and will be getting a pension. He has ten more years of good earnings before he retires, and he has paid off his house and seen his children through college. Unconsciously, Larry is determined to replay one of his unresolved issues, the negative emotion of feeling weak and helpless. When he worries about money, he's imaging being unable to take care of himself and his wife. He imagines how he'll feel when, short of funds and no longer able to work, he's overwhelmed by bills and other financial obligations and placed at the mercy of the kindness of others.

Unconsciously, he overlooks the fact that his worry is irrational. Instead, he secretly wants to indulge in feeling weak. As part of this, Larry is inclined to experience feelings of lacking in intrinsic value in himself, and so he makes himself emotionally dependent on the sum of his monetary value in order to feel substantial and whole. Now, however, even plenty of money won't feel like enough because he constantly reverts back to this inner default position which is his attachment to feeling that he lacks value.

Todd, Alisa, and Larry believe their worry is somehow warranted. Occasionally, they might say, "Oh, I worry too much." But they fail to see the deeper problem, their unconscious willingness to replay (or indulge in) negative emotions having to do, respectively, with rejection, criticism, and unworthiness. We simply hate to see how, in our psyche, we so blatantly act against our best interests. It offends our sensibilities. We can't believe we would be so blind as to do this to ourselves.

These unconscious dynamics get even more interesting. Not only is worry in itself a way to suffer, it's also, as mentioned, employed unconsciously as a defense. Here's how that works:

Todd's inner critic has an intimate "awareness" of the contents of his psyche. The inner critic knows about his attachment to feeling rejected and abandoned, and it uses this knowledge to mock and bully him. His inner critic accuses him of wanting to feel rejected: "You like it, don't you! That's what you're looking for, you wimp." Todd reacts to the accusation with an unconscious defense: "I don't want to feel rejected or abandoned. Look at how much I worry that it might happen. My worry proves I don't want to experience those negative emotions." Unfortunately for Todd, he has to produce plenty of worry in order to make this defense stick.

Reacting to her inner critic, Alisa makes this claim: "I don't want to feel criticism (or self-criticism) for failing to get praise for my work. I'm very worried that might happen. My worry proves that I don't want it to happen." Alisa also has to produce worry, and suffer with it, in order to erect a defense that covers up her attachment to criticism. Should this defense become unstable, she might have to worry more intensely and painfully, and produce anxiety and fear, in order to maintain the effectiveness of the defense.

Larry is also using worry as a defense. He chooses unconsciously to feel helpless and lacking in intrinsic value. He experiences the need to cover up this self-defeating choice: "Look at how much I worry. That proves I hate feeling helpless and unworthy." All it proves, though, is his determination to resist becoming more conscious. He's loath to expose his attachments to feeling helpless and lacking in value because doing so, it feels to him at a deep unconscious level, would shatter his ego-based sense of self.

We can remove the distress and anxiety of worry when we begin to bring inner truth into focus.

16. Indecisive No More

There's something important that chronically indecisive people need to understand: *They're not actually interested in making a decision.* Since this statement flies brazenly in the face of common sense, let me restate it differently.

Indeed, as these individuals anguish intensely over the pros and cons of a given option, they think they want to be decisive. But they're fooling themselves. Behind their apparent sincerity, they're cozying up to an old unresolved negative emotion (inner passivity) which involves feeling weak, helpless, and lacking in the sense of their own authority. This old joke satirizes the emotional predicament: "Once I make up my mind, I'm full of indecision."

Through this emotional weakness, indecisiveness haunts a significant percentage of people. When we finally do make up our mind—after agonizing and procrastinating long enough—we're likely to start being indecisive over some other matter.

The misery and self-defeating consequences of our indecisiveness are the prices we pay to cover up an inner conflict. What is that conflict? On the surface of our awareness, we *do* indeed want to be decisive. We want to feel the pleasure and sense of authority that goes with making a good decision on our behalf. Deeper down, it's a whole different matter. We don't want to feel decisive. It's too tempting instead to "know ourself" through unresolved inner weakness. We want to experience ourselves through the old self-doubt, uncertainty, and sense of unfitness that is an emotional default position. At a deep level, we've known ourselves through that familiar frailty as far back as we can remember.

People can shift away from that old identity and experience the pleasure of wisdom, discernment, and decisiveness. The quickest way is to expose inner passivity and begin to understand how it gets entangled with inner aggression (inner critic or superego).

Let's try to bring this into focus. When compulsively indecisive people do finally make up their mind, what often happens? They start to worry that they have made the wrong decision. They start undermining themselves and second-guessing their own authority. Why does this happen? Their sense of authority comes under attack from their inner critic. They feel they will be harshly condemned from within if their decision turns out to be a bad or costly one. Their sense of authority collapses because, in the face of the self-aggression that emanates from the inner critic, they have retreated into inner passivity.

Medieval philosopher Maimonides said, by way of advice: "The risk of a wrong decision is preferable to the terror of indecision." Why did Maimonides offer these words of wisdom? He must have seen among his fellow Jews, Arabs, and Spaniards that they tended, in their passivity, to prefer the terror of indecision to the risk of a wrong decision. Ah yes, human nature hasn't budged in 1000 years, and the inner critic still backs us into a lose-lose corner: It hammers away at us, as in the first instance, for daring to express inner authority, and, in the second instance, for being too passive.

Indecisiveness is one of the many painful symptoms that arise because of the major conflict in our psyche between aggression and passivity. The conflict puts us, as mentioned, in a no-win situation: If we hold off indefinitely on making a decision, our passivity, taunted by the inner critic, causes us to feel terrible; if we do finally make a decision, we fearfully and passively experience self-doubt in conjunction with the sense of being held accountable by our inner critic for possibly having made a bad choice. Similar dynamics are involved with procrastination: We feel terrible when we procrastinate, yet our inner passivity keeps us trapped in that behavioral predicament.

With indecisiveness (and many other emotional difficulties), there are two dimensions of the problem: one is the reality dimension, the other the unconscious dimension. We can look at an example to see how these two dimensions become entangled. Consider the case of Roger, a neuroscientist who is plagued with indecisiveness about whether to leave his wife for another woman. He has been debating the question with himself for more than three years. All Roger considers, though, is the outward reality dimension, the pros and cons in his mind of leaving his wife. What he doesn't see—from the unconscious dimension—is that he's acting out his version of an inner conflict that troubled his father who for many years had complained of feeling trapped on a dead-end career path. So Roger is clinging to an unsatisfactory situation (the reality dimension) and failing to trace his predicament to the identification he made during childhood with his father's conflict (the unconscious dimension). Roger is determined to go on experiencing himself in a passive way because doing so is such a major ingredient in his sense of self. This determination constitutes an inner blind spot as well as stubborn resistance to inner growth. In a way that is both literal and figurative, he has an emotional addiction to the feeling of being passive.

Indecisiveness can also serve as a defense against realization of one's determination to be passive. It constitutes, in its stubbornness and in the mental effort of weighing pros and cons, a smattering of strength that provides the individual with the illusion that he is acting—albeit very slowly—in his best interests. "I'm not being passive," the unconscious defense reads, "I'm trying very hard to make up my mind. Look at the effort I'm making. It's just taking me some time." This tact recalls the wisecrack, "If I decide to be indecisive, that's my decision."

Indecisiveness crosses over into procrastination and also ambivalence. *Ambivalence* is the experience of two contradictory feelings toward the same person or situation at the same time. Again, ambivalent people can't decide how they really feel. They may like a particular person, but through their own unresolved issues they get triggered by the words, behaviors, or personality quirks of that person.

Often when an indecisive person finally makes a decision, she might feel she was compelled or browbeaten to do so by the insistence of others. Again, inner passivity is the problem. Even if caring friends pushed her into making a good decision, she can be resentful due to her unconscious determination to feel forced, controlled, or dominated. Keep in mind that inner passivity, which constitutes unresolved negativity in our psyche, always goes looking for opportunities to be experienced. In my books, I have described hundreds of the self-defeating ways in which it is experienced. Inner passivity, which inhibits us from identifying with our true, authentic inner authority, can be understood as a hindrance to freedom.

If you look online for guidance or understanding about indecisiveness, you're likely to find only advice, not insight. An article[30] at Forbes magazine, written by a psychiatrist, offers seven ways to conquer indecisiveness, including trust your gut, channel Winston Churchill, and flip a coin. Advice like this is cheap if not worthless; in contrast, insight is precious. We're simply not going to become wiser and more intelligent when we fail to see the deeper dimensions of our struggles with a behavioral and emotional problem such as indecisiveness.

17 . A New Understanding of Bipolar Disorder

---

[30] http://www.forbes.com/sites/stevenberglas/2012/01/10/seven-ways-to-cope-with-indecision/

About 5.7 million American adults experience the particularly burdensome affliction known as bipolar disorder.[31] Psychiatric experts are uncertain as to its origins, yet depth psychology does have a theory to explain one possible cause.

Depth psychology is usually not effective for people with schizophrenia and other psychotic disorders. Yet people with bipolar disorder, while they sometimes have psychotic breaks, usually return to a fully functional state between episodes. At such times these individuals can strengthen themselves and become more stable by learning self-knowledge that pertains to their affliction. Researchers pursuing medical and neuroscience investigations of bipolar disorder can also sharpen their science by considering the influence of these psychological dynamics.

Cognitive-behavioral therapy, in combination with medications, is known to help bipolar sufferers cope with their affliction. This therapy is advice-oriented, while depth psychology tries to uncover the influences of inner conflict and help to resolve that conflict. Understanding the deeper psychological factors in bipolar disorder can greatly help sufferers because the knowledge, when absorbed, enhances the individual's intelligence and strengthens self-regulation.

Inner passivity, in particular, appears to be a factor in bipolar disorder. This passivity can be traced to the universal experience of infantile helplessness. All of us, not just people with bipolar disorder, are to some degree under the influence of inner passivity. The condition causes adults to cling to an emotional-mental

[31] http://www.medterms.com/script/main/art.asp?articlekey=2468

identification involving self-doubt and helplessness. This passivity, as mentioned, is attributable to the many childhood years that we all spend experiencing ourselves as dependent and subordinate. In adults, this passivity still lingers in our psyche (unconscious mind) where it occupies a kind of no-man's land that has not been claimed or even recognized by our intelligence or consciousness.

Inner passivity, as mentioned, describes the internal mental-emotional position that people most often represent in the psychological conflict between inner aggression (as represented by the inner critic or superego) and inner passivity (as represented by the unconscious or subordinate ego). This unconscious part of our ego battles ineffectively and defensively on a daily basis against our harsh inner critic. The inner situation compares to a courtroom drama where we face an aggressive cunning prosecutor (inner critic) while being represented by a weak inept defense lawyer (inner passivity).

Bipolar disorder appears to be, at least in part, a symptom of this primal clash in our psyche between aggression and passivity. To explore this idea, we can start by looking at bipolar disorder's symptoms. (It's not necessary here to distinguish among bipolar I disorder, bipolar II disorder, and the other subsets of the disorder because they share essential similarities at the level of the unconscious mind.) Bipolar disorder features mood swings between a manic phase and a depressive phase. According to the depth-psychology model presented here, the manic phase—in its display of pseudo-power, hyper-activity, and inappropriate aggression—is an unconscious reaction to inner passivity. This reaction also serves as a psychological defense against one's recognition of the deep emotional identification or resonance with inner passivity. Other common symptoms of inner passivity include self-doubt, indecision, fear, and feelings of being overwhelmed.

Naturally, the bipolar individual is unable to physically sustain the huge output of energy required to maintain the manic phase. He or she soon collapses back into inner passivity, as represented by the depressive phase. Here the individual, now even more emotionally entangled in the passive side of the inner conflict, is swallowed up in an emotional swamp, an inner no-man's land where he or she is unable to muster enough strength, energy, power, or vision to thrive or flourish in a healthy way.

Again, let's look at some symptoms to illustrate how, in the bipolar-sufferer, passivity and aggression play off one another in a way that is painful and self-defeating. Let's first look at the symptoms from the manic phase, since during this phase there is a reaction to (and defense against recognition of) the deep identification and emotional resonance with inner passivity. Individuals in the manic phase can feel heightened self-esteem or grandiosity, a decreased need for sleep, loquaciousness, excited hopefulness, racing thoughts and surges of creativity, purpose and drive, and aggression. All of these symptoms—in being so fleeting, exhausting, and illusory—fail the test of being true aggression and power. Yet illusion and manic pleasure, though third-rate gratifications, are sufficient to serve, at least on a temporary basis, as defenses that cover up the underlying passivity. (People are almost always in denial of inner passivity and defend vigorously against recognition of it.)

On the depressive side of the conflict, the individual experiences a significant loss of energy, diminished ability to think or concentrate, indecisiveness, depressed moods (feeling sad, empty, hopeless, or suicidal), boredom, and insomnia. All of these symptoms show evidence that the individual has collapsed back into the passive side of the inner conflict, the original default position.

Consider the actions and words of a boy, James (diagnosed with bipolar disorder), who is reading aloud a story and speaking to his mother.[32] Note the rapid swings here between his mania, as expressed aggressively, and his passivity:

> When his mother asked a question, the roil of frustration that nearly always seethes just under James's surface, even when he is happy, sloshed over. . . "If you listened on the first page, it says it!" he scolded her, then collapsed hopelessly beside the coffee table. "You don't get anything. Now I lost my place. Forget it. I give up." He crossed his arms on the table and rested his head in them. Mary [his mother] waited quietly in her chair. Sure enough, a minute or two later James began reading us a list he had concocted of 50 ways to get rich. The next time his mother spoke, he bellowed: "I wasn't talking to you! I'm not reading it now!" He threw the paper down and stalked out of the room.

It's quite possible that bipolar disorder is a depiction or representation of the irrational part of the infantile mind.

---

[32] http://www.nytimes.com/2008/09/14/magazine/14bipolar-t.html?_r=1&

A primitive dimension of the infantile mind reverberates with the intense contradiction between the reality of being profoundly helpless and the illusion, induced through megalomania, of being all-powerful. (Read, "A Chaos Theory of the Mind.") The bipolar individual appears to be expressing elements of this infantile conflict.

It's very important to understand how the aggressive and manic side of the conflict serves as a psychological defense. As mentioned, the manic side, especially when expressed aggressively, is both a symptom of inner passivity as well as a defense that covers up realization or acknowledgement of this passivity. The rules of our psyche call for us to cover up (or defend against recognition of) the ways that we can be deeply identified with the passive side of the inner conflict. So the bipolar individual produces a defense to cover up his or her emotional affinity for this passive, negative side. In a typical example, the unconscious defense takes this position: "I'm not indulging in feeling powerless or helpless, or identifying with myself through those feelings. Look at how much pleasure (mania) I have when I'm energized and feeling powerful. That proves I don't want to feel weak." This claim of the defense, of course, is false: The individual is determined to continue to experience the unresolved passivity because it has become an emotional attachment, or an emotional default position in the psyche, or a major aspect of one's self-identification.

Our defenses are unstable. They often have to become more extreme or self-damaging in order to maintain their effectiveness. In the case of bipolar disorder, this can lead to psychotic episodes when the individual "ratchets up" the illusion of having power. A psychotic break can be associated with an illusion of "transcendence," or a flood of megalomania or omnipotence, whereby one has the impression of having escaped the bounds of human limitations to become god-like.

Some people do recover from this psychological affliction through conventional treatments which include drugs, therapy sessions, and support groups. Yet, as my clinical experience with bipolar individuals attests, they not only can recover but they can go on to become highly insightful and evolved when they understand the nature of their affliction in terms of inner passivity and its conflicted relationship with the inner critic.

18 . The Futility of Compulsive Approval-Seeking

Using brain imaging, researchers have discovered that pleasure is activated in the brain when people get positive feedback concerning their reputation or character.[33] These researchers do not appear to understand that such pleasure is not necessarily genuine or healthy. A psychological defense, for instance, feels good when it successfully covers up some truth that an individual does not want to see about himself.

Few people, experts included, know or address the hidden reasons why we generate such pleasure in

---

[33] http://journal.frontiersin.org/Journal/10.3389/fnhum.2013.00439/abstract

receiving praise and validation. Typical is this explanation:

> These results [from the research cited above] may explain why Facebook is so popular. It likely isn't Facebook itself . . . it is all of the self-promoting features that it offers: posting what *you* are thinking, posting pictures of *yourself*, giving *your* opinion on what others post via "likes" . . . throw in a little intermittent reinforcement (e.g., not knowing when the next time someone will "like" or comment on your post) . . . and Facebook has a winning formula . . . Or at least one that gets us hooked.[34]

Yes, but why do we get hooked? Why in heaven's name do so many of us feel the need to go through the day constantly assessing ourselves and looking for validation. This emotional neediness often shows up as inner dialogue in which we're trying to establish our importance either to ourselves or to others. Mark Twain noted this peculiarity of human nature more than 100 years ago when he famously said, ". . . the Sole Impulse which dictates and compels a man's every act" is "the imperious necessity of securing his own approval, in every emergency and at all costs."

We feel pleasure in producing self-approval for two main reasons. *(Warning, you're about to descend into your psyche's murky waters. Put on your breathing gear and thinking cap.)* First, in compulsively seeking self-approval, we're trying to counteract the self-doubt that

---

[34] http://www.huffingtonpost.com/dr-judson-brewer/social-media-addiction_b_4079697.html?utm_hp_ref=gps-for-the-soul&ir=GPS%20for%20the%20Soul

pervades, in various degrees, the inner life of most of us. Even those of us who appear supremely confident can have residues of self-doubt in our psyche. When we go hunting for approval, it means we're living more at the surface of ourselves, dependent on our ego and personality to prop us up and provide a sense of substance.

At a deep level, most people, extroverts and strong personalities included, are not connecting strongly enough with their value, goodness, and inner authority. In a way that can be mostly unconscious, we all tend to identify with ourselves, at least in part, through feelings of unworthiness, weakness, and insignificance. Unconsciously and in varying degrees, we're all emotionally attached to this identification that lingers from childhood experiences. Our mental and emotional "software" is coded with powerful memories and experiences of refusal, helplessness, rejection, and criticism, along with a variety of baby fears.

To cover up or deny (or defend against) our attachment to (or identification with) these negative associations, we're eager to produce a defense that proclaims how thrilled or happy we are to cast ourselves in the best possible light or to imagine that others see us in this rosy glow.

As it happens, such approval is a defense against recognition of our unconscious willingness to absorb inner criticism. This criticism emanates from our inner critic in the form of negative self-judgments. When the defense of self-approval is effective, it produces "pleasure vibes" that brain imaging can detect.

The pleasure says, in effect: "Hey, I'm not looking to be criticized. See how much pleasure I feel when being validated and praised." This pleasure is felt only on a temporary basis, and its intensity—as a "reward" for covering up inner truth—depends on the effectiveness, at any given moment, of our defense. The pleasure, even at its peak, still pales in comparison to the rich sustained satisfaction and enjoyment of being creative, generous, brave, free of negativity, or committed to a noble cause.

The pleasure of self-approval helps us to avoid seeing how willing we are to go on "knowing ourself" through old painful memories of helplessness, humiliation and defeat. As our mocking, sarcastic inner critic piles on with accusations of our alleged defectiveness and unworthiness, we don't want to see how passive we are to that cruel, primitive agency of our psyche. Meanwhile, no amount of approval or positive attention feels like enough when our inner critic is breathing down our neck.

Self-approval applies coats of whitewash to our idealized self-image. The whitewash produces a feeling of relief, or excitement in our brain: We're getting away with covering up certain unpleasant inner truths. However, this cover-up and denial tend to produce injurious symptoms, among them failures of emotional and behavioral self-regulation.

As mentioned, our psyche is a battlefield between the forces of aggression (emanating from our inner critic or superego) and the defensive guerilla tactics of our inner passivity (located in our subordinate ego). The inner critic attacks and inner passivity defends. But our inner passivity's tactics are weak. It employs passive-aggressive behaviors, half-hearted negotiations, desperate compromises such as the acceptance of guilt and shame, and unstable defenses. Often this passivity is expressed in the plaintive inner voice of self-pity.

We can resolve this conflict through our deepening awareness of it. If we don't resolve it, we find ourselves trapped inside the conflict, identifying with either the passivity or the aggression, often alternating back and forth in our identifications. As we acquire more awareness of the conflict, our growing intelligence is able to resolve it. Our authentic self emerges from the fray as the conflict is being resolved.

The second reason we produce pleasure through self-approval is related to the first reason. While our inner critic lords it over us, it also mocks us for our passivity. Accordingly, it finds fault not only with our inability to deflect its aggression but also with our passive willingness to absorb that aggression to the point of feeling shame and humiliation. This is the same dynamic whereby a bully is at his cruelest when mocking and ridiculing the submissive aspects or passive tendencies of his victims. Now one's compulsive striving for self-approval can feel like a life-saving necessity, the psychological equivalent of gasping for air.

In summing up, our inner critic uses any pretext, even just alleged transgressions that happen only in our imagination, for its campaign of disapproval. Hence, when in our mind we can create storylines or narratives that cast us in a good light, we're eager to do so, and we feel an accompanying pleasure that's usually short-lived. Meanwhile, we're pretty clueless about these inner dynamics. Through compulsive self-approval, we struggle for some relief from the distress, anxiety, depression, and general unhappiness that our inner conflict produces. Because we don't see the dynamics of the conflict clearly enough, our intelligence doesn't have the knowledge it needs to liberate us from this suffering.

Self-understanding is the necessary ingredient in any recipe for happy brain waves. Right now people hate to look so deeply into themselves because doing so shatters our self-image, as it also exposes our ego (and the self-centeredness that accompanies it) as a flawed or inadequate operating system for the modern world.

19. The Human Weakness behind Alcoholism

Many alcoholics and addictive personalities resist the idea that their plight is in any way due to character weakness. Any such allegation, they feel, categorizes them as substandard people who are to blame for their troubles. Weakness of character or "moral weakness" is *not* what causes alcoholism, one addiction website states emphatically.[35] This is true; it's not about moral or character weakness. Yet we can't ignore the influence of a specific kind of inner weakness in the psyche.

There's an essential reason alcoholics are sensitive to this allegation that character weakness is behind their out-of-control drinking: Inwardly, this accusation is directed at them on a daily basis by their inner critic. The inner critic berates alcoholics with allegations that range in intensity from "You should be trying harder to

[35] http://www.the-alcoholism-guide.org/causes-of-alcoholism.html

stay sober!" to "You worthless no good loser! Look at you! You're truly disgusting!"

Everyone has an inner critic, and for many of us that part of our psyche has assumed the role of master of the personality. As mentioned, it can harass and scorn us for the slightest misdemeanors. Our inner critic can attack us for a wide variety of alleged "crimes," most viciously for the idea that we are somehow a failure or a loser. In some people, the inner critic is an absolute tyrant that causes much of their unhappiness and suffering.

Unconsciously, we give credence to these allegations. We become inwardly defensive and absorb emotionally the negative charges directed against us. As alcoholics struggle defensively to deflect these charges, they might say, "It's not that big a problem" or "I'm trying, it's not my fault, I don't know what comes over me." Even as they defend in this way, they still "buy into" the allegations or harassment dished out by the inner critic. This means they absorb the negative criticism and take it to heart. Consequently, they can experience considerable shame and self-loathing.

All of us have inner weaknesses, and we usually can overcome them when we understand them and take remedial steps. If, for instance, we want to excel at some endeavor or sport, we work on our weaknesses. With tennis, for example, a person might have to work on a weak backhand or weak serve. If we want to play the game of life and excel at it, we have to consider what weaknesses might impede us. Some people are weak athletically, or intellectually dull, or socially awkward. Alcoholics are weak in emotional and behavioral self-regulation, as are people with many other kinds of psychological challenges. We can empower ourselves with deeper self-understanding.

For the most part, alcoholics could just as easily be addicted to drugs or struggling with an eating disorder. Their addiction is not about alcohol *per se*. The heart of their addiction lies in their inability to stand up to the cruel and unjust allegations of their inner critic. They don't know how to live in inner freedom or how to liberate themselves from inner conflict. This is a psychological weakness, not a moral or character weakness.

Alcoholics and other addicts are attracted to the disease theory of addictions because that theory provides them with a psychological defense against the inner critic. The theory says that addiction is a disease of biological, chemical, neurological, or genetic origins. By embracing it, they can, at least temporarily, deflect the inner critic's harassment. Through their unconscious defense system, they're able to say, "But it's not my fault! I have a disease. If I didn't have this disease, I would certainly be doing better!"

Depth psychology's theory of addiction recognizes that our psychological weakness can be exacerbated by genetic flaws or other biological factors, yet it identifies unconscious conflicts in our psyche as the main problem. When we understand these conflicts, we can resolve them. Doing so strengthens us on an inner level, producing enhanced self-regulation. As part of this inner strengthening, we learn to keep our inner critic at bay. We see the inner critic more objectively as a part of us that has no business holding us accountable or passing judgment on us. We also see the part in us—inner passivity—that serves as an enabler of the inner critic.

As we acquire insight and strength, we no longer give credence to the pronouncements of the inner critic. The inner critic retreats into the background and becomes less problematic.

Factors cited for causing alcoholism include high levels of stress, anxiety, tension, or emotional pain. Yet where do these high levels of distress come from? They can certainly arise when a harsh inner critic is bullying us and getting away with it. Our challenge is to understand clearly the nature of this major conflict in our psyche. Our inner critic dishes out self-aggression while our unconscious ego traps us in inner passivity. When we learn to stand up to the self-aggression emanating from our inner critic, we're in the process of resolving the inner conflict. That conflict can only continue when, through inner passivity, we allow the inner critic to get away with its unwarranted and frequently cruel intrusions into our life. Our inner critic has no business butting into our business and passing judgment on us. Yet due to our inner weakness it gets away with bullying us. To become stronger, we have to stand up to it. We begin to develop an authentic self that represents us on an inner level.

Tormented by their inner critic, many alcoholics descend into self-loathing, self-condemnation, and even self-hatred. Unable to connect with the self and with their own goodness and value, they can't recognize or affirm the goodness and value in their family members, nor can they protect them from emotional instability, financial danger, and social disgrace.

A study published in 2013 says that former alcoholics who feel shame about past drinking are more likely to relapse.[36] That shame is produced by an inner critic that refuses to go away, even during abstinence.

With a harsh inner critic, people find it very difficult to feel good about themselves. The inner critic can belittle and ridicule us to the point that we become depressed. (Read, "The Hidden Cause of Clinical Depression.") Meanwhile, inner passivity makes some of us more likely to come under the unhealthy influence of drinking buddies who have no interest in our well-being. Through inner passivity as well, people can also be more easily influenced by advertising that portrays drinking in glamorous terms.

Alcoholics Anonymous has had success for a variety of reasons, chief among them the warmth and kindness of its members. Alcoholics are warmly welcomed to the organization. Each alcoholic is accepted unconditionally. Each person is important, and members strive to help each other. This emotional generosity is a powerful antidote to the harsh belittling inner critic. The individual can use the kindness of the group to counteract the effects of the inner critic. Armed with evidence of one's value, the individual can cause the inner critic to retreat—yet this approach doesn't eliminate it. The inner critic can return with a vengeance, particularly when a relapse occurs. Typically, a relapse comes about as a result of the compulsion to plunge back into the unresolved inner conflict and to face once again, in the clutches of inner passivity, the wrath of the inner critic.

The "Big Book" of Alcoholics Anonymous urges members to admit they are powerless over alcohol and to seek the

---

[36] http://psychcentral.com/news/2013/02/07/shame-about-past-alcoholism-ups-risk-of-relapse/51303.html

help of a "higher power." Through depth psychology, in contrast, the higher power is developed from within. This connection with one's essential self, encompassing a new quality and depth of consciousness, emerges within us as the conflict between self-aggression and inner passivity is resolved. The resolution of this inner conflict greatly invigorates our intelligence and will to thrive. Through the new sense of self that emerges, we connect with our goodness, value, and strength. A craving to drink, should it arise, is no longer overwhelming. We see the craving for what it is—the temptation to plunge back into passivity. Now we acquire the determination and ability to support ourselves emotionally.

Alcoholism is just one way among many that psychological weakness manifests. When we examine the true sources of our self-defeat, we acquire emotional and behavioral self-regulation.

20. The Mysterious Allure of Kinky Sex

Sadomasochistic consensual sex play may be gaining some acceptance as a socially or culturally sanctioned sexual orientation. *The New York Times* reports in a featured story, "A Hush-Hush Topic No More," that a significant effort is underway in the United States and Canada to "defend the rights" of kinky-sex adherents and to acknowledge the practice as an expression of freedom and normal sexuality.[37]

---

[37] http://www.nytimes.com/2013/02/28/fashion/bondage-

The recent best-selling books in the *50 Shades of Grey* trilogy have achieved their wide popularity (70 million copies sold worldwide) by exploiting the strange, mysterious human weakness to "libidinze" (eroticize or make pleasurable) the experience of being dominated, violated, abused, or otherwise mistreated. One popular website reports quite seriously that the books are introducing youths "to a brave new bondage-loving world."[38]

Kinky sex in a playful setting doesn't have to be a big deal in itself, providing one can take it or leave it. But behind the scenes, deep in our psyche, sexual arousal that is sadistically or masochistically produced tells a remarkable story about human nature. If adherents to sadomasochistic sex play were to examine these psychological dynamics, many would find their kinky pleasures less appealing. With greater understanding, we prefer real love to cheap thrills.

Pursuing sexual pleasure from sadomasochistic practices cultivates a deeper problem. Many people extract unconscious *nonsexual* gratification (a third-rate kind of pleasure) from their unwitting, stubborn allegiance to painful old hurts, memories, regrets, and sorrows. When sexual sadomasochism is practiced, this dark side of the psyche is awakened and stirred up. The consequences can include considerable emotional disturbance and disharmony, along with the possibility of psychological regression.

---

domination-and-kink-sex-communities-step-into-view.html?pagewanted=all&_r=1&
[38] http://www.thedailybeast.com/articles/2012/12/20/50-ways-fifty-shades-of-grey-has-changed-the-world.html

Sexual sadism and masochism are just the visible tip of a vast unconscious mass of psychological intrigue. To varying degrees, human beings become entangled in painful negative emotions that harbor elements of nonsexual masochism. People who frequently feel deprived, refused, controlled, criticized, rejected, and abandoned are likely to have "libidinized" their suffering. This means that, through the function of libido, their suffering is made into a bittersweet, third-rate gratification that, registered mostly unconsciously, becomes a compelling experience.

Libido often refers to the sex drive, yet it can be defined more broadly as the pursuit of the experience of pleasure. Pleasure is needed, of course, to make life bearable, and it's a feature of the sex drive that compels animals to procreate. Libido does indeed serve to produce many healthy forms of pleasure. Yet some pleasures are obviously perverse. The so-called pleasure experienced by bullies, rapists, and pedophiles all have to do with experiences of power and submission, as do sadomasochistic pleasures. The libido of a rapist or pedophile is activated in the process of victimizing others, and it can also be activated by thinking about or imagining such behavior.

Many "normal" people, in the form of spite, can take perverse gratification in seeing others suffer. They might wish for misfortune to befall celebrities, competitors, coworkers, liberals, conservatives, the rich, the poor, members of other religions and races, and so on. Their penchant for doing this has a sadistic aspect. At the heart of this spite is a primitive side of human nature, one that, when we dare look at it, offends our idealized self-image. Yet it's important for us to see clearly how many of our actions and behaviors arise from our subconscious emotional life rather than our more conscious mental life. We tend to act out what is unconscious, and much of these inner dynamics have a negative, self-defeating bias. To tragic effect, modern psychology turned its back on Freud's essential premise that libido constitutes a biological drive that shapes our personality, influences our behaviors, and frequently produces suffering and self-defeat.

Libido acquires a masochistic flavor even from early childhood. Think of the child who, in part, experiences life through impressions of being controlled, helpless, criticized, rejected, unloved, betrayed, and abandoned. These impressions live on in the adult psyche as emotional attachments. On the surface, we think we hate these negative feelings and very much want to avoid them. But this negativity, which is churned up by inner conflict, doesn't easily go away. People can feel, for instance, that they want to be respected and loved at the same time that, unconsciously, they're unresolved with feeling disrespected and unloved. Unconsciously, we expect to encounter these old hurts. We live in fear of them, yet we don't quite know who we are without them. We fear these negative emotions, yet unconsciously we're attached to them. These negative emotions, as mentioned, become "libidinized," meaning we acquire a stubborn willingness to recreate and recycle them. As we become entangled in feeling victimized, oppressed, disrespected, and unworthy, these negative impressions then feed a sense of being unjustly treated by others and the world.

As discussed earlier, we develop an unconscious psychological defense system that's designed to cover up our emotional attachment to old negative experiences. Through our defenses, we often blame others for our negative reactions, convinced their (alleged) ignorance and malice are the causes or sources of our failure, disappointment, self-doubt, or anger. We convince ourselves we're victims of injustice and cruelty. Few of us are eager to acknowledge that our emotional suffering is produced by our willingness and determination to keep recycling it. Humans tap into this unconscious masochism when they experience sexual pleasure from various forms of abuse or denigration. For some, this kind of pleasure is intense and addictive. One individual who wrote to me said that, in his view, the "heroin of sexual arousal" is "hotwifing" or "cuckolding," a behavior in which a husband is intensely aroused when passively present while his wife is having sex with other men. Any recurring behavior that involves such a surrender of integrity and self-respect will have serious psychological and emotional consequences.

It's important to understand, as well, that sadists are really masochists at heart; they get their thrills by identifying unconsciously with the passivity of the masochist. (Even everyday people who take glee in seeing others suffer are identifying with what, in their imagination, that suffering entails.) Sadists claim to get their pleasure from feeling power, but this claim is an unconscious defense against their underlying passivity: "I'm not looking to feel passive or helpless—Look at how much I enjoy this feeling of power." Rapists and pedophiles, for instance, are extraordinarily passive, as evidenced by their unwillingness or inability to curb their criminal inclinations. Pedophiles and people addicted to child pornography have libidinized their unresolved passivity, mainly through their unconscious identification with the helplessness and degradation of the children they victimize.

Sometimes both men and women, through their imagination and in fantasy, enter into emotional experiences of passivity, shame, or worthlessness in order to have an orgasm during intercourse. In such cases, they may, even as they're becoming more conscious of the inner dynamics, be unable for months or even a few years to stop the libidinization of negative emotions that are producing the arousal they require to reach an orgasm. If this applies to you, don't fret about it. Go ahead and have your sexual satisfaction in this manner, and be patient with your intention to emerge from this limited way of making love. If you're impatient, you're more likely to be in conflict. Make it your intention to become more whole and healthy so that, at some point, you'll enjoy your orgasms in the spirit of love, wholeness, and union rather than as a lesser experience.

The dark side of human nature hides out in us all. It constitutes, for the most part, an emotional affinity for negative experiences. This is humanity's basic neurosis, and it can produce many varieties of self-defeat and suffering that include defensiveness, apathy, self-pity, self-absorption, as well as cruelty, greed, hatred, and violence. We can make this dark side conscious and overcome its negative influence if we're brave enough to see ourselves objectively.

21. A Hidden Reason for Suicidal Thoughts

Suicidal thoughts are quite common, and even people living good lives can experience them now and then. For many, suicidal thoughts are fleeting considerations from which they soon bounce back to their everyday sense of self.

Others are haunted by these thoughts on a regular basis. The risk of committing suicide is increased for a person who begins to think often on how to do it.

Experts say the causes of suicide are varied. Suicide is associated with bipolar disorder, schizophrenia, mood and personality disorders, depression, sleep deprivation, work failure, and drug abuse. Another cause cited among suicide-prevention websites is the feeling of helplessness.

This feeling of being helpless (overwhelmed, trapped, and unable to cope) appears to be a universal emotional experience among people with either fleeting or persistent thoughts of suicide. Suicidal thoughts often arise in people who are no longer able to cope with what they experience as an overwhelming situation. The situation can involve the death of a loved one, financial problems, serious illness, or the breakup of a relationship. Of course, it's not the situation in itself that's overwhelming. Rather, the individual's emotional weakness, frequently brought about by inner conflict, makes the challenges feel overwhelming.

An inner weakness in our psyche, one that goes largely undetected, produces the tendency for some people to collapse into helplessness. This weakness is sometimes felt quite acutely even by people coping with just everyday routine matters. We don't need to be facing life-or-death situations to experience this debilitating weakness. This weakness, which I identify as *inner passivity* and discuss throughout this book, can also instigate the other factors listed above that contribute to suicidal thoughts, particularly drug abuse, depression, work failure, and sleep deprivation. (This discussion deals with emotional issues, not the physical pain from various diseases or conditions that might also induce suicidal thoughts.)

Here's how this feeling of helpless was described at the suicide-prevention website of WebMD.com:

> People who seriously consider suicide feel hopeless, helpless, and worthless. A person who feels hopeless believes that no one can help with a particular event or problem. A person who feels helpless is immobilized and unable to take steps to solve problems. A person who feels worthless is overwhelmed with a sense of personal failure.[39]

People contemplating suicide "perceive the future as being hopeless," says the American Association for Marriage and Family Therapy. Many "feel so buried under so many little things that have gone wrong that they feel like they are drowning."[40]

When people fail to rise effectively to deal with life's challenges, they've likely come under the influence of inner passivity. Our inner passivity tries to represent us in the ongoing conflict with our inner critic, but it often feels overwhelmed, defeated, and rendered helpless by

---

[39] http://www.webmd.com/mental-health/tc/suicidal-thoughts-or-threats-topic-overview

[40] http://www.aamft.org/imis15/content/Consumer_Updates/Suicidal_Thoughts.aspx

the persistent, primitive, and authoritarian stance that our inner critic assumes.

When we have large deposits of inner passivity in our psyche, our inner critic tends to become more intrusive. The inner conflict between aggression and passivity is intensified. Ideally, the inner critic has no business butting into our life and curtailing our inner freedom. Yet we still need some inner strength to neutralize and shut down this inner aggression. A person with large deposits of inner passivity can be harassed and bullied by the inner critic to the point of experiencing helplessness against it and acquiring self-loathing and self-hatred in the process.

More people now recognize how we live under the spell of egotism, our mind's chief operating system. Many people also recognize the extent to which we're harassed by our inner critic. But a much smaller percentage of the population know about inner passivity. It's the source of a defeatist mentality, which is a "who cares, I don't care" approach to life. Chronic complainers—the "I got screwed, I was taken advantage of" contingent—exhibit inner passivity as they cover up their affinity for experiencing helplessness and victimization. Inner passivity contributes to worry, anxiety, stress, and fear as people entertain feelings of being at the mercy of bad things happening. Many sufferers with inner passivity identify with their mind and find themselves spinning their mental wheels in futile attempts to make decisions and emerge from confusion. Others feel swamped by the chaos of their emotions.

People with suicidal thoughts are often very critical of themselves. When we're particularly enfeebled by inner passivity, we put up little resistance against the inner critic. This gives the inner critic license to be particularly harsh and merciless. As the American Association for Marriage and Family Therapy says, some individuals contemplating suicide "may be experiencing a steady decline in the quality of their lives, and may blame themselves and think that something is wrong with them. The more they blame themselves, the less worthy they feel of having success, having friends, or having fun."[41] They blame themselves because, through an inner collapse caused by extensive inner passivity, they soak up the negative, aggressive insinuations and condemnations being issued by the inner critic. People in this predicament frequently succumb to clinical depression, which is itself a factor in suicidal thoughts. (Read, "The Hidden Cause of Clinical Depression.")

Other negative emotions, as well, can produce suicidal thoughts, among them painful feelings of being unloved and abandoned. Such experiences, however, still relate to inner passivity because, through inner passivity, individuals have difficulty supporting themselves emotionally. When we can't support ourselves emotionally, we are, in effect, failing to appreciate or respect ourselves, and hence we're abandoning ourselves. Suicide becomes the ultimate act of giving up on oneself.

Now we come to quite a startling consideration. Suicidal thoughts, as well as acts of suicide, appear to be psychological defenses designed to cover up our unconscious participation in (or emotional attachment

---

[41] http://www.aamft.org/imis15/content/Consumer_Updates/Suicidal_Thoughts.aspx

to) the experience of inner passivity. Because we are desperate to deny our passivity (to keep it unconscious), we try to "prove," as a psychological defense, how much we hate to experience the helplessness. For the defense to work, we're required to accentuate the sense of our misery. The defense goes like this: "I'm not looking for the feeling of being helpless. I'm not wallowing or indulging in that feeling. In fact, I hate the feeling so much that I'm wishing I were dead and didn't have to feel anything." Also driving suicidal thoughts is the individual's temptation, out of profound inner passivity, to perceive the act of suicide as a display of resolve and aggression. But this sense of aggression is an illusion because it is self-defeating self-aggression.

As mentioned, psychological defenses work in such a way that, in order to maintain their effectiveness as inner conflict intensifies, we often have to ratchet up the self-damage. Ghastly though it is, people kill themselves to "prove" they are innocent of any collusion in self-suffering: "I hate my suffering and now I'm going to end it." Consciously, we do hate our suffering. But unconsciously we cling passionately to it and fervently deny our collusion in the experience of it. When we understand this, we can stop suicidal thoughts in their tracks.

22 . Oh Shame, Where is Thy Secret Source?

Shame is a powerful and self-damaging emotion, and many books in recent years have tackled the subject in search of its roots. Shame has been called "the quintessential negative emotion" because it influences so many different moods and behaviors. While shame can saturate our emotional life, most sufferers don't understand its roots deep in our psyche.

Shame is the painful sense that there exists a dark secret or an exposed truth about some vile, disgusting, or pitiful aspect of oneself. The negative emotion sometimes lies dormant until triggered by a situation or event in a person's life. Other times, shame is active within us on a daily basis. Whether we're conscious of our shame or not, it can play an important role in obesity, addictions, depression, crime, violent behaviors, sexual offenses, social phobias, career failure, outbursts of anger, and other self-defeating behaviors.

Shame is often associated with external variables such as our appearance, clothes, social skills, and a sense of physical and mental ineptitude. It's also associated with inner fears such as being exposed as a fake or phony, and it surfaces when experiencing or imagining ridicule over our handling of money.

Shame itself is a byproduct of forces, drives, and conflicts in our psyche. It's more likely to be a problem for us if we were bullied, humiliated, and unfairly or severely punished in childhood. We're more likely to have acquired a deep sense of being flawed, defective, unworthy, inferior, and bad. Chances are we'll grow up with a compulsion to punish ourselves for allegedly being a misfit or a loser, and we can use shame as a means of administering that punishment. The blushing associated with shame represents the anticipation or acceptance of punishment, as in the reddening effect on the skin of being beaten.

The shame-filled person "buys into" the allegations of others (or the allegations from his or her inner critic) of being a vile, disgusting, or pitiful creature. The allegations or accusations are often completely irrational and false. They're unfair and unkind, and have no bearing on reality. Nonetheless, shame-prone people accept and even embrace the accusations because the condemnation feels so familiar, right, and true. The condemnation they once absorbed in childhood (and now absorb from their inner critic) causes them to resonate inwardly with the "truth" of the accusations. They're convinced emotionally that their very being is genuinely associated with dishonor, disgrace, and unworthiness. They feel deserving of condemnation and punishment.

We can have problems with shame even when we had good, kind-hearted parents. Genetic factors can play a role in whether we'll be emotionally strong or emotionally unstable. These factors can influence how sensitive we are to the normal rough-and-tumble of childhood. It's also common for us as children to misinterpret events and situations, and to be determined in our self-centeredness to feel that we don't get enough love, support, recognition, and encouragement. In this way, too, we end up with low self-esteem, which means that we're essentially passive, that we don't have a strong center that can protect us and represent our interests against the aggressiveness of others as well as against the mean, irrational inner critic that we all acquire. Shame is an emotional weakness that's often associated with shyness and with how able we are to stand up for ourselves.

Shame is a common experience for the adult children of alcoholic parents, religious fundamentalists, narcissistic or depressed parents, and parents who embarrassed themselves and exhibited pronounced character weakness. The shame we felt for parents and the weakness we saw in them become our own shame and weakness.

Shame often originates, then, out of a profoundly passive position in our psyche. The individual is accepting punishment not for "crimes" committed but for his or her very existence. Shame says, "I'm sorry for who I am and I accept punishment for who I am." This is an exceedingly passive self-assessment that borders on unconscious, non-sexual masochism. "Doubt," wrote psychoanalyst Erik Erikson, "is the brother of shame." Research professor Brené Brown has written, "Shame corrodes the very part of us that believes we are capable of change." Put another way, both inner passivity and the inner critic are parts of us that believe we're *in*capable of change.

Parents as well as some religions have used shame as a means of control ("For shame!" or "Shame on you!") in order to render a person compliant and passive. One father regularly subjected his daughter to the harsh judgment, "You blew it!" Unable to stand up to his bullying, the daughter was a passive recipient of this condemnation. People who are bullied, and have been passive to the bully, typically feel shame in themselves. Child victims of sexual abuse are thrown into profound passivity by the experience, and much of their shame comes from the horror of their helplessness and paralysis against the power of the perpetrator. The expression, "It's a crying shame," also signifies a connection to passivity.

In essence, shame is produced through our surrender to the bullying of our inner critic. Because of inner passivity, we fail to stand up for ourself. It means we are a party to our own self-abuse, which may be the most shameful circumstance of all.

Literature contains examples of the connection between shame and inner passivity. Here's an excerpt from *Till We Have Faces: A Novel of Cupid and Psyche*, by C.S. Lewis:

> –I felt ashamed.
>
> –But of what? Psyche, they hadn't stripped you naked or anything?
>
> –No, no, Maia. Ashamed of looking like a mortal— of being a mortal.
>
> –But how could you help that?
>
> –Don't you think the things people are most ashamed of are things they can't help.

In Antoine de Saint-Exupery's *The Little Prince*, the passive connotations of shame, in association with a lack of self-regulation, are illustrated in this passage:

> –Why are you drinking? demanded the little prince.
>
> –So that I may forget, replied the tippler.
>
> –Forget what? inquired the little prince, who was already sorry for him.

–Forget that I am ashamed, the tippler confessed, hanging his head.

–Ashamed of what? insisted the little prince, who wanted to help him.

–Ashamed of drinking.

The tippler is ashamed of his weakness with regard to self-regulation, and that weakness is directly related to inner passivity.

It's important to know that shame emerges from inner passivity. As a symptom of a deeper issue, shame can be impervious to a direct approach. It can, however, be undermined from below when we burrow deep enough to expose its roots in inner passivity. We can begin to eliminate inner passivity as we see how, through it, we allow ourself to be harassed and bullied by our inner critic. We become empowered as we begin to take responsibility for having let our inner critic get away with being a bully.

Inner passivity is also the weakness within us that makes us defensive in our dealings with other people. When we begin to recognize and put a stop to our inner and outer defensiveness, we are shifting our consciousness away from (or out of) inner passivity. The inner strength we begin to feel makes us very pleased— not at all ashamed—to be who we are.

23. Cultivating a Life of Disappointment

Strange but true, many of us actively cultivate a life of disappointment, meaning we unconsciously look for ways to feel disenchanted, disheartened, and dissatisfied. Whoever would have thought that we humans, so sensible and smart according to conventional wisdom, would be harboring such a self-defeating proclivity?

Well, we're full of mischief, for sure. But some of our antics, including our flirtations with disappointment, can leave us bruised and bloody. When we expose our misadventures in our unconscious mind, we won't so easily succumb to emotional temptations that degrade the quality of our daily life.

There are so many little ways to feel disappointed. I had a client who frequently counted the money leftover in his wallet just after he had bought something. When I told him that behavior meant he was looking for the feeling of disappointment, he objected to the idea at first. But as he thought more about it in the weeks that followed, he said, "It's true. I can sense it—it's subtle, but I almost always have a sense that the money that's left in my wallet will be less than I'm hoping."

The same principle can apply when people check to see how their bank account is holding up or how their investment portfolio is performing. We do, of course, have to check up on our assets periodically in order to be responsible for our well-being. But we can do the right thing for the wrong reasons, meaning that, in behaviors that on the surface are otherwise innocent and reasonable, we can be tempted to experience unresolved negative emotions such as feeling deprived, denied, refused, and helpless. We can easily feel, in the case of money, that our limited resources somehow reflect on our alleged unworthiness or insignificance. This version of disappointment arises from self-doubt, that lingering uncertainty about our intrinsic value that resides in our psyche.

Often we cultivate the feeling of disappointment through our imagination. When I lived in Santa Fe, New Mexico, I had a client who experienced disappointment every time he walked downtown to sit in the Plaza. The Plaza had a scruffy, neglected look when seen with a particular aesthetic eye. My client would sit on a bench and feel what a shame it was that city officials didn't take steps to beautify it. Sitting there, he imagined all the different ways the Plaza could be made more attractive. Yet this use of his imagination produced more displeasure than pleasure. He couldn't quell the disappointment that kept arising within him. He told himself he wasn't going to visit the Plaza as often, and he harbored critical thoughts toward city officials for being indifferent to aesthetics. His musings were part of a psychological defense that went like this: "I'm not indulging in the feeling of being let down and disappointed. Isn't it obvious that I want to see something beautiful that makes me happy! How could I be indulging in disappointment when I'm thinking about not coming back to this place? Besides, I'm not the problem. The problem is those people who don't have any aesthetic sense."

Disappointment can be cultivated in our feelings toward loved ones. Parents sometimes see their sons and daughters as disappointments, when often these parents are simply projecting on to their children the disappointment they have in themselves. Many of us can feel that our whole life has been a disappointment in the sense that we didn't fulfill our expectations for success. Even people who have been successful can feel their success still falls short of expectations. They're unable to appreciate their accomplishments or to commend themselves for a job well done because their unconscious determination to experience self-criticism and disappointment trumps the reality of their worthy effort.

After many years of marriage, men and women sometimes begin to see their partner as a major disappointment. Men and women who are absorbing inner accusations of having been a failure or at least a big letdown can attribute their sense of disappointment to the alleged shortcomings of their spouse. The defense reads, "I'm not looking to indulge in the feeling of not measuring up. My feeling of disappointment is due to my wife who has let me down and not measured up." This distortion of reality can lead to considerable suffering and unnecessary divorce, particularly in men going through a mid-life crisis.

It's also common for people to be disappointed in political leaders. Sometimes these leaders are indeed weak and ineffective, yet our criticism of them will not be constructive when it emerges from our own unresolved issues. Even politicians who are doing a decent or excellent job can become targets of the negative projections of others. To be responsible citizens, we need some insight and discernment. We have to know when our disappointment in others covers up our emotional entanglement in self-disapproval or when we use others as targets for our determination to feel marginalized or victimized.

In a sense, we're all geared up for disappointment. We can live through desires and expectations instead of living in grace and gratitude. It's helpful to see desires and expectations as camouflage that disguises our emotional entanglement in disappointment.

There are, as mentioned, many subtle ways we can cultivate disappointment. Many of us wander repeatedly into the kitchen throughout the day or evening and peer into a cupboard or the refrigerator at the food offerings inside. We stare at the foodstuff for a while, finding nothing interesting. We go away, only to wander back an hour later to stare forlornly at the same provisions. During such moments we are, however subtly, cultivating feelings of disappointment. Consciously, we're convinced that we're looking for a tasty treat to snack on. We think we're pursuing pleasure. However, we keep coming back to look for the tasty treat that's not there. Even when we do choose something to eat, we can feel we settled for second-best.

We can, in particular, feel very disappointed in our efforts. Failure with food plans and dieting constitutes one such area of disappointment. Frequently, people get enthused and excited about their prospects of succeeding at a new attempt to self-regulate with food, only to be disappointed a week later by ensuing failure. That initial enthusiasm frequently is a set-up to repeat a painful pattern of defeat. The enthusiasm can serve as a defense that contends: "Look at how determined I am to succeed. I know I'll do it this time!" The feeling can cover up one's anticipated plunge back into familiar, unresolved issues concerning passivity and failure.

We can also be experiencing disappointment when we glance at our reflection in a mirror or shop window. We're consciously thinking that we want to see how good we look, yet deeper down we often experience some disappointment, some feeling of being let down by what we see. The more compulsively we check up on our reflected image, the more we're looking to get "hit up" with a twinge if not a jolt of disappointment.

Henry David Thoreau once wisely said, "If we will be quiet and ready enough, we shall find compensation in every disappointment." This statement, when considered as a psychological insight, means that we can benefit from our encounters with disappointment when we look into our psyche for the source of those feelings.

24 . Cynicism, the Battle Cry of the Wimp

Cynicism is the bravado of the faint-hearted, the strut of the weak-kneed, the battle cry of a feeble voice. This negative mentality, while self-defeating for its practitioners, seems to be gathering like storm clouds in the West. Barack Obama delicately brought this dysfunction to our attention when he noted at a campaign stop that "it's fashionable right now for people to be cynical."

Fashionable, indeed! A cynical view of the world has become a form of conviviality, like social drinking, that's perceived as cool by many students, professionals, and sophisticates when they get together to talk or party.

It's cowardly, though, not cool. Cynics fly the white flag of surrender thinking it's a rebel flag.

Cynicism is a cleverly disguised expression of passivity and hopelessness. It's the art of being disgusted by hypocrisy and corruption without being moved to action. We can see its self-defeating effects in our faltering will to solve public and social problems, as well as in the loss of confidence in leaders and public and private institutions. Should America decline in self-defeat, we'll have our cynical selves to thank. We can stop being cynical, though, by understanding its roots in our psyche.

Cynics tend not to see their inner weakness with any objectivity. They think they're sophisticated realists entitled to take refuge in mockery, sarcasm, biting wit, and a know-it-all attitude. Yet the personality they present to the world is a defense against recognition of passive elements in their psyche. As part of their defense, they take morbid satisfaction in their unconscious denial of inner weakness.

Cynics feel power in their aggressive contempt toward others and their scorn for the state of the world. Their display of (phony) aggression feels so good because it covers up frightened weaklings who are overwhelmed by life's complexity and challenges. The greater the person or institution they're attacking, the juicier the illusion of their power and superiority. Such cynicism can quickly become malicious.

Their wit is seen as bold and daring and their perceptions as a mark of superiority. Cynicism tends to become more toxic over time, however, because people who employ it as a defense are forced to intensify its feeling and expression in order to maintain its effectiveness as a defense. Sometimes this causes them to overstep the mark and become overbearing, though they can be adept at backtracking, claiming they're only joking and need not be taken seriously.

Nevertheless, cynics do scramble to sign up allies who agree with their negative perceptions. This provides them with more deniability for their emotional entanglement in passivity and fear. Allies can provide the cynic with the group rapture of collective denial. They now have more "evidence" for their inner defense: "Look, my negative attitude to life is justified because lots of people agree with my point of view." They have even more "evidence" when they cite doom-and-gloom headlines about the economy, the environment, political dysfunction, and financial-industry lawlessness.

A cynical outlook also tends to deepen the underlying passivity. Once "we decide that we're powerless, our passivity becomes a self-fulfilling prophecy, a habit of mind that's harder and harder to shake," writes Paul Rogat Loeb in *Soul of a Citizen: Living with Conviction in Challenging Times* (St. Martin's Press, New York, 2010).

In an excerpt from his book, Loeb writes:

> Cynical resignation salves the pain of unrealized hope. If we convince ourselves that little can change, we don't have to risk acting on our dreams. If we never fight for what we believe in and aspire to, we'll never be disappointed. We can challenge destructive or duplicitous leaders with contrary information and counter-examples, stories about how the powers-that-be have misled us. But what can possibly challenge an all-

encompassing worldview that, in the guise of sophistication, promotes the bleakest possible perspective on the human condition—the notion that our world has become so irredeemably corrupt that whatever we do, we cannot change this?[42]

Loeb makes good points—yet he probably shouldn't be expressing the idea, even if intended ironically, that "cynical resignation salves pain" or that "we'll never be disappointed" if we don't fight for what we believe in. Cynical resignation is a product of inner passivity which itself is a measure of self-doubt and a defensive, wary default position in our psyche. Inner passivity becomes very painful when it blocks our human mandate to grow, evolve, and fulfill our destiny. When inner passivity gets the best of us, it can activate our death drive and produce depression, despair, and a collapse of self-regulation.

As well, we'll be painfully disappointed if we don't fight for what we believe in. Life is either a daring adventure, or nothing, Helen Keller once said. That "nothing" is the agony of acute disappointment in one's self. Cynics are in danger, particularly late in life, of being crushed by the truth of their failure to have practiced integrity and courage.

A remedy for overcoming cynicism involves a learning process through which we begin to see the phony nature of that form of aggression. Cynicism is not true aggression. Rather, it's a coping mechanism (or psychological defense) intended to portray a semblance

---

[42] http://www.huffingtonpost.com/paul-loeb/soul-of-a-citizen-excerpt_b_482264.html

of aggression for the purpose of covering up self-doubt, fear, and inner passivity. It also helps us when we see that the negative aggression we direct toward others is a reflection (and reaction to) the negative aggression our inner passivity absorbs from our inner critic.

All of us, cynics and non-cynics alike, are entangled to some degree in inner conflicts involving fear, self-doubt, inner aggression, and inner passivity. This is no cause for shame or embarrassment. It's not our fault—it's human nature at this point of evolution. We just have to be smart and brave enough to uncover this repressed content. In the light of self-knowledge, our intelligence then goes to work resolving the conflicts and creating more harmony with life.

25 . **Overcoming Incompetence and Its Miseries**

One way to be happy (or happier) is to operate in the workplace at a higher level of competence and effectiveness. Performing at our best is a great source of pleasure. Performing at our worst is, well, just ask Dilbert.

The comic strip featuring that forlorn character and his experiences of workplace incompetence is said to be the most photocopied, downloaded, faxed, and emailed in the world. Obviously, people are well aware of the pervasiveness of the problem. Let's hope the comic strip's ridicule of such incompetence blunts the misery of it and even inspires higher levels of achievement.

Incompetence involves, as one writer put it, "a positive genius for selecting the wrong approach to a given problem." Yet being incompetent and acting stupidly are not inborn tendencies or weaknesses. We humans are plenty smart enough. The problem stems from unresolved psychological conflicts that limit and impair our creativity and intelligence.

These conflicts soak up a lot of our mental processing. The processing is used counter-productively to generate rationalizations, denials, and other defenses. It's ironic, but through unconscious, self-defeating processes we're quite efficient at producing inefficiency. Dilbert would love it!

The worst incompetents typically don't know how incompetent they are. Often, they don't even think of themselves as being incompetent. They're more likely to think of themselves as being bright. However, they can't entirely avoid reality, and so they usually suffer considerably through the frustration of their ineffectiveness and their lack of success and validation.

Incompetence features a range of issues. For instance, people can have a psychological aversion to thinking through a problem. They're failing to muster some inner power or strength to bring concentration and focus to the problem. At times, all of us can come up against a degree of self-doubt that starts to produce mental inertia and even mental paralysis, at which point we might stop believing in ourselves and our abilities. Here self-doubt is the problem.

The problem of incompetence also includes contempt for facts. People can readily minimize important facts if they're intent on feeling clever or special for their unique—though flawed—way of perceiving problems or challenges. Out of weakness, they chose self-validation over objectivity. Facts can also undercut one's own cherished beliefs, threatening an individual at an emotional level. As the philosopher Hegel said ironically, "If the facts are against me, so much the worse for the facts." When we oppose objectivity at the front door, our folly sneaks in the back.

Sometimes incompetents are unable to see the essentials of a situation. They focus on the non-essentials, often out of malice. A literary critic, as a random example, might be determined to be critical for unconscious reasons. This individual might find fault for the sake of finding fault. He or she focuses on minor flaws or perceived flaws, overlooking the value of the overall work. The excellence of others can be threatening to some of us, especially when we have dodged the challenges that might have raised us to that higher level of achievement. We can be tempted to bring others down a peg (in order to dull our inner critic's rebuke for our shortcomings). Hence, the writings of such a literary critic are not objective, and his spiteful, incompetent writing shortchanges readers.

Other facets of incompetence include fear of making a decision, lack of organization, forgetting steps or obligations, and remaining silent when verbal prowess is called for. These failings are usually produced by self-sabotage rather than an innate deficiency.

Incompetents fear making decisions because, should the decision be flawed or wrong, they fear having to face the disapproval of their superiors (or the wrath of their inner critic). If we are stronger emotionally, our inner critic is not such a dominant force in our psyche. Hence, we're not limiting ourselves in order to please authority figures. If it happens that our decision is flawed, we learn from the experience in order to do better the next time.

A lack of organization can facilitate incompetence—and vice-versa. When individuals lack organization to a self-defeating degree, they're displaying an unconscious affinity for inner passivity, which means they're comfortable with, or at least familiar with, feelings of being confused and overwhelmed. Unwittingly, they decline to become better organized because they're emotionally attached to experiencing their environment through the feeling of being hampered or frustrated by it.

When people chronically forget steps or obligations, they can be acting out an unconscious emotional attachment to feeling criticized and to experiencing themselves as a disappointment to others. When being inappropriately silent is the problem, the individual can be failing, through inner passivity, to access the thoughts and words that represent his or her position and value.

These examples of incompetence present just the bare bones of the problem. I provide more insight in my book, *Freedom from Self-Sabotage*.

26 . When Sexual Desire Covers Up Self-Sabotage

We can easily get turned on sexually by people who spell trouble.

What are some important features of human sexual desire? Two neuroscientists falter in their attempt to answer the question in their book, *A Billion Wicked Thoughts: What the World's Largest Experiment Reveals About Human Desire* (Dutton, New York, 2011).

Scouring internet data, the authors, Ogi Ogas and Sai Gaddam, analyzed millions of web searches, websites, erotic videos, erotic stories, personal ads, and digitized romance novels. The resulting behavioral data produced, among other findings, the allegedly "shocking truths" that men prefer plump women to thin ones, women enjoy reading about two heterosexual men having sex, men often seek erotic videos featuring older women, and male sexual cues are very different from those of women.

The authors claim to have initiated "a revolution in the scientific study of sexual attraction." But their findings are of limited value. The superficial information they have produced does very little to help us understand the vitally important ways that sexual attraction can be an ingredient in how we sabotage relationship harmony and success.

A basic tenet of depth psychology informs us that we become sexually attracted to (and emotionally entangled with) people with whom we can more easily recreate the unresolved psychological conflicts that linger from our childhood. In other words, we can easily get "turned on" by people who we can feel, at an unconscious level, are candidates to help us to replay the unresolved issues from our past.

For instance, a man or woman with low self-esteem, who is under the influence of childhood impressions of having been unappreciated or neglected, is often sexually, compulsively attracted to people who are withholding emotionally, who have serious character flaws, and who are unwilling to commit to their partner. Other times, people can find themselves hopelessly infatuated with someone who is in another relationship and not available. Or, in reverse, some people back away and are "turned off" by a person of good character who is available to them.

In our psyche, we retain memories of feeling refused, controlled, criticized, rejected, abandoned, betrayed, and unloved. Even when we had decent parents and a relatively happy childhood, we felt these emotions strongly at times because of childish sensitivities. These negative emotions remain unresolved in our psyche, and we're compelled to continue to experience and replay them, even when that's painful for us.

Sexual attraction is often a defense against realization of one's self-defeating tendencies. For instance, a woman who is attracted to a self-centered man might claim in her unconscious defense, "I'm not looking for the feeling of being unsupported and unappreciated—Can't you see how turned on I get when he pays attention to me and makes love to me."

Promiscuous individuals often have strong sexual attractions for others, yet their promiscuity can be an expression of self-loathing, produced by unresolved issues involving rejection, self-rejection, and even self-hatred. This individual's sexual attractions and activities serve as defenses that attempt to "prove" he or she wants to feel loved, or at least an illusion of love, to cover up an affinity for feeling unloved. We can be attracted to the sexual passion of a promiscuous person because, in our self-doubt, we interpret that passion as an emphatic validation of us.

The examples are endless. A man who had a cold, detached mother is prone to being sexually attracted to similar kinds of women. A woman who had a father who was passive and submissive to his wife can be sexually attracted to passive men. A man who had a dominating mother will tend unconsciously to seek out women to whom he can be passive. People who felt they were a disappointment to their parents will act out being a disappointment to their partners, or they will alternate between being a disappointment and seeing the partner as a disappointment.

After the initial courtship, the thrill of sexual attraction typically starts to abate, at which time the unrecognized emotional issues start to be acted out, bringing pain and suffering to both parties in the relationship.

Of course, we all want love and happiness. But unconsciously we're compelled to replay and recreate unresolved emotions from our past. To recap, until these emotions are resolved with insight and awareness, we're in danger of recreating unpleasant dramas in our present circumstances through which we relive the pain. In fact, we can be driven or compelled to pursue such dramas, all the while fooling ourselves with rationalizations that we are sincerely chasing after love.

My late wife, Sandra Michaelson, wrote three in-depth books on relationships. She wrote in *LoveSmart: Transforming the Emotional Patterns that Sabotage Relationships* (Prospect Books, 1999):

> Sex often serves as an antidote for low self-worth or as a means to perform or please, rather than as a genuine physical expression and extension of one's love. Sex is also used as a way to disguise our inability to be intimate and to deny the alienation we feel from ourselves and others. When our hearts and bodies are closed to intimacy due to self-rejection, inner fears, and emotional conflicts, we need more extreme forms of stimulation to experience pleasure (p. 224).

A few pages later, she wrote:

> Much of what looks like a powerful libido can be in reality a quest for domination and power. Rapists, in particular, uses sex as a way to dominate and reduce a woman, as a defense against their underlying identification with the woman's helplessness and humiliation. Thus sex can be used to control others, to get revenge, release aggressive needs, meet our yearning for validation or attention, boost our self-image, and relieve stress. Addictive or compulsive sex is another way of acting out emotional problems in the sexual arena. Those who use sex to channel their emotions or hidden feelings find it rarely brings relaxation and release but rather a need for more sex. Constant sexual tension is often confused with potency, but it is more likely an indication of the futility of using sex to get the emotional satisfaction we are unable to give to ourselves.
>
> Many couples become sexually aroused by dramatic outbursts in their relationship. A series of fights and reconciliation, followed by intense sexual activity, characterize their relationship.

They are often convinced this way of having sex is healthy. However, such people use conflict, as opposed to tender love, to generate passion. (p. 226).

We'll deprive ourselves of pleasure, intimacy, and love when we don't see the illusions of reality that sexual attraction can produce.

27. Four Favorite Ways to Suffer

If you're looking for attention, try wearing a T-shirt with this question embossed across the chest—Who Will I be Without my Suffering? These words have a thunderous effect on an unconscious level. That's because we often experience ourselves and identify with ourselves most profoundly through our suffering.

We all need to make sense of our world and find our place in it. We look for orientation through our beliefs, ego, athletic ability, intelligence, skills, character, body image, personality, sum of knowledge, and possessions. Underneath these external values, though, we can also experience and know ourselves in hidden recesses of our psyche as victims of injustice and malice, as failures or phonies, or as individuals who are insignificant and unworthy.

We have, in particular, four favorite ways to suffer. We can engorge ourselves at the trough of human misery through feelings of *deprivation, helplessness, rejection*, and *criticism*. Chances are good that when we're miserable, we're entangled in one or more of these negative emotions. Symptoms such as anger, anxiety, fear, procrastination, and depression often have their roots in these four opportunities to suffer.

With a little insight, we can check in with ourselves to determine pretty accurately whether we've tumbled into one of these four pits of pain. We can get ourselves out with self-awareness and insight. Most of the time, people in the pits find it hard to escape because they can't see their own blindness. They can't understand how and why they plunged into the pit in the first place.

(Before proceeding, I wish to note that some of the following knowledge and principles have already been discussed. However, this content is now being presented from a slightly different perspective. My expository writing compares with the use of a stereoscope, a device used for depicting right-eye and left-eye views of separate images of the same scene to produce a single three-dimensional image. To be assimilated, knowledge about our psyche has to be brought into the best possible focus, and these variations on perspective are a technique for achieving that end. Our mind is baffled by the counter-intuitive character of depth psychology, and this attempt at "three-dimensional" clarity improves our chances of learning the material.)

If you're living a life of relative abundance, yet still feel anxious that something is missing in your life, you're likely entangled an emotional attachment to deprivation (the first of the four ways to suffer). This means that you are *unconsciously determined* to see and experience the glass as half-empty. This propensity to see and experience our life through negative impressions is a quirk of human nature. We often are unaware of how easily we can slip over to the negative side and stay there, even as we complain about how unpleasant it all is.

Envy is a symptom of the unconscious determination to feel that something is missing in our life. Greed is also a symptom of that feeling. Envy, greed, and selfishness result from our emotional entanglement in deprivation. Unconsciously, we prefer to experience ourselves as poor and deprived rather than as blessed by consciousness and life. (More is said on this subject in "Hooked on Deprivation.")

Our second favorite way to suffer is through the negative emotion of helplessness. We were born into the world in a profound state of helplessness. Years have passed, but emotional memories of childhood helplessness linger in our psyche. Now we can feel helpless to influence loved one, to get ahead in our careers, and to have an impact on local or national events. Most painfully, we can feel helpless to regulate our emotions and behaviors. Two common symptoms of our entanglement in helplessness are procrastination and the feeling of being overwhelmed.

The problem is that helplessness can become a kind of default position—we hate it, and yet we can't imagine how we can make it any different. We have to begin to recognize the unconscious choice we are making to stay in the passive mode of self-doubt and indecision. Every time we recognize that we have slipped into our default position of helplessness (inner passivity), we're nudging ourselves into the clear and getting away from it. We have to be careful, though, that we don't try to spring out of it with inappropriate, negative, often angry aggression. This is just flipping over to the other extreme, mainly for the purpose of denying the underlying passivity.

Next comes rejection. Rejection hurts the most when we take it personally. In taking it personally, we're going to a weak spot in our psyche. In childhood, we were very sensitive to feeling rejected. For instance, if Mommy or Daddy gave our brother or sister what we thought was too much attention, we could feel rejected. If Mommy and Daddy went off for a weekend get-away, we could feel rejected. Ideally, as we age, we develop more objectivity and wisdom. If someone is actually rejecting us, we understand that the rejection is likely happening because of the other person's unresolved issues and flawed perceptions. If we are emotionally strong enough, we consider the possibility that some characteristic or behavior on our part may have contributed to the rejection—and we try through insight to rectify that weakness of ours. We make the situation into a learning experience instead of an opportunity to suffer.

If, as adults, we're experiencing rejection repeatedly and taking it personally, we're using rejection as a favorite way to suffer. Consciously, we want to be accepted and loved; unconsciously, we expect rejection and are "programmed" to keep experiencing it and making it happen. The rejection hurts so much because we use the pain of it to cover up or deny our attachment to it: "I'm not attached to the rejection—Look at how much it hurts and how much I hate it."

The last of the four is criticism. Many of us depend on our skills, intelligence, and personality to feel okay about ourselves. Many children are raised with the sense that their value in the eyes of their parents depends on how clever or competent they are. We can, it often feels, be appreciated much more for our performance and cooperation than for our essential self. So when criticism comes our way, it can feel as if the ground is giving way beneath us. Whether the criticism is unfair or whether it has some validity, we allow it to penetrate into our uncertainty about our self. This means that, as with rejection, we absorb the negative implications about our worth and value. Unconsciously, we give to others the power to invalidate us with their judgments and comments. This happens when our connection to our own self is weak and unstable. When we're stronger, we don't take criticism personally. If we're wise, we examine the criticism objectively to see if it has any validity. If it does, we try to learn from it without feeling hurt. If it doesn't, we just deflect it and go about our business without being emotionally upset.

It pays dividends in happiness to know if you have an emotional attachment to one or more of these four ways to suffer. Through your awareness, you can avoid getting entangled in them. You won't suffer when you expose the hidden ways that negative emotions have been sneaking into your daily life.

28. Get Rid of Guilt with Deeper Insight

The great novelist John Steinbeck once remarked, "I have never smuggled anything in my life. Why, then, do I feel an uneasy sense of guilt on approaching a customs barrier?" Steinbeck's guilt was irrational because, as he said, he had nothing to hide. So where did his guilt come from?

As he approached the customs barrier, he was aware that he was soon going to be dealing with an authority figure, namely the custom agent. This agent was going to view Steinbeck as someone who might be trying to smuggle something over the border. The agent would question him and hold him accountable. The agent, who might be a gruff fellow having a bad hair day, was going to use his authority to find out whether Steinbeck was a law-abiding citizen or some low-life smuggler.

Steinbeck, of course, had a great imagination. To write so convincingly, he had to be able to feel what his characters felt. It would be easy for him to imagine being a smuggler, just as it would also be tempting for him to imagine being a smuggler who got caught and was then arrested and punished. As he approached the crossing, Steinbeck would, somewhere in his unconscious mind, have likely become emotionally entangled in feelings associated with the possibility of being exposed as a lawbreaker. At this point, his guilt was likely aroused because he identified with the predicament of someone being caught and exposed. Such feelings are common to human nature. Even the healthiest among us can at times slip into such negative ruminations.

Steinbeck could also have experienced guilt simply because he was starting to feel a bit passive about his impending encounter with the custom agent who, in his imagination as he approached the border crossing, would soon be looming over him with black, suspicious eyes.

One of the great cosmic laughs at our expense is that, when it comes to crime, punishment and even small misdemeanors, we don't actually have to do the "evil" deed to suffer the penalty. In our unconscious mind, we only have to imagine ourselves involved in some transgression to pay a price in some degree of guilt or shame. Movies and literature, for example, have frequently depicted young novices in religious orders expressing intense guilt or shameful mortification for their "bad" thoughts. Blushing is deemed to be evidence that someone has been "caught red-handed" having naughty thoughts. Our inner critic is happy to expose us for our thoughts as well as for our deeds.

So we can feel guilt for our slightest slip-ups, misdemeanors, or idle thoughts. We sense that we deserve our guilt because we have allegedly done something wrong. But often the guilt is produced when, deep in our psyche, we absorb negative accusations from our inner critic that are unjust, untrue, or simply make-believe.

Sometimes the misdemeanors we feel guilty about occurred ages ago. One client could still feel guilty because she had gotten angry for a few hours in her mother's presence during her mother's long, fatal illness over thirty years ago. The mother was sick for more than three years, and my client had been a conscientious daughter who tried her best to be helpful and ease her mother's pain. But she still regretted that one-time outburst of anger and frustration. She said she had forgiven herself many times for the outburst, but the painful memory of it, and her guilt for allegedly having been a "bad daughter," kept coming back.

I told my client, "The only reason you're still feeling guilty and suffering in this way is because your inner critic is still able to hit you up with negative accusations about that long-ago incident. Those inner accusations of having been a "bad daughter" are unfair and quite irrational. Typically, our inner critic is unforgiving and cruel. It ignores the fact that we can't be perfect. Even though, as you said, you forgave yourself for your angry outburst a long time ago, that forgiveness means nothing to your inner critic. Your inner critic is still able to weasel its way into your thoughts and to pass judgment on you. You absorb that negative accusation, which means you feel that the accusation has some validity. That causes the guilt."

As mentioned, we absorb aggression and negativity from our inner critic because of our inner passivity. This passivity is an inner weakness, a place inside our psyche that we have not yet claimed (or infused) with sufficient consciousness. The dimensions of this inner passivity, which affects men and women equally and causes us all sorts of problems including clinical depression, come clearer to us as we study our psyche and acquire self-knowledge.

People can put themselves in a no-win situation with respect to guilt. Consider a man who, on one particular day, is asked by his wife to leave work early in order to pick up his son at school. He feels guilty about leaving the office early, yet he knows he'll also feel guilty if he tells his wife that he can't do it. The guilt is felt because the man is allowing himself, through inner passivity, to feel trapped in a quandary. Through his passivity, he's enabling his inner critic to get him, coming or going. Absent this passivity, he would make his choice more easily, and then, free of all guilt, he would follow up on that decisiveness.

A scientific study from 2012 shows the relationship between guilt and depression. The study, published in the journal *Archives of General Psychiatry*, compared brain images of people prone to depression with people who never got depressed to show significant differences in the regions of the brain associated with guilt.[43] Freud famously said that depression was related to feelings of guilt and self-blame, which is how it differed from normal sadness. The self-blame Freud refers to is the action of the inner critic or superego as it assails or berates the personality for alleged faults, foolishness, and wrongdoing. As mentioned, the guilt arises because the individual, through his or her subordinate ego or inner passivity, unwittingly absorbs this aggression from the inner critic. The individual feels the guilt as a consequence of his or her unconscious submission, meaning is this case the individual's willingness, through inner passivity, to absorb the aggression and to "buy into" the allegations of wrongdoing. When we understand this conflict and can objectively observe this inner dynamic, we can occupy with our self-knowledge and consciousness the area in our psyche that harbors inner passivity. In doing so, we claim that inner territory in the name of our conscious self. Now, instead of absorbing aggression from the inner critic, we're able to deflect or neutralize it. As a result, we experience neither guilt nor depression.

---

[43] http://www.forbes.com/sites/alicegwalton/2012/06/06/oh-the-guilt-the-neurobiology-of-blaming-yourself-for-everything-when-youre-depressed/

As we get stronger and eliminate our unconscious passivity, we successfully shut down our inner critic and live guilt-free and in greater harmony.

29. Understanding Anorexia

Recently I watched a YouTube clip of Phil McGraw (Dr. Phil) counseling a 79-pound woman with anorexia, and it was a sad sight indeed.[44] My sadness was felt both for the plight of the woman and for the plight of all people who get only shallow psychological knowledge from so-called experts and the media.

In this video clip from 2012, Dr. Phil succeeds only at shaming the woman for her anorexia. The woman already lives with considerable inner shame, and the unwitting Dr. Phil is only piling it on.

Anorexia can be treated and cured when its psychological origins are uncovered. Yet prominent websites on the subject—such as WebMD.com, MayoClinic.org, and MedlinePlus, the website of the National Institutes of Health—provide only scanty and shallow psychological information. The National Institutes of Health, which favors a medical approach to understanding and treating eating disorders, claims that, "Family conflicts are no longer thought to contribute to this [anorexia] or other eating disorders."[45] I disagree with this statement, and I provide evidence in this

---

[44] https://www.youtube.com/watch?v=xAWJE3anhXE
[45] http://www.nlm.nih.gov/medlineplus/ency/article/000362.htm

article that family conflict, along with inner conflict, does indeed contribute to these disorders. When anorexics understand their inner conflict and how they act out that conflict with others, they have a decent chance of escaping their painful condition.

A statement at HelpGuide.org, which operates in collaboration with the Harvard Medical School, provides some psychological insight into the causes of anorexia:

> Believe it or not, anorexia isn't really about food and weight—at least not at its core. Eating disorders are much more complicated than that. The food and weight-related issues are symptoms of something deeper: things like depression, loneliness, insecurity, pressure to be perfect, or feeling out of control. Things that no amount of dieting or weight loss can cure...
>
> People with anorexia are often perfectionists and overachievers. They're the "good" daughters and sons who do what they're told, excel in everything they do, and focus on pleasing others. But while they may appear to have it all together, inside they feel helpless, inadequate, and worthless. Through their harshly critical lens, if they're not perfect, they're a total failure.[46]

This is all true, yet there's more to consider. Let's explore the psyche for a better understanding of one of the indicators mentioned above—feelings of

---
[46] http://helpguide.org/mental/anorexia_signs_symptoms_causes_treatment.htm

helplessness. I explain these painful feelings in terms of inner conflict and inner passivity.

Anorexia is one symptom among many that is caused by an individual's entanglement in feelings of helplessness. This painful emotion, as mentioned in earlier discussions, is usually experienced in conjunction with a lessening of one's capacity for emotional and behavioral self-regulation. Why does the individual have such feelings in the first place? Many of us are unable to completely shake off the feelings of helplessness that we're born with. We all strive and struggle through childhood and adolescence to come into our own sense of power and autonomy. Yet helpless feelings persist. Even everyday normal people experience it when they're worried if not tormented by a fear of not being able to take care of themselves financially or otherwise. This is the fear that we'll somehow be rendered helpless as we make the journey through life.

Feelings of helplessness are often associated with emotional issues related to control and domination. We can feel our helplessness most acutely when it seems that we're at the mercy of others or are required to submit to others or to some imposing situation. In our unconscious mind, we can start to identify with ourselves through this feeling of helplessness. The feeling can begin to define us to ourselves. We don't know who we are without it, even though it's often quite distressful and painful. Consequently, we can be said to be emotionally attached to the feeling of helplessness. Common sense tells us that only a fool or a hopeless neurotic could be attached to feeling helpless. And hence we defend psychologically, on an inner level, against realization of this attachment. We deny the existence of the attachment even as it exists as an emotional default position that greatly limits our powers of self-regulation and sense of autonomy.

The following examples can help us to understand emotional attachments as they relate to eating disorders. The examples also provide clues as to how the underlying inner conflicts can be resolved. The first example looks at a boy with anorexia, and the second discusses the plight of a girl with bulimia. The examples are taken from my book, *Secret Attachments: Exposing the Roots of Addictions and Compulsions*.

A gaunt nineteen-year-old anorexic, living at home with his divorced mother, was managing to torture himself with the word *should*. He agreed with his mother and others that he *should* be doing better and eating properly, yet he was failing quite miserably to do so. The boy's refusal of food represented "a refusal of mother," and the behavior was a passive-aggressive defense to cover up his attachment to feeling controlled by his dominating mother. His anorexia had caused serious health problems, and he had been admitted to hospital several times. The mother was emotionally insecure, and she required her son to behave according to her demands and needs. Unconsciously, she did not want the boy (who looked no more than sixteen) to grow up. On the surface, the boy went along with her control and domination. He was emotionally captivated by her intense though neurotic preoccupation with him. Still, his unconscious dynamics required that he cover up (or defend against realization of) his attachment to feeling controlled by her. As part of this dynamic, he tormented himself with thoughts that he *should* try harder to please his mother and be a nicer boy for her sake.

But that sentiment was in vain. He was compelled to act out a self-damaging defense against his attachment to feeling controlled and dominated. His defense (and resulting self-damage) was based on an unconscious formulation that produces an illusion of power: "Mother doesn't control me. On the contrary, *I* refuse to eat her food. *I* refuse to comply with her demands. *I* even control her feelings and get her upset. True, she doesn't like me behaving like this, but at least *I* have some sense of power. It is *my* behavior that is controlling her."

This claim to power was, of course, self-defeating. Yet it "worked" to some degree as a defense, even though it produced guilt and shame. In fact, the defense produced a great deal of guilt, shame, and low self-esteem, amounting to a considerable degree of suffering. The boy's emotional entanglement in helplessness and passivity meant that on an inner level he was less able to keep his inner critic at bay. In absorbing the inner critic's attacks for allegedly being a bad or naughty boy, he felt considerable shame and guilt. Unconsciously he counteracted these inner accusations concerning his "naughtiness" with defensive claims that he wanted to be a good boy and knew he *should* be a good boy. (A girl and her mother could be involved, of course, in the same unhealthy dynamic.)

Inner conflicts are also associated with bulimia, which is characterized by binge eating and purging. One of my clients with a history of alcohol and drug abuse was concerned that her father would think less of her if he were to find out she was also bulimic. He was a successful businessman, and she was convinced he would see her as incompetent and a failure in her life. On the surface, she desperately wanted approval from him. But anyone who is desperate for approval is unconsciously attached to feeling disapproval. This woman had an emotional attachment to the feeling of being seen as a disappointment or in a negative light. By imagining her father thinking less of her, she produced negative emotions (such as anxiety or anger) through her inner conflict which, in itself, involved wanting approval but expecting (or being attached to) disapproval. After psychotherapy, which addressed this conflict as well as conflicts involving deprivation and control, her bulimia became inactive.

This excerpt below from *The Human Spark: The Science of Human Development* provides more evidence, as I see it, that an unconscious emotional attachment to helplessness (inner passivity) is a significant factor in producing anorexia and bulimia:

> Most anorexics are perfectionists with a strong need to be in control of all aspects of their lives because they want to avoid unpredictable and unwanted events. An inability to tolerate uncertainty over the immediate future is a characteristic common to many . . . These individuals continually think about the possibility of unwanted surprises occurring during the next moments, days, or weeks and try to do something to prevent them. Because the slightest mistake or failure is an unwanted surprise, they are often incapable of deciding on an action, even one as innocent as purchasing a ballpoint pen, if they haven any doubt about the correctness of their choice. They resemble bronze statues with a half-raised arm frozen in indecision.[47]

---

[47] Kagan, Jerome. The Human Spark: The Science of Human Development. New York: Basic Books, 2013.

A variety of inner conflicts are associated with eating disorders, and this discussion provides only a very small sampling. People in need of treatment have every right to expect and demand more insightful psychotherapy than what mental-health professionals are now providing.

30 . Hooked on Deprivation

We've always known that being generous feels good, but now there's proof. New research from the American Psychological Association says "the warm glow" and "emotional benefits" that result from spending money on someone else rather than for personal benefit appear to be a universal response among people in rich and poor nations.[48] The international survey comprised more than 234,000 individuals.

The researchers conclude that such generosity has served our species as a "mechanism" that may have carried "long-term benefits for survival over human evolutionary history." While that may be true, the APA report doesn't answer the Big Question: Why do people continue on behaving with a lack of generosity even when doing so feels "bad" or, at least, not so good. To answer that, we have to look to depth psychology.

People who are lacking in generosity are likely to be entangled to some degree in emotional conflict. That

[48] http://www.apa.org/news/press/releases/2013/02/people-giving.aspx

conflict produces negative emotions that shut down the impulse to be generous. What is the nature of this inner conflict? When we're unable to be generous, we're likely entangled in conflicts having to do with feeling deprived or refused. Many of us tend to know ourselves to a significant degree through the feeling that something important or even essential is missing in our life. As a result, we can be burdened with painful impressions of deprivation or refusal. Often we're not aware of how much we're being influenced by these negative emotions. If we were to find words to express this emptiness and negativity, we might say something to this effect: *The suffering in my life, even my sense of self, can be measured through the chronic dissatisfaction of what I don't have and what I may never possess. If I don't acquire these possessions, or fill myself with the recognition and validation of others, I am ultimately worthless and my life is a failure.*

Feelings of deprivation, refusal, and loss are unresolved emotions from early childhood. *To get* or *not to get* is a primal conflict. A little kid wants some other kid's toy or wants what's shown on TV or what he sees in the toy store. *Not getting* that object can produce intense emotions and even tantrums. Later as adults, we can remain painfully entangled in feelings of *not getting*. This painful feeling is the result of an inner conflict: Consciously, we want *to get*; unconsciously, we're stubbornly prepared, even determined, to experience particular situations through the familiar unresolved feeling of *not getting* or *not having*.

When some people think about giving or being generous, they become emotionally preoccupied with the sense that they'll now have less for themselves. This sense of deprivation blocks the impulse to be generous, leaving us to experience a sense of emptiness along with some degree of suffering. With this mentality, we're also more preoccupied with what we expect from life and thereby less concerned about what life might expect from us.

This problem could be called "the Deprivation Conflict." At a conscious level, we want to feel gratified and fulfilled, yet at an unconscious level we haven't resolved an expectation, dating back into early childhood, dealing with impressions of being refused and deprived. We're often not aware of possessing this poverty mentality, and we believe that "wanting to get" is a worthy pursuit and that our desire or instinct to accumulate goods or wealth is commendable. On the surface of awareness, we take our emotional life for granted, providing it's not excruciatingly painful, and hence we fail to detect the underlying pangs of unfulfilled desire.

People can also feel that because, as they perceive it, life is refusing to give more generously to them, they in turn will refuse to be generous to others. Based on their psychological or emotional interpretation of their situation, their lack of generosity feels like a normal response to life. Another conflict is to be hungry for recognition and attention while, simultaneously and unconsciously, being attached, through one's disconnect from self, to the feeling of *not* being appreciated, recognized, or respected.

This underlying preoccupation with what's missing in our life is strong enough that it can be understood as an emotional attachment or an emotional addiction. The feeling has lingered in our psyche from the oral stage of childhood. Babies have a highly subjective sense of reality, and they can become frustrated when their desires for oral gratification aren't instantly accommodated. The subsequent feeling of being refused or deprived lingers in our psyche, and as adults we can experience our world through these unresolved emotions. This hodgepodge of unconscious negativity doesn't support the spirit of generosity.

Our ego hates to acknowledge that we could still be clinging to expectations of deprivation or refusal, and so we produce an unconscious defense which claims, "I'm not looking to feel refused or deprived. I want to *get*. My desires (and my credit-card debt) prove how much I want to *get*." Hence, greed, envy, and fear of loss serve as unconscious defenses (just as they're also painful symptoms) of the underlying conflict.

Even when people have all they need, they can still accentuate in everyday ways the feelings of being deprived. Compulsive spending and shopping are self-defeating activities that are fueled by "the Deprivation Conflict." Our instinct to "prove" we want to get (to cover up our unresolved emotional attachment to feeling deprived or refused) is so powerful that many of us unwittingly enslave ourselves in the form of debt obligations. When debt-ridden, we heighten the sense of feeling deprived while producing the self-sabotage that accompanies inner conflict. The spirit of generosity wanes under these psychological impediments.

Acting out these unconscious attachments also produces another form of self-sabotage. Modern consumerism is, in part, a product of our instinct to cope with the inner emptiness that frequently accompanies neurosis. In rampant consumerism, we've created a monster with a huge appetite for the planet's natural resources. It's depleting and polluting the planet, impoverishing us and future generations. Consumerism creates the illusion that we're rich. Yet the goodies of the marketplace are trinkets compared to the value of the Earth and the value of our essential self. Who was fooled the most, the Native Americans who sold Manhattan to the Dutch for strings of beads, or you and me who are selling the Earth to its defilers for odd shapes of plastic, vinyl, and treated wood?

Another negative emotion is involved with the lack of generosity. Many people, in identifying with their ego, have a powerful desire to feel superior to others. For them, it's either feel superior or feel inferior. They don't like seeing people raised up from poverty because they no longer can easily feel superior to them. Hence, they feel no need to be generous. In fact, the impulse is to refuse to be generous. When they do give money, it can be for pet causes that promote their own narrow values or for the purpose of ego gratification (looking good in their own eyes and in the eyes of others). Such pseudo-generosity is less pleasurable than heart-felt generosity.

We need to be smarter about the underlying psychological dynamics that drive our behaviors and emotions. When we comprehend, for instance, our emotional attachment to feeling deprived, our intelligence can now resolve the inner conflict (the desperate desire to *get* versus the unconscious determination to feel deprived and refused).

When this conflict occupies our inner space, we cannot feel or know ourselves with any intimacy. Enthralled by materialism, our essential being and imperishable value fade into insignificance. We can't cherish nature and absorb its magnificence because our consciousness has not yet struck, for most of us, the gold in our own nature. We hesitate to be generous because our emptiness feels even more painfully depleted when we think about giving to others.

31. The Missing Link in OCD

You can't touch it, see it, or smell it. But it's there all the time, the hidden instigator of numerous human ailments and miseries including obsessive-compulsive disorder.

Experts attribute obsessive-compulsive disorder to various sources such as genetic factors and dysfunctional brain processes, as well as allergies and sensory problems that produce anxiety and stress. Yet a common cause of OCD—inner passivity in the psyche—is hardly ever mentioned. The fingerprint of inner passivity can be found on all the common expressions of OCD.

Readers, at this point, are becoming familiar with my descriptions of inner passivity. Throughout this book I show how inner passivity is an emotional weakness or attachment that is linked to many painful and self-defeating experiences and behaviors such as anxiety, depression, procrastination, shame, guilt, panic attacks, and addictions. In this discussion, I provide explanations that show how inner passivity is the common link among the primary types and symptoms of OCD.

Inner passivity, as I've been saying, is a hidden glitch in human nature, and it can plague us even when in daily life we're capable of being assertive and effective. As one of its most striking features, inner passivity, when experienced acutely, causes us to become emotionally entangled in a sense of helplessness and to feel overwhelmed by the everyday challenges of life.

How does this correlate with OCD? One of the most common symptoms of OCD is called "checking." People become anxious that they've failed to lock a door, switch off lights, or turn off the stove or toaster. Some OCD sufferers have persistent fears of hitting pedestrians while driving. After hitting a bump on the road, they might stop the car, and check under the car or along the road to see if they hit someone. In such cases, people are feeling profound self-doubt (a primary symptom of inner passivity). They can't trust themselves to know what's real and true. A nagging inner voice of self-doubt keeps saying, "What if …what if …" OCD sufferers are failing to access their sense of inner authority, that confident part of us, our authentic self, that can take charge and can tolerate uncertainty (one of life's inevitable challenges) without feeling overwhelmed by it.

The nagging voice of self-doubt is, in fact, the voice of inner passivity. Unresolved inner passivity, like our inner critic, is determined to make itself felt and heard, if only unconsciously. The weaker we are emotionally, the more we can let inner voices that are expressions of inner chaos and conflict, determine the manner in which we experience everyday situations. OCD sufferers are frequently haunted by persistent, intense thoughts, feelings, impulses, and images, and find themselves unable to moderate such inner experiences. They feel overwhelmed by these intense thoughts and impulses, which is another painful way in which their inner passivity is experienced.

People with OCD sometimes live in acute fear of the self-condemnation they'll experience should they do something wrong or "bad." Their fear is that, in leaving the stove on, the house could burn down. If they leave the door unlocked, an intruder could enter their home and cause damage or harm others. Their fear is largely irrational especially since they take such exhaustive, obsessive precautions to avoid these outcomes. Yet through their emotional imagination they experience a sense of the inner condemnation they would absorb from their inner critic if they were to be even marginally at fault for a consequence of such magnitude. Unconsciously, they're unresolved with inner condemnation. Throughout each day they absorb harsh criticism from their inner critic for minor transgressions or alleged shortcomings. Their inner passivity allows the inner critic to punish them in this way. Inner passivity blocks them from assuming inner authority (being more decisive and confident), and consequently their inner critic fills the vacuum.

The odds are remote that an OCD sufferer's alleged negligence would cause a house fire, so their fears are irrational. Nonetheless, through their emotional imagination *they can feel a sense of self-condemnation* even though the catastrophe of a house fire, conjured up in their imagination, has only a flimsy semblance of reality. This prospect of self-condemnation, along with the inability to protect oneself against it, produces acute anxiety which is a primary ingredient in obsessive-compulsive behaviors.

Why do OCD sufferers produce these unreal worst-case scenarios? I'll repeat in this context what I've been saying all along. We're all compelled to experience whatever is unresolved in our psyche, even as we also experience forms of suffering such as anxiety and fear in the process. Through inner passivity, we absorb self-aggression and self-condemnation. Any one of us, of course, would feel some degree of self-condemnation for hitting a pedestrian while driving our car. OCD sufferers, in comparison, acutely feel self-condemnation (at either a conscious or unconscious level) just thinking about (or imagining the possibility of) hitting and killing someone. Their obsession and fearfulness about doing so is a defense that covers up their emotional attachment to the inner aggression of self-condemnation. The unconscious defense reads: "I'm not looking for or anticipating self-aggression. I don't want to feel condemned for hitting a pedestrian. Look at how fearful I am that it could happen."

OCD sufferers are also unconsciously entangled in feelings of being at the mercy of life. One misstep, they're prepared to feel, and life will crush them. Through inner passivity, they're emotionally attached to this negative impression. As a consequence, they're often attracted to the sense or illusion of having power. They frequently believe that their ideas, thoughts, feelings, impulses, or images have power to influence events, and that their aggressive or horrific impulses can do harm to others. They fear, for instance, that they will impulsively hurt others, especially children, just because they can do so. The thoughts become obsessive and are appraised as dangerous. These individuals now feel helpless and powerless as they try to suppress the thoughts. They swing back and forth between feeling power and feeling passive, mimicking the conflict in their psyche between inner passivity and the aggression of the inner critic. Because these individuals are so entangled in inner passivity and lack real power, they tend to produce these counterfeit impressions of power and aggression.

People with OCD can also act aggressively against their own body, cutting their skin or picking at it and pulling out their hair. In these cases, they become instruments of their condemning inner critic, attacking themselves physically in the manner in which their inner critic attacks them emotionally, while passively mimicking the inner critic's primitive impulse toward self-aggression.

Sufferers who wash their hands compulsively and avoid hand contact with objects obsess about contamination. Unconsciously, they're entertaining feelings of being overwhelmed by germs and rendered helpless against some imagined contagion. Others experience intrusive sexual images and fear of becoming a pedophile or rapist. Their inner passivity is tempting them to embrace out-of control feelings and to display a lack of self-regulation. Hoarders are also experiencing inner passivity, particularly through their indecisiveness about discarding objects. They also experience acute inner emptiness (a symptom of inner passivity), and use clutter to give them a sense of value or completeness.

Inner passivity is a hitch or glitch in our consciousness, and also a wayside ditch that could stall our evolution. It is, as mentioned, quite invisible. It can be identified, however, through many of our painful and self-defeating symptoms. As we bring it into focus, we become emotionally stronger and more capable of self-regulation.

32 . **Wallowing in the Lap of Bitterness**

Bitterness is rat poison we feed our memories. It's the tedious self-torture of desolation row.

Bitterness cavorts with evil. It causes people to disown their children or to seek revenge, while it sends others off on maniacal shooting rampages. It shatters the political unity of great countries. And it ravishes joy with its lust for malice.

Bitterness is stupidly self-inflicted by people who refuse to be open to understanding, knowledge, and compassion. Even when bitter people manage to avoid doing evil to others, they do evil to themselves: They prefer to defile the carcasses of festering memories than to dance at the festival of life.

Our mind, when it lacks consciousness, can easily interpret old or new memories to conjure up negative emotions. Bitterness is produced when we indulge in these emotions until our splurge of intemperance scorches the soul. To make matters worse, we can hold on to those painful interpretations as if they were the family jewels. "That which is bitter to endure," said historian Thomas Fuller, "may be sweet to remember."

Some resolutely bitter people caper about on their tiny plot of moral turpitude, hardly knowing the range of freedom that extends beyond their emotional boundaries. Others can recognize their bitterness but are unable to divest themselves of it, in part because they believe their sullen rancor is a valid or legitimate reaction to what they perceive as the hurts and injustices inflicted by the cruel world and the malice of others.

"Whenever one finds oneself inclined to bitterness," wrote social critic Bertrand Russell, "it is a sign of emotional failure." Indeed, it's a sign of emotional weakness and psychological ignorance. Bitterness is really just one symptom of how unconscious conflict in our psyche is processed. It's one of the many forms of suffering we endure for not being sufficiently astute about the battleground of our psyche. Through this lack of awareness, we're inclined to stir up certain negative emotions that can produce the bitterness. What are some of these negative emotions?

We can produce bitterness when we react to emotional conflicts that involve inner passivity, loss, rejection, criticism, betrayal, abandonment, and feelings of being devalued. Let's start with inner passivity. People can feel bitter about failures and disappointments in their careers. Their bitterness is usually directed at "bad luck" or the insensitivity of others, though at times it circles back to haunt us as self-condemnation or self-hatred. We attack ourselves for allegedly having been foolish, lazy, or stupid. Yet the real culprit behind our misfortune or failure is often inner passivity, which is our identification with a weakness in our psyche that's causing the misfortune or failure in the first place.

Philosopher Paul Valéry described the bitterness produced through such passivity:

> Latent in every man is a venom of amazing bitterness, a black resentment; something that curses and loathes life, a feeling of being trapped, of having trusted and been fooled, of being the helpless prey of impotent rage, blind surrender, the victim of a savage, ruthless power that gives and takes away, enlists a man, and crowning

injury inflicts upon him the humiliation of feeling sorry for himself.

People entangled in such suffering are convinced they're helpless pawns of larger forces that restrain and trap them in hopeless inertia. Their resentment accumulates over time until it finally boils over into bitterness. Any comfort they might find in the notion that their failure wasn't their fault is overwhelmed by the inner need to blame others or circumstances for their plight. The pain of bitterness is inwardly accepted in order to produce a cover-up and maintain a semblance of self-respect.

The American Psychiatric Association had considered adding bitterness to its latest edition of the *Diagnostic and Statistical Manual of Mental Disorders*. The condition would have been identified as a mental illness under the name "post-traumatic embitterment disorder." This manual, the diagnostic bible of mental illnesses, is a list of emotional symptoms and their characteristics. Unfortunately, the manual doesn't identify the source in our psyche of the many symptoms it identifies. So including bitterness in its pages would not likely have helped people to liberate themselves from the painful condition.

As mentioned, bitterness is a product of emotional conflict in our psyche. Our intelligence and knowledge, not pills, liberate us from this pain. Take the example of people who become bitter over financial loss. When such loss becomes a painful, lingering emotion, the individual is *indulging* in the loss. He or she is emotionally entangled in the feeling of loss and won't let go of that feeling, even though holding on to it is obviously painful and potentially self-defeating. It's *not* the loss in itself that's causing the pain. It's the individual's unconscious determination to use the loss as a way to suffer. The following unconscious defense produces the bitterness: *I'm not indulging in the feeling of loss; look at how bitter I am that the loss has occurred.*

This individual, on one hand, wants to feel gain instead of loss; on the other hand, this person is unconsciously choosing, through the experience of loss, to suffer with old unresolved feelings of being deprived, of missing out on something of allegedly great value, and of being a lesser person because of the loss. Bitterness is a symptom of the unconscious wish to cling to this suffering.

We want to expose or make conscious this unconscious choice we've been making to suffer. When we expose this unconscious folly, we're strengthened emotionally. We see the inner "games" of self-suffering and self-defeat. Now, as we absorb this new awareness, we're able to step away from our emotional entanglement in inner conflict and liberate ourselves from bitterness.

The same principles apply when people feel bitter over experiences of rejection, criticism, betrayal, and abandonment. We begin to recognize our participation in the cultivation of these negative feelings. If, for instance, we felt rejected as children, we'll be inclined to replay this emotion in the new contexts of our life. We'll actually expect rejection and go looking for it. Or, conversely, we'll strive narcissistically to become objects for the admiration of others.

We can sometimes feel that holding on to our bitterness is a fight for justice. In other words, if we drop our bitterness we'll thereby be acquitting or forgiving the cruel, insensitive person or persons who allegedly contributed to our suffering. This is a rationalization for our wish to hold on to our suffering. Some experts believe that forgiveness is an antidote for bitterness. Sometimes forgiveness of others is appropriate, but often such forgiveness in itself fails to recognize our own role in having created a bad situation in the first place.

Finally, vanity or egotism can contribute to bitterness. Our vanity and self-centeredness cause us to become offended at even minor slights. As these "offenses" pile up, we're likely to become bitter. Here we want to understand that vanity and egotism are byproducts of underlying self-doubt. We're sensitive to feeling devalued because, deep down, we harbor self-doubt in our psyche. We can become upset and then bitter when others, from our perspective, treat us with disrespect. The bitterness arises, though, because of our emotional attachment to the underlying self-doubt and its accompanying sense that we're somehow lacking in value.

Our existence is precious. We know this truth and feel it when we liberate ourselves from vanity and unresolved negative emotions. This achievement washes away all bitterness.

33. When You Feel Bad About Yourself

One common form of suffering involves the feeling of shriveling up inside from allegedly being bad, unworthy, flawed, and defective. People who experience this anguish often anticipate being seen by others in a negative light. They expect that they might, at any moment, be exposed as a fake or a phony.

Some people feel this nauseating sense of self every day, and others only occasionally. The disagreeable feeling is often a lingering shame associated with one's fear that some embarrassing fact will become public knowledge or that we'll appear foolish or inept in a public situation. (See also, "Oh Shame, Where is Thy Secret Source?")

We can be convinced mentally and emotionally that this pain, which originates in our psyche, signifies some wretched, hidden flaw or loathsome defect at the core of our existence. Hence, we might be unable to establish friendships and intimate relationships because we don't feel worthy of being admired and loved. As Groucho Marx put it, "I don't care to belong to a club that accepts people like me as members." He might have got a laugh, too, if he'd said, "The only club I'd care to join is one that won't have me as a member."

Often, we have no inkling where the bad feelings come from. Our parents might have treated us with kindness and respect. We might also know—mentally at least—that we're honorable and good. Still, we're hurting at the core of our being and can't figure out why.

In an email, a visitor to my website put her emotional predicament in these words:

> I am 23, and overall, I can describe my childhood as a happy one (no abuse, loving parents, siblings) but ever since I remember I've always thought that I simply don't deserve to be loved. In high school, I had a boyfriend (7 years older than me),

and I always thought I was too young and too simple for him. As it turned out, he found some other girl (though he insisted that was untrue) and we broke up. I felt sad, neglected, angry and, after some time, apathy. Since then, I've been unable to be close to anyone – and I naturally assumed no sane person could be interested in me.

Paradoxically, I want to be loved and at the same time I avoid men – sometimes I'm even afraid to look random ones in the eye when I walk down the street. I'm thinking that I'll be alone the rest of my life.

Also, recently, much to my surprise, a friend from high-school contacted me and we started conversing. I used to like him a lot and I'm now willing to see how this could turn out – but I am at a loss what to do. I have the same feelings as before – yet even I can see that he's interested in me. But I'm simultaneously assuming this cannot be true.

I don't want to hurt him with my doubts, but I can't help having them. I really wish I could change my way of thinking.

Some of us can feel a lack of self-acceptance because we're holding on to old, familiar feelings of being rejected, abandoned, and unloved. In the above case, however, this woman didn't feel rejected or unloved by her parents. So something else is likely causing her suffering. Let's try another perspective—from the heart of classical psychoanalysis—to help us understand where the affliction she describes could possibly come from.

While many of us want to blame our parents for our dysfunction, our behavioral and emotional problems as adults can connect directly to childhood impressions, fantasies, and experiences that have little to do with how our parents treated us. Associations and memories dealing with the taboos and forbidden knowledge of childhood huddle in our psyche, beyond our conscious awareness. How did this emotional content get there? Children experience self-doubt and confusion when they're told or made to understand that it's forbidden to touch and look at certain things, such as their genitalia and mother's or father's nakedness. Sexual interest in brothers and sisters is also forbidden. In weaning, children are refused the breast. Next, they're not even allowed to look at it. To do so is bad or naughty.

Civilization does rightfully require decorum, protocols, and taboos, and it would be helpful if parents had more skill or knowledge in explaining them to their children. The problem is that children, who easily take things personally, can associate taboos with insinuations of wrongdoing and wickedness on their part, especially since the taboos are so enticing to their imagination. It's in the nature of our biology that the forbidden can excite our imagination with fantasies and secret pleasures.

A peeping or visual instinct is strong in children, and they like to look. But even curiosity, especially related to genital regions, is discouraged and then prohibited. Soon children are aware that parents have secret lives in the bathroom and bedroom. Imagining what goes on there is felt to be wrong. Forbidden erotic wishes drift through their consciousness. What are parents up to? Why are these sights forbidden to them? Using their imagination, children begin to peep. They peep into the darkness of what is forbidden, trying to understand this secretive world, all the while wary of the formidable powers of moral reproach, guilt, and punishment which parents and caregivers can dispense.

Repression begins at an early age because the material can be so painful, shameful, and guilt-laden. At the same time, children find the subject too intriguing to relinquish entirely. The child creates an inner receptacle, a department of secrets in the psyche. This private place is conscious in early childhood. That changes when the child's developing inner critic gains full access to the content of the psyche. The inner critic, now fulfilling its function as a harsh conscience and dispenser of punishment, begins to object to the child's erotic longings, wishes, and curiosities. The inner critic becomes a caricature of disapproving parents. Through the inner critic, the parent's prohibitions now apply to the child's department of secrets.

Children now have to contend with external and internal prohibitions. In self-protection, they unconsciously deepen their repression. They move forbidden material out of conscious awareness into unconscious regions of their psyche. This repressed material, however, is not expelled or even dormant. Instead, it creates mischief in the form of anxiety, stress, and unhappiness since it's so rich in painful, shameful, and guilt-laden content. It can also simmer quietly, producing a low-grade state of uncertainty and unhappiness. Out of this inner turbulence arise emotional and behavioral problems associated with lying, bullying, stealing, and snitching, along with insecurities concerning one's personality, intelligence, and physical appearance.

The repressed content can cause us to feel, as we enter adulthood, that something rotten dwells inside us. The sense is that we're harboring something that's unacceptable, bad, or wretched. This can produce the irrational impression that we're flawed, defective, or unworthy. Life now feels like a struggle to justify a tainted existence.

Related emotionally to repressed sexuality is the function of elimination. With self-doubt, it's easy to feel worse about ourselves when we realize our body produces what appears to us as a disgusting byproduct. Modern society may have a particular problem of shame with this bodily function because the flush toilet shrouds it in privacy and even secrecy. A children's book, *Everyone Poops*, became a big seller because parents sense a need to reassure their children of the function's universality. One parent wrote in a customer review at Amazon.com: "My 2-year-old is obsessed with 'poopy'. When we started to potty train her, she was upset when she did a poopy. To address this problem, we bought *Everyone Poops*. She loves it and the phrase, 'It's OK, because everyone poops!' has become a favorite in our household. I highly recommend this one!"

In summary, we can feel unloved and unlovable not because our parents didn't appreciate us but because we go on living with the repressed feeling that a wickedness, inherent flaw, disgusting aspect, or sinfulness resides within us. This repressed material can burst into our emotional life with explosive power to precipitate out-of-control behaviors, emotions, and astounding feats of self-defeat. Often the inner fear associated with this repressed material surfaces in adults as phobias and self-defeating behaviors. In maintaining our repression, we also waste a lot of the vital energy required for joyful living.

Understanding the source of our rotten feelings exposes the nature and extent of the underlying irrationality, which helps us to release guilt and shame so we can now respect and honor ourselves at a deep level.

34. Desperately Seeking Validation

Watch out for people who lean on you to validate their pain and misery. They may be using you to justify their unconscious decision to hold on to their brand of suffering. They're willing to load you up with their negativity, and often they'll dismiss as worthless anything you might say or do.

Sometimes, of course, we can help others in their suffering as we listen to them and comfort them. It's appropriate for friends and family members to reach out to us at times of need for our emotional support.

It's a different story, though, when we're being used by others for the purpose of helping them to *cover up* or deny their own participation in their suffering. We're dealing here with the weird and wacky determination of people to use whatever means necessary to deny their affinity for pain and misery.

Here's an example. Suppose that Tom is really angry at Jane because she rejected him and took up with another guy. In his hurt, Tom tells his friends how mean and cruel she is. He paints her in the worst possible light, portrays himself as an innocent victim, and in passionate intensity convinces his friends that he was grievously wronged.

Tom, however, is blind to his own true role in the drama. He has an unresolved issue with feeling rejected. It's how, in part, he interpreted emotionally his relationship with his mother who lacked a nurturing sensibility. Tom has been rejected by previous girlfriends. He has been completely unaware of the dynamic in his psyche through which he repeatedly acts out the experience and feeling of being rejected. He hides this inner weakness from himself. He can't handle this truth. It's "too much" for his ego to bear. He blames others in order to cover up his own role in his recurring self-sabotage.

As part of his defense, he enlists friends and relatives to agree with him that Jane is the villain. Why is he so desperate to get this validation from them? In the courtroom of inner reckoning, Tom is under an inner accusation from his inner critic that he's indulging in the feeling of being rejected. Tom instinctively feels the need to defend against this accusation. One of his defenses contends: "Look, it's natural that I'm suffering, considering the way Jane rejected me. My friends agree that she was cruel to me. Jane is the problem, not me."

When Tom adopts this defense, however, it causes his pain to linger. It means he's not willing to let go of his suffering. As part of his resistance, it can feel that "letting go" and moving on lets Jane off the hook. It also means he's likely to repeat the experience of being rejected with another woman because he isn't getting the insight or self-knowledge that could resolve his inner conflict. The conflict involves two opposing emotional positions. Tom might express the conflict in the following words, if he were to become conscious of it: "I truly wish to avoid the feeling or experience of being rejected, yet I expect to be rejected and I'm tempted, because the negative emotion of rejection is unresolved in me, to go looking for rejection and to indulge in experiences of it." This powerful insight exposes the conflict, and that exposure leads to the possibility of reform.

Ironically, while he complained fervently to others about Jane's alleged meanness, he likely was (or had been) provoking her to reject him. This is accomplished with subtle or not-so-subtle comments and quirks of behavior. While these comments and quirks are intended to provoke rejection, Tom, for the most part, produces them unconsciously.

If you have a friend like Tom who's blinded by his defenses, you can be a true friend by telling him in a kindly way that he may be overlooking his own role in the disharmony. You might tell him that it's common for people to relive the old hurts from their past without realizing that they're doing so.

Be careful, though. People can react quite defensively or negatively when they're "called out" on their unconscious determination to suffer. Recently on the *Psychology Today* Facebook blog, a psychologist posted a story in which he wrote perceptively, "If you think that validation [from others] is what you need, you will try to get someone to confirm that your pain is *justified*. This keeps you hyper-focused on the pain and the reasons for it."[49] Some readers of his post objected vigorously, claiming that the writer got it wrong and that empathy

---

[49] http://www.psychologytoday.com/blog/anger-in-the-age-entitlement/201104/pain-suffering-and-validation

from others was vitally important in the healing process. The psychologist then wrote a subsequent post in which he apologized for "a regrettable misunderstanding" concerning his earlier post.[50] In my opinion, he should *not* have backed down from his original position. Unfortunately, psychologists and mental-health counselors frequently do back down when confronted by a client's vigorous denial of how he or she unwittingly participates in producing misery and self-defeat.

Another example involves a visitor to my website who sent me an email about an article I posted there. The article, "Avoidable Miseries of the Workplace," describes some of the unconscious ways we chose to be miserable in the workplace, even when we hold excellent jobs. In her email, the reader emphatically chronicled the (alleged) reasons why she had no choice in her workplace but to suffer. She makes her case convincingly, as these excerpts from her email attest:

> Hello Kind Sir, I was wondering if you could assist me ... In my trade, graphic designer, I need to maintain 100% concentration at all times ... Repeatedly, I have kindly asked the owner of this small company to please keep the noise levels down (barking dog, loud walking, and distracting talking), but that suggestion was repudiated by the owner. Not only was my plea for solitude disregarded, but the noise level seems to have increased ... Not only does this owner micromanage my every move by looking over my shoulders every 15 minutes, I have to deal with a barking dog, too. . . (The owner will accommodate

---

[50] http://www.psychologytoday.com/blog/anger-in-the-age-entitlement/201112/what-i-should-have-said

AND respect the DOG'S WISHES- BUT NOT MY PROFESSIONAL CONCERNS.) ... at lunch the dog sits next to my desk waiting for me to offer it food and the owner will pass by my desk, witness this behavior, and walk on as if this type of nonsense is acceptable. What total disrespect!!!!!!!!! This owner just doesn't care!!!! If I make even the smallest mistake, due to the excess noise levels, the owner goes completely BONKERS – I MEAN LITERALLY ALRIGHT CRAZY...totally insane, out of her mind, off the charts screaming, stooping around like an angry, irate and pouting child. Which takes the word out-of-control to a new level of CRAZY. I'm at my wit's end AND depressed. I have never worked for a Company like this before and hope NEVER AGAIN to encounter such tacky behavior that exemplifies morbid disrespect, malice and unprofessionalism... In my opinion, this owner is a micromanaging dictatorial self-serving diabolical hovering control freak... Owner is also exceptionally nosy and condescending LIAR. I am so miserable.

I wasn't going to validate her suffering. I sent back this brief reply, for which she later thanked me.

It sounds as if you do indeed have a difficult work environment. Nonetheless, it's your job, and since you're working there you can try your best to minimize the aggravation. You might be embellishing emotionally on the feeling that your boss doesn't respect you or care enough about you to tone down the noise. Sometimes, as well, we can unconsciously be embellishing on the feeling of being at the mercy of the control of others, which makes us feel more trapped and restricted. If so, that will make the situation more difficult for you. You would want to trace that trapped feeling or the feeling of being disrespected back into your own psyche. Keep reading my posts. My writing is designed to help people see these trigger-points in themselves and clear them up. Do your best to acquire self-knowledge. Thanks for writing. Best of luck.

It can feel like walking a tightrope when dealing with people, especially among family and friends, who seek validation for their unconscious choice to hold on to their suffering. Be kind yet firm. You want to have enough self-respect not to let yourself be used in this way.

35 . The Origins of Feeling Overwhelmed

One sufferer described the misery of feeling overwhelmed this way: "Has anyone seen my brain? It ran off this morning flailing and screaming about being overwhelmed. I'd really like it back."

As the comment suggests, the feeling of being overwhelmed can be agonizing. Paradoxically, though, the feeling is sometimes delightfully associated with love or with wonder, as when astronomer Carl Sagan contemplated "the overwhelming immensity" of the sky. For this post, however, I'm writing about the feeling as a disagreeable, painful experience. We can ease this form of suffering when we expose the source of the feeling in our psyche.

The feeling is widespread in modern life. Another person described a common rendering of the experience: "I constantly feel overwhelmed—busy, busy, busy! I ask myself, 'How can I possibly get this all done?' I'm living on the edge of chaos, and I tell myself, 'This is crazy, insane!' I go to bed, get up in the morning, and it starts all over again." He later admitted, "Every day I load myself up with too many tasks and too much work, so I know I contribute to the problem."

Feeling overwhelmed can sometimes be a normal reaction to very difficult circumstances, as in the plight of some single parents or the predicament of underemployed people struggling to pay bills. Some people, indeed, are pushed to the limit, especially when struggling to stay employed, raise their children well, and manage a variety of other challenges. Yet many people would be coping more successfully, with less tension and stress, if they were not embellishing emotionally on their sense of being unduly burdened. Our psychological issues are often making challenging circumstances more difficult and painful than they have to be.

People can feel overwhelmed as they try to tackle the straightforward challenges of everyday life. While some of us go with the flow, others get caught in the undertow. Why do some of us feel overwhelmed on a daily basis by work, sadness, fear, children, choices, finances, or the obligations of a busy life? Often times, too, we feel overwhelmed by things we can't influence, for instance when we start worrying about dire possibilities that are unlikely to occur. We tend to believe that difficult circumstances are causing us to feel overwhelmed, that we're being bogged down by our complicated rat-race life and suffocating in endless demands and obligations.

While we may indeed be feeling bogged down, we're unwittingly contributing to that impression. It's not the outside world or demanding circumstances that are solely responsible for producing the unpleasantness. Rather, one or more unresolved negative emotions inside of us are producing much of the suffering. Unconsciously, we're willing to live through the experience of those negative emotions. Much of the time that negative emotion is associated with feeling helpless, weak, and even defeated.

When feeling overwhelmed, we often react by being frantically busy, by procrastinating, or by doing things clumsily or inefficiently. Let's briefly look at the problem from the perspective of procrastination. When a person is experiencing the paralysis of procrastination, he or she is suffering the pain and consequences of inner conflict. This pain is the product of helplessness, apathy, psychological paralysis, and a disconnection from one's intelligence, self, and will. I tell my clients that they're entangled in the primary conflict between inner aggression and inner passivity. On the passive side, the conflict consists of their conscious (sometimes desperate) wish to feel inner strength versus their unconscious determination to continue to experience themselves through unresolved feelings associated with helplessness.

Feeling overwhelmed is a primary *emotional* symptom of inner passivity, while procrastination is a primary *behavioral* symptom. When mainstream psychologists discuss the misery of feeling overwhelmed, they overlook its roots in our psyche. Superficial behavioral advice is often offered, such as recommendations to take walks, breathe deeper, relax one's muscles, and take mental breaks. This is like giving candy to a kid with a toothache, hoping the sweetness will make her feel better.

Let me briefly digress. Many experts feel confident in discussing symptoms (such as feeling overwhelmed) because the symptoms are there for all to see. These experts feel less confident in identifying the underlying causes because these causes, as they see it, are of mysterious origins and haven't been "scientifically validated." But is unconscious bias at play? Are scientific psychologists, wringing their hands in dismay, not tempted to avoid certain propositions and fields of inquiry concerning the wild, chaotic, imponderable unconscious that insists on remaining mysterious? In any case, the scientific method, while obviously a powerful tool for discerning what's real and true, might not be able to produce any more definitive answers about our inner space than it can about outer space. Like depth psychology, astrophysics and neuroscience are disciplines based on imagination, evidence, observations, and basic principles. However scientific these disciplines or any others may be, they're as unlikely to illuminate the essence of consciousness as they are to disclose the meaning of life. Only the consciousness of transcendence, mystics might say, could hope to access that level of understanding. In the meantime, sensible humility keeps us grounded. We do our humble best to decide what's real and true as it applies to our basic wellbeing.

Let's get back to the topic of feeling overwhelmed and, using humble intelligence, try to make sense of this common affliction. Logical analysis can trace the feeling back to its source in inner conflict and inner passivity. Let's apply some deduction. Feeling overwhelmed is often produced through the common tendency to churn up mental speculations and considerations that are difficult if not impossible to resolve or to answer. This is the mental equivalent of "spinning our wheels." This futile, out-of-control thinking gets us nowhere, but it does accentuate the feeling of being overwhelmed by life's many choices or complexities. In other words, it appears quite plausible that people "spin their wheels" for the unconscious purpose of intensifying the feeling of inner passivity and, hence, they experience as a symptom the feeling of being overwhelmed. Keep in mind this axiom of depth psychology: We're compelled to recycle and replay whatever is unresolved in our psyche. Inner passivity, in its confrontational dynamic with the inner critic, is part of an unresolved conflict. It's also an emotional attachment that can be experienced as distress, anxiety, fear, confusion, and indecision. Until we make inner passivity conscious, we continue to experience it in ways that are either self-defeating or that limit our potential.

It helps us in understanding this concept when we see that the feeling of being overwhelmed actually serves as a psychological defense. As a defense, the feeling covers up inner passivity, which is our emotional attachment to experiencing ourselves as weak and helpless. The unconscious defense goes like this: "I'm not attached to (or willing to recycle and replay) that old feeling of being helpless and at the mercy of circumstances. Look at how I hate feeling overwhelmed. I want to get things done! I want to be on top of things! Look at how much I suffer by feeling overwhelmed. That proves I don't want to feel helpless!" The defense, however, only proves how convincingly we can deceive ourselves.

Students sometimes feel overwhelmed at the prospect of reading and assimilating the knowledge they're required to learn. Their thick textbooks can look and feel like treatises in perplexity. Because of inner passivity, students may be tempted emotionally to experience the full curriculum in its totality, as a body of knowledge that has to be digested whole rather than in parts or segments, and hence feel paralyzed by the immensity of the task. Students who do poorly or who fail their courses are often sabotaged by this inner conflict between wanting to learn versus being determined to experience themselves through the old, familiar passivity. The solution is to recognize the attachment and how it produces a willingness to experience the learning challenge through a sense of inner weakness. Armed with this knowledge, students can begin to feel some satisfaction, power, and pleasure in absorbing the knowledge one page or one lecture at a time, trusting in themselves to produce the inner resources for success. Related to this is the problem of illiteracy. When trying to read, people who are illiterate are experiencing their powerlessness to penetrate into the meaning of the words. They feel overwhelmed by the challenge of making the words comprehensible. Unconsciously, they're holding on to the feeling of their passivity, even though in doing so they produce such painful self-sabotage. Beneath their shame about their illiteracy is the deeper shame of their inner passivity.

In another situation, a person who frequently complains about being too busy, or who constantly reiterates, "I'm so busy, I'm so busy," is in that moment feeling acutely the sense of being overwhelmed. The busyness, in itself, doesn't have to be painful or overwhelming. But through the busyness, the individual is able to accentuate or intensify the emotional attachment, namely the familiar feeling of being helpless to regulate one's experience in a more agreeable way. This is what, to some degree, we all do with inner passivity—we go looking for the feeling of it, and then we submerge ourselves in it, no matter how unpleasant it is in that moment to do so.

36 . Stubbornness: The Guts to Fight Reality

Stubbornness is, essentially, a determination to fight a losing battle with reality, while accepting as a "reward" for the effort the gift-wrapped deadweight of rigidity and resentment.

My apologies to Frank Sinatra fans, but I believe the theme song or anthem for stubbornness is the old favorite, "My Way." One stanza stands out:

> Yes, there were times, I'm sure you knew/ When I bit off more than I could chew./ But through it all, when there was doubt,/ I ate it up and spit it out./ I faced it all and I stood tall,/ And did it my way.

Sure—my way or the highway! When we're smart and wise, we don't put the emphasis on *my way* or relish self-congratulatory conceits that *I stood tall.* We're just pleased and grateful to find a good, sensible, or brave way to travel "each and ev'ry highway."

People can mistake stubbornness and perseverance. The latter quality is at play when we adhere bravely to a sound principle or effort in the face of opposition or indifference. Stubbornness, in contrast, is negative in nature, and it can be recognized by a defensive evasive mantra: "Look, I am what I am. Either you like it or you don't. Take it or leave it!" The stubborn person is self-centered and willing to sacrifice you—toss you out of his life—rather than meet you halfway.

Stubbornness and denial are two bad apples in the same basket. The former tends to be a conscious expression of opposition, as in a lady's stubborn refusal to reunite with an estranged family member, while the latter is likely to refer to an unconscious form of the behavior, as in a man's denial that his drinking problem is going to get him fired.

Stubbornness is usually a reaction to underlying emotional attachments. If we can make these attachments conscious and keep them in focus, we have a good chance of letting go of our mulish attitude and the suffering it brings on. Basically, obstinacy is a symptom of three different emotional issues in our psyche.

The first issue involves our ego and our instinct to protect it and save face. The ego, which is usually stronger in men than in women, often creates the feeling that we can't back down and concede that we're either wrong about something or are failing to see the whole picture. Our ego, which hates to feel diminished, interprets the act of backing down (and even concessions to reality) as a feeling of losing, being reduced, being humbled, and, hence, being a lesser person. An emotional impression washes over us: "If I'm wrong, I'm lacking in value. If that person is right, she's better than me. She'll feel she's triumphed over me." Obviously, being wrong about something doesn't make anyone a lesser person. But much of the time our emotions trump our reason. We can't figure out what is real and true. Our gut instinct, influenced by inner conflict, tells us something is true when it's not. Yet we'll stubbornly embrace the error of our ways in order to avoid upsetting our self-image, even when doing so is painful. Consequently, we start thinking less clearly and can even become stupid in what we believe.

The more pronounced our egotism, the less stable we are emotionally. This means we depend on our ego for our orientation in the world. When our ego is threatened, we can start to feel what we've been repressing all along—our underlying self-doubt. When activated, this self-doubt is quite painful and can produce acute anxiety. Self-doubt is essentially an irrational conviction that we're seriously lacking in value and significance. Our instinct is to avoid this anxious feeling at all costs. So truth becomes secondary to our perceived need to protect the beliefs that in turn protect our ego and ease our anxiety. When we hang on stubbornly to a flawed belief or perception, we're dependent emotionally on being "right." Saying "Sorry, I was wrong" feels to our ego like a smack to the jaw. We can't maintain such bullheadedness without paying a price: Our stubbornness is likely to lead to increasingly painful deviations from truth and reality.

The second issue involves power and submission. Many of our daily dealings with others involve who is in a dominant position and who will prevail. Of course, we're inclined to resist when we feel pushed around, controlled, and dominated. However, people with unresolved emotional issues are easily triggered when it comes to feeling controlled. A problem for the weak person is that he or she can feel controlled and dominated even when the other person, the alleged controller, is only being appropriately helpful or legitimately forceful. The weak person enlists stubbornness as a way of coping with his or her own weakness. As one observer put it, "Stubbornness is the strength of the weak." British writer W. Somerset Maugham also got it right: "Like all weak men he laid an exaggerated stress on not changing one's mind." The feeling is that, "If I'm not stubborn, people will walk all over me." So stubbornness feels like power to a weak person, but typically it is a self-defeating third-rate kind of power.

Stubbornness can be understood as an illusion of power that covers up the feeling of being overwhelmed and out-gunned by reality. Once an individual emotionally interprets a situation in such a way as to feel controlled, he or she is likely to slip into passive-aggressive resistance. This is a kind of cowardly aggression—a sly, unspoken refusal to cooperate, for instance—yet it feels to the weak individual like actual power. Any port in a storm, the saying goes. In feeling forced to comply, passive-aggressive people might say to themselves, "No, I won't, and you can't make me!" Often they don't even register consciously this inner defiance. They seem agreeable on the surface, but their resistance and behaviors soon exhibit the rigidity of passive non-compliance.

The third issue involves our tendency to hold on fiercely to our grudges. In this version of stubbornness, we refuse to let go of some real or imagined insult or affront to our person. Injustice collectors, for instance, hold on obstinately to the big and small slights they feel have wounded them over the years. At this point, stubbornness becomes quite simply a determination to suffer. This is why stubborn people are often unable to give a clear reason or explanation for their refusal to budge. I remember one time, probably 25 years ago, being in a snit over some alleged unkindness that I felt my wife Sandra had inflicted upon me. Looking back, I vaguely remember it as some trifle. Anyway, I sat at my desk in a very dark mood, brooding resentfully, determined at the very least to hold this grudge against her all night long and into the following day. Next thing I knew, though, she was sitting down close to me, talking to me in sweet consideration, wondering if we could clear the air. I didn't want to. I wanted to stay resentful. She kept talking patiently, expressing warm feelings toward me, pondering the nature of conflict and unhappiness. Within minutes, my misery began to melt away. In less than ten minutes I was soaking up inner peace and harmony, marveling at how much suffering her kind intervention had spared me.

37. The Dire Determinants of Divorce

The list is long of the sundry ways we can suffer in a marriage or romantic relationship. We can, for starters, feel controlled, trapped, restricted, deprived, refused, criticized, belittled, disrespected, betrayed, rejected, abandoned, undervalued, and unloved.

If we're really eager for punishment, we can feel many of these painful emotions at the same time, for much of the day and night. This inevitably produces growing resentment against one's partner because we blame our partner for the misery that we ourselves are determined to activate and experience.

On the surface of our awareness, we all want tender love and intimacy. But deeper down we can have an unconscious program in place to act out negative emotions that are unresolved from childhood and have now become emotional attachments. (See also, "The Bittersweet Allure of Feeling Unloved.")

Of course, happy marriages and romantic unions exist in large numbers. Yet the more we are dysfunctional or neurotic, the more likely we are to turn our relationship into a turbulent free-for-all that is doomed to end in separation and divorce.

Why are our unresolved issues so eager to be acted out in marriages and intimate relationships? We're unconsciously interested in re-experiencing old unresolved emotions and conflicts, no matter how painful they are. It's so easy to act out these issues with the people we're closest to, and unconsciously we can't resist doing so. The hurt of feeling wronged by someone we're intimate with can be so much more intense. Thwarted love can be the greatest of all hurts, especially when we're blind to the depths of our own contrariness. Because of inner conflict, the thrill of new love is often a homing beacon for the desolation of rejection, betrayal, and abandonment. Divorce is usually a result of our failure to escape the clutches of self-suffering. We lug into marriage our toolkit for making misery; we stagger way from the divorce settlement unwilling to part with that baggage.

Unconsciously, we go looking for opportunities to recycle and replay those painful emotions that are unresolved from our past. In failing marriages, even as divorce and its agonizing effects on a family loom ever closer, estranged partners typically will resist looking objectively at how each one is contributing to the dysfunctional relationship. We stubbornly hate to see our ignorance and contrariness, and we accept much self-defeat and self-damage to keep it all a secret.

Nonetheless, some couples do come into an awareness of this self-defeating dynamic. The knowledge produces great empathy for each other. Each one's self-understanding supports the other as they struggle together, usually successfully, to overcome the vagaries of human nature. Our own progress or self-development can proceed at a faster clip when we're in a partnership with someone who shares these aspirations. A marriage that narrowly avoids divorce can end up, in the ensuing fulfillment of love and intimacy, being the means by which one's life is gratifying and even triumphant.

Try to imagine the vast difference between suffering in a relationship that's headed for divorce and one that tumbles into the satisfaction of deep, abiding love. There's a vast chasm between the emotional poverty of painful separation and the richness of union with one's beloved. The difference can be just a matter of understanding some basic principles. In my opinion, a large percentage of divorces could have ended up as happy marriages if the partners had accessed this knowledge and applied it to their situation. We usually do succeed in creating intimacy and great mutual respect when we overcome our resistance to seeing our own contribution to the disharmony.

Injustice collecting is one notable way that partners create and hold on to strong feelings of animosity toward each other. *Injustice collecting* is a psychological process whereby we gather and accumulate an inventory of grievances concerning our subjective perceptions of having been mistreated by others or by the circumstances of our life. Injustice collecting reflects our unconsciousness interest in remaining stuck in negativity. In marriage, we often can collect injustices through our irritation over trifles. Partner A can feel great annoyance over some harmless idiosyncrasy or behavior pattern displayed by partner B because, like a child who for a moment hates mother because she denied him a candy, partner A has not outgrown intense infantile reactions to small events.

Injustice collecting, when it belittles our partner, also serves the purpose of providing an outlet for the manner in which we allow our inner critic to devalue our own self.

Negative transference and projection soon kick into action. Now we are ready to feel refused, controlled, and criticized by our partner, based on old emotions that go back to childhood. We start to see and hate in our partner the flaws that we cover up in ourselves.

We convince ourselves we would be happy if our partner didn't have the flaws and behaviors that we increasingly dislike. Our conviction is that he or she "causes me to feel this way." As we shift more blame and criticism toward our partner, he or she begins to react in a way that provides us with what we are unconsciously looking for, namely some deepening experience of our unresolved negative emotions. The couple descends into an increasingly painful acting out of their individual issues. Unwittingly, they provide for each other the opportunity to act out all the unresolved inner conflicts.

Soon, hatred and bitterness sweep away what love there was. Restoring love can mean that we have to let go of our defenses—the main one being our determination to blame the other. We also want to explore the roles that egotism, stubbornness, and resistance play in how we experience our partner. As mentioned, we can be reluctant to see clearly our role in the dysfunction, often out of fear that seeing the sabotage produced by our own issues will translate emotionally into some hopeless sense of being beyond redemption.

Here's another example of the kind of insight that can help to avoid divorce. Gary frequently imagines that his new wife Glenda is having disagreeable feelings or thoughts about him. He does nothing to investigate whether this impression is valid. He declines, for instance, to initiate a discussion with her to determine whether indeed she's having such critical thoughts. Instead, he silently endures his inner anxiety. The more he's silent, the more acutely he feels the discomfort. What valuable insight could Gary learn about this situation?

He has emotional attachments to feeling unworthy and unloved. He's afraid to talk to Glenda about how he feels because, in part, he's afraid she'll confirm that his anxiety is indeed based in reality, meaning that she does indeed harbor negative thoughts and feelings toward him—and rightfully so. He's also passive, and he's thereby inclined to refrain from initiating a conversation with her that would explore what's really going on. He feels these painful moments through a sense of being helpless to do anything about them. But this is his unconscious intention: He's emotionally attached to inner passivity and to feeling unworthy and unloved, and, unwittingly, he's prepared to experience life through these negative emotions.

At it happens, he's misreading the situation entirely. Glenda has a tendency to be non-demonstrative, but for the most part her feelings toward him are either neutral or affectionate. When she thinks about him, it's mostly in a kindly way. (The danger, though, is that she may soon start having negative thoughts and feelings toward him if he continues to live as if that's already the reality. When in conflict, couples give to each other what the other is unconsciously expecting or willing to endure.) Gary can free himself of his false reading on reality and its accompanying distress by understanding his emotional attachments to feeling unworthy and to inner passivity. However, his resistance and defenses block him from seeing this deeper truth. This is the stumbling block he has to get over.

Try to understand that the topics that couples are arguing about tend to be of secondary importance. It's not the topic *de jour* that's the problem but instead it's the unconscious compulsion to act out inner conflict with each other, fueled by the inner conflict that's occurring in the psyche of each participant. Also, try approaching marital conflict as if dealing with a no-fault situation. The dysfunction is not your fault or your partner's fault. Both of you are decent people who are struggling with the vagaries of human nature. Just set your sights on becoming more conscious. Be open with yourself and with each other. As inner conflict subsides, so will the conflict between you. When your own negativity is out of the way, you'll very likely respect and love the person you're with. Recognize the value of self-knowledge and the acquisition of deeper insight.

38. Nagging: Love Destroyer, Marriage Killer

The media are *not* providing the level of intelligence on psychological issues that our world desperately needs. An article on relationship disharmony in the *Wall Street Journal* —titled "Meet the Marriage Killer"—illustrates the point.[51] The content of the article fails completely to get to the heart of the widespread nagging problem.

Both my headline above and the one in the *Journal* are not precisely correct: Nagging is just a symptom of a deeper psychological conflict, so nagging in itself is not the real marriage killer. Nonetheless, the problem of nagging is widely experienced and dreaded.

The article starts out satisfactorily, and it provides an adequate definition of nagging:

> Nagging—the interaction in which one person repeatedly makes a request, the other person repeatedly ignores it and both become increasingly annoyed—is an issue every couple will grapple with at some point. While the word itself can provoke chuckles and eye-rolling, the dynamic can potentially be as dangerous to a marriage as adultery or bad finances. Experts say it is exactly the type of toxic communication that can eventually sink a relationship.

---

[51] http://online.wsj.com/news/articles/SB10001424052970203806504577180811554468728?mg=reno64-wsj&url=http%3A%2F%2Fonline.wsj.com%2Farticle%2FSB10001424052970203806504577180811554468728.html

However, never at any point does the article ask (let alone answer) the question of how "toxic communication" arises in the first place. The author of the article summarizes the views of experts with this paragraph:

> The first step in curbing the nagging cycle, experts say, is to admit that you are stuck in a bad pattern. You are fighting about fighting. You need to work to understand what makes the other person tick. Rather than lazy and unloving, is your husband overworked and tired? Is your wife really suggesting she doesn't trust you? Or is she just trying to keep track of too many chores?

Let's take a look at this paragraph, sentence by sentence. It's true that couples caught in the nagging cycle "are stuck in a bad pattern." But what exactly is this pattern? There's usually a large unconscious component to behavioral patterns. Such patterns, when self-defeating, are caused by our compulsion to repeat what is unresolved in our psyche. We can be recycling and replaying, through our partner, the conflicts that are unresolved within us.

We are, the article says, "fighting about fighting." It is much more precise to say that we displace our inner fights or conflicts with ourselves on to our partner. As mentioned earlier, we're fighting on the wrong front (through our partner) rather than addressing the conflict in ourselves. The fights we have with each other mirror the fights we're having in our own psyche. The external conflict—the nagging from one partner and the resistance from the other—is an externalized rendition of the conflict occurring within. Often the inner conflict is between our inner critic and the passive-aggressive resistance to our inner critic, as channeled through our inner passivity.

The next sentence in the above excerpt reads, "You need to work to understand what makes the other person tick." In part, this is true. But the advice can be based on faulty premises such as, "He or she *causes* me to feel upset," or "The other person is the problem, not me." The best advice would say, "You have to understand what makes *you* tick." You need to see clearly your own role in the dysfunction. When couples chronically act negatively toward each other, each is being compelled to act out an emotional drama that's unresolved from his or her past.

In the paragraph quoted above, three questions are asked. The questions focus on what one's partner may or may not be experiencing rather than on one's own inner experiences.

Question One: "Rather than lazy and unloving, is your husband overworked and tired?" Now if one's husband is "overworked and tired," how is knowing that going to significantly change anything? As a solution to the problem, it's too simplistic. Does it mean the wife is supposed to coddle him because he's tired? Does this mean she has to bottle up her resentment as she does all the housework? And how does this question address the husband's responsibility to bring cheer and positive energy to his marriage?

Question Two: "Is your wife really suggesting she doesn't trust you?" Isn't it obvious that the wife isn't trusting her husband to do what she asks? More relevant questions would ask, "Isn't this woman's nagging an ineffective way to address the problems between them?"

and "Is her nagging simply a symptom of her passivity, namely her inability or unwillingness to express true power to convince her husband to take her more seriously?" In itself, her distrust is just a symptom of their compulsion to act out their own unresolved issues with each other. Focusing on symptoms doesn't get to the root of the problem.

Question Three: "Or is she just trying to keep track of too many chores?" Indeed, she may be trying to keep track of chores, but what is *too many*? Who's going to keep track of them if she doesn't? Again, this point about "too many chores" is far removed from the much bigger issues and dynamics at play in their dysfunctional relationship.

The *Journal* article quotes a couple in California who said they had been helped by a specific approach to understanding their nagging problem. Here is the passage:

> Noreen ..., 44, of Westlake Village, Calif., says she used to give her husband frequent reminders to take out the garbage, get the car serviced or pick up the kids from school. "I thought I was helping him," she says. Jose..., 47, often waited a while before doing what she asked. The couple would argue. Sometimes Ms ... would just do it herself.
>
> A few years ago, they got insight into their nagging problem after taking a problem-solving assessment test, the Kolbe Assessment. Ms. ..., a business coach, learned she is a strategic planner who gathers facts and organizes in advance. Her husband, an attorney, learned that he is resistant to being boxed into a plan. Now, Ms. ... says, "I

don't take it personally when he doesn't respond." "There is a sense of recognition about what's happening," Mr.... says. "It's easier to accommodate each other."

Obviously, this couple feels they have received help, and they might not be interested in any deeper understanding of their situation. That, of course, is up to them. The problem is that none of the experts, to judge by the *Journal* article, are providing them with an opportunity to explore deeper psychological knowledge that could eliminate the source of their disharmony.

There's a danger for this couple that underlying issues, if not made conscious, will reappear or be acted out in other harmful ways. Certain vital insight could be helpful in a case such as theirs. A wife could be nagging because she's ready to feel, repeatedly, that her needs aren't important and that her value as a person isn't being recognized. This could be an unresolved feeling from her relationship with, say, her mother, father, or both. Without understanding transference and her compulsion to continue to feel what is unresolved emotionally, she would be driven to repeat this pattern with her husband, even though doing so is very painful for her.

A husband in a situation of this kind might be resistant to feeling controlled or boxed into a plan. This could mean that he's emotionally attached to that feeling (it's unresolved from his past, and likely related to his relationship with his father or mother). Because the feeling of being controlled is unresolved, he's compelled to continue to keep feeling it, even though his wife may not actually be trying to control him but only trying to keep her household organized. His resistance to her overtures for household assistance is a passive-aggressive defense that covers up his unconscious willingness to remain entangled in the old, familiar feeling of being controlled or boxed in. Both husband and wife are "conveniently" acting out their unresolved issues with each other, locked into a painful battle that complements their inner issues.

As the *Journal* article notes, women are more likely to be the naggers, men the resisters. However, the underlying issues affect men and women equally. Men are more likely to be the resisters because of their lingering emotional associations with the mother-figure who once made them submit to toilet training and childhood socialization. The narcissistic offense felt in the process of early childhood development is typically more pronounced in men than in women. Women are tempted to nag because it does give them some sense of power, however illusionary, when faced by passive-aggressive resistance.

39. The Temptations of the Injustice Collector

In matters large and small, we all want to see justice done. A lot of us, though, suffer greatly—more than actual situations call for—in seeing injustice, or what we identify as injustice, being done to others or to us.

We magnify injustices out of proportion, holding on fiercely to feelings such as being wronged, deprived, controlled, criticized, disrespected, or rejected. An example is the unfortunate partisan divide in American politics that is fueled, at least in part, by the willingness of people to complain about all the injustices that the other political side is allegedly inflicting upon them.

If we're classic injustice collectors, we whine incessantly about the unfairness of life. We're upset on a daily basis about all the alleged affronts we have to endure. We're figuratively dangling upside-down in a shaft of self-pity, clutching a charge sheet of outrages, piercing the darkness with night-vision goggles to see more "bad things" to moan and groan about.

Unconsciously, some dysfunctional people amass their collection of grudges the way a miser hoards his gold or a hoarder saves old newspapers.

There are two kinds of injustices. The first is *actual* injustice caused by human folly or the capriciousness of life. Faced with this injustice, we know logically that it's best to avoid extrapolating emotionally upon the sense of being victimized. If actual injustice is being done to us, we try to respond appropriately, which may include asserting our rights and seeking legal redress. At the same time, we strive at an emotional level to minimize the conflict or the unpleasantness of the situation. We can, for instance, not take personally the malice or insensitivity of others. We may be in a difficult situation, but we don't need to make it worse by having our emotional strength collapse inwardly upon us.

The second kind of injustice is based on our subjective impressions. Take the example of a fellow, let's call him Paul, who is suffering a feeling of injustice because he didn't get a raise he expected. If he wants to make more money, he could conceivably start looking elsewhere for work. If he decides to stay where he is, he obviously doesn't want to suffer unnecessarily. However, the injustice collector in him can be quite willing to take this "injustice" and use it to recycle and replay some unresolved negative emotion in his psyche. Paul could unconsciously experience the smaller paycheck as a way to feel deprived, forced to submit, or unappreciated. Such negative emotions are commonly experienced in childhood, even when parents try to be supportive and sensitive. It's easy for us as adults to continue producing these unpleasant emotions, especially when we have a real or alleged injustice with which to "validate" or "justify" our determination to suffer.

Paul, in fact, might not be a victim of injustice at all. He may simply not be performing at a level that merits a raise. His boss might be withholding the raise to motivate him to work at the higher level he believes Paul is capable of. Paul, however, is unable to be objective about his situation. That's because he's determined to experience the situation subjectively and negatively, based on his inner conflicts and emotional attachments.

Often we're not really concerned about the particular injustice we're complaining about or feeling upset over. Instead, as mentioned, we're just using a particular injustice, or alleged injustice, to justify our secret interest in remaining entangled in an unresolved negative emotion. Such negative emotions are powerful. We have to be as conscious as possible to identify them and then to protect ourselves from them. They can sweep into our life at any time, and usually we're conscious only of the symptoms such as anger, resentment, and a sense of injustice. The negative emotions themselves—the underlying, unresolved attachments—exist more subtly in our psyche. They tempt us or induce us, as I've been saying, to feel deprived, refused, controlled, rejected, devalued, disrespected, and abandoned. When we get triggered by these emotions, we react with anger or helplessness to the sense of being victimized by others or by external situations.

Usually, we don't want to acknowledge our readiness or willingness to go on experiencing those unresolved emotions. One way we cover up or deny our participation in this self-suffering is through injustice collecting. This tricks us into believing that the negative feelings we're experiencing are justified by the "bad things" that are happening to us.

The more injustices we collect, the more negative and unhappy we're likely to become. As we hold on to the injustices, we continue to reap the negative effects of our unresolved emotions. Remember, whatever is unresolved in this way (I must have said this 20 times by now) is determined to be experienced by us, even when that's very painful.

40. Deeper Issues that Produce Meanness

Tired of being mean? Tired of being on the receiving end of meanness? The nasty trait produces a lot of unnecessary suffering, both for the person who's being mean (the "hell of your own meanness," a character says in *Jane Eyre*) and for the recipient of the meanness. Meanness is often a compulsive behavior that's difficult to remedy without deeper insight.

Puzzled by his meanness, a fellow wrote to me to say: "Every time I see a girl I like I always end up being mean to her. I try not to, and I know that I'm doing the wrong thing, but I just can't help it. I don't know why. I'm really nice to my friends who I know really well, but to people I'm attracted to I end up being mean. Can someone give me some tips on how to fix that?"

"Tips" or advice are most likely too shallow to help resolve an emotional problem such as meanness. Insight is the better tool. Mean people have psychological issues that can be resolved with insight. People who are frequent targets of meanness also have their issues, since unwittingly they can be attracting negative, aggressive behavior from others.

Meanness has many dimensions. It's a factor in domestic abuse, schoolyard bullies, children and adults who mistreat or torture animals, and bosses or supervisors who mistreat their subordinates. It commonly arises in elderly people who no longer can repress their unhappiness, regrets, and unresolved issues. It's also common for the elderly, in their helplessness and passivity, to be on the receiving end of such treatment. A variety of issues influence its emergence from our inner life. Often it's simply the spill-over from an individual's accumulation of unresolved negativity. The mask of a charming or good-natured persona wears thin after a while. Underneath, some people have nothing much to offer but their unresolved negative emotions.

At the other end of the spectrum, people who are frequently on the receiving end of meanness need to consider their contribution to the problem. Often, for instance, one partner in a relationship is particularly mean, while the partner on the receiving end of the meanness is passively tolerant of what amounts to relentless negative comments and disrespect. The passive person can, unwittingly, be absorbing the abuse or negativity because of his or her low self-esteem or lack of inner strength. One passive person told me, "As far back as I can remember, I've always considered myself the victim of the inconsiderate behavior of others." The mean or inconsiderate person is inclined to continue behaving that way when the person on the receiving end remains passive and unwittingly receptive to the abuse. A strong person would not tolerate constant exposure to meanness. So the weak person has to examine the aspects of his or her weakness, rather than simply blaming the dysfunction on the mean, aggressive person or making excuses for him. Often the passive person has to grow psychologically before the passive-aggressive dynamics of meanness are overcome. Certainly, someone has to grow, or the primitive passive-aggressive dynamics remain locked in place.

Meanness can escalate into mental torture and serious malice, particularly so when, through our inner critic, we can be particularly mean to ourselves. To be kind to ourselves and to others, we have to recognize and resolve the primary sources of meanness in our psyche—inner conflict and emotional attachments.

Let's take a deep breath and dive into the issue, using as an example the situation described by the fellow quoted in the second paragraph of this discussion (I'll call him Riley). His meanness could be a symptom of his unconscious expectation that he's going to be rejected or seen in a negative light by others. More is at stake for Riley emotionally when the problem involves a girl he likes. If she sees him in a negative light, he feels the rejection more deeply. Consciously, he wants her to like him. Unconsciously, he likely expects her to reject him or to see him as inadequate or defective. Riley is psychologically entangled in the feeling of rejection, which means that, even though it's painful, he's attached emotionally to rejection or to being seen in a negative light. Instinctively, he feels the need to deny (defend against or cover up) this emotional attachment. A defense called "pleading guilty to the lesser crime" is invoked. By acting mean toward her, he can claim that his meanness causes the rejection to happen: "I'm not looking for the feeling of being rejected—the problem is I get mean and cause it to happen." Now, in hanging his hat on this defense, he acquires an illusion of control over his situation, even as he feels bad and guilty for being mean.

Once Riley sees through the defense and understands the underlying attachment—his unconscious expectation of rejection and his readiness to feel it—his meanness will evaporate. The more self-knowledge we bring to a situation such as this, the more capable we are of navigating our way forward while avoiding the sharp shoals of suffering and self-defeat. Our psyche is a mysterious realm where all sorts of peculiar processes take place. Yet if we're smart enough to be computer literate, we're smart enough to be "psyche literate."

Here's another way to understand Riley's psychological predicament. He might be afraid that others will see him as being unworthy of their attention or respect. That means he's emotionally attached to that negative feeling. As a defense to cover up his resonance with that feeling, he beats them to the punch. In other words, his meanness toward them enables him to disrespect them first. Through his meanness, he treats them in a way that corresponds with how, unconsciously, he imagines they are evaluating him. This is because he has not cleared out of his psyche his attachment to the emotional sense of being unimportant or unworthy. Even though he's likely a good person, his emotional perception of himself is, deep down, quite negative. He wants to believe he's a good and worthy person, yet he still feels wrong about himself at some deeper level.

Another fellow wrote to say, "Last night my ex-wife told me I was mean. I've worked hard on changing myself into a better man but when it comes to relationships, I might as well not even try. I know it stems from my mom and dad abandoning me and abuse, and so on. I just don't know how to heal it." Meanness such as this can simply be a result of the accumulation of unresolved negative emotions. The mean person has to find a starting point to begin to clear up these issues. (The discussion—"How to Be Your Own Inner Guide"—is a good place to start. However, the knowledge presented in that article has to be assimilated. You have to learn it and then make it an awareness that threads through your daily life.)

Spitefulness, a variation of meanness, is often the perverse pleasure that a person takes in the torment or misfortune of others. Such spite can be expressed quite passively, as when a person purposely dawdles in a restaurant or at a parking space when others are waiting. In such cases, the spiteful person can be identifying with the helplessness of those people who are at his mercy, or he could be identifying with what he imagines to be their experience of being marginalized or devalued. The perverse satisfaction of spitefulness arises through the individual's resonance with (libidinization of) a negative emotion, in this case either of helplessness or of the feeling of being marginalized or unimportant.

41 . Panic Attacks Arise from Within Our Psyche

The public is not getting the best insight into a wide range of psychological ailments, including panic or anxiety attacks. Books on the subject downplay the role of the psyche or unconscious mind, and ascribe the problem, as one author wrote, to the intrusions of the conscious mind.

Sufferers from panic attacks are typically offered "solutions" that include relaxation exercises, breathing exercises, and behavioral strategies. These approaches overlook essential self-knowledge related to the problem. Deeper insight can help those sufferers who are willing to learn some basic facts about the psyche.

One description of panic attacks includes this following statement:

> *Lack of assertiveness*—A growing body of evidence supports the idea that those who suffer from panic attacks engage in *a passive style* of communication or interactions with others. This communication style, while polite and respectful, is also *characteristically un-assertive.* This un-assertive way of communicating seems to contribute to panic attacks *while being frequently present* in those that are afflicted with panic attacks [*my italics*].[52]

As this passage suggests, passivity clearly plays a role in panic attacks. The passivity described in this passage is the surface manifestation of what I call inner passivity. Individuals can free themselves from painful panic attacks by understanding the inner passivity that dwells in the human psyche.

Other risk factors for panic attacks are also associated with inner passivity. In describing panic attacks, the Diagnostic and Statistical Manual of Mental Disorders (DSM-5) says under risk and prognostic factors:

> Negative affectivity (neuroticism) (i.e., proneness to experiencing negative emotions) and anxiety sensitivity (i.e., the disposition to believe that symptoms of anxiety are harmful) are risk factors for the onset of panic attacks. History of "fearful spells" (i.e., limited-symptom attacks that do not meet full criteria for a panic attack) may be a risk factor for later panic attacks.[53]

All of the above risk factors, I believe, are produced in large part through unresolved inner conflicts and the accompanying attachments to (unconscious affinity for or emotional resonance with) negative emotions.

The most common conflict in our psyche, as mentioned, is between aggression and passivity. Aggression is dished out by the inner critic in the form of mockery, scolding, accusations, harassment, and rejection. Our

---

[52] http://en.wikipedia.org/wiki/Panic_attack

[53] American Psychiatric Association. (2013) *Diagnostic and Statistical Manual of Mental Disorders (DSM-5).* Washington, D.C. 216.

inner critic gets away with its unwarranted, harsh intrusion into our life, and presides as master of our personality, because our inner passivity (our self-doubt, defensiveness, and separation from our authentic self) is unable to protect us from it.

Through inner passivity, as mentioned, we fail to stand up to our inner critic. Hence, we're more exposed to the onslaught from our inner critic and more at its mercy. This creates inner fear. Such fear can easily escalate in intensity from worry to anxiety to panic. Most people live in some degree of fear (mostly unconscious) of the accusations and condemnations of their inner critic. When a person's inner passivity is pronounced or acute, he or she can be terrorized by the inner critic.

This knowledge from classical psychoanalysis is discounted by modern psychology. In his book, *Don't Panic: Taking Control of Anxiety Attacks 3rd Edition* (Harper, New York, 2009), Reid Wilson writes that the unconscious approach is the wrong approach. "It's the conscious mind's intrusion that is the problem—that little voice that says, 'What if these sensations get worse? Something bad will happen. Watch out!"

That little voice, indeed, is sometimes conscious, though often the voice or the message is muted and therefore experienced only unconsciously. Whether the voice is actually "heard" or is registered unconsciously, it still arises out of our unconscious. That should be obvious. Why would someone consciously produce that fearful, negative voice? Anyone doing so might look as hopelessly pathetic as Gollum, the corrupted, conflicted hobbit from *The Lord of the Rings*. The "little voice" to which Dr. Wilson refers, and which he declines to ascribe to unconscious conflict, is likely the voice of inner passivity. It does communicate its emotional nature to us, particularly as fear, helplessness, and self-doubt. Compulsively, we can repeat that voice in our head, and absorb unconsciously its message of weakness, no matter how self-defeating it can be to do so.

Dr. Wilson notes that many sufferers of panic attacks are plagued by the thought or expectation of losing control at some point in the future. This means, as I see it, that these individuals, in the moment of feeling "plagued," have become emotionally entangled in their inner passivity. Whenever someone looks to the future with worry, anxiety, or fear, the person is "getting hit up" with an experience of inner passivity right at that moment. This is a direct, unpleasant encounter with one's inner passivity. For all of us, inner passivity can be easily and quickly felt. It's the default position for all our self-doubt.

It is, in fact, impossible to understand panic attacks without understanding inner passivity. Yet, as I've acknowledged, inner passivity is a difficult concept to understand. My book on the subject—*The Phantom of the Psyche: Freeing Ourself from Inner Passivity*—explores and tries to map this *terra incognita* of the psyche. That book was originally published in 2002 (with a new edition in 2015), and I have continued to write on the subject since then. Inner passivity becomes comprehensible when its many symptoms are described and then correlated with the symptoms that appear in a wide variety of behavioral and emotional problems plaguing humanity. For example, people prone to panic attacks display the tendency to be lacking in assertiveness and to practice a passive style of communication, and these two symptoms are also symptoms of inner passivity.

Looking at another example, Shakespeare's Hamlet is a passive character who is anxious, indecisive, and overwhelmed by circumstances. It seems to me the prince of Denmark has a number of what might be considered panic attacks. At one point, he utters the famous words, "To be or not to be, that is the question." He's ostensibly expressing his indecision about committing suicide, but his words have resonated deeply down the centuries because they succinctly express what might be the most vital, deep challenge of our humanity: Do we become fully human, connecting deeply with our authentic self and our powers of self-regulation, or do we perish in our own fear and passivity? Do we live on the surface of awareness, content with behavioral and cognitive techniques for wisdom and self-regulation, or do we plunge deeper into our psyche where our unresolved negative emotions maintain a life of their own?

When we arise out of the non-being of inner passivity (choosing "to be" rather than "not to be"), we connect with our authentic self. As this connection deepens, we're in the process of overthrowing the tyranny of the inner critic, resolving the conflict between inner passivity and the inner critic, and assuming our rightful place as master of our own personality.

While most people have in their psyche some measure inner passivity, they don't usually experience panic attacks. It's all a matter of degree. And it can indeed be a mystery as to why some people experience their underlying passivity in the form of panic attacks and others in the many other variations of emotional distress and behavioral self-defeat. The symptoms, or the reason why one particular individual has a certain symptom or set of symptoms, may be less important to our knowledge base than our understanding of the underlying cause. Invariably, the cause can be traced in part to inner conflict and emotional attachments. This knowledge makes it possible for us to become our own healers and to establish more independence from experts.

In the process of identifying the conflict and resolving it, we discover our authentic self, which is the realization of our goodness, our value, our wisdom, and our power of self-regulation. Our unique, authentic self protects us from danger, self-defeat, and suffering.

42. The Hidden Cause of Clinical Depression

Crippling confusion governs our treatment approach to the mental-health epidemic of clinical depression. Typically, sufferers who ask what causes their depression are told it's a mysterious and complex brain disorder.

This answer does a grave disservice to the many millions of people who suffer worldwide from depression. So-called experts have dragged depression sufferers into a limbo of ignorance, dependency, and escalating misery. Meanwhile, with no cure in sight, the percentage of Americans taking anti-depressants has grown by 400 percent in the last 23 years.[54]

---

[54] http://usatoday30.usatoday.com/news/health/story/health/story/2011-10-19/CDC-Antidepressant-use-skyrocketed-in-past-20-

Many factors can contribute to depression, including social circumstances, environment, diet, exercise, genetics, and seasonal weather effects. The problem is that a major cause of depression—the inner conflict described in this discussion—is almost completely overlooked by the prevailing medical-model treatment approaches. Wikipedia has an 18,000-word entry under "Major depressive disorder" (clinical depression), and only about one percent of that content (180 words) approaches the psychological heart of the problem—and even that is couched in vague terminology.[55]

According to depth psychology, inner conflict is a primary contributor to depression. Hard science, however, has been unable to identify within the brain any biochemical or energetic dynamics that correspond to psychological conflict along the lines of what I've been describing. Psychiatrists have conceded that they don't know the origins of depression, and there's no laboratory test for the condition. A recent report—"Massive Search for 'Depression Gene' Comes up Empty"—appears to back up my contention that depression is at least as much of a psychological problem as it is a medical or genetic one.[56] The evidence shows depression runs in families,[57] and both neurotic psychological dynamics as well as genetic factors are passed along in families from generation to generation. Even when genetics, biochemistry, or brain anomalies do contribute to depression, we don't have to be

---

years/50826442/1
[55] http://en.wikipedia.org/wiki/Major_depressive_disorder
[56] https://www.sciencenews.org/article/depression-gene-search-disappoints
[57] http://www.webmd.com/depression/features/depression-when-its-all-in-the-family

helpless victims of this condition. It's likely that inner conflict is present in most cases of depression, and we can strengthen ourselves emotionally and cognitively by understanding the nature of the conflict and thereby resolving it.

Through depth psychology, we learn that our psyche is a battleground between inner aggression and inner passivity. Much of our thoughts and feelings, whether conscious or unconscious, are reflective of the emotional nature of one or the other of these opposing factions in our psyche. Depression is the emotional price we pay when, in our unconscious effort to minimize the threat of our hostile inner critic, we accept the punishment of emotional suffering. The suffering of depression is the pound of flesh we pay to the inner critic. As mentioned, this inner agency harasses us with accusations, sarcasm, mockery, and ridicule. On an inner level, we fight back, usually rather weakly, through the thoughts, feelings, and instinctive defensiveness of inner passivity. We can't win this battle through inner passivity. It simply can't represent us effectively. Through inner passivity we end up making a compromise: We can get the inner critic to back off if we concede that its ill treatment of us is justified by our supposed flaws and defects. We pay this pound of flesh as, figuratively, we hang our head in guilt, shame, and self-disgust, accepting sufficient punishment in demoralized self-debasement to satisfy the inner critic.

At such times, the inner critic can run people down and demoralize them to the point that they sink into apathy, hopelessness, self-rejection, despair, and depression. The inner critic's accusations against us are usually negative, unfair, and unjust. While we do try to deflect this inner assault, we still absorb much of the aggression. We would be able to protect ourselves from the inner critic if our authentic self were alive and well. But it's buried under the weight of the conflict. Our weak sense of self, meanwhile, simply shifts back and forth under the influence, in one moment, of inner passivity, and, in the next moment, of the inner critic.

Many of the symptoms associated with depression are the same symptoms associated with inner conflict. Depressed people, according to Wikipedia, "may be preoccupied with, or ruminate over, thoughts and feelings of worthlessness, inappropriate guilt or regret, helplessness, hopelessness, and self-hatred."[58] These painful feelings also arise from the inner conflict between inner aggression and inner passivity. Our inner critic assails us with accusations of our worthlessness, and through inner passivity we experience helplessness, hopelessness, and guilt.

Many people have a particularly harsh inner critic, and genetic factors may account for much of this. Such an inner critic is particularly vicious and cruel. Without insight, the person presumes, at least on an emotional if not mental level, that the harsh criticism or hatred he or she is feeling is somehow validated by his or her faults and failures. The individual can absorb the negativity to the point that he or she becomes increasingly passive. This individual is in danger of descending into self-rejection and even self-hatred. Often, a person with self-hatred is especially hateful toward others.

It's also the case—likely for genetic reasons as well as childhood exposure to passive parents—that some of us are particularly burdened with large deposits of inner

[58] http://en.wikipedia.org/wiki/Major_depressive_disorder

passivity in our psyche. Still, we don't have to be victims of genetics or childhood experiences. In many instances, consciousness in the form of psychological astuteness and self-knowledge can trump genetics or at least mitigate the worst influences of genetic factors.

Another common feature of depression sufferers is the presence of guilt. This guilt has a complex undercurrent. It's associated with the degree to which the individual is unconsciously willing to soak up or absorb the negative, aggressive energy of the inner critic. Unlike the pound of flesh analogy presented earlier, this situation, now viewed from another perspective, involves unconscious, non-sexual masochism. I mention this masochism several times throughout this book, and I can feel at times an impulse to apologize for suggesting that such a disagreeable trait is a feature of human nature. The word does denote the manner and degree to which we unwittingly hold on to negative emotions and go looking for new experiences of them. This thesis, originally advanced by Freud, contends that the guilt is produced as part of our defensive effort to deny recognition of the masochism. If such masochism does indeed exist as a feature of human nature, we can easily imagine how some individuals would soak up the inner critic's aggression to the point of becoming congested with negativity, hence "psychologically sick" or depressed. Even when clinicians suspect this or know it to be true, many of them can't bring themselves to say it to their patients. It's just not a "nice thing" to say to someone. Many people, as well, are mortified and offended by the allegation. This indignation (they "doth protest too much") ought to be considered evidence for its truthfulness.

Many people suffering from depression frequently blame themselves for their failures and troubles. This corresponds with the inner critic's readiness to blame us for our real or alleged faults and failures. Without any awareness of what they're doing, some people, on a daily basis, repeat negative mantras (such as "What am I doing wrong?") that are replays of a steady stream of accusatory insinuations from their inner critic. Our inner passivity, as well, grapples with the venom dished out by the inner critic, although inner passivity often tries to shift the blame to some allegedly "lesser crime," hoping the inner critic will agree to a plea bargain. Depression is also associated with bodily tension and stress, and such physical symptoms are byproducts of the anxiety produced by inner conflict.

Some experts say that depression arises when we're unable to attain our needs or realize our potential.[59] Again, inner passivity in particular creates an inner blockage to creativity, purpose, confidence, and the full range of our intelligence. We can be very smart and capable, yet through inner passivity we remain bewildered and overwhelmed by the demands of achieving success.

Depression sufferers can apply this knowledge to relieve their suffering. In this process, relief from depression involves a learning process. We learn the dynamics of the conflict (between inner passivity and inner aggression) that produces depression, and we become insightful enough to see these dynamics at work in our own psyche. This strengthens our intelligence and consciousness. For now, very few psychotherapists, even among psychoanalysts, practice a method that

[59] http://en.wikipedia.org/wiki/Major_depressive_disorder

employs this knowledge. So individuals who wish to try the process may have to learn it and apply it on their own. (Read, "How to Be Your Own Inner Guide.")

Insight isn't always necessary to emerge from depression. Many people escape their depression by engaging in healthy and enjoyable pursuits and activities. Through whatever means, they "snap out" of inner passivity. Some residue of inner strength comes to the rescue and enables them to take control of their life. Through this expression of inner strength, they also make their inner critic less troublesome and their depression abates. Without the knowledge of inner conflict, however, their chances of relapse are higher.

Psychological insight bestows personal power upon us. We're no longer dependent on expensive medications that are little more than pain-killers. Inner knowledge belongs to us. We can use it to make sense of our life as we extend our intelligence into realms we once ignored.

43. How Inner Fear Becomes Our Worst Nightmare

Some people like digging around in the past—geologists, historians, archeologists, and genealogists—because the past is the foundation of the present and has a lot to tell us. Our own past in early childhood is also worthy of study because, for one thing, it has a lot to tell us about the levels of fear that permeate society.

Much is said and written about fear, yet seldom is it traced to its irrational psychological core. To overcome inner fear, we have to see its existence in our psyche instead of denying it or trying to justify it by imagining Armageddon or "seeing" evil intent in others. Deeper insight makes us more conscious of our fear's irrationality.

It's easy to stoke our fears because we all have *inner* fears that have an infantile basis. Toddlers can burst out crying when getting a haircut, seeing a costumed character at the fair, even when meeting a neighbor's new puppy. Children can also have fears of darkness, of falling, being dropped, chopped to pieces, accosted by bogey-men, and flushed down the toilet. This fear is likely, in part, an instinctive remnant of humankind's early history when primitive conditions made the environment more dangerous.

In any event, baby fears are perfectly understandable because babies are so vulnerable. They're profoundly helpless, at the mercy of the kindness of others. As well, their powers of reason are still unformed, so they can easily feel menace or danger where none exists. As adults, of course, we no longer fear being flushed down the toilet. But fear itself remains in our psyche, bound up in unresolved emotional memories and associations. Despite our capacity for reason, this inner fear, which can be part of our identity, is unconsciously transferred and projected on to imagined dangers as easily as real dangers. Even common *worry* is a form of fear. Worry can fester in our psyche, becoming more problematic when it intensifies into anxiety, fear, and panic.

Many people rush out to buy handguns because they believe their fears are justified and real. They're fooled into believing that the inner fears they're unconsciously projecting into the environment are somehow validated by allegedly dangerous circumstances. As we brandish these guns, innocent people die.

Diminishing our fear is vitally important because fear can cause enormous suffering. It might also have the potential to destroy humanity. The nuclear arms race was, in part, propelled by the fear that we would be attacked and destroyed by our enemies if we didn't invest substantial amounts of our wealth in national security. In an irrational way, we can also be fearful of change, and so we hesitate to institute the changes needed to curb man-made climate change, even as evidence is being presented that these changes can be made without major disruptions.

It's true, of course, that bad people exist in the world and we need to protect ourselves from them. But we must avoid doing so in a manner that's self-defeating. Through psychological dynamics, we can contribute to the undesirable outcomes that we fear the most. Fearful people unwittingly create the circumstances though which their fears become more real. For instance, the technology that we pour into our advanced weapons systems spreads throughout the world for others to use against us. At some point, the danger becomes overwhelming.

If we had less inner fear, we would have more power to influence others in a positive way. We would be more effective at neutralizing the dangers through the "soft power" of integrity, morality, and wisdom. Others would be more likely to trust us as honorable people and to lay down their arms and dissolve their hatred.

What's blocking us from transitioning from hard power to soft power? Our worst enemy is our resistance to inner growth and progress. We aren't making the transition from hard power to soft power because we're stubbornly resisting the imperative to evolve.

Let me explain. Inner fear, which is often unconscious, is encountered in many ways, including fears of death, poverty, starvation, the unknown, change, nothingness, and the idea of our insignificance or unworthiness. The biggest fear, however, may be the fear of our own self. This is the fear of having to abandon our old identity, and give up our favorite forms of suffering, as we see and are challenged to embrace the noble stranger we are destined to become. Fear and passivity lurk behind the cynicism that refuses to believe in our capacity for a sudden spurt of wisdom and consciousness.

Our fears also jeopardize democracy. We lose power through our fears. Unscrupulous politicians play on our fears in order to pose as our guardians or protectors. We're afraid to employ our constitutional right "to petition the Government for a redress of grievances." We give up freedom in exchange for protection and the illusion of security.

Often when we try to reform a system, we encounter fear. Sometimes the fear is entirely rational, as when millions risk death in the struggles in recent years to overthrow oppressive governments in the Middle East. Other times we face mostly inner fear, as when we wonder: "Do I have this right to demand reform? Am I substantial enough in myself to expect to be taken seriously?" We all encounter doubt and fear, along with fierce resistance, as we struggle to evolve and make progress toward democratic development and personal self-development.

It is understandable that we struggle with fear. As Stuart Walton writes in *A Natural History of Human Emotions*:

> If it were possible, as some evolutionary psychologists maintain, to decide which of humanity's emotions is the oldest, then fear would surely enter the strongest claim. To our very early ancestor knit groups, the world was an intimidating, haunted place, in which violent storms, the threat of fire, unfathomable disease and suffering, all held awesome power over them. So it was, in the beginning, that lack of understanding gave rise to primal terror.[60]

Now we can acquire more understanding. While much of our fear is irrational, we can see rationally from where it originates. Inner passivity causes us to doubt our wisdom, strength, and power. Fear would logically be associated with this self-doubt. At the same time, our inner critic tyrannizes us with its primitive aggression. Fear would logically be associated with this inner tyranny. People who are defensive by nature, and inwardly passive are usually greatly intimidated by this "higher" authority in their psyche. These fears have kept us child-like, unable to successfully manage our modern world and challenge those who would corrupt it. Seeing these fears as phantoms, we now can pass confidently through them.

---

[60] Walton, Stuart. *A Natural History of Human Emotions*. New York: Grove Press, 2004.

Experienced meditators have a technique that's particularly helpful in eliminating inner fear and banishing the inner critic. They close their eyes and then set aside their ego by stilling their mind. They then try to accept or even embrace the emptiness or nothingness behind the inner silence. All identifications with family, friends, beliefs, possessions, and self-image fall away, leaving only pure consciousness. There's nothing to fear when we're not afraid of the inner void. This true essence at the core of our being is all we really have—and it's more than enough. Not even death, it feels, can take it away.

If I might digress into personal preferences, I don't recommend that anyone make this particular form of meditation a general practice. It's been my experience that, when performed on a regular basis, it can engender a passive approach to life just when we're struggling to overcome passivity. People who meditate can remain more grounded and engaged in the world by meditating or reflecting on the word "Am." I don't do any reflections on the term "I am" because, in my view, that puts too much emphasis on the pronoun I, thereby activating some ego. As a mantra or daily reflection, this one word "Am" calls forth our essential being, our authentic non-clinging self, to install its fearless soul in the seat of benevolent power and in the community of life.

44 . The Dreary Distress of Boredom

Yawn. Nothing interesting going on today. Day after day, the same old thing, going around in a daze, inwardly dead. Life used to be more fun. Why is the world so dull? Why am I bored so much of the time?

Hey, it's natural enough to be bored while waiting two hours in a doctor's office or at a garage getting your car repaired. It's better if you can enjoy the wait, of course, perhaps by relaxing deeply, feeling good about your life, or boning up on current events by reading every magazine in sight. But some boredom or restlessness at such a time goes with the territory and needs no psychological intervention. It's *clinical* or *chronic* boredom that we want to avoid. A whole range of painful symptoms—from drug addiction to compulsive gambling to poor performance at work and school—are associated with chronic boredom.

Some people believe that boredom is normal. In *Boredom: A Lively History*, Prof. Peter Toohey concludes his book by writing that, "Boredom is a normal, useful, and incredibly common part of human experience. That many of us suffer it should be no cause for embarrassment. Boredom simply deserves respect for the, well, boring experience that it is."[61]

It's wrong, however, to say that boredom—a negative experience that can be painful as a toothache—is normal and useful. Boredom is a bummer, a form of unnecessary suffering, when, in its chronic form, it's a significant part of one's daily experience. Toohey's book

---

[61] Toohey, Peter. *Boredom, A Lively History*. Yale University Press, 2011.

touches on superficial psychological ideas concerning boredom, but he doesn't explore the knowledge of depth psychology where the remedy can be found.

Boredom results from a failure to activate one's imagination, creativity, and sense of wonder. The bored person inwardly renounces pleasure. Even when pleasurable options or activities are suggested to this person, he or she might decline the opportunity to experience such pleasure. The bored person, in other words, is unconsciously determined to suffer from the blahs.

What are the dynamics in our psyche whereby our imagination shuts down? (By now you likely have a good idea what I'm going to say.) Unresolved negative emotions—arising out of inner conflict—are the culprits. Until we become more conscious, we can be entangled in negative emotions, including feeling refused, deprived, and helpless. Such emotions, first experienced in early childhood, linger in the adult psyche. As adults, we can be compelled to filter our experience of the world through these lingering emotional attachments. As evidence of this fact, many of us are able to activate our imagination, sometimes to a vivid degree, only when torturing ourselves with visualizations of worst-case scenarios and impressions of being refused, deprived, helpless, and rejected.

Consciously or unconsciously, we're always trying to rationalize our suffering. In the case of boredom, the rationalization, presented as an inner defense, might be expressed along these lines: "I'm not secretly indulging in the feeling of self-doubt and emptiness. I'm not entangled in a stubborn rejection of pleasure. I'm not soaking up the passive feeling of being unable to activate my imagination and my vitality. Look, the world is a boring place. How could anyone feel happiness and joy in such a boring place!"

In adopting this defense, the individual is now required to truly suffer in the depths of boredom. He or she must indeed make the world out to be a boring place. In clinical language, the individual, through the unconscious or subordinate ego, offers up this suffering to the inner critic in exchange for secretly being able to maintain his or her wish to go on experiencing one or more unresolved negative emotions.

This may sound complicated, but once we begin to consider the knowledge, we can "see" the dynamics at play in our psyche. This raises and strengthens our intelligence which can now be applied to the resolution of the underlying inner conflict.

Other dynamics or aspects in our psyche pertain to boredom. Here are four, very briefly described:

1. As children, we experience some activities of our imagination, particularly sexual interests, as forbidden material. An active imagination can be a source of pleasure. Yet such pleasure can be associated emotionally and irrationally with forbidden content. For instance, much fear can reside in the psyche around infantile incestuous wishes that remain in place and have not, through one's lack of inner awareness, been renounced. The individual, as a defense, avoids using his or her imagination for any pleasure at all.

2. When our fear of the inner critic is more substantial, we might empty our psyche of all "incriminating" material. The defense now reads, "I'm not guilty of

secret wishes to hold on to all my hurts and painful memories. In fact, I'm not in possession of *any* such material in my psyche. There is *nothing* in my psychic chamber—I am empty." Now, of course, the individual does indeed feel empty and bored.

3. Many different defenses cover up our willingness to carry our suffering to the grave. One is called the "negative pseudo-moral." It's an unconscious statement or posture of childish defiance that says to one's parent or educator, "My feelings and behaviors show how little you had to offer me, thereby leaving me feeling bored." This defense serves the self-defeating purpose of blaming others for one's entanglement in painful feelings of emptiness.

4. We can harbor an unconscious willingness to go through life feeling disappointed with oneself and with what life has to offer. The individual might have felt from an early age that parents or life were refusing to life up to expectations. Now he or she is determined to continue to live with the sense that life has nothing much to offer. Chronic disappointment also denotes a consciousness that's inhibited by the inability to feel one's intrinsic value. Now everything in one's environment is taken for granted. A person's parents may have displayed this emotional approach to life, making it more likely that the son or daughter will adopt the same perspective.

This can all produce a state of consciousness that's too conflicted to register the wonder of being alive and the magnificence of creation. With unresolved issues, we tend to be self-absorbed, often floundering in misery. Boredom can even feel like welcome relief from the other more painful options to which we're drawn.

45. Problem Gamblers Are Addicted to Losing

Problem gamblers typically believe, as they head out the door to the nearest casino, that their full and sincere intention is to win money. Little do they know they're acting out an emotional attachment to the feeling of losing.

Such gamblers typically do become, in the fateful sense of the word, losers. They can lose their money, happiness, self-respect, and perhaps their home and loved ones as well. At this point, indeed, we see them as losers.

Yet it doesn't occur to them that they actually *want* to lose. Why would anyone, even "losers," be determined to lose? That level of folly defies common sense. Consciously, of course, problem gamblers *do want to win*. On the surface, winning money is their all-consuming passion. But unconscious dynamics in their psyche are playing a different game—a game of self-sabotage and self-induced misery.

The dynamics of our psyche require us to experience repeatedly our unresolved negative emotions, however painful. A person who is sensitive to feeling refusal or loss, for instance, typically goes through life repeatedly experiencing this suffering. The impression of being refused likely started in childhood, and it continues through life as a psychological conflict: The adult is desperate to get some reward or benefit, at the same time that he or she is expecting refusal or loss. This person will be burdened with the suffering the conflict produces, unless the conflict is resolved with insight and awareness.

The chronic gambler is typically an injustice-collector. Unconsciously, he's intent on proving how badly life treats him. He's acting out an unconscious wish to experience that fate is against him. This impression that life is refusing to support him can be based on an unresolved attachment from childhood to feelings of being denied or refused by parents or caregivers.

Problem gamblers have another inner conflict. They're desperate to feel the drug-like euphoria of winning in order to cover up their deep affinity for feelings of emptiness, loss, refusal, worthlessness, and passivity. Those negative emotions are powerful, and the thrill of winning is able to cover them up—if only temporarily. These negative emotions can also include feelings of deprival, helplessness, self-rejection, and self-hatred. The more that chronic gamblers lose, the more intensely they feel this unresolved negative congestion within themselves.

Problem gambling is simply one means among many for acting out one's deeper emotional addiction to painful, unresolved inner conflict. If, for some reason, a problem gambler found himself with no gambling opportunities, he would likely act out his inner conflict in other ways, perhaps through substance abuse, job failures, or relationship problems.

Edmund Bergler writes in *The Psychology of Gambling*:

> It must always be remembered that the gambler acts irrationally. He allows himself to be pushed

into an unequal fight against superior forces, forces he cannot control, and which make him into an *object*. The gambler's preference for being the object, and not the *subject* in the gambling setup, demonstrates his deeply rooted passive tendencies. This factor may be somewhat mitigated, but not basically changed, by the pretense of exclusive interest in the "intellectual" aspects of the game.[62]

Gamblers typically display optimism as, from day to day, they venture forth to risk their money. This optimism is probably, at least in part, an expression of lingering infantile megalomania and omnipotence. Behind their passivity is the conviction that they possess some hidden power to prevail. They believe in their special powers to defy the odds, as if they have magic on their side. This irrationality might be expressed as such: "I'm going to win because I can feel it. I know it's my day!" The more acutely they feel this special power, the more intensely they're covering up the underlying passivity. They can also be deluded into thinking that their risk-taking is a form of aggressive behavior. "I'm not passively putting myself in harm's way," their defense reads, "I'm the aggressive taker of risks."

To some degree, we are all challenged by self-defeating inner dynamics. Not only can we feel the pain of unresolved negative emotions—we are compelled, as mentioned, to go on feeling them. It's as if we're programmed to feel and to act out whatever is unresolved within us. Figuratively, our inner coding is askew. That inner software needs to be upgraded.

---

[62] Bergler, Edmund. *The Psychology of Gambling*. International Universities Press, Inc., 1974. 237.

Through our intelligence, insight, and knowledge, we can penetrate our psyche to bring us up to speed.

46. A Common Ingredient in Human Misery

What do binging, hypochondria, and hoarding have in common? On the surface, they appear to be unrelated. Yet all three of these behaviors have the same source in our psyche.

That source—inner passivity—is an unconscious sense of identity situated in our psyche that determines, in varying degrees, our happiness and vitality. I make the case throughout this book that inner passivity contributes to a wide range of dysfunction, including depression, addictions, compulsions, phobias, cynicism, obesity, procrastination, anxiety disorders, criminal behaviors, and so on. Now I'm adding the three above-mentioned symptoms to the list.

Before embarking on that discussion, some background is helpful. As I've been saying, the clash in our psyche between inner aggression and inner passivity is a primary source of unhappiness and suffering. Fortunately, one side of this clash between inner aggression and inner passivity does get some recognition from mainstream psychology. Many psychologists appreciate the significance of inner aggression or self-aggression. A Google search of the term "inner critic" turns up thousands of references to it, including a Wikipedia entry.

The other side of the conflict—inner passivity—is much less recognized. A Google search of that term turns up mostly references to my posts and books. Of course, passivity itself is widely recognized as a human trait. But *inner* passivity is something more. It's an unconscious identification with (and emotional attachment to) a state of nonbeing and inherent weakness. Inner passivity, as I've said, can inhabit the psyche of even successful, aggressive individuals. Their success and aggression, as with workaholics, is not always a measure of wisdom, character, and decency.

Inner passivity is also the behind-the-scenes emotional experience that produces bingers, hypochondriacs, and hoarders, along with many other behavioral and emotional problems. An estimated eight million men and women in the United States struggle with binge eating. Studies show that binging among men and women is often linked to depression and to a feeling of being out of control (both symptoms of inner passivity).[63] One sufferer said his binge eating was, in part, his attempt to fill the "emptiness, loneliness, and emotional void" that he frequently felt in his life. These painful feelings—along with confused and chaotic thinking, and an inability to access resourcefulness, self-regulation, and a sense of one's personal value—are all symptoms of inner passivity.

Binge eaters often are able to regulate their food intake during the day, only to lose control at night. This behavior corresponds with the tendency of many people to experience inner passivity more intensely during the

---

[63] http://well.blogs.nytimes.com/2012/08/13/binge-eating-among-men-steps-out-of-the-shadows/

night's quiet times when, undistracted by daytime activities, they're alone with their thoughts and feelings.

After a bout of binging, individuals are likely to feel ashamed of themselves and disgusted at their behavior. Such reactions follow from the intrusions of the inner critic which is expressing disapproval and condemnation for the binging. The negative accusations are absorbed to a degree that produces shame, disgust, and guilt.

The next symptom—hypochondria—is an expression of fear based on the belief that physical ailments, even minor ones, are indicative of serious illness or impairment. Often no medical evidence is found to justify such concerns or fears. Though the fears are irrational, they feel very real. That's because, through inner passivity, these sufferers create emotional experiences of feeling overwhelmed, overpowered, helpless, and confused. They sense in themselves a great weakness which they associate with physical ailments. To cover up their indulgence in these negative feelings, they produce the sense or conviction that the feelings are justified by the likely prospect of serious illness.

Hypochondria is the fear that one's life is being taken over (or will be taken over) by a serious condition or malignant disease that renders one helpless. It's the feeling of being possessed and defeated by an alien force. The suffering of hypochondriacs makes sense (even given its irrational basis) when we understand their attachment to inner passivity.

The last of the three symptoms of inner passivity has its own TV reality show, "Hoarding: Buried Alive." The dysfunctional behavior draws viewers mesmerized by the mountains of useless junk stuffed into homes. Neuroscience has been investigating the brains of people with hoarding disorder, and it has found abnormal activity in the brain regions known to be involved with decision-making.[64]

Indeed, hoarders are decidedly indecisive. Normal decision-making requires us to make daily choices that facilitate our life. We access a sense of authority within us, a part of us that we trust to know what's best for us at any given moment. We can be quite lost to ourselves and prone to very painful emotional predicaments and self-defeating behaviors without this inner guidance system.

Obviously, hoarders are lacking in inner authority. They can't make a simple decision to discard certain items. Technically, they do make a choice—*to keep* all their possession. But this is a passive or default choice. Their behavior is clearly a symptom of inner passivity.

Many hoarders also feel overwhelmed by the clutter. Yet they unconsciously create an environment that enables them to maintain and deepen the feeling of being overwhelmed. This behavior reflects the nature of inner passivity—we unconsciously go looking for the feeling of it, and we create situations in which we feel it more intensely.

---

[64] http://www.livescience.com/22140-hoarders-brain-why-they-cant-ditch-stuff.html

IV - MORE EXAMPLES OF INSIGHT

47 . **Obesity and the Dopamine Fallacy**

The Flip Wilson Show was America's second most-watched TV show for its first two seasons in the 1970s. In his role as the sassy Geraldine Jones, Wilson, a comedic genius, had a trademark line, "The devil made me do it," that his character declared when she needed an excuse for her impulsive or questionable behavior.

Another trademark line is being trotted out, this time by neuroscience, to account for the nation's obesity epidemic. Nobody is laughing, though we should, when they tell us, "The dopamine makes you do it."

Yes, dopamine, we're told, has taken possession of the brains of obese people and turned them into sugar and fat addicts, slaves of the midnight snack and prisoners of the cookery. "It's not your fault," they're told, "the dopamine makes you do it." Hang in there! Great minds are working on a pill.

Professor Gary L. Wenk, author of *Your Brain on Food* (Oxford, 2010), posted the essence of the dopamine explanation at the Facebook page of *Psychology Today*:

> Initially, scientists assumed that obese people were simply addicted to food in the same manner that someone becomes addicted to heroin, i.e. food produces happy pleasant feels, and therefore eating lots of food would produce extremely

pleasant feelings. Not so. A few years ago scientists discovered just the opposite was true; the brain's reward center decreased its response to eating tasty foods. This induces people (and animals in experimental studies as well) to consume ever greater quantities of fat and sugar in order to mitigate the diminished rewards that were once experienced by consuming only one scoop of ice cream or a small donut.

The neurotransmitter in the brain for rewarding us for eating is called dopamine. Everything we do that is pleasurable requires the release of dopamine within the brain ... Needless to say, eating fat and sugar induces the release of dopamine. In both obese humans and animals, dopamine function is significantly impaired. The key thing to point out is that this dysfunction occurs in response to many years of poor diet; dopamine dysfunction does not occur first. Our behavior leads to the dysfunction in this important pleasure-inducing neurotransmitter.

A recent study published in the *Journal of Neurochemistry* reported that dopamine's normal function is enhanced in the feeding centers, leading to increased craving for high calorie foods, while its function is decreased in our reward centers, leading to a decrease in the pleasure that obese people can derive from eating tasty foods. Thus, ultimately, obese people are driven to eat more but enjoy it much less. The main value of this recent study is that it offers hope that one day it might be possible to correct this dopamine dysfunction with medication.[65]

Prof. Wenk appears to have science on his side. Yet he and his colleagues are taking narrow findings from science and using them to make broad generalizations. For starters, science is finding only that dopamine dysfunction becomes a factor following "many years of poor diet" and that the brain's reward center is experiencing less pleasure. It doesn't follow from this scientific knowledge that dopamine dysfunction compels—or *induces*, as he puts it—obese individuals to eat more for the same amount of pleasure.

What exactly does Prof. Wenk mean by that word *induces* (in the first paragraph of the excerpt)? Is he saying that people have no control or willpower at all? Are we driven solely by our impulses, cravings, and desires? Smelling lovely flowers presumably produces a dopamine effect? Yet we don't apparently have a problem of flower-smelling addiction. Prof. Wenk's article makes no mention of overcoming weaknesses of self-regulation through the personal attributes of common sense, courage, concentration, mindfulness, patience, or consciousness. The practice of these attributes can moderate or eliminate the cravings. In themselves, cravings can simply be a side-effect of the emotion attachment to helplessness.

We know that certain behaviors such as overeating reduce the quality of life and lead to health risk. What does it say about the consciousness of people who act against their own best interests? Certainly, some foods, particularly sugar, can produce an addictive-like effect. The cravings can be more intense with certain physical conditions such as adrenal fatigue. Yet increased self-

---

[65] http://www.psychologytoday.com/blog/your-brain-food/201201/why-is-obesity-so-hard-defeat

awareness helps us to get to the heart of the problem, namely the manner in which our will is weakened by inner conflict and unresolved negative emotions. It's not just our will power that's weakened, but also our will to thrive and flourish. Inner conflict intensifies the passivity and aggression in our psyche, which can push us to embrace the dark path of self-destruction.

In the excerpt, Prof. Wenk appears to equate human behavior with animal behavior. On what basis does he make this assumption? Where is the scientific evidence that animals trapped mercilessly in cages for experimental studies behave just like animals in the wild? The caged animals would of necessity be passive, and they would then be more likely to lack self-regulation.

Conceivably, the long period of poor diet or nutritional self-abuse that leads to dopamine dysfunction could in itself be reducing the conscious or awareness of individuals. What is the educational level of obese people and how does it compare to people who eat in a healthy way? What is the correlation between the passivity involved in not becoming well educated and the failure to take good care of one's health? Are obese people, for the most part, inherently passive individuals encumbered with unresolved psychological issues and emotional weakness? What is the emotional weakness of those individuals who are dynamic and successful in life, except for their struggles with overeating? These questions are being ignored.

While the dopamine effect from eating tasty food might be lessened over time, there's much more to the pleasure of eating than just the question of how tasty the food happens to be. We can feel pleasure because we care enough about ourselves to eat healthy food. Healthy, organic food can taste delicious, in part because we appreciate it for its vitality and nutritional benefits. We can also feel pleasure in the self-regulation of eating moderate quantities. Pleasure is often felt only when it is registered consciously, for instance in absorbing beauty in nature and art. People who practice conscious eating, in which they slowly eat a moderate amount while fully registering the pleasure, feel satisfied and fulfilled with smaller food portions. We can also certainly feel pleasure because we're slim, healthy and physically active and perhaps athletic. Why aren't obese people accessing these forms of pleasure? This question needs to be addressed.

The world needs more consciousness, not more pills. With consciousness come wisdom, power, and self-regulation.

Higher consciousness involves awareness of one's psychological weaknesses. This awareness raises one's intelligence, in the sense of seeing the fuller picture of what's involved in self-defeating behavior. In the case of obesity, common weaknesses include the following: unconscious injustice collecting; an unresolved emotional attachment to the feeling of refusal; an attachment to helpless feelings in the face of food cravings; the expectation of being a disappointment or being seen in a negative light by others; and the unconscious willingness to continue to experience familiar self-criticism and self-negation. Resolution of these psychological weaknesses is attainable when our educational system raises the quality of what it teaches.

48. The Pain We Lock Away

It's so important to see through our psychological defenses if we want to become emotionally strong and escape from suffering. Through our defenses, we lie to ourselves in much the way that parents lie to children to protect them from life's harsher realities. (This discussion is a sequel to "Get to Know Your Psychological Defenses.")

Some experts believe that psychological defense mechanisms serve a good purpose. One expert, writing at the *Psychology Today* website, said, "Psychological defenses are forms of self-deception we employ to avoid unbearable pain."[66]

"They also protect you," said another writer at the same website, "from the anxiety of confronting your weaknesses and foibles."[67]

"They work as shock absorbers and help a person deal with pain," according to another website.[68]

Wow! Thank goodness for these defenses. Without them, we'd apparently be bouncing and rattling down the road in spasms of pain.

---

[66] http://www.psychologytoday.com/blog/shame/201211/the-psychological-defense-emotional-lie
[67] http://www.psychologytoday.com/blog/fulfillment-any-age/201110/the-essential-guide-defense-mechanisms
[68] http://www.buzzle.com/articles/common-psychological-defense-mechanisms.html

Wait a minute! What is this "unbearable pain" that we're protecting ourselves from? Wouldn't it be better if we were to see it clearly? Wouldn't that give us a better chance to heal or resolve it? Our defenses, it seems, are preventing us from seeing ourselves more objectively. Well, what is it we don't want to see? What reality or pain is so dangerous or threatening that we must navigate life's highways in a truth-proof armored vehicle with jolt-free shock-absorbers?

One of the above writers provides the following answer. She says that (in a situation in which the defense of denial is being used to cover up a person's substance abuse) that "you protect your self-esteem" by refusing to acknowledge the harmful behavior. But this statement doesn't make any sense. What kind of self-esteem is it that needs to be protected from reality? It's a flimsy self-image that needs such protection, not true self-esteem.

It's true that our defenses can protect us from some anxiety and pain, but usually that emotional pain is not overwhelming. It may be nothing more than the intensity of feelings that invariably accompany inner growth. For the most part, anxiety and pain of this kind, as well as our defenses themselves, are elements of our resistance to inner growth and freedom. Like a baby blanket, we cling to the old self, the old order—however dysfunctional we may be. Inwardly, we're afraid of change, afraid of the new self. Yet we won't make much inner progress, or be able to protect and enhance political freedoms and environmental integrity, until we stop using our defenses as baby-blankets.

Our defenses protect us from being humbled at the realization of the vast extent of unconscious psychological dynamics to which, through our ego, we have been completely unaware. Our ego, the limited self with which we identify, experiences inner growth as the process of its demotion, even as a form of death. The feeling is that, were we to embark on a voyage of self-discovery, we'll lose all our familiar landmarks and risk falling off the edge of our world into emptiness or nothingness. Our resistance to this undertaking is activated in the form of anxiety and fear. The anxiety and fear are mainly childish emotional associations, along with manifestations of our resistance.

We all harbor inner fear left over from the helplessness and irrational conjectures of childhood. Inner fear is also experienced when our inner critic (superego) harasses and bullies our subordinate ego (the seat of inner passivity). It feels as if we need to defend ourselves (through the subordinate ego) or we'll be crushed or annihilated by the inner critic. Our psychological defenses, in large part, are mustered in an attempt to fend off our inner critic which harasses and belittles us.

We can go deeper still. Our psychological defenses are protecting not only our ego but something that is actually quite amazing. This is not something we have to be afraid of, though it does produce anxiety and pain when we approach it.

What is that deeper issue that lurks behind our delicate self-image? Just about every one of us tends to identify, to some degree, with a sense of unworthiness, the deep-down sense of being a fake, fraud, or nobody. This is a Big Enchilada of human nature. It's also a major cause of shame, anxiety, and guilt. This is what many people anxiously defend against, the realization of how emotionally attached they are, how identified they are, with this irrational belief. (An earlier post, "When You Feel Bad about Yourself," discusses the childhood origins of this painful irrational belief.)

If you want to break free from this inner pain, you have to own or acknowledge your emotional attachment to the irrational belief in your unworthiness. To do so, it helps to understand that self-centeredness (or egotism) serves as a defense against this realization. Our ego is a complicated phenomenon—part illusion, part necessity—that can become a mental-emotional compensation for our deep, repressed sense of having little value, being hollow at the core and insignificant in the world. The greater our repressed self-doubt, the more self-centered and narcissistic we can become in compensation. The more we tout our individuality and superiority, the more we're defending against realization of deeper truth, namely our identification, to a significant degree, with this conviction of our unworthiness. Our defenses "protect" us from this realization, as they simultaneously prevent us from accessing the inner truth that can liberate us from suffering.

The idea from religion that we are abject sinners in need of salvation arises from this deep conviction. This sense of unworthiness is an emotional construct, a lingering existential pain from childhood, not the truth about our place in the world. The problem is complicated by the fact that, unconsciously, we identify with this pain. This repressed identification with inferiority and self-rejection causes us to lose sight of who we are and who we can become.

Author and teacher Eckhart Tolle recognizes this deeper aspect. He writes in *A New Earth: Awakening to Your Life's Purpose*: "The underlying emotion that governs all the activity of the ego is fear: The fear of being nobody, the fear of nonexistence, the fear of death."[69] I see it slightly differently, and the distinction is important. It may be more precise to say that the underlying factor that governs much of the activity of the ego *is our fear of discovering our emotional attachment to (or identification with) the repressed sense of being nobody.* Resistance can be understood as our unconscious determination to hold on to that painful identification. We chose the suffering self we know over the mysterious stranger we don't.

This is a challenging concept, yet there's historical evidence for it. People resist inner growth and fiercely hold on to painful identifications rather than move toward higher consciousness. It often takes revolutions to force people to break free from their identifications with feelings of inferiority. A century ago in America, men believed themselves superior to women who were not allowed to vote. The feeling of superiority was a cover-up for their identification with women, meaning that, through women, men could slip into the familiar old feeling of what it was like to be regarded as inferior. The defense went like this: "I don't want to identify with the weakness and inferiority of women. They really are inferior, in the sense of being unsuitable to participate, on an equal footing with men, in social and political life. Rather than identifying with them, I wish to keep them restricted to the home and kitchen."

The same process was acted out in the American Civil Rights struggle. White racists fiercely held on to their unconscious identification with feelings of inferiority,

---

[69] Tolle, Eckhart. *A New Earth: Awakening to Your Life's Purpose.* New York: Plume, 2006.

which they covered up psychologically by projecting their unconscious inferiority-complex on to blacks. Gays have also been subjected to this unconscious behavior, in the form of decrees proclaiming the inferiority of their sexual orientation. Sexual and racial slurs can hurt so deeply because they go to the heart of this issue. Issues of inferiority are also at play in class struggles and widening income disparity and by impulses to feel disdain toward the poor. The situation is worsened by the tendency of many poor people to resonate, even if only unconsciously, with the idea of somehow being lesser citizens. As another example, the Nazis, in a grotesque rendering of unconscious humankind striving for self-importance, were egotistically mesmerized and stupefied by presiding like demigods over large-scale life and death. They actively projected upon the Jews the belief in worthlessness that they harbored and despised in themselves. The projection of this negative belief is clearly a factor in the psychological origins of intolerance.

We hate to reveal our true selves to a psychiatrist, one psychiatrist wrote, because we fear "we'll be judged, criticized, or rejected in some way." And even worse, he went on, some worry they "might be labelled crazy, locked up in an asylum, medicated into oblivion, or put in a straitjacket."[70] I believe it's not so much the psychiatrist that people are afraid of. Rather, we're afraid to uncover the repressed material in our unconscious, much of it involving guilt and shame, which we hide from ourselves. We'll also be mortified to realize the feeble extent of our awareness and our abundance

---

[70] http://aeon.co/magazine/being-human/have-psychiatrists-lost-perspective-on-mental-illness/

of inner conflict. Bursting with resistance, our ego does not welcome such revelations.

But the knowledge is so powerful! It enables us to break the spell our ego holds over us. With our ego pushed aside, we can look with some detachment and equanimity upon the true circumstances of our inner life. When see our attachment to the impression of being unworthy or insignificant, we can say with deep understanding, "That's not the real me—that's just an old emotional association. Nonetheless, it feels real, and I have to be insightful and vigilant not to be drawn into it."

As we see deeper into reality, we feel our goodness and value more fully. Our ego, which separates us from the feeling and the knowing of the goodness that exists in ourselves and others, steps into the background. We're each great in our self, while at the same time very much part of (and dependent on) something greater than our self. With this awareness, we no longer need artificial defenses because we have nothing to hide.

49 . **The Private Joke behind Our Laughter**

Insight is a good thing, and insight into where our laughter comes from not only can spare us a lot of misery but is worth a laugh in itself. Still, as one witty writer said, "Analyzing humor is like dissecting a frog. Few people are interested and the frog dies of it." Despite the risk, I'm putting humor and laughter on the dissecting table. I love humor as much as any cutup, and, obviously, I have no wish to fracture its funny-bone or to see it croak.

Humor, bless its existence, is often a byproduct of the clash in our psyche between inner aggression and inner passivity. The voice or "intelligence" of inner passivity (our unconscious ego) often produces humor for the purpose of deflecting and reducing to absurdity the harsh pronouncements and judgments of inner aggression (our inner critic or superego). The online "Rumble in the Air-Conditioned Auditorium" between TV personalities Jon Stewart and Bill O'Reilly serves to illustrate this point.

Stewart, the easy-going liberal humorist and host of "The Daily Show," sees and relates to the world from the perspective of inner passivity. He generates much of his humor by cleverly mocking the pretentions and inconsistencies of the establishment and the Right Wing. O'Reilly, in contrast, is a gruff conservative commentator known for his denouncements of liberal positions. His persona, while capable of humor, is a caricature of our authoritarian inner critic. Each man represents an opposing side of the major clash in the human psyche between inner aggression and inner passivity. Stewart provided some evidence of this unconscious connection when he said, "O'Reilly is like comfort food for me. I feel like I grew up around these guys. He's my shepherd's pie." Since O'Reilly is the embodiment of Stewart's inner critic, Stewart obviously feels right at home dueling with him.

The two men are friends, and it's a tribute to them that they've connected with some measure of goodwill, despite coming from opposing positions in the psyche. Still, when watching their "rumble" we're like children giggling at two quarrelling puppets when we don't appreciate the "intelligence" (unconscious dynamics) pulling the strings behind the scene. If humor is the best medicine, deeper awareness of humor's substructure enhances the joke.

Humor comes in many guises, among them wit, irony, sarcasm, jocularity, buffoonery, and whimsy. Jocularity often holds people up to ridicule; someone is made the butt of a joke. Yet why should human foolishness or suffering be laughable at all? Instead of laughing, we could be callous, scornful, or compassionate, as indeed we often are. However, we very much desire the delightful pleasure of laughter, and we grasp for it when we can. Laughter comes easily as an intense momentary release of inner freedom, like the toot of a safety valve or the exalted cry of an escaping prisoner. We're liberated momentarily from the considerable weight of inner reproach and disapproval that comes at us from our ubiquitous inner critic. When a joke identifies someone else as the fool or failure, he or she is offered up as a prisoner to our inner critic: "This person is obviously a better object of ridicule than me," we unconsciously proclaim, "and much more deserving of disapproval." In that moment, we're experiencing sharp relief that someone other than ourselves has been "captured and condemned" by the inner critic.

TV comics Jay Leno and David Letterman have for decades roasted celebrities and politicians on their shows. Leno cracked me up a few years ago when he said, "Today, Mick Jagger is 65 years old—and it's also the 30th anniversary of him looking like he's 65." The laughter is all sporting, good-natured fun; the iconic singer himself would probably chuckle. Still, technically, the joke is at his expense. For the joke to work, he's sacrificed for our emotional relief. I laughed gleefully because I felt—*instantaneously*—at that moment: "Imagine looking 65 when you're only 35. I never looked *that* ridiculous."

This reveals the degree to which, on an inner level, we live under the inner critic's constant, hostile surveillance and oppression. Our inner critic, as mentioned, is the tyrant of the psyche and the hidden master of our personality. It constantly holds us accountable and questions our actions and decisions. It's important for us to recognize this in ourselves. Otherwise, we function to a considerable extent in a state of inner passivity, unable to neutralize our inner critic and continuing to waste much mental and emotional energy doubting and defending ourselves against its relentless assault.

Like Leno and Stewart, people who become comedians have from an early age made a fine art of deflecting inner attacks by directing them on to others or by reducing them to absurdity. While such people can confound the inner critic, as well as authority figures in society, the effect is temporary. Their unwitting use of political and sarcastic humor is not going to overthrow the tyranny of the inner critic, nor will it trouble a corrupt or tyrannical economic and political establishment. The court jester, a specialist at self-preservation and a dogged approval-seeker, is no threat to the king. His humor is too defensive and too much employed for self-preservation.

While some humorists present artificial victims to their inner critic, others present themselves as the victims. This is the Rodney Dangerfield self-derision persona, where a comedian makes himself an object of ridicule. Once again this humor gets laughs because people are happy to see someone other than themselves—it doesn't matter who—dangling from the butt-end of life. This formula applies, too, to the "insult comedy" of Don Rickles and the "big oaf" persona of Jackie Gleason. Some "humorists" of the Rush Limbaugh School practice an especially vicious variety that's fired off like cannonballs of cynicism, with hostile sarcasm for gunpowder. Their explosive cynicism draws in people who are eager to blame others for their own suffering. This "humor" registers high collateral damage because it serves not to placate inner aggression but to direct it unmercifully and unjustly toward others.

Humor as a form of defending ourselves from the inner critic is passive and unstable. It's like playing chess against a supercomputer—one nervous twitch and you're done. Some famous comedians have died young from drug abuse—notably, Lenny Bruce, John Belushi, and Chris Farley—because intense inner conflict undermined the power of self-regulation. *Scientific American* reports that British researchers gave 500 comedians a personality test that assesses traits associated with schizophrenia and bipolar disorder. They found that the comics scored unusually high on a range of psychotic traits. This is evidence, in my view, that comedians have, on an inner level, a particularly harsh inner critic, and that they resort to absurdity and humor in their shaky, unstable attempt to deflect that inner aggression. The study appeared in the *British Journal of Psychiatry*.[71]

When we become stronger on an inner level, we don't compulsively resort to humor as a way to maintain our

---

[71] http://bjp.rcpsych.org/content/early/2014/01/02/bjp.bp.113.134569.abstract

inner equilibrium. Nor will we laugh at stupid jokes that present the folly or misfortune of others solely for our selfish glee. In inclusive laughter we express the spirit of joyfulness.

50 . Why We Fear and Hate the Truth

Men occasionally stumble over the truth, but most of them pick themselves up and hurry off as if nothing ever happened. – Winston Churchill.

We fear and hate many of truth's disclosures because they're often accompanied by narcissistic insults. What's a *narcissistic insult*? It's a bulletin from reality that, while capable of smartening us up, offends our ego. To avoid such insults, we cling to our illusions and limit our intelligence and inner freedom.

The evasion of truth has many manifestations, one being our denial of the fact that our methods of producing and using energy are sickening our planet. We slip and slide around this idea. Deep inside, we whisper to ourselves: "If climate change is a real threat to future generations, what does that make me? Does my indifference to my carbon footprint make me an accomplice in mass destruction? No, that's not me! That's not the kind of person I am!"

Many of us embrace the idea that we're rugged self-sustaining individuals rather than participants in a delicate web of life. Hyper-individualism is naked narcissism, a byproduct of our repressed fear of being insignificant or unworthy. Our esteemed self-delusion resists unlocking its defenses when its assumptions are challenged. Studies have found that misinformed people, particularly those loyal to their politics, rarely change their minds when exposed to corrected facts in news stories.[72] Instead, they often become more strongly set in their beliefs, refusing to digest even the smallest fragments of truth. Individuals also see a political candidate, in terms of how they perceive the physical characteristics of that person's face, according to their political preferences.[73]

This restriction of intelligence may be humankind's most baffling and self-destructive problem. The world's complex challenges won't be solved by stubborn brains cells revolting against reality.

Our anxiety begins in the depths of our psyche where inner weakness makes the unknowns of life more frightening. We tend to create an identity—often an idealized sense of ourselves as individuals and as a group—that's based on fixed beliefs. Those beliefs can be religious, secular, personal, cultural, and social, and they carry a lot of emotional baggage. When we stay on the surface of awareness, we use beliefs as a substitute for an emotional foundation in our own being, our own self. Emotionally, we're needy: We need our beliefs to be true. Self-doubt is buried beneath the assertion, "I believe it, and therefore it's true." Such beliefs are

---

[72] http://www.boston.com/bostonglobe/ideas/articles/2010/07/11/how_facts_backfire/
[73] http://www.sciencedaily.com/releases/2013/12/131212113042.htm

designed to allay our fears and bolster our sense of value and significance.

Not surprisingly then, many of us experience anxious, inner turmoil when our beliefs are directly challenged by opposing ideas and beliefs (or, even more distressingly, by *facts*). We can feel a frightening cognitive dissonance when facts undermine our belief system. The emotional impact might be, "Who am I, who will I be, without my beliefs?" The ground seems to give way beneath us, and we're cast out into the unknown like *A Space Odyssey* nursling floating in an orb of light.

We downsize the mystery of life and package it into bite-size convictions. Psychologically, we're still children who fear spooks hiding under our bed. To avoid feeling overwhelmed, we close our minds and refuse unconsciously to accept inconvenient facts. Unconsciously, we feel that, "My beliefs protect me from so-called facts that try to undermine me and cause self-doubt. I've figured out my beliefs for myself, and nobody's so-called facts are going to take them away." Unrecognized stubbornness produces an illusion of certainty, safety, substance, and power.

To be strong, we need to become more comfortable with uncertainty. With greater emotional strength, we can accept—sometimes even *embrace*—the emptiness and uncertainty that permeate existence like an invisible dark energy. Mystics say that highest wisdom and sense of freedom come to us as we're able to transcend our ego and merge our consciousness with oneness. In this equanimity, we have the best of both worlds, the richness of our authentic self along with the pleasure of transcending our aloneness. Yet this option is resisted because it undermines individualism, that precious illusion of an ego-based self that ultimately is maintained by inner fear.

Deep down, we identify with a limited self. We believe in our own unworthiness, and we fear exposure of our identification with this flawed self, even though such awareness leads to peace and freedom. The healthier we become psychologically, the more we "know" ourselves and the more we're able to manifest the virtues of integrity, honesty, empathy, generosity, courage, and concern for truth. Old identifications disappear, replaced by the knowing of our goodness and value and by the freedom of our spirit.

Typically, our intelligence is impeded or clouded over by fear of inner truth and by accompanying emotional issues such as low self-esteem, depression, and anxiety. An unconscious process of repression is active in our psyche, covering up old material from our past that's painful, shameful, and guilt-laden. Mental energy, which ideally is used productively and creatively, is wasted in the unconscious repression that fear of truth necessitates.

Mental energy is also wasted in inner defensiveness that protects a delicate, idealized self-image or ego. Truth and reality are sacrificed as we concoct defenses that cover up the most feared and hated truth of all—the mind-blowing realization of the extent of our unconscious participation in suffering and self-defeat. We proceed to uncover such truth as we expose our self-deception and our fear of our better self.

We have only a specific amount of mental energy at our disposal. The more we waste in inner conflict and the cover-up of inner truth, the less creative energy we have to navigate our way forward.

51. Underlying Dynamics that Breed Bullies

If we want our society to put a stop to bullying—an excellent goal, of course, one embraced by Barack Obama,[74] educators, and celebrities[75]—we can help the cause by better understanding the underlying psychological dynamics of bullying and by teaching this knowledge to our kids.

What are these underlying dynamics? The bully—girl or boy, man or woman—appears bold and confident on the surface. But this person is emotionally entangled in substantial self-doubt. As I've been saying, all of us grow up with some degree of self-doubt. This feeling can be quite conscious and intense, or it can be latent and repressed. Our self-doubt produces uncertainty concerning our value, significance, strength, goodness, and worthiness. Even more so, it can produce deep emotional convictions that we're lacking in value, deeply flawed, and undeserving of respect.

Self-doubt is a universal condition. We compensate somewhat for the painfulness of it when we're able to soak up recognition, acceptance, praise, and validation

---

[74] http://abcnews.go.com/blogs/politics/2012/03/obama-introduces-bullying-documentary-on-cartoon-network/
[75] http://abcnews.go.com/blogs/politics/2012/03/obama-introduces-bullying-documentary-on-cartoon-network/

from others. The existence of self-doubt is evident in the human passion for fame, glory, power, and wealth, all of which bestow an illusion of value and superiority. Self-doubt is also evident in bullies who belittle and abuse others in their desperate need to feel superior and more powerful in themselves.

What is the source of our self-doubt? Many thoughtful people, of course, have tackled this age-old question. One answer, I believe, lies in our emotional conviction that somehow our intrinsic, authentic self was never fully recognized and appreciated as we were growing up. Now we're unable to bestow this recognition upon ourselves. Unspoken words, addressed to one's parents, convey the feeling: "You don't really know who I am." The feeling is personalized: "If you don't know who I am, then I'm probably not worth knowing." These feelings can be present even when we had kind, decent parents. Whether decent or not, the problem often is that parents are not conscious enough to bestow deep reflective recognition upon their children. Why is that? Adults as well as children tend to have too much inner conflict to be able to bestow this level of recognition upon themselves. If we could fully grant it to ourselves, we would at this moment be much more willing to make sacrifices on behalf of our descendants (as extensions of ourselves) to minimize the effects of climate change.

Our limited sense of self is tied in with our subjective experiences of early childhood development. The need for parents to subject us to the necessary process of child-rearing—highlighted by toilet training and the battles of the "terrible two's"—can leave us convinced emotionally that some essential part of us was unacceptable, even wrong and bad. Such feelings live in our psyche at a deep, repressed level.

Bullying begins deep down inside of us. Our self-doubt supports the existence of an inner bully—our inner critic or superego—that operates in our psyche. We experience self-doubt most emphatically when our inner critic whispers or even seems to shout in our ear, belittling us and our accomplishments. This voice from our inner critic mocks, harasses, and torments us on the pretext that we somehow deserve to be subordinate and to be treated with this disrespect.

How does our inner critic get away with bullying us? How come we put ourselves at such a disadvantage? It only happens because we're not sufficiently conscious of these inner dynamics. The human race has simply not been able to come to terms with the fact that we have a fundamental inner battle in our psyche between aggression and passivity. This war between inappropriate aggression (our bullying inner critic) and inner passivity (our defensive unconscious ego) is waged on the battlefield of human evolution with the ammunition of false accusations, weak defenses, and emotional punishment.

Every psyche has aggressive and passive deposits. Usually, people don't mind being identified as aggressive, but they invariably hate being identified as passive. So our instinct is to disavow our passivity. Bullies are inherently passive individuals who are often neglected or treated roughly at home. Inwardly, they feel devalued, unworthy, and passive to parents or siblings. At the same time, they may see their parents in the grip of these same painful emotions. Their instinct is to cover up this self-doubt, and they can do so by becoming aggressive with other children who are smaller or more passive. Now, for the moment, their self-doubt vanishes. Bullies feel they have the power and are the better person, as they torment the one they have identified as a lesser person.

The aggressive behavior of bullies doesn't allow them to escape from their emotional entanglement in self-doubt. That's because, unconsciously, they identify with the victim of their bullying. Emotionally, they "sneak" into the skin of their victim, and through identification with their victim they feel what it's like to be bullied. The victim typically feels enormous self-doubt. As the entertainer Lady Gaga, a victim of bullying in her childhood, said in an interview, "I was so ashamed of who I was."[76] Victims of bullying can be taught to become stronger emotionally so they feel better about themselves and are less likely to be targets of bullies.

Some bullies can't resist the sadistic gratification they feel. The sadist, like the bully, appears to get this perverse gratification by feeling power and superiority over the victim. However, the perverse pleasure is ultimately of a masochistic nature. It is produced, as mentioned, mainly through the aggressor's identification with the helplessness and worthlessness that the victim is presumed to be feeling. Bullies will think twice before acting out if they're taught that their impulse to mistreat others is based on their unconscious wish to identify with the alleged inferiority or helplessness of their victims.

Bullying is a psychological defense. It attempts to cover up the bully's identification with the victim's passivity and sense of having little value. "Look, I'm the aggressor," the bully's defense maintains: "I'm the one

---

[76] http://www.nytimes.com/2012/03/01/opinion/kristof-born-to-not-get-bullied.html?_r=1&hp

who is superior. This is what *I want* and this is what *I like*—to feel superior to this worthless weakling and more powerful."

This makes their bullying a compulsive behavior. All of us can be quite compulsive when it comes to using various self-defeating behaviors to cover up what we don't understand (and don't want to acknowledge) about ourselves. Hundreds of various self-defeating behaviors are used by people to cover up our unresolved emotional attachments to feeling deprived, refused, controlled, rejected, criticized, betrayed, abandoned, and disrespected.

Bullying is essentially an instinctive acting out of the conflict in our psyche between aggression and passivity. Bullying also serves as a psychological defense that covers up the bully's emotional attachment to feeling self-doubt in the forms of passivity and lack of value. With consciousness or self-knowledge, we're able to resolve this inner conflict, which then nullifies both the instinct to act out being a bully and the tendency to feel deserving of being bullied.

52. The Three Amigos of Woe

The Three Amigos of Woe are not as well-known as their compatriots in suffering, the Four Horsemen of the Apocalypse—conquest, war, famine, and death. Yet the three amigos are just as big a danger to health, happiness, and prosperity.

Each of the three amigos—the beggar, the slave, and the orphan—represents a negative, painful state of mind. For most of us, our psyche is contaminated with at least one of these miseries, and many of us are burdened with a trace or more of all three.

The beggar represents those of us who, however bountiful our life may be, suffer with an inner emptiness. It feels as if something vitally important is missing in our life. The beggar can be rich or poor, the distinction isn't relevant. A poor person's regular purchase of lottery tickets can be an expression of this mentality. The feeling is, "If only I were rich (or if only I had this or that) I would be happy." A rich person's desire to feel special or superior or to possess even greater wealth also reflects this mentality. On the surface, beggars are eager to accumulate or to acquire things, whatever those things might be. Deeper down, they're on the scent of deprivation.

The beggar mentality is a product of our lingering emotional attachment to feelings of deprivation and refusal. We're still the little kid who once screamed in angry frustration when he didn't get something he very much wanted. As adults, the painful feeling lingers. It becomes the sense that our existence and our self as we know it are not enough. It feels that our goodness and our consciousness count for little. So we minimize these essentials of happiness, and we go out into the world begging for scraps of validation and coveting the trappings of success. Oral cravings for food and drink are also symptoms of the beggar mentality.

The next amigo, the slave, goes through life suffering with feelings of being controlled, trapped, dominated, and helpless. The slave who lives in a democracy may not be able to fulfill the responsibilities of citizenship because he or she is likely to be emotionally aligned with feelings of being oppressed, rendered powerless, or having nothing of value to offer.

Slaves can express a second-rate power that is mostly negative. They have the "power" to complain and to rage against the "forces of oppression." They can rebel—often only passive-aggressively—but they can't reform the situations they complain about. That's because they give unconscious consent to feelings of being manipulated, controlled, oppressed, and discounted. Despite their claims to the contrary, they're not interested in reform. They're too identified with the slave mentality, and they don't know how to live in inner freedom.

An emotional entanglement in feeling controlled arises during the "terrible twos," when toddlers loudly object to feeling reined in, to toilet training, and to the process of socialization. As adults, they hate feeling controlled, yet the feeling is familiar and unresolved. Sometimes they become controllers—the ones who do the controlling—in reaction to their fear of being controlled.

Slaves are likely to be weak at self-regulation, so they're often addictive and compulsive personalities. They're also likely to be codependents and to be passively ensnared in dysfunctional relationships. Sometimes the only experiences of power they can muster are angry defensiveness and self-defeating stubbornness.

The final amigo, the orphan, chases after love and never seems to find it. He or she tends to disappear into the background, or, narcissistically, strives for recognition and acclaim. This person carries the perpetual pain of feeling alone, abandoned, unwanted, and unloved. Orphans are often entangled in acute self-centeredness, a mentality that constantly recycles this mental and emotional conflict: "I desperately want them to like me and appreciate me, but I remain attached to the hurt and the pain of their indifference and their rejection."

The orphan is blocked from being a more loving person because of the emotional preoccupation with feeling unloved. This preoccupation means that this individual sometimes dislikes, rejects, and even hates himself or herself.

No matter how much love the orphan receives, it may never be enough. More is always needed, and still it's not enough. In this emotional neediness, the orphan often turns on those who are doing their best to be friendly or loving, blaming them for his or her suffering.

Promiscuity is one behavioral consequence of an orphan's desperate yearning for love. The yearning is a defense that claims, "I'm not looking for the feeling of being unloved; look how desperate I am and how anxiously I pursue love." Orphans can be tormented by jealousy and expectations of betrayal. As well, they can fail to achieve true intimacy in their marriages and relationships because they settle for the pretense of love. The orphan runs away from true love because the feeling would overwhelm his or her determination to live through the emotional attachment to feeling unloved.

All three amigos are acting out major elements of what is unresolved in the human psyche. Like the four horsemen, they can, while acting out their inner conflict, wreak havoc upon others.

53. The Problem with Positive Psychology

Most everyone is looking for happiness. The shopping malls of the self-help industry feature thousands of different methods, beliefs, and practices for finding it. Many of these approaches are of limited value, and we do ourselves a big favor by avoiding them.

According to Martin E.P. Seligman, founder of positive psychology, people who apply his method "are the people with the highest well-being I have ever known." Seligman's approach encourages us to apply determination and grit in order to increase our positive emotions and relationships. We flourish, he claims, when we focus on engagement, accomplishment, and a sense of meaning. A recent book of his is titled, *Flourish: A Visionary New Understanding of Happiness and Well-being* (Free Press, New York, 2011).

Seligman's approach can produce a temporary boost of happiness, or an illusion of it, but it doesn't improve our intelligence or deepen our wisdom. It risks turning us into smiley-faced puppet people instead of real and authentic individuals who are evolving through deeper awareness. Positive psychology advocates a kind of willpower-on-steroids programming that insists we can feel fulfilled and happy by believing we are making it happen. This system does not appreciate how, through unconscious conflict in our psyche, we compulsively replay and recreate unresolved negative emotions.

When we try to dodge or repress our psyche's inner dynamics, we encounter inner rebellion that produces a wide variety of suffering and self-defeat. To become smarter, wiser, and more conscious, we have to understand the inner mechanisms and drives in our psyche that induce us to chase after old hurts, cling to painful regrets, and indulge in a variety of other unresolved emotions.

We have two layers of negativity in our psyche. At the deepest layer, we encounter *unconscious* negativity. As mentioned, this negativity is unconscious in the sense that often we don't realize it's even there. It's also unconscious in the sense that we don't realize that we're attached to it, and that we go looking for ways to continue to experience it. This negativity, as I've been saying, involves impressions left over from childhood of being deprived, refused, controlled, helpless, criticized, rejected, betrayed, abandoned, and unworthy. Most people are entangled, to some degree, in this unconscious negativity, and their emotional attachment to the various expressions of this negativity is a major determinant of their suffering and unhappiness.

The second layer of negativity is more superficial and frequently conscious. It consists of painful feelings such as anger, loneliness, fear, envy, greed, resentment, bitterness, and depression. These negative experiences are symptoms of the deeper negativity, and the symptoms can be used as defenses that cover up awareness of the deeper negativity. As mentioned, we're able to free ourselves from the deeper negativity as we become more conscious of the dynamics that hold it in place.

Positive psychology doesn't come within a mile of this understanding. We can't, for instance, just plaster a smiley-face over the plight of compulsive shoppers. Typically, compulsive shoppers feel empty, anxious, or depressed after a shopping binge. That's because their compulsive behavior is a defense intended to "prove" that they want to get something of value, when in fact they're entangled in powerful feelings that something vital is missing in their life. This underlying unresolved emotion—the deep negativity—reasserts itself when the shopping binge is over. These individuals are likely entangled in emotional issues involving deprivation and refusal that go back to childhood. They often harbor deep feelings of being unworthy and lacking in intrinsic value. Their compulsion can also be traced to feelings of helplessness and passivity that produce their lack of self-regulation. They can also, through lack of insight, be unable to resolve a recurring conflict in their psyche in which the inner critic assails them for their excessive spending, while they accept punishment for their unwise "naughty" behavior in the suffering of guilt and shame.

Positive psychology is like a guest that barges into someone's home (our psyche) through the front door, giving orders and demanding compliance. This guest may at first appear to get his way, but the host (the conflicts and emotional attachments in our psyche) soon rebel to restore the old order. A wiser, more humble guest (depth psychology) has waited to be invited. Observing the occupants, procedures, and interactions of the home, this guest is intent on learning from the host while offering the host something of great value, and is at peace with whether the host accepts or declines the offerings.

Positive psychology, which Seligman claims has produced "a tectonic upheaval in psychology," cannot see through illusions or penetrate defenses. In *Flourish*, for instance, he writes, "I now think that the topic of positive psychology is well-being, that the gold standard for measuring well-being is flourishing, and that the goal of positive psychology is to increase flourishing." This emphasis on well-being is misguided. Americans had a sense of economic and social well-being in the years and decades leading up to the financial crash of 2008. Our well-being was an illusion. We were in denial as corruption, greed, and stupidity prevailed beneath the surface. A sense of well-being is an impression we can unwittingly produce to rationalize or justify our denial. In other words, our sense of well-being can be blissful ignorance, a kissing-cousin to denial of both inner conflict and social-economic-political dysfunction. Without insight, we can't tell when our sense of well-being is being employed as a defense or whether it is legitimate in its own right. At the moment, we have a sense of well-being in terms of the earth as our sanctuary, even as we rush about creating environmental impacts that might soon wash or blow away that illusion.

The goal of psychology ought *not* to be well-being. The focus on well-being is too individualistic and egotistical. How can we trust that our sense of well-being accords with reality when we deny the reality of unconscious inner dynamics that shape our desires, impulses, intentions, and motivations? Human development needs a more expansive sense of where our intelligence and consciousness can lead us. Better goals for psychology include the development of more self-trust, autonomy, and wisdom. We need to learn to let go of fear so that we can see reality more clearly, acquire the inner strength to accept reality, and the enhanced intelligence to deal effectively with it.

Seligman also writes, "We often choose what makes us feel good, but it is very important to realize that often our choices are not made for the sake of how we will feel. I chose to listen to my six-year-old's excruciating piano recital last night, not because it made me feel good, but because it is my parental duty and part of what gives my life meaning." Again, Seligman doesn't seem to see the bigger picture. We can't separate good feelings from what gives our life meaning. Good feelings of the highest quality are produced when we're fulfilling our duty to others and finding meaning and purpose in life. He ought to feel very good while in attendance at his son's "excruciating piano recital" because even inexpertly played music need not dampen the pleasure of being in the right place at the right time.

In an earlier book, *Authentic Happiness*, Seligman made a similar claim. He wrote that happiness has little to do with pleasure and much to do with developing personal strengths and character. Again, happiness has a lot to do with our capacity to experience pleasure, and the pursuit of personal strengths does indeed produce pleasure. It's true that in pursuit of self-development we often wrestle with painful issues such as fear and cravings. Yet the pursuit and acquisition of personal strengths and character contains within it the pleasure and happiness of knowing we're trying our best to do what's right. Seligman also says our level of happiness cannot be lastingly increased—and that we can only hope to live in the upper reaches of our natural range. How ironic that positive psychology makes such a nihilistic prognosis. Our happiness can indeed be lastingly and dramatically increased. This is achieved through deeper insight and a willingness to acknowledge and to understand our unconscious mind's commanding presence in our daily life.

54 . A Question of Forgiveness

Many mental-health experts claim that we need to embrace forgiveness if we want to let go of anger, resentment, and thoughts of revenge after someone we care about has hurt us.

I disagree. Often, we don't have to forgive them at all. Our peace of mind isn't necessarily about forgiving others. It's about seeing how, in our emotional reactions to the behaviors of others, we're likely to be replaying our own unresolved issues and stumbling unnecessarily into suffering.

Forgiveness is sometimes appropriate, of course, especially when we have been gravely victimized. But much of the time we get triggered by the behaviors of others due to our own emotional attachments. When we understand how we got triggered and how we're trying to cover that up by blaming others, we see there's nothing to forgive.

Contributing to the confusion, the Mayo Clinic, a medical institute known for its research and education on health matters, has on its website an article written by its own staff, titled "Forgiveness: Letting go of grudges and bitterness," that reads in part:

Nearly everyone has been hurt by the actions or words of another. Perhaps your mother criticized your parenting skills, your colleague sabotaged a project or your partner had an affair. These wounds can leave you with lasting feelings of anger, bitterness or even vengeance — but if you don't practice forgiveness, you might be the one who pays most dearly. By embracing forgiveness, you can also embrace peace, hope, gratitude and joy.

This advice implies that letting go of grudges and bitterness depends on forgiveness. As a remedy for conflict, forgiveness can easily be misused and misunderstood. To understand the shallow nature of the Mayo Clinic's advice, let's take a close look at each of the three examples from the institute's posting.

1) Your mother criticized your parenting skills. Such criticism would only hurt you or make you angry if you yourself were sensitive to the feeling of being criticized. Otherwise, you would calmly consider whether your mother's observation had any merit, and you would take into account what she has to say. Or you might dismiss her words as an expression of her critical nature and not take them personally.

Perhaps your mother has always been a critical person. That would likely indicate that, as a child, you absorbed criticism from her, or else you identified with others in the family who were criticized by her. This means you would have an unresolved conflict regarding criticism: You hate the feeling of it, yet you remain emotionally attached to the experience of it. Now, when mother criticizes your parenting skills, you get "hit up" once again with that old unresolved feeling of being criticized.

You're the one, however, who "takes a hit" on the feeling. To cover up your unconscious participation or collusion in this suffering, you feel offended by your mother and get angry at her. All along, you might have unconsciously provoked her in order to replay this old dynamic between the two of you. If so, what is there to forgive? What you need in this situation are insight and self-knowledge. Forgiveness in such a situation entails self-deception: You're refusing to see how and why you got triggered by her, and you're making her responsible for your anger or resentment.

Before moving on to the second example, it's important to note that the Mayo Clinic's posting does say at one point far down in the text: "Move away from your role as victim and release the control and power the offending person and situation have had in your life." This bit of advice is vague, and it also comes too late. The remark is basically just a footnote that's provided long after the emphasis on forgiveness as a remedy in itself has been established. This passing comment is also too sketchy. It's just *advice*; it doesn't provide *self-knowledge*. It's not helpful because we likely can't release "the control and power of the offending person and situation" when we don't see or understand how, unconsciously, we're interested in magnifying the effect of that control and power.

2) Your colleague sabotaged a project. If you feel that forgiveness of your colleague is the solution for your bitterness, what might you be overlooking? You could be holding a grudge toward him as part of a cover-up of your unconscious determination to replay old unresolved feelings of being betrayed or victimized. Or you could be a party to a situation in which your own unconscious expectations of failure are being acted out. This raises the question of whether you might have chosen a partner who's prone to sabotage. You might say you had no reason to suspect such a possibility, but chances are you ignored many warning signs. That means, rather than being bitter, you have some soul-searching to do in order not to repeat your own inclination toward self-defeat.

Your colleague's sabotage likely arises from his or her own unresolved issues regarding failure and being seen as a disappointment to others. When such emotional weaknesses are unconscious and unresolved, all of us can be compelled to act out in a way that produces self-defeat. If you were to respond appropriately to your partner's sabotage, you might, rather than indulging in the hurt done to you, be concerned about his and your own emotional attachments to some unresolved issues having to do with failure and self-defeat.

The situation, if confronted honestly and bravely, can become a valuable learning experience for all, not something you have to bring yourself to forgive. Forgiveness also is so patronizing and unfair to your partner: It makes him the one who is solely responsible for what was likely acted out by the both of you.

3) *Your partner had an affair*. This is the most complicated of the three examples and, indeed, some forgiveness may be called for. (The more grievous the offense, and the more our own innocence is undeniable, the more that forgiveness is an appropriate option.) Nonetheless, if you're interested in the best possible outcome for you and your partner, you need to examine your role in his or her infidelity. Usually before infidelity happens, an intimate relationship has begun to careen off course. Each individual is party to the growing divide.

Let's look at your possible role. Were you taking your partner for granted? Were you lacking in the ability to affirm your love? Is betrayal or abandonment a theme in your live? Are you afraid of intimacy? Were you passive or codependent in the relationship? Did you overlook your partner's past history of disloyalty? Are you more negative and more difficult to live with than you realize? What you might have to struggle with, more so than whether to forgive your partner, is self-forgiveness as your inner critic assails you for allegedly being a foolish dupe of your partner's disloyalty.

Clearly, the act of forgiveness is misused when we use it to identify unfairly the other person as the prime culprit, conveniently covering up our own dysfunctional participation in the contentious situation.

The Mayo Clinic is only one of many providers of skimpy psychological knowledge. What we might need to forgive are our "experts" in mental health who have been providing us with such poor fare.

55 . Oh, Sweet Narcissism

Centuries ago our ancestors, in the throes of self-centeredness, cherished the commonly held belief that the Earth was right smack at the center of the universe. Even the poorest peasant could find solace in the notion of being at the center: "If the Earth is at the center, then I am, too." What a sweet narcissistic way to perceive reality!

Copernicus and then Galileo, wielding scientific knowledge of our solar system, exposed the fallacy of that self-centeredness. Another narcissistic hurt, applied by Charles Darwin, informed the proud lords and ladies of the Industrial Revolution that they were descendants of early primates. Darwin was indignantly denounced by millions of people. To accept his proposition was to be humbled, offended, and belittled. A century and a half after Darwin, many millions still deny the science.

It appears that, at some point in history, we slipped through a little warp in the doorway of perception and placed our mind at the center of existence. We were proud of our clever mind and believed it elevated us far above other creatures. We fashioned God in our image and required that He focus his attention on us, confirming our special status. This narcissism stands on shaky ground. One minute we're jubilant in our pride, the next we're shaking in anger at being slighted or offended. Behind narcissism is the feeling, as one client put it, "that I won't exist and they'll forget me if I don't get recognition."

Narcissism has its genesis in the self-centeredness of the infant. An infant experiences its existence through self-centeredness. An infant, lacking experience and the development of intelligence, knows only its own sensations. For infants, nothing exists beyond their sensations. The infant has no ability to perceive reality with any objectivity. Each child places himself or herself at the center of a little universe. Childhood development (as well as adult development) is a process of learning to overcome this distorted perception and become more objective and discerning.

Most adults get only part way there. We're still seeing ourselves and the world with childish eyes. In a primitive way, our intelligence is held hostage to our lingering self-centeredness and egotism. It feels to us, as part of our resistance to inner growth, that we'll crumble into nothingness if we part company with our now-outdated mental-emotional operating system.

We fiercely protect the mental and emotional conclusions of self-centeredness, among them a rigid individuality, sense of separation, distinctions about alleged superiority and inferiority, and even a dog-eat-dog mentality. Many of us can't fathom, as climate change intensifies, that we could become extinct. When reality intrudes upon this self-centeredness, we stubbornly hole up behind the barricades of willful ignorance.

Another narcissistic hurt was inflicted by Freud when he said we're not masters in our own house. We're powerfully influenced by unconscious dynamics that can produce suffering and self-defeat. This notion didn't sit well with our ego-centered point of view. Through this mentality, we hate the idea that our sense of reality could be shaped, without our knowledge or consent, by processes we know so little about. The situation compares to an insecure king who becomes enraged at the discovery that his minister of state is conducting the kingdom's internal affairs behind his back.

The ego is going to fight back. Enlisted perhaps by their own ego, experts rushed forward to develop ego psychology, along with positive psychology, behavioral-cognitive approaches, and other systems that downplay the irrational side of human nature. Some experts, especially among academic psychologists, have treated

Freud as a charlatan and mock his work. While a few of Freud's findings were incorrect or imprecise, his basic findings about the unconscious mind's irrationality and influence are now accepted by modern science.[77]

The next narcissistic hurt, largely unknown, is such a grievous hurt that it has been almost entirely repressed. This is the hurt that, in large part, I've been addressing in this book. It involves the understanding that, in addition to *not* being masters in our own house, we're also perpetrators of our suffering and self-defeat. Unconsciously, we make choices to hold on to unresolved negative emotions from our past. This causes us to replay and recycle these painful emotions, even while, through psychological defenses, we strive to cover up our collusion in generating these negative experiences. In other words, we're inwardly programmed for suffering and self-defeat.

This knowledge was first introduced by Freud (read, "Finding Inner Longitude") and developed in much greater detail by Edmund Bergler. He wrote that we carry in our psyche a deadly flaw that he called unconscious masochism. This masochism, Bergler said, is the life-blood of all neurosis. The masochism is psychological, with a biological basis, and sado-masochistic sexual activities are only one of the many fields of human activity in which it can be acted out. Humanity is doomed to perpetual self-damage, he believed, unless this unconscious flaw is exposed and addressed.

This deep knowledge Bergler uncovered activates our unconscious resistance to the point that, in ironic

---

[77] http://www.ncbi.nlm.nih.gov/pmc/articles/PMC2440575/

retaliation, we have unconsciously denied his existence. His work is hardly ever mentioned in university courses or programs, though no one has set out in any systematic way to try to refute his theories. From what I can determine, never in the history of the world has such a prolific writer, published by so many prestigious establishments, been so completely ignored after death. A book of mine, appearing almost 50 years after his death, is the only one written about his work.[78] The shunning of Bergler's discoveries is one of the ego's great victories over reality. Unfortunately, Bergler can more easily be dismissed because he made one serious mistake: Reflecting the mid-twentieth-century ethos, he stated in several of his books that the homosexual orientation is neurotic.

Humanity faces still another narcissistic hurt. We don't want to come to terms with the oneness of all life. We cringe in the face of non-duality. Most of us perceive life through a sense of duality—you and me, us and them, my country versus yours, my rights and money versus your needs, my beliefs as opposed to others, the value of my life versus that of another person, my entitlements versus the preservation of organic life. This outlook is rigid and myopic. It causes us to operate like self-interest machines, each programmed by our egotism (and, deeper down, painful self-doubt) to live for our little acquisitive self and for whatever pleasures and benefits we can grab for the moment. Yet we're not meant to be isolationists inside thick skulls. A more evolved consciousness understands that, metaphorically

---

[78] http://www.amazon.com/Why-We-Suffer-Understand-Unhappiness-ebook/dp/B004WOVLR6/ref=sr_1_1?ie=UTF8&qid=1389636371&sr=8-1&keywords=why+we+suffer+michaelson

speaking, we are points of light in a great web of life. We're all dependent on each other's goodwill, generosity, and intelligence. This is a reality we can bring into some focus when we enlist our imagination, dispense of our negatively oriented self-centeredness, feel the strength to be humble, and activate our compassion.

People are becoming more conscious. We're in a paradigm shift, and each of us influences the tipping point. Human beings may be an invasive species fated to self-destruction by a deadly flaw. Yet we're also wonders of nature, destined to become champions of the Earth. It's a glorious battle between darkness and light, delusion and truth, which gives meaning to existence.

56 . **Overcoming Fear of Intimacy**

For our personal growth and self-development, the psychological establishment is feeding us baby food. We'll have difficulty fulfilling our destiny without better educational nutrition.

Let's consider the problem in light of what mainstream psychology is telling us about the self-defeating behavior known as "fear of intimacy."

We won't find abiding love, of course, when we're afraid of intimacy. So how do we fix the problem? An online search for information turns up hundreds of articles and numerous books. Much of this self-help literature does a decent job discussing the experiences and characteristics of fugitives from intimacy. But it does a lousy job providing real insight that can dramatically improve their lives.

One mainstream explanation says that intimacy-dodgers have *a fear of rejection* (being rejected or abandoned by the loved one), along with *a fear of engulfment* (feeling controlled and dominated by one's partner, along with losing oneself in the relationship).

Indeed, these two fears are felt by individuals who flee from intimacy. But where do these fears come from? Relationship experts are not explaining the true source of these fears. They say the fears can be due to a social phobia, an anxiety disorder, or a history of abuse. Yet even when these factors are aspects of the problem, we still are in need of knowledge that goes beyond a diagnosis or the wounds of victimization.

For true insight, we have to penetrate into the nature of emotional conflict. On one side of the conflict, people with fear of intimacy often suffer from acute loneliness and desperately want to find love. On the other side of the conflict, however, they could unconsciously expect to be rejected or abandoned. They might also be lacking in self-respect, and as a result they anticipate being passive or submissive and thereby "losing themselves" in an intimate relationship.

Such conflicts, unresolved in the person's psyche, are processed fruitlessly and painfully in the many forms of self-defeat and self-sabotage that dysfunctional relationships can take.

People are typically aware of one side of a conflict, namely the fact that they do sincerely want to find love.

They're less likely to be aware of the other side of the conflict, where they're unconsciously expecting and even compelled to experience the old unresolved negative emotions of rejection and passivity. The psychological establishment is not recognizing (or at least not educating the public about) this side of the conflict.

Most of us experienced negative emotions as children, even when we had decent parents. As adults, we can still know ourselves and identify with ourselves through old painful emotions. In other words, we haven't liberated ourselves from our attachment to negative emotions such as rejection and passivity. We may be free people living in a democratic country, but we have yet to acquire real inner freedom, meaning a life that is free from the compulsion to recycle unresolved negative emotions.

To raise our emotional intelligence, we need better insight. To illustrate that insight, I'll compare a mainstream article on the fear of intimacy with the more valuable deeper self-knowledge that I provide in this book. This mainstream article,[79] published at The Huffington Post, is correct in some of what it says about fear of intimacy. Yet it presents only a superficial analysis. Here's an excerpt from the article:

> The fear [of intimacy] exists, not because of the experience itself, but because you don't know how to handle the situations of being rejected or controlled. The secret to moving beyond the fear of intimacy lies in developing a powerful, loving, adult part of you that learns how to not take

---

[79] http://www.huffingtonpost.com/margaret-paul-phd/fear-of-intimacy_b_884536.html

rejection personally, and learns to set appropriate limits against engulfment.

Yes, agreed. Yet the author doesn't answer essential questions: *Why* don't you know how to handle situations of being rejected or controlled? *Why* do you take rejection personally? We have to see our unresolved entanglement in feeling rejected or controlled. Whatever is unresolved in our psyche is going to be felt by us, no matter how painful. Without deeper awareness, we have little choice but to continue to feel what is unresolved. The negative emotions are powerful, and they can swamp our best efforts to stay positive.

Through these unresolved emotions, we unwittingly enhance whatever negativity and pain can be extracted from a given experience. If it seems that our partner has rejected us or might reject us in the future, we get "triggered" or "take a hit" on the feeling of rejection. Even in instances where rejection is not intended, we can experience a situation emotionally as if rejection is actually happening. To cover up our unconscious willingness to once again feel that painful old unresolved emotion, we get angry or upset at our partner, thereby blaming our partner for what we ourselves are unconsciously willing and compelled to experience.

Fear of intimacy, then, serves as an unconscious defense. This defense makes this claim: "I'm not interested in 'taking a hit' on (and indulging in) that old feeling of rejection. Look, I'm backing away from the relationship. I'm playing it safe and keeping a distance. That proves I'm not looking for rejection."

The person sacrifices love and intimacy to "prove" he or she is not interested in feeling rejected. But the individual is, in fact, entangled in the negative emotion of rejection and compelled to go on either experiencing it or fleeing from it. What saves us is growing awareness of our emotional attachment to the rejection. We see we've been making an unconscious choice to feel that old hurt and to indulge in it.

We do this also with respect to the second fear mentioned above, the fear of engulfment. Here the individual's unresolved inner passivity means that he or she unwittingly gives up power to the other person in the relationship. This individual then experiences self-loathing, as well as animosity toward the partner, and engages in various forms of passive-aggressive reactions while failing to bring his or her inner weakness (or participation in the sense of powerlessness) into focus.

The Huffington Post article also says:

> When you learn how to take personal responsibility for defining your own worth instead of making others' love and approval responsible for your feelings of worth, you will no longer take rejection personally. This does not mean that you will ever like rejection; it means you will no longer be afraid of it and have a need to avoid it.

These words are not just baby food, they're empty calories. How can you take personal responsibility for defining your own worth when you're completely unaware of being emotionally attached to rejection? In this predicament, you're likely also to be experiencing strong doses of self-rejection that are being spooned out by your inner critic and that you unwittingly swallow. A rejecting partner is only doing to you what, through your inner critic, you're doing to yourself. If you want to feel your worth, you have to go toe-to-toe with your belittling inner critic. You have to subdue it so that you become the master or mistress of your personality.

The Huffington Post article goes on to say: "When you learn how to speak up for yourself and not allow others to invade, smother, dominate and control you, you will no longer fear losing yourself in a relationship." But the author says nothing helpful about how you learn to speak up for yourself. To various degrees, our psyche is infused or contaminated with inner passivity, a weak yet persistent identification that separates us from our authentic self. Through this weakness, such people can't represent themselves with power (though they can represent themselves with pseudo-power such as anger or passive-aggressive power such as spiteful withholding), and they easily lose themselves in relationships. At the same time, through inner passivity, such people are not representing themselves with power vis-à-vis their inner critic.

Why are we still swallowing the baby food of mainstream psychology? We're afraid of deeper self-knowledge, and our stubborn clinging to a small sense of self becomes our baby blanket. We're also afraid of the loving, authentic self—the mysterious stranger who's consciousness will complement our own—who will emerge when we pick up the pace and really start evolving.

57 . Vital Knowledge for Marriage Intimacy

There's a reason men and women are creating better marriages than ever before. We're living in the era of what some have termed *self-expressive marriages*. Many married people are now more interested than ever in personal growth and self-fulfillment, and they see marriage as a means, through mutual exploration and supportive partnership, to achieve those ends.[80]

I've acquired some personal know-how on this subject. My first marriage ended in divorce in the 1970s because I was too neurotic to make it work. My second marriage was a mutual adventure in personal growth. It lasted 21 years, until my dear Sandra, an author and psychotherapist like me, died of breast cancer in 1999. Now I'm happily married to Teresa Garland, an occupational therapist who gives training seminars around the country on autism, ADHD, and sensory disorders. She's my editor and I'm hers. Her first book, *Self-Regulation Interventions and Strategies*, has just been published.[81] We're devoted to each other, and we actively support each other's pursuit of personal and professional fulfillment.

The desire for intimacy is a prerequisite of good marriages. Intimacy depends on mutual trust, respect, and affection. It's also a measure of the openness and

---

[80] http://www.nytimes.com/2014/02/15/opinion/sunday/the-all-or-nothing-marriage.html?src=me&ref=general&_r=2
[81] http://www.pesipublishing.com/ECommerce/ItemDetails.aspx?ResourceCode=PUB082195

sincerity of each partner. Intimacy also hinges on a couple's ability to refrain from acting out, with each other, each one's own unresolved personal issues. (In the previous essay, I approached this subject from another perspective.)

Of course, many individuals resist doing the inner work of self-development. That means they're likely to have more difficulty dismantling the personal issues that block intimacy. The divorce rate has remained at a steady 45 percent since the 1980s and mediocre marriages abound. I'm sure the divorce rate would fall substantially if more people had a better understanding of psychological dynamics. In any case, more couples than ever are willing and determined to facilitate each other's personal growth. They can sense they have a better shot at success and happiness with a trusted, loyal spouse who's on the same mission.

Seldom does the openness and trust of a loving union occur by chance. Intimacy has to be simmered in the cauldron of conflicting needs, desires, patterns, and beliefs. To get the best results, some self-reflection is needed to enhance our awareness of what makes us tick. What are some important components of this self-reflection? We start by looking into our old hang-ups or trigger-points, understanding, for instance, how it happens that we can so easily "go negative."

Ideally, you develop the feeling you have nothing to hide, either from yourself or from your partner. As you feel more openness, you can share that evolving sense of self with your mate.

Intimacy is also a source of great pleasure. Smart people are able to grab hold of (and hang on to) that pleasure. And they understand—more than previous generations did—the individual and mutual processes through which intimacy is created.

You and your partner might be an ideal match, but don't expect him or her to make you happy. It's your job to make yourself happy. You have to look within to consider the issues that, independent of your partner, can make you unhappy. These include unresolved sensitivities left over from childhood such as feeling refused, controlled, criticized, rejected, slighted, and abandoned. We can be quick to "go negative" or get triggered, and turn against those we love, whenever we become entangled in these negative emotions, as invariably we do when they remain unresolved.

In the initial stage of romance, our partner certainly can make us happy. We're feeling so accepted, validated, and loved by the intense admiration and affection of the other person. This admiration overrides our own inherent self-doubt. But that pleasant effect is soon going to wear thin when we harbor sizable unresolved issues in our psyche.

Unconsciously, we're always ready to act out these inner conflicts with our spouse. Unwittingly, we can even provoke our spouse into a fray in which these issues are experienced. When one partner, for instance, has unresolved conflicts concerning control or criticism, the other partner will unwittingly play into this dynamic and either become critical or controlling or become passive to being criticized and controlled. In this way, we bring out the worst in each other. Lacking self-knowledge, we tend to give to each other the negative experiences that the other is unconsciously looking for.

The *Journal of Marriage and Family* reports in a recent study that people who had difficult relationships with their parents are more likely years later to experience rocky romances.[82] (Most people do feel they had a difficult relationship with at least one parent.) The study only confirms what depth psychology has known all along. We act out with our romantic and marriage partners the same basic issues we experienced with our parents. Much of our psychological profile can be traced to childhood and how we experienced those early years. As mentioned, even with good and decent parents, children (who are subjective in their appraisal of what's happening) can at times feel refused, deprived, controlled, criticized, or rejected. These negative emotions continue to be trigger-points for us as adults. We can, of course, act out these emotions with bosses and friends, but a spouse is always "so handy."

We unconsciously pick romantic partners who remind us of traits and characteristics we experienced with one or both parents. This means we're ready to go on living through old experiences, even unpleasant and painful ones. For instance, someone who had a cold, rejecting mother is likely to pick a partner with those traits. Or, conversely, the individual who had the cold, rejecting mother picks a partner who is going to be, for the most part, unconsciously inclined to be on the receiving end of that treatment. In this case, the one who now doles out the rejection still resonates with that familiar pain because he or she identifies unconsciously with the one on the receiving end of it.

82
http://www.sciencedaily.com/releases/2014/02/140206101103.htm

In this regard, an important concept to understand is *transference*. As mentioned earlier, this refers to our expectation that someone (such as a spouse) will relate to us emotionally in line with (according to) how we're unconsciously prepared to suffer. We transfer on to our partner the expectation that he or she will frequently relate to us in, say, a critical or controlling fashion. We're now prepared, in such a situation, to experience criticism or control even when none is intended.

This self-knowledge is a great asset to the marriage. The couple understands that negative acting-out is a compulsion based on ignorance of underlying dynamics. Once the dynamics are made conscious, people lose interest in acting them out, and they can now more easily refrain from doing so. (The dynamics of transference, projection, and identification were discussed in "Three Great Truths from Psychology." Because of the importance of understanding them, I'm reviewing them again, with some new wording, in the context of marriage intimacy.)

It's also of great value to understand the role that the psychological dynamics of projection and identification play in a marriage. Through *projection*, one partner can see and hate in the other partner what this first partner is refusing to acknowledge in himself or herself. This dynamic often occurs in issues involving passivity. A wife might hate it when she sees her husband acting passively, and she gets upset or angry at him for his passivity. In this process, she's covering up her readiness to feel the passivity within herself. In other words, she resonates with her own passivity, and her annoyance or anger at him is a defense that serves to cover up this passivity. In fact, she may, in large part, have chosen him as a mate because of his passivity (particularly if she had a passive father), since unconsciously she's compelled through her own unresolved attachments to associate emotionally with passivity. So, in fact, both are harboring unresolved passivity and, unconsciously, both go looking for opportunities to act out their attachment to that negative emotion.

If she sees this and, through insight, begins to resolve her attachment to passivity, she'll be able to stop getting angry at her spouse. Now she's able to help herself (as well as him) resolve the passivity that's hurting both of them and blocking intimacy.

Through *identification*, a husband might get triggered, say, by his wife's critical assessment and rejection of his father. The husband identifies, through his father, with the feeling of being criticized and rejected. He instinctively defends his father, which leaves his wife feeling isolated and misunderstood. So the husband is not objective because, emotionally, he's prepared to take on feelings of criticism and rejection and then to defend against the realization that he's doing so. Again, he likely was attracted to his wife in the first place because he sensed her capacity for criticism and rejection, thereby enabling him to recreate and replay those old unresolved hurts. Though he's attached to feeling his wife's criticism and rejection, he hates it when it's happening and gets angry at her. The anger serves as a defense that covers up his attachment: "I don't expect or want to feel criticized—Look at how angry I get when it happens."

When couples understand these dynamics, they're able to resolve them. With this understanding, they communicate much more objectively and honestly. This clearing of the fog of inner conflict creates greater intimacy.

58. When Money Enriches Our Suffering

Money is important—it's the grease in the economic machine. Some of us, though, get that grease all over our clothes, hair, and skin. When our body is overlaid with it, and every pore sealed up, the smear of cold cash turns our humanity blue.

Money can be greasy to the touch, whether we have a lot of it or a little. A shortage of it provides us with the opportunity to feel deprived, refused, helpless, abandoned, unworthy and unloved. A big stash of it enables us to feel smug, intolerant, greedy, and fearful of losing it. We can use money to feel elation and to know despair. Like sex, romance, and food, it offers us a smorgasbord of positive and negative emotions.

How do plain old dollar bills get so entangled in our emotional life? All of us have unresolved conflicts in our psyche that produce emotional and behavioral difficulties, including self-doubt. This sense that we're lacking in value is a widespread human weakness. For many of us, it's part of our identity. Sometimes it's just a vague, uncertain sense of uneasiness. Giving up (or letting go of) this self-doubt can be difficult, even when we know we're good people trying our best to do what's right.

Self-doubt can stick to us like pennies dipped in Crazy Glue. Some people are strongly attached to the negative feeling, to the point where it produces self-pity, depression, and despair. Often we scramble to cover up, with psychological defenses, our attachment to (or resonance with) this painful self-doubt. Money, it turns out, can buy a lot of suffering and self-deception—and we don't even have to spend it. We can simply accumulate it, or we can long desperately to possess it. The more money we have or the more we want, the more we're using money (or *misusing* it) as a prop to avoid seeing our unconscious, emotional entanglement in feelings of unworthiness and helplessness.

In this manner, our high regard for money and our striving to accumulate it "prove" that, in denial of the underlying reality, we're not emotionally entangled in feelings of unworthiness. Our fondness for money, we claim, establishes our fervent desire to feel and portray our value. The more we value money, this rationalization claims, the more we can establish our own value by accumulating and hoarding money and by flashing it around.

This approach, of course, rests on a thin veneer. If the money is spent, stolen, or lost, we will easily collapse into a painful sense of physical and emotional destitution. People can thus become highly dependent on their wealth, and they're determined "for safety's sake" to accumulate more.

Money is also a counterfeit coin for measuring success and avoiding a sense of failure. Financial success can be associated emotionally with one's alleged superiority, while financial failure (or simply less-than-spectacular success) can be evaluated as an indication of inferiority.

On the playing field of our psyche, the desperate person slices and dices reality to "prove" his value and feel his "power." Typical risks associated with this interpretation of success include a ruthless ego, greed, a workaholic schedule, and cold-hearted ambition.

The miserly person—the kingpin of greed—displays an unwillingness to part with money in conjunction with an intense desire to accumulate more of it. Both of these behaviors are defenses. The first proclaims, "I'm not a weakling who can easily be separated from my money. I aggressively hold on to it. Not even the taxing authorities can get at it." The second defense might proclaim, in some cases, "I'm not a frightened weakling. Look at how aggressively I go after money. My professional money managers are the best and most aggressive in the business. I don't even care if they rob from the poor." Deep in their psyche, though, such individuals can live in anxious fear of being taken advantage of in money matters and losing what they do have. Their mentality underscores the power of unresolved negative emotions to torment us—even when all we're doing is *imagining* worst-case scenarios—no matter how much (or how little) money we have.

The hurt of deprivation also comes into play. A person can feel deprived just through the impression or the prospect of loss. Real loss is not needed for suffering to occur. We can plunge into discontent or distress simply by using our imagination to produce an impression that our assets are not as significant as we would like them to be. In the process of spending money or being asked for it, some of us can feel sharply reduced of assets, even if the amount spent or requested is a tiny percentage of what we own. It's as if who we are and what we have is cut in half. If, deep down, we're mired emotionally in a devaluation of our own personhood, $50 out-of-pocket can feel like forfeiture of a pound of flesh.

When asked for money, some people erupt in indignant anger: "You good-for-nothing! Go out and make your own money!" Instead of calm refusal, they express outrage. The outrage is a form of aggression that's employed to cover up inner passivity. Money neurotics feel that the requests made to them for money indicate that they're seen as an easy mark. No one would dare to ask them for money, their skewed reasoning goes, if they were a more formidable figure. The allegation that they're an easy mark comes from their inner critic, and they absorb the negativity contained in that criticism. In turn, they lash out critically at the one who requested the money. They also perceive, in the moment of being asked for money, weakness in the person who requests it, and they identify with that weakness. Their indignant anger is their attempt to cover up that identification.

All of us can embellish on the feeling that we'll be rendered helpless, and perhaps homeless, if we run out of money. True, if it happens we're likely be in a messy pickle. But people who worry about running out of money often never do. That means they worry for nothing. All their suffering is unnecessary. Still, they're determined to suffer in this way because of the human compulsion to feel and recycle unresolved negative emotions such as helplessness, abandonment, and unworthiness. To stop doing this, we just have to see more clearly into the irrationality of our worry, while exposing our secret desire to recycle unresolved negative emotions.

Our relationship to money is a huge national problem. Money in politics is corrupting our democracy. We all contribute to this corruption when money greases our inner conflicts instead of the economic machine.

59. **Being Seen in a Negative Light**

Many of us have had experiences of walking into a social situation and feeling shy, awkward, hesitant, and even fearful. Other times we can feel that people are scoffing at us because we apparently said something silly or foolish. We can also believe that our physical appearance or clothing is drawing critical attention, or that everyone was laughing at us when we played ineptly at the picnic volleyball game.

In self-centeredness, we typically exaggerate the degree to which people notice us or think critically about our appearance. Mentally or intellectually, we know that people have better things to do than to make us the center of their attention. They're often too preoccupied with their own lives to even pay us much notice. Emotionally, though, our impression can be very different: We can feel that others not only focus a lot of their attention on us but also think less of us. This is partly because, through our unresolved inner conflict, we make ourselves so much the center of our own attention and dwell on our alleged flaws and defects.

This feeling of being judged negatively comes and goes. Sometimes it seems to live inside us like an intestinal worm feeding off our entrails. We tell ourselves we're as worthy and good as anyone else. Yet our emotions often say otherwise. Our subjective impressions don't correspond to objective reality. Why is that?

Many of us are encumbered with an emotional attachment to the feeling of being seen in a negative light. This problem stems from an unresolved inner conflict. In our *conscious* mind, we want to be liked, admired, and respected. However, in our *unconscious* mind where our irrational emotions are rooted, we can expect to be seen in the opposite manner, as if we're unworthy of being liked, admired, or respected. As it happens, that's exactly how our inner critic usually regards us and treats us—or how, through inner passivity, we allow it to treat us.

Even though our unconscious expectation of being regarded negatively is irrational, it's still a powerful attachment in our psyche. We "know" ourselves through that feeling. This means that, in part, we identify with ourselves through the feeling. It's as if the negative feeling is an essential element of who we are. We won't be able to recognize ourselves without this feeling. We feel lost, disoriented, and even panicky without the reassurance of our familiar identity. Deep down, we remain emotionally unresolved with a sense of being unworthy, badly flawed, or just plain bad. Guilt and shame are usually associated with this painful sense of self, yet still we're locked in to this negative self-regard.

When it comes to being seen in a negative light, we're first in line to do it to ourselves. Our inner critic is a dependable backstabber, while our inner passivity keeps supplying it with knives. When we're watchful, we can see this conflict in ourselves. I had my own attachment to being seen in a negative light. One day 24 years ago, while working on my first book, I wrote a few thousand words that I felt were creative and insightful. That night I had a dream in which I was promoted to the rank of general and sent off to an overseas war-zone. Crowds cheered me on the way to the Tampa airport in an open-air limousine for my flight to the Middle East. In this dream (called "a dream of refutation") I tried to establish a defense (that I wanted to be cheered and admired) to cover up my unresolved attachment to being judged critically and, as it related to my book, having my work rejected. My identification with the general and my thrill in waving to the cheering crowds were intended to "prove" that I really wanted acceptance and admiration. By seeing through this defense and others like it, I've acquired the insight that reduced this inner conflict, and I've been able to acquire more self-respect along with a higher degree of writing proficiency.

Typical conflicts consist of wanting to be admired while expecting to be belittled, or anxiously seeking approval or validation while painfully anticipating or experiencing disapproval or rejection, or wanting to be powerful when inwardly programmed to revert to self-doubt. All of these involve experiences in which we feel others are seeing us in a negative light or in which we're seeing ourselves in such a light.

The interconnectedness of the mind and body is well documented, so it is no surprise that we are *physiologically* entangled in this painful identity. Our emotional life shows up, of course, in our facial expressions and body language. Many neuroscientists say that our sense of self emerges out of the staggering complexity of our brain's component parts. Does that mean that, according to this theory, our identity, our sense of self, consists of our brain's "hardware?" We might want to stop and ask, "Is it hardware or is it software?" That's a debate for the ages. In any case, how will knowledge of the brain's hardware and all the accompanying organic complexity help you and me to intervene at a personal level to relieve our suffering? Software, at least, can be updated and improved upon, which is what happens in our psyche when inner conflicts are resolved.

We know how to upgrade computer software, and now we're being challenged to upgrade our brain's software—in particular, our inner operating system—so that our perceptions correspond with objective reality and we avoid suffering for nothing. This enhancement of brain function involves raising the level of our consciousness. This means that those of us who are emotionally attached to being seen in a negative light become aware of this attachment. Otherwise, we'll be compelled to go on experiencing ourselves and behaving, as one example, according to the negative sense of how we believe the world sees us. This is a highly passive orientation.

Let's make insight the new world currency. It's a billion-dollar insight, as one example, to understand why people make such a cultural sport of seeing others in a negative light. Malicious gossip—along with florid media coverage of dishonorable, disgusting, and dopey behaviors—captures our attention because the subject provides us with some inner relief from self-criticism. "You see," our unconscious defense claims, "I'm not nearly as bad as that person." We are also eager to be offended by the questionable or foolish behaviors of others because we're so ready to cast them in a negative light. Through such insight, we see ourselves with new understanding, as creatures who have been held accountable by the primitive, negative inner critic. Through this inner dynamic, we've been treating ourselves like second-class citizens. When we seize upon this knowledge, we can stop seeing ourselves the way our inner critic sees us. Now that we see this inner truth, we know we want to rise above it.

Remember, too, that any tendency we have to seeing others in a negative light dovetails with our own emotional attachment to being seen that way and seeing ourselves that way. When we stop being judgmental or comparing ourselves to others, we step out of the shadow of negative light.

V - THE PSYCHE'S INFLUENCES ON SOCIETY

60. **How Inner Passivity Robs Men of Power**

An acquaintance of mine (I'll call him Sam) was arrested recently for obstruction of justice. He was pulled over by the police because his vehicle fit the description of one that had been stolen. Though innocent, Sam, who's in his late-twenties, became rude and uncooperative. When he could produce only an expired vehicle registration, he was handcuffed, taken to jail, and his vehicle impounded. His case was later dismissed, but he paid a price in time, money, and misery.

I've spent some time in Sam's company and I know something of his state of mind. He's a smart, caring, and loyal person. But he has a significant emotional weakness. He's quick to feel that people are trying to control, dominate, or oppress him, and he's adopted an anti-authority outlook on life that can be traced back to this emotional weakness. Because of this, he interprets authority as something unpleasant or bad that needs to be resisted.

Deposits of inner passivity are contained in Sam's psyche. Inner passivity, as I describe it here and in many of my other books, is a feature of human nature. It's a leftover mental-emotional residue from the stages of helplessness and dependence we experience through our childhood years. It tends to remain in our psyche as an emotional default position. When we're not aware of it, we can fall prey to its influence and become weak, ineffective, and prone to self-defeat. Instead of possessing true power, we're likely to react unresponsively, passive-aggressively, or with belligerent self-defeating aggression.

When Sam was pulled over, he obviously reacted unwisely to the authority of the police. Normally, we grant to police officers the expectation that they'll handle their authority appropriately. If stopped by them, we're wise to be polite and cooperative, thereby showing that we command respect. However, when inner passivity is acting up in our psyche, we can easily feel intimidated by a policeman's authority. His authority feels like a form of oppression or domination. We sense we're being (or going to be) bullied or that we'll become victims of an injustice. When we experience legitimate authority through inner passivity, we're obviously being weak. Yet, paradoxically, we can be inclined to react with hostility or belligerence to "prove" we're not weak. In this way, Sam's sense of freedom is limited and he can't trust himself to stay out of trouble.

When stopped by police, he slipped into defiance as a reaction to (and cover-up of) his unconscious predisposition to emotionally misinterpret the policeman's authority. When inner passivity is triggered, our unconscious mind prompts us to cover up (or defend against realization of) our affinity in that moment for feeling controlled, dominated, or oppressed. At such a moment, passive-aggressive resistance is the only sense of strength we're able to muster. The resistance is an unconscious defense which claims, "I'm not being weak or passive. Look at how resistant and defiant I am." Of course, the real strength in such a moment is to be calm and non-reactive.

It's irrational to interpret all forms of authority as oppressive or bad, and that irrationality arises out of inner conflict. As I've said, the primary conflict in the human psyche is between inner aggression (inner critic) and inner passivity. Our inner aggression, as mentioned, is a primitive force that possesses little kindness or justice. This aggression can rule our inner life, particularly when we enable it (or facilitate its existence and power) through our inner passivity. Our inner aggression is a form of injustice and harassment, though often we're unaware of its existence. This inner experience is then transferred into the world around us, which means that authority vested in others (e.g., coming from parents, teachers, bosses, the police, corporations, and government) can now be experienced by us as abusive or oppressive. Out of such inner weakness, we're now in danger of making oppression a self-fulfilling outcome.

Inner passivity, of course, is a problem for women as well as men. Both sexes are equally susceptible to it. This discussion, however, examines more aspects of its impact on men. More so than women, men are held accountable by their inner critic when they fail to establish a satisfactory career or when they're unable to project a forceful presence in their circle of family and friends. (Though women are not necessarily more passive than men, they can more easily find social acceptance, and hence inner acceptance, for their passive tendencies.) Even men who others regard as successful frequently grapple with an inner critic that claims they still haven't done enough or haven't lived up to expectations.

Again, individuals with substantial deposits of inner passivity resonate emotionally with feeling oppressed because they allow themselves to be oppressed by their inner critic. They say they hate oppression, but oppression is a familiar inner experience. They're even emotionally attached to this feeling, and it shapes in large measure their identity or sense of self. Some men give up and stop trying to fulfill themselves through work or careers, or even as husbands and fathers. This capitulation can serve as a psychological defense which, expressed unconsciously, claims: "I'm not interested in feeling powerless or overwhelmed by my options or situation. On the contrary, I'm quite comfortable with just being a passive observer of life." They may temporarily numb themselves to their malaise, but emotional complications can loom in their future.

Many cultural and economic influences challenge the male psyche. Experts agree that boys and young men are less aggressive and less resilient than previous generations. Several possible causes are cited, including a lack of mentoring and good male role-models, intrusive parents, overprescribing of psychiatric drugs, the prevalence of illicit drugs, the presence of toxic endocrine disruptors in the environment, the influence of education that some say favors feminine values, and the influences of video games, online pornography, and gaming. Certainly, commercial forces are pandering to human weakness and likely reinforcing it, as violence is displayed ever more graphically in the movies and while casinos are presented as reputable entertainment centers and sexual prowess is packaged in prescriptions. Young men face much more competition in the workplace from women who, much of the time, are smarter, especially in communication skills. For boys and young men, modern life is very complicated with all of its distractions, options, and challenges, so they need emotional strength and better psychological knowledge to avoid feeling overwhelmed.

Men are bombarded daily with thousands of subliminal impressions that imply they're not measuring up. Many TV commercials present men as passive patsies who cower to celebrities or who won't be whole or complete without some particular product or lifestyle choice. During elections, negative advertising often presents male politicians as incompetent fools. Perhaps most trying of all, a difficult labor market and high unemployment create the impression that one's contribution to the world, if not one's very being, is not valued. If unemployed or under-employed, they can't point to work and income as ways to validate and appreciate themselves.

Sensual gratification can be achieved passively through virtual friends and copious entertainment and social media options. If these experiences aren't making you happy, the implication goes, something's wrong with you. Without meaningful work, however, it's not easy to avoid depression, apathy, cynicism, and anti-social behaviors. With consumerism, an entitlement mentality, and individual gratification driving the economy, the lure of drugs and the specter of mental illness may harken. How many men who would otherwise remain stable are sinking into the clutches of paranoid, antisocial, narcissistic, obsessive-compulsive, depressive, dependent, and avoidant personality disorders? Men returning from war with post-traumatic stress disorder can face steeper uphill struggles.

Nevertheless, we must believe these difficult challenges aren't going to defeat us. More awareness of inner passivity offers powerful guidance for moving forward.

This hidden aspect of human nature, a leftover from childhood experiences and a flaw in our biology, is neither good nor bad. It's *not* a disease or a mental illness. It's more like a hurdle in the path of human evolution. If we don't see it, we just keep crashing into it. When we begin to bring it into focus, we connect with our goodness and power.

61. The Psychological Roots of National Disunity

To judge by the extent of social incivility and political conflict, Americans seem to be suffering from an epidemic of neurosis. I attribute this discord, in part, to the fact that academic psychology has turned its back on depth psychology and neglected to give prominence to the role that inner conflict plays in personal and national dysfunction. We aren't being taught what we need to know.

Too much inner conflict produces too much outer conflict. What could be more obvious?

Consider, for instance, the moral philosophies of individualism and solidarity. They clash upon the withered plain, battling for the soul of America. As moral positions, both individualism and solidarity obviously have commendable aspects. Individualism represents self-reliance and independence, while solidarity or community represents social unity, common cause, and an expansive understanding of what constitutes self-interest. All these aspects are important to our well-being.

Conservatives, for the most part, stand behind the former philosophy, while Liberals are tied to the latter. An intense conflict is disuniting the people, and we're all suffering. There need not be such division and antagonism between these two moral positions or between Liberals and Conservatives. Their positions are not mutually exclusive. The clash over which philosophy ought to prevail turns negative and hostile only because the human psyche is, in itself, so conflict-ridden. (Many people are neck-deep in politics, so I'll try in the following pages to cross the Potomac without splashing cold water on partisan sensitivities.)

Millions of people vote in state and national elections on the basis of negative emotions and self-centered perspectives that are often unconscious. People often vote according to their particular brand of resentment or bitterness. On the surface, we can deceive ourselves with righteous posturing and displays of moral superiority that cover up varying degrees of fear, helpless feelings, and an instinct to be critical and negative. Consequently, there's insufficient levity or lightness of spirit.

It's our unconscious mind that's contaminating the debate, widening the divide, and creating unnecessary misunderstanding and hostility. Often we align ourselves with one side or another of a political or social conflict for personal, emotional, or psychological reasons that are hidden from our awareness and have nothing to do with the merits of the debate. We sometimes take stances on political issues to keep our personal blind spots covered up. Political and social beliefs or alignments that are adopted for hidden psychological reasons are likely to be rigidly held, hostile to opposing views, and self-defeating.

Let's consider some hidden reasons that cause people to become partisans for individualism. (Further on, I discuss hidden motivations for embracing solidarity.) Individualists see the government as a dispenser of dependence in the form of welfare, health care, food stamps, social security, disability payments, Medicare, and so on. Many of these individuals, far from simply asserting a preference for standing on one's own two feet, are forced by inner weakness to assert a passionate dislike for any form of dependence. They're denying or covering up their entanglement in unresolved negative emotions such as helplessness, passivity, fear of change, and self-doubt. They project their own weakness on to the recipients of government benefits, which means that, with intense dislike, they "see" in these recipients what they refuse to see in themselves.

Many conservatives and individualists can be found among the poor. These individuals often feel marginalized, ignored, rejected, and unworthy. These painful impressions, incidentally, often reflect how, psychologically, they can feel about themselves. By placing individualism in such high regard, they're able to produce a sense of personal value and power. In other words, emphasizing one's individuality can serve as a psychological trick for giving oneself a feeling of importance and strength. As another psychological defense to cover up inner weakness, they're tempted to identify with the right-wing's more aggressive military tilt regarding international challenges.

People from all classes can favor individualism because they believe that freedom must be measured primarily through the rights and privileges of each citizen. This belief, when accompanied by refusal to recognize economic opportunity and government protection as important measures of freedom, can denote an entitlement mentality. Moreover, we can't trust individualism to stand alone as a healthy guide to wise action and behavior because our conflict-ridden psyche produces too much self-sabotage, willful ignorance, and self-serving behaviors. Tens of millions of individual Americans are floundering in unhealthy, unwise, and dysfunctional behaviors. If *individually* we can't be trusted to do what's right for ourselves, how can *individualism* as a guiding principle be trusted on its own to do what's right for the nation or the world?

Let's cross to the other side and take a look at issues concerning solidarity. Behind the embrace of solidarity can lurk a psychological attempt to compensate for feeling insignificant, unworthy, and powerless. Deep down a person can feel, "I have value because my group sees my value and champions my rights." But this sense of value isn't grounded in one's own person. This illustrates how we can have different defenses—such as the emotional misuse of either the concept of individualism or that of solidarity—for the same underlying dysfunction.

It's true, of course, that solidarity (as it applies to labor unions, for instance) can represent genuine political or economic power. However, it's not an intrinsic or psychological power. Solidarity that's not grounded in our self-development can be crushed by determined opponents. When that happens, people who relied on such solidarity for their sense of standing and well-being can be left feeling empty and vanquished.

People on the Left, too, can have an entitlement mentality. Out of inner weakness or lack of consciousness, many people on both the Left and Right take themselves and life for granted. Now they also can take their government and its largesse for granted, leading to the development of an entitlement mentality.

Everyone at times deals with deep feelings and fears of being utterly alone. Childish fantasies of being powerful and special can collapse into emptiness, passivity, and feelings of abandonment. All that can save us, it might feel to those on the Left, is the cohesion of the collective. From this weakness, they can also embellish upon the sense of being innocent victims of the alleged malice of private interests, with only their group and the government to protect them.

Meanwhile, both sides can contribute to widening the divide when it feels that the other side is "forcing" a point of view down one's throat. This negative feeling is an emotional reaction to humanity's widespread tendency to feel oppressed, controlled or dominated—even when actual control or domination is not the intent of the other side. Many of us don't know how to live free from a sense of oppression. We may have been raised in a family where one or both parents—and siblings—bullied us, bossed us around, or demanded in a mean-spirited or self-centered manner that we submit to their authority. As adults, we can still feel that we have to answer to someone, whether a boss, spouse, or faceless bureaucrats. In this frame of mind, we can experience society's well-founded rules, protocols, taxes, and other prerequisites of civilization as forms of oppression. Meanwhile, we also live intimately with the domination of our own inner critic, making oppression an even more familiar feeling.

Our emotional attachment to feelings of being oppressed are invariably covered up through denial and other psychological defenses. As evidence, the Left and the Right spend a great deal of time complaining about how things *are* and lecturing about how things ought *to be*. Our greater good is served by our determination to maintain our integrity and keep our spirits up—and fight our civic battles, if need be—even when political or economic conditions are far from perfect.

Both sides of the political divide fear being oppressed, one side by the private sector and the other by the public. Both resonate with old irrational fears, and both can display an entitlement mentality. We're all still emotionally unresolved, in varying degrees, with childhood feelings of being passive, helpless, and at the mercy of others. We also fear being seen as worthless and crushed underfoot. Because inner conflict is reflected in political and social situations, both sides produce someone or something to be in conflict with. As well, conflict with our compatriots is close to home, which replicates the intimate proximity of inner conflict.

We're more alike than we thought. Insight into our shared psychology makes it easier to transcend our differences. As we heal the discord in ourselves, we feel the unity of humanity. Recognizing our shared nature, we see our commonality.

Around the world the complexity of modern life contributes to personal distress, as does the effect on us of misguided leaders and anti-democratic forces in government and corporations. Yet our psyche, like a Model-T Ford sputtering along a superhighway, remains our primary weak spot. Psychologically, we operate according to old-fashioned principles. We're quick to blame others for allegedly causing our pain. We want to attribute our neurotic suffering to the stupid beliefs and rotten behavior of others. The more we blame the other, though, the more we dislike or hate the other and the less clearly we see the essentials of our predicament. We also suffer more acutely from our own unresolved negative emotions.

To avoid a dire fate, we need to see how our psyche is a cauldron of drives, wishes, defenses, aggression, and passivity. We need to become smarter in order to regulate our psyche's byproducts: irrational beliefs, phony defenses, negative impressions, resistances to facing reality, cravings for distractions, and self-defeating reactions. Much of modern psychology is far too superficial to be of help.

This old political order in the human psyche needs to be upgraded. Life is now too perilous. We have to start operating at a higher level of intelligence and consciousness. We certainly can't trust the elites to lead the way. We have to do it ourselves. When more people engage in astute self-reflection, we'll see the futility and foolishness of mutual animosity. Negativity will be replaced by the ability to engage the other side rationally and heartily in the battle for our psyche's liberation and democracy's soul.

Harmony will follow when we better understand the hidden dynamics that bind us to conflict. We find inner balance when our personal issues are recognized and resolved, at which time political and social harmony come along for the ride.

62 . Stressed Out in America

The 134,000-member American Psychological Association recently published its annual report on stress.[83] The report is trademarked: Stress in America.™ Yet this official stamp of self-approval can't hide the hollowness of the report.

Millions of Americans are struggling to keep their stress levels down. It's vitally important that mental-health professionals provide the media with high quality psychological knowledge concerning this epidemic of misery. This knowledge should be made available at every opportunity. As in previous years, however, the APA's latest report offers mostly numerical findings and percentage comparisons. Such information fails to provide deeper understanding about the origins and causes of high stress.

The report's numbers really only disclose that a bad situation appears to be getting worse: During the school year American teenagers experience more stress than adults, and teens believe the stress they're experiencing far exceeds what might be considered healthy. Only 16 percent believe their stress level is on the decline, the report says, while twice as many teens say their stress level has increased and will likely continue to increase. The report is based on a survey done last summer of 1,950 adults and 1,038 teens.

The APA does mention that money and work continue to be the most commonly mentioned stressors for adults, adding that "these issues are complex and difficult to manage, often leading to more stress over time…." Yet

---

[83] http://www.apa.org/news/press/releases/stress/index.aspx

the report says nothing that might at least hint at how and why issues concerning money and work "are complex and difficult to manage." (I come back to this point further on.)

The APA notes that the majority of teens say the challenges they face at school are a major source of their stress. However, no details are provided that might explain why the school experience is so stressful. The report says, "Many teens also report feeling overwhelmed (31 percent) and depressed or sad (30 percent) as a result of stress." This statement implies that the stress itself is causing those negative emotions, but it can also be the other way around: Negative emotions caused by inner conflict are producing the stress. Yet the APA does not mention how such *internal* factors, in addition to external ones, contribute to stress.

It's true that our world can be intense and feel stressful. We're also dealing with new stress factors such as the ever-increasing assault of noise.[84] Yet we get a respite, too, because we don't live in a violent, lawless society as many of our ancestors did, and modern medicine provides us more security from illness or accident. When it comes to stress, what matters most is not the actual conditions of our life but how we *experience* our life *and* ourselves. One person experiences anguish and paralysis from the same source that motivates another. Our problem with stress has to be considered in the context of our own personal psychology. Insight into our own issues can greatly relieve our stress.

---
[84] http://www.nytimes.com/2012/07/20/nyregion/in-new-york-city-indoor-noise-goes-unabated.html?_r=3&

Some stress is unavoidable, of course, given life's many challenges. Yet stress is also produced unwittingly within us, often to a degree that becomes quite painful. The following example looks at self-induced stress concerning the issue—money—that's cited in the report. Money can cause stress, of course, when people don't have enough of it to pay their bills or buy food. The following example, however, looks at the situation in which people with sufficient money become stressed because they feel it isn't enough. (This discussion covers issues mentioned earlier—see "When Money Enriches Our Suffering"—but here I make a more direct connection to stress.)

Money can be exceedingly important to teenagers and adults as a form of status. Having status is a way to feel accepted and even to feel superior. It's common for us to experience ourselves through feelings of self-doubt, emptiness, and unworthiness. Many smart people making their way in the world harbor conscious and unconscious self-doubt. Deep down, many of us brush up against feelings of being inauthentic or phony. We can't feel our goodness or integrity. The problem can be traced to an inner conflict: While we consciously want to feel good about ourselves, we're prone to experiencing painful self-doubt that results from unresolved inner conflict.

Hence, an asset such as money can become exceedingly important. The money serves as evidence or "proof" of having value. People are now using money for an impossible purpose, to fill an emotional hole. Money becomes inordinately important to them, and they can feel anxiety, tension, and stress in their belief and fear that they don't have enough.

The psychological solution is to recognize one's emotional attachment to, or identification with, the notion or impression of lacking value. Usually that attachment is unconscious. Of course, we're really not lacking in value. Each of us is just as valuable and worthy as the next person. But our emotions have a life and a "rationality" of their own. Though our impression of lacking value is irrational, we tend to remain entangled in such unresolved negative emotions from our conflicted and subjective impressions of childhood.

When fretting over money in this way, the individual can now become aware of his or her attachment to the impression of lacking in essential, intrinsic value. The person becomes conscious of the unconscious choice he or she has been making to feel that emptiness or unworthiness and to recycle that feeling.

When we see this choice, and bring the inner conflict into focus, we can now say "No Thanks" to the negative experience and free ourselves from it. Of course, we usually have to do this repeatedly over time to make it stick. That means we have to learn this knowledge—this particular insight about the nature of our suffering—and be willing to apply it with attention to our everyday experiences.

We can also acquire insight by understanding the psychological defense that keeps the attachment from becoming conscious. We can begin to understand that the yearning for money serves as a defense. The unconscious defense contends: "I'm not interested in feeling insignificant or unworthy. Look at how good I feel when I have money. This is how I want to feel." This is, of course, a lie (albeit, an unconscious one) we tell ourselves. When we see the truth behind the defense, we become conscious of what was previously unconscious. Now we benefit by knowing what is true and real about our inner life, even as it's a bit humbling to see this truth.

When money is used as a prop in an unstable defense, the individual becomes stressed-out about money. This person is actually required over time to be more anxious about money, and thereby to feel the stress more acutely, in order to maintain the effectiveness of the defense.

Seeing through this defense raises our intelligence. We now see our own role in producing stress. We have now identified the conflict: "I want to feel value, but I'm attached to *not* feeling value." We understand how money is being used as a defense, and that the defense is part of our resistance to seeing ourselves objectively. This awareness makes it possible for us, through our enhanced intelligence, to resolve the conflict and reduce the stress. Of course, there are many other ways that money, work, and other facets or life are involved in emotional conflict, and all of these ways can be revealed, published, and learned in order to help lessen our stress.

Money is also an "antidote" and defense for people who are determined unconsciously to go through life feeling deprived or refused. These two negative emotions, which produce the-glass-is-half-empty syndrome, are left over from childhood. When unresolved, these negative emotions produce greed, envy, anxiety, and stress.

Knowledge such as this can be learned by just about everyone. The APA and other mental-health organizations have to make a better effort to get beneath the symptoms and to dispense relevant knowledge—not just a bunch of statistics and percentages—about all the ways we produce stress from within.

63. Lincoln's Integrity, Our Integrity

Integrity, as personified in Abraham Lincoln, has gone missing in the American soul, like Bernie Madoff's billions. The nation's future harmony and prosperity may depend on restoring this vital virtue.

We can understand integrity if, through our imagination, we step into the spirit of Lincoln, our secular saint. First, let's consider what integrity (and the lack of it) means.

The lack of this virtue in American life is like a trillion-dollar campaign contribution to national self-sabotage. Wall Street's financial follies, as one example, are a study in the art of manifest unscrupulousness. With this fraudulency comes enormous grief and misery.

Corrupt financiers and self-serving politicians must be among the unhappiest people in the world. That's because integrity is a necessary ingredient in stable, lasting happiness. Integrity is an expression of self-respect. The virtue of integrity develops as we feel our intrinsic goodness and care about our personal honor. For this reason, integrity guides us to do the right thing even when nobody's going to know whether we did so or not.

Our integrity won't allow us to tarnish that precious feeling of our essential honor and self-respect. When integrity guides us to do what's right, we essentially do it for our own sake.

Integrity also accesses inner truth and thereby raises our intelligence. We start to realize that other people have as much value and goodness as we can feel in ourselves. When we feel true self-respect, we know that everyone else is entitled to that same sense of inner value. Even criminals get respect, in the sense that we profess an ideal that gives them a fair trial, humane imprisonment, and a chance at rehabilitation.

The Greek words 'integritas' and 'integra' mean whole. Our integrity requires wholeness, almost holiness. We protect the sanctity of our mind and body. We care about the sanctity of life because we feel that in ourselves. The feeling of integrity is our guide to wisdom and truth. We feel the virtues of openness, kindness, and generosity—and we act accordingly. Now we can access the meaning of liberty, which is to live in a society where laws, custom, and civility afford us and others full respect. The spirit of liberty and the social pact of mutual respect constitute the foundation of American democracy, more so than laws that can be twisted and contorted.

If we don't have this consciousness, meaning the knowing that our own well-being is intimately associated with the needs and happiness of others, we descend into the hollowness of egotism, narcissism, entitlement, and individualism. Wholeness and integrity are shattered.

The testimony is overwhelming that Lincoln had a great respect for all of life. Lincoln "had an unusually intense sympathy with the suffering of his fellow creatures," writes William Lee Miller in *Lincoln's Virtues: An Ethical Biography* (Alfred A. Knopf, New York, 2007).

This sympathy extended also, as is not always the case with animal lovers, to his fellow human beings: to the old Indian who wandered into the camp; the woman whose drunken husband beat her; the farm boy who is going to be shot for falling asleep on sentry duty; the coffle of slaves on the boat in the Ohio, chained together like fish on a line.

In his reflections on slavery, writes Miller, Lincoln was constant in his adherence to the idea that the United States "was founded upon the proposition that all men are created equal, as stated in the Declaration of Independence." In the finest meaning of integrity, all parts of the whole are of equal value. As Lincoln understood, the whole can't be broken down into lesser values. The whole and the parts are one, hence the Union.

The word integrity applies to a code of moral values. Lincoln, writes Miller, displayed "a distinct quality of tact, generosity, and civility" in his dealings with supporters, opponents, editors, and clients. Lincoln also applied the principles of integrity to his concept of the nation. Throughout the Civil War, Lincoln never wavered in his commitment to the *integrity* of the Union. In his mind, the Union was unbroken. For Lincoln, the Civil War was a rebellion or insurrection, not a war between two sovereign states. Because he had personal integrity and hence inner union, he could stand more forcefully against the threat to the integrity of the Union.

How do we raise our level of integrity? We all can be lacking in integrity to the degree that we're entangled in hostile, negative feelings toward those who don't see or interpret the world as we do. We need to close the gap between the ideals we profess and the negativity we feel.

In part, the process involves personal insight into our own emotional or psychological weaknesses. Self-knowledge that is assimilated overcomes personal dysfunction. Inner conflict is resolved. We break the stranglehold of unresolved negative emotions. Individually, we become *integrated.* We establish an *inner union* as the contentious dynamics and forces in our psyche are subdued.

Imagine being Lincoln. There's a lot of power in coolly walking up to a recognized political adversary and being genuinely friendly. Being negative, in contrast, is the path of least resistance, the approach that triggers opposition. (Read Sun Tzu's *The Art of War* for lessons on the importance of "knowing yourself" and winning without falling into the pits of negativity.) Of course, Lincoln was also ruthless in his pursuit of victory. Yet that didn't tarnish his integrity because there was no malice or self-aggrandizement in his ruthlessness. Dwight Eisenhower displayed similar character during World War II.

Integrity is a quality that helps us to ensure success and victory. With integrity, we have the courage to be true to our beliefs. Integrity won't tolerate moral failure. That means we avoid being apathetic, passive, or emotionally entangled in the victim mentality. With integrity, we're able to avoid the psychological pitfalls of inner passivity—willful ignorance, cognitive dissonance, omission bias, and the other means of sidestepping issues and reality.

Integrity enables us to be powerful. We need the power not just to resist bad things but to reform bad things. Yet weak people often associate power with being negative. They can't feel power unless they're angry or condemning of others or feeling cynical. If we're too negative, malice and self-centeredness will override our integrity, and we'll be stuck in inertia, cynicism, and the deadlocked status quo.

64. A Participant in National Self-Sabotage

Who dares suggest the American dream could be thwarted by an indistinct entity a mere two letters long? The CIA certainly doesn't have a dossier on it. Yet one ingredient of personal suffering and national self-sabotage is the *id*. Yes, I know that's an odd, whimsical word, one that many of us, should it zip across our mind, dismiss as harmless jargon.

Yet psychoanalysis has taken the id very seriously. The discipline defines the id as the primitive, unconscious part of our mind that induces us to pursue self-centered gratification, often at the expense of wise self-regulation. For reasons I'm about to discuss, the id appears to be particularly virulent in the American psyche.

The id is like a virus or bug of the unconscious mind. And it can wreak as much havoc on the national scene as swarms of computer viruses. We have an impressive national-security apparatus in place to block out hackers. But in blindness to the enemy within, nobody's minding the id.

Civilization and national life are extensions of our consciousness. Despite that direct correlation between the inner and outer world, the media hardly ever talk about the psychological dysfunction of our leaders or write much that's insightful about the mental-emotional components in everyday political and social conflicts. To give them some due, the media are beginning to explore the psychological dynamics of family life and to look deeper into the roots of financial instability.

Any media discussion of the enemy within is usually a reference to domestic terrorists. The inner world of our secret motivations and intentions seems to be taboo. Yet psychological dysfunction is at play in our financial meltdowns, no-win political brinkmanship, nuclear-weapons proliferation, and climate change. One aspect of self-sabotage is our stubborn refusal to speak more openly about these subversive realities.

The id is one such reality, a secret inner saboteur that can be kept in check with more insight and awareness. I refer to the id metaphorically as a bug or virus, but it's more accurately understood as a psychological drive. It compels us to pursue the pleasure principle, often rambunctiously in the form of a craving for excitement and often at the expense of restraint, self-regulation, and healthy living. It subscribes to the ideologies of self-aggrandizement and hedonism. Our id is *not* infused with the consciousness of evolving humanity, so it pursues the base, instinctive forms of pleasure associated with sensation—sex, aggression, power, superiority, and accumulation. It has no affinity for integrity, wisdom, and compassion. Sometimes it is moderated by our superego and unconscious ego, which are other agencies of our psyche I have been writing about. Fortunately, the id answers at times to common sense, social mores, and guilt. Other times the law, when it's up to the task, keeps its most wanton thoughtlessness and impulses in check.

Still the mischief it makes in our psyche spills into national life. It incites, for instance, our entitlement mentality, as it denies the need for active acknowledgement of climate change or self-regulation of unrestrained individualism. It probably fuels, in part, the profit motive, that base instinct of capitalism that puts the accumulation of money ahead of the virtues of integrity and wisdom.

What conditions have enabled the id to dominate the personality of so many Americans? Centuries ago an aggressive, laissez-faire mercantile culture was transplanted here from England and elsewhere in Europe, and it may have fused with a "take-all-you-can-get" approach to conquering and possessing the limitless wilderness. After the yoke of English oppression was lifted following the Revolutionary War, the jubilant American psyche, ravenous for the perks of manifest destiny, appears to have produced the conqueror and hustler archetypes. These two exuberant sub-personalities swept across the frontier uttering the mantra, "We can now take and have whatever we want." In the 1790s, as Joyce Appleby describes in *Capitalism and a New Social Order*, the definition of virtue underwent a reversal—from putting public interests above private aspirations to pursuing personal gratification in an opportunistic new world.[85] This ideology, wedded to the American Dream, has since kept at bay attempts to upgrade to a more balanced system of national life, one that will produce much more overall happiness than does self-preoccupation.

Even Ivy League colleges, our best centers of learning, have stumbled blindly into the embrace of arrogance and further tipped the inner psychic balance in favor of the id. Andrew Delbanco, director of American studies at Columbia University, writes that Harvard, Yale, and Princeton were founded by "stringent Protestants" on the belief that the elite were granted their status through God's mercy, not through any worthiness of their own.[86] Accordingly, members of the elite were expected to work and live on behalf of others. Now, according to Prof. Delbanco, the elite college culture "encourages smugness and self satisfaction. . ." Deans and presidents greet new students "with congratulations for being the best and brightest ever to walk through the gates." They are taught, he says, that those who don't attend an Ivy League or equivalent school are beneath them. What they aren't taught, however, is basic self-knowledge. They aren't being humbled and enlightened by the ego-shattering revelations of depth psychology.

Our psychological ignorance is not something for which we are to blame. The inner world—the *terra incognita* of our psyche—is our last frontier, and the time has come

---

[85] http://www.barnesandnoble.com/w/capitalism-and-a-new-social-order-joyce-appleby/1101386844?ean=9780814705834&itm=1&usri=9780814705834

[86] http://www.nytimes.com/2012/03/09/opinion/colleges-and-elitism.html

to begin to populate the backwoods of our being with our humanity and our consciousness. We'll go on producing self-sabotage and suffer greatly if we don't make a conscious effort to raise our individual and collective awareness. We experience humility when we uncover the mysterious dynamics of our psyche because we expose the blindness of our egotism and the marauding of the id. That humility becomes the foundation of wisdom and inner power.

65 . **A Singular Cause of War**

Political scientists and other experts say there is no simple cause of war. Human nature, they say, is just another ingredient in the recipe for war, along with varying portions of racism and religion, geography and language, and economics and culture. This notion that war arises from highly complex factors conveys the idea that ordinary people are simply not going to understand it. In other words, war is too complicated for us to prevent.

Conveniently, that lets our leaders off the hook for starting wars and it lets us taxpayers off the hook for financing them. War, to put it in the guilt-free passive tense, just happens. In fact, war can be understood in simple terms that enable us to take responsibility for this continuing shame upon the honor of our species.

Many people believe that war is necessary to protect ourselves from mortal enemies. For a time, certainly, we have to be positioned to protect ourselves from the brutal mentality that taints much of humankind. It's that primitive, brutal mentality that's the enemy, not the people themselves. When we eliminate this mentality in ourselves, we'll be eliminating it in the world.

Most people cite aggression as a primary cause of war. However, underneath the aggression, deep in our unconscious mind, resides the passivity that enables war to occur. This inner passivity largely takes the form of self-doubt about one's value and significance. Inner passivity is a void, a heart of darkness pulsating in an empty chamber. A main cause of war is our difficulty in recognizing this emptiness, this waste land in our psyche where our consciousness and humanity have not penetrated. When this inner landscape of non-being is extensive, we can't more fully feel our humanity. We're much more likely to feel our brutality instead. From that vantage, we can't feel the horror of war or the shame of being associated with it. We can't connect with our authentic self which would decline to be involved in war.

Our self-doubt or lack of inner authority is expressed in these terms: "Who am I to question authority and say I know the truth of what is right or wrong?" When we're growing in consciousness, however, we do know, more precisely than ever, what is right and wrong. We're able to take personal responsibility for wars fought in our name. We begin to experience—in our families, communities, and workplaces—the capacity to resolve conflict without violence or even rancor.

What are some ingredients of this mentality? Our self-doubt or inner passivity produces, along with doubts about our value and significance, something even more sinister: a deep conviction of our worthlessness. As mentioned, we repress (keep secret from our awareness) our identification with this passive, negative feeling. Our egotism, narcissism, and entitlement mentalities—along with religious fundamentalism and ideological certainty—are all compensations for this underlying identification with ourselves as marginal voices or inconsequential representatives of humanity.

We can see evidence for this in the appeal of violent movies and video games. It's exhilarating or emotionally satisfying for moviegoers who are secretly harboring a sense of worthlessness to see people being slaughtered. Real or alleged villains and innocent bystanders are identified as worthless or expendable as they are gunned down or blasted away. Their demise is more likely to be met by cheers than tears because, on the surface, viewers identify with the aggressors, the violent "heroes" who prevail. In the case of violent video games, the viewer or player is the aggressor, a role that's addictive for passive boys and men. Their defense goes like this: "I'm not emotionally identified with my own worthlessness and passivity; if anything, I identify with the righteous, powerful aggressors!"

The same inner process is at play with cop shows on TV. Consciously, the viewers, largely from among the poor, identify with the police, though their real psychological intrigue is in their identification with the "worthless" misfits, the strays from their own class, who are featured in the broadcasts. The real emotional resonance for most of these viewers is with these petty criminals and their friends and families, not with the police.

Our wars are byproducts of our unconscious need for enemies. In our wars, we behave like the ancients, making human sacrifice to the gods, in our case to the gods of our psyche. Our psyche demands, as our price for our unconscious determination to go on resonating with feelings of worthlessness, that we project that worthlessness on to others. With our drones and missiles, we don't even have to get our hands dirty. When we fight others violently on the pretext that they might endanger us at some point in the future, we have identified them as worthless in the present moment. Even if, as in Vietnam and Iraq, we fail to win our wars, we still have succeeded in identifying the "enemy" as beneath us. We also sacrifice our wealth, even our souls, to cover up this dark stain on our psyche, this truth that threatens our ego and self-image, that we possess uniformly and universally the same psyche, one that harbors a smirking Gollum, the prince of our dark side and the saboteur of our humanity.

The rich and the elite are as unconscious as the poorest among us. How many members of the elite feel that, without ego and wealth, they are nothingness itself? Their insensitivity to the rest of us is their unresponsiveness to their better self. Does their war-profiteering testify to their disgust with the commonness of humanity? Do they avoid looking into the eyes of the poor because they see themselves reflected back? Meanwhile, we're trapped along with them in the kill-or-be-killed Matrix, with many of us loitering in the den of good and evil. This is why our labor can be bought so cheaply, our health system denies us the right to life, racism lurks in the hearts of the repressed, and poor criminals are punished much more severely than rich ones.

More evidence for this inner condition is seen in the cult of celebrity. People become "electrified" on seeing a celebrity in the flesh because their own inner poverty, their separation from their own value, comes into sharp contrast with the "grandeur" of the celebrity. People can either feel diminished by the greatness of others because they feel their own inner poverty more intensely, or they can feel better about themselves when they are able, through scandal or gossip, to reduce the value or majesty of the celebrity.

The aggressive arrogance of fascism was able to arise in Germany because the German people, vanquished and dispirited following World War I, were desperate to regain the old illusion of power. They concocted the idea of a supreme Aryan race while they projected their repressed sense of worthlessness on to the Jews. On a smaller scale, a city gang member might lash out violently at anyone who looks at him "the wrong way" in alleged disrespect. His sensitivity to disrespect is a measure of how deeply he resonates with feeling worthless and is inwardly disrespected by his inner critic. As well, many of our politicians strive desperately for the prestige of high office to lessen that painful inner burden.

Inwardly, we all disrespect ourselves through the auspices of our inner critic. To cover up our resonance with the scorn we absorb from our inner critic, we produce egotism, narcissism, and a great sensitivity to any signs of disrespect or allegations of our unworthiness. We temporarily ease our inner conflict when we pass along to others our own sense of unworthiness, and we feel relief and validation when, in warfare, they are defeated or eliminated. In this way, like Gollum in *The Lord of the Rings*, we would all perish in the lava pits of Mount Doom, clutching our golden ring—our invincibility in precious self-image—while wars rage on and reality crashes down around us.

66. The Overlooked Factor in Criminal Behavior

One way to suffer greatly is to break the law and go to jail. More than two million people are incarcerated in the United States, so there's a lot of suffering going on behind bars and in the hearts of the relatives of imprisoned people. Our society is addressing the problem rather ineptly because we don't understand an important ingredient in juvenile delinquency and adult criminality.

Numerous competing theories—including biological, sociological, psychological, economic, and political—are proposed for the cause of criminal behavior. Little consensus is established among the experts. Supporters of each theory barricade themselves and their doctrines against all comers.

These different schools agree on one point, though. They all identify as a decisive factor the criminal's devotion to aggressive behavior and the discharge of aggressive acts. However, criminal aggression is not what it appears on the surface. It springs out of inner passivity. Criminals are extremely passive and weak in the sense that, much of the time, they're not accessing the powers of self-regulation and self-protection. They're failing to act wisely or appropriately on their own behalf. They are not accessing true power, which is the ability to flourish with integrity and civility.

As a caveat, let me say that many criminals have suffered—through childhood poverty, neglect, and abuse—more insult and injury than the rest of us. Their dysfunction can be due to many biological and environmental influences. I'm simply attempting in this discussion to introduce an important yet overlooked psychological factor.

Knowledge of inner passivity's effects is important because it can help many criminals to become rehabilitated. As mentioned, all of us, to some degree, are "carriers" of inner passivity. While this aspect of human nature produces a psychological disorder in criminals, it can cause much suffering and self-defeat among the rest of us. Most of us at times react to our inner passivity with displays of phony or reactive aggression, sometimes in the form of angry outbursts or retaliation. Aggression, when neurotic, is easily provoked. It's sometimes expressed as "rage against the machine," an emotional state that arises when a person's underlying issues involving passivity and helplessness react to ignorance, corruption, or oppression with impotent fury. Such armchair rebellion often takes the form of cynicism or bitterness.

Both the so-called normal person and the criminal, when acting out reactive aggression, manifest the unconscious expectation of failure and defeat. The level of self-defeat is a matter of degree: A criminal's reactive aggression is more likely to lead to jail time, while the inappropriate aggression of everyday neurotics is better regulated and, though it can be riddled with painful shame and self-recriminations, typically produces less self-damaging results.

Our success and well-being require healthy aggression as we make our way in the world. However, a criminal's profound inner passivity makes it more difficult for him to function at this level. His inner passivity causes him to feel overwhelmed by the requirements of living appropriately and wisely. Healthy aggression in the pursuit of socially approved success is not an option for criminals because their overflowing reservoir of inner passivity overrides the capacity for self-protection and self-advancement.

However, criminals must compensate in some manner for their passivity to save face and avoid the appearance of being weak. They seize on negative aggression as a compensating sense of power. This aggression, of course, is only an illusion of true power. Their negative aggression is their instinctive path of least resistance, and it's entirely reactive and phony. It's a self-defeating force rebounding off their profound inner passivity.

This entanglement in passivity can be described, as mentioned, as an emotional attachment or addiction. In other words, one's impulse to interpret experiences through passivity is an emotional default position. The inner passivity of criminals, for instance, can become triggered simply by the sight of a police cruiser passing by. Instinctively, they deny their readiness to feel passive to authority figures. Their hatred and aggression can be understood as defenses that cover up their emotional entanglement in profound passivity. Thus, their hatred of authority is an unconscious defense that makes this case: "I am not hopelessly entangled in feeling passive. Can't you see how much I hate it when someone (an authority figure) tries to restrict me, control me, or tell me what to do!" For passive people, anger and hatred produce an illusion of aggression and power.

As a defense, their aggression also claims, "I'm not passive. No one is going to push me around. Let them try and they'll see how aggressive I really am." Yet they can be extremely passive to their leaders in a criminal hierarchy, in part because of their emotional alignment with the criminal mentality, along with the fact that their passivity requires them to find people or situations with which they can experience or act out that passivity.

Criminals unconsciously bargain for punishment. Evidence can be seen in their unnecessary provocations and in the "silly mistakes" they frequently make that lead to their apprehension and incarceration. The criminal recreates this inner dynamic: He feels helplessly trapped and limited by his inner passivity (often he's emotionally attached to the feeling of being trapped), and he subsequently ends up in a prison cell trapped and pinned down by the authorities. Just as on an inner level he is profoundly passive, he "acts out" by becoming a passive cog in an extensive justice system.

Not only is the criminal's unconscious ego (the seat of inner passivity) especially weak, his inner critic or superego is particularly corrupt and demanding. On an inner level, the passivity of criminals makes them targets of self-condemnation and self-hatred directed from their superego through their unconscious ego. Inwardly, they absorb from their superego high levels of self-disparagement, self-abuse, and self-hatred, which then cause them to relate to the world with the same negative insensitivity with which they are treated by their inner critic or superego.

These facts can be taught to criminals in the penal system. Many of them could absorb this psychological knowledge, even as they might be inclined on the surface to scoff at it. At least they should be given the chance to make use of this knowledge. Many of them could be rehabilitated by understanding that their aggressive tendencies have been covering up underlying passivity.

67. Terrorism and the Death Drive

The day I was writing on this subject, *The New York Times* published a photograph on the front page of the aftermath of a suicide bomber's horrific attack on a group of Afghan Shiites taking part in a religious ceremony. Human perversity sometimes seems unfathomable, but we must keep trying to make sense of it.

Terrorists provide clear evidence for one of Freud's theories. He was right about a lot of things for which people have been reluctant to give him credit. He insisted that the human psyche harbors a death drive, a self-destructive instinct and unconscious desire to flirt with death if not to embrace it.

Freud put forward the idea after observing the horrors of World War I. He wanted to explain the human compulsion to engage in personal or collective acts of self-destruction that produced such suffering. The death drive, he stated, can often override the pleasure principle, the instinct or drive for pleasure, progress, and harmony.

While terrorists are overtly entranced by death, the impulse toward self-destruction operates more subtly in many of us. Daredevils and people who engage in dangerous sports are driven by the thrill of flirting with death. Reckless or risky behaviors of other sorts—involving finances, relationships, violence, and alcohol and drug addictions—can also indicate a flirtation with our own defeat or demise.

For now, let's stick to the psychology of Islamic terrorists. What are some ingredients of their death drive? What produces the instinct or impulse to engage in such fiendish behavior?

Terrorists of all stripes are steeped in a victim mentality. In the case of Islamic terrorists, they feel violated, oppressed, and marginalized by Western power and culture. They experience the social and political dynamics of the West through feelings of deprivation, helplessness, domination, disrespect, and defeat. Their unconscious interest is not in reform or progress but in the ongoing experience of themselves as victims of alleged injustice and oppression. This means that they harbor in their psyche large deposits of passivity.

Their restrictive, insular mentality makes them their own worst oppressors. Inwardly, they impede their own self-development. They're bound up in an inner conflict between their aggression on one hand and their passivity on the other. They cover up awareness of their unwitting participation in this conflict, and deny the self-condemnation and self-hatred it produces, by raging at the West and hating our freedom.

Such individuals don't recognize their unconscious willingness to experience and recycle the feeling of being controlled, harassed, dominated, or persecuted. Inner oppression is a great weakness at the heart of human nature. It affects many decent, law-abiding people who suffer in varying degrees with feeling, say, oppressed by a boss or family member. The healthier we are, the more we can avoid entanglement in these negative emotions and, certainly, refrain from reactive self-defeat and primitive violence. Some individuals, criminals and terrorists among them, have greater deposits of inner passivity, perhaps for genetic or other biological reasons.

As a psychological defense, they produce distorted views of the world, with convoluted dogma and reactive behaviors to match, that enable them, on an inner level, to plead innocent to any participation in their own sense of oppression. Rather than acknowledge their emotional weakness, terrorists resort to blaming others. Psychologically, it's easier for them to blame rather than to accept responsibility for their emotional attachments to helplessness, victimization, and a sense of unworthiness.

They're also swept up by another of inner passivity's symptoms, namely the craving for intense excitement. This craving for excitement provides an unconscious defense: "I'm not inwardly separated from my own essence, nor am I dead to myself. I want to feel the excitement of being engaged in a noble cause! Look at how much pleasure I can feel in my passion for justice and revenge. I want to feel empowered. I'm thrilled to be a martyr, a person of great substance who will die for a just cause." In pursuit of a "just cause," political extremists in a democratic country can operate according to the same principle. While they might not be willing to die for their cause, they're willing to sacrifice the wellbeing of others.

In pleading innocent to any passivity, terrorists are required to produce hatred and rage against their alleged oppressors in order to make their inner defenses work. Their defensive rationalization contends: "I'm not looking to feel oppressed or defeated. Can't you see how much I hate my oppressors!" At this point, their hatred necessarily becomes acute. A higher pitch of hatred is required to make the inner defense effective. This hatred now constitutes a primary ingredient of their death drive because it is ultimately self-directed as well as outer-directed. A person can't produce such intense negativity, thinking only to direct it toward others, without being contaminated himself.

The terrorist is now willing to embrace death and become an agent of death because the decision to do so feels to him so much like courage and power. For the sake of this defense against recognition of his underlying passivity, the forfeits his mind, his will, and—if need be—his life.

The terrorist believes not only that violent actions represent power and strength but that even his fantasies of violence constitute such power. In the grip of the death drive, his fantasies of destruction become intoxicating in themselves. But being an armchair terrorist has its drawbacks. If he procrastinates and fails to act on his fantasies, he can be accused by his inner critic of being passive. Now he's having to circle back to accusations of passivity from which he originally tried to flee. At this point, he can become trapped in a downward spiral—an intensifying inner conflict—in which he has to act on his fantasies or face increasingly painful scorn and mockery from his inner critic.

Ultimately, he's desperate to display some form of strength, however demented that may be, to cover up his enmeshment in feelings of powerlessness and weakness. The more destruction his terrorism produces (or that he imagines it producing), the more he convinces himself that he's powerful rather than weak. As mentioned in the previous discussion, this same psychological mechanism operates in juvenile delinquents and adult criminals, and obviously their path of destruction can also be deadly.

The terrorist's passivity is revealed by the fact that he allows his mind and emotions to be taken over by dogma or by the agenda of others. He's a bewildered soul, separated from his own truth and his own self. He embraces a cause that makes him feel real or powerful, enabling him to claim as a defense that he want to feel power, not the helplessness, passivity, and self-doubt in which he is mired.

His avoidance of inner truth renders him infantile, like a child who slaps another child who touches his toy. Like a child, he feels entitled to act on his primitive emotions, particularly when he becomes bonded with a cadre of similarly psychologically impaired individuals.

If the underlying weaknesses and psychological defenses of terrorists were more widely understood and publicized, potential terrorists could be influenced in a positive way by these revelations of inner reality.

68 . The Secret Allures of Pornography

Lots of people, men in particular, are addicted to pornography. They are sexually aroused by the visual stimulation, and they return compulsively to the activity, looking for that pleasure. However, it's often a pleasure that comes with a price.

Many feel shame after feasting on the stimulation. They might also feel guilty if they have a partner who is being kept in the dark about it. They can also feel bad about themselves because they know the voyeuristic activity is induced by inner weakness or because they can't stop doing it. All of us can suffer with guilt, confusion, worry, and anxiety whenever we're losing what may be life's greatest struggle: to maintain self-regulation of behaviors and emotions.

Pornography has dimensions to it of the impersonal, mechanical, tawdry, and boring. So how does a person become addicted to such voyeurism? Several hidden psychological components are at play. When the consumption of pornography is addictive, it means the individual, in part, is acting out his inner passivity. He doesn't have the power to act consistently in his best interests. This is the same inner weakness that leads one to be indecisive, to procrastinate, and to feel overwhelmed. This individual replays an unresolved emotional issue that involves the feeling of not being in charge of his or her own life. Such individuals frequently find themselves in fixes in which they're lacking in self-regulation, as with compulsive gamblers and those with obsessive-compulsive disorders.

Pornography has the added element of being related to the *visual drive*. This refers to the powerful impulse to seek gratification through visual stimulation. Visual craving is not necessarily unhealthy. It's a source of pleasure when playing video games, watching movies, cruising along the highway, and seeking out beauty in art and nature. But the craving can be indiscriminate and self-defeating, depending on what emotional factors are driving it.

For one thing, the individual watching pornography can be identifying with the degradation of the actors or models, most particularly the women. Through a perverse manipulation in our psyche, such degradation can be turned into sexual pleasure. It's the same mechanism that occurs when a sadistic person is "turned on" by his abuse of a passive or masochistic person. In a non-sexual way, it's similar to the pleasure a schoolyard bully feels when he abuses a passive boy or girl. Typically, the abuser feels superior, which covers up his or her identification with the humiliation and passivity of the victim.

With pornography, then, one source of the sexual pleasure arises from the individual's unconscious (secret) identification with the sense of worthlessness that the degraded, passive actor may or may not be feeling. The negative feeling (degradation or a sense of worthlessness, or a sense of brute power over a passive individual) is "libidinized." This clinical word, as mentioned, refers to the action of libido, the pleasure drive, which is capable of turning displeasure into pleasure in some circumstances, with masochism and sadism being examples of sexual pleasure.

Every one of us can at times feel self-doubt and wonder about our ultimate value. We can feel a sense of relief, even a perverse pleasure, when someone other than us is identified as being the unworthy person. (This perversity is a factor in racism, where someone feels a kind of third-rate gratification in identifying others as allegedly being inferior or worthless.) Even when we try to cover up our identification with the degradation, failure, or demise of the other (through our defenses and rationalizations), this unconscious identification of ours produces some form of suffering, often guilt and shame.

It's tempting when watching pornography, for instance, to resonate with the shame that one might imagine the actors ought to feel in exposing themselves so brazenly. In resonating with them in this way, a person can, through identification, rekindle old feelings of shame that are associated with childhood memories of engaging in what is forbidden. As children, we encountered many sexual situations involving the forbidden. Seeing naked parents or siblings, even inadvertently, was often considered wrong or shameful. Men often hide their compulsive voyeurism from their wives or girlfriends, and then feel shame when caught and confronted. As little children, they may have been tempted into doing what was "bad" by the thrill of defiance and the wish to feel "liberated" from parental "oppression." Or, if they remained obedient, they may have secretly wished they were bold enough to defy their parents. As adults, they can still be aroused, this time sexually, by unresolved childish impulses involving forbidden behaviors.

This same ability to turn intensely negative emotions into perverse pleasure can lure some highly neurotic individuals into child pornography. Instead of identifying directly with debasement, those individuals who are addicted emotionally to child pornography are typically identifying with the children's helplessness and victimization. The compulsion of the pedophile also involves inner passivity, meaning in this context that the pedophile experiences pleasure via sexual masochism in the process of identifying with the helpless victimization of the children.

Another hidden element in the addiction to pornography is the feeling of disappointment. When pornography is first viewed, the excitement and pleasure can be intense. Before long, however, the pleasurable effect wears off. Now disappointment sets in. Pornographers introduce material that is increasingly sensational, bizarre, and perverse in an attempt to avoid the sated feeling. Yet the sated feeling persists, and it can in part be attributed to the disappointment that many people are unconsciously determined to feel in both sexual and non-sexual ways.

The Peeping Tom, for one, is driven not by his apparent wish to see naked women (which he can legitimately see in any strip club or online) but by his determination, as he slinks through back alleys, to experience the disappointment of being refused the sight of nakedness by "uncooperative" women who "refuse" to bare themselves for his eager eyes. Keep in mind that we are compelled to experience repeatedly our unresolved negative emotions—in this case feelings of refusal and disappointment.

69 . Rebutting 9/11 Conspiracy Beliefs

More than ever, we need to discern what's real and true about the events and circumstances of modern life. Unresolved emotions can clutter our mind, obstructing access to objectivity and wisdom. This is happening with 9/11 conspiracy buffs, many of whom believe that powerful individuals in the United States government orchestrated the attacks on the World Trade Center and the Pentagon.

It's commonplace knowledge that various beliefs are strongly influenced by our emotional issues. These issues, often relating to inner fear, are usually unconscious. People often aren't aware of how, for emotional reasons, they can unwittingly be discounting or misreading relevant evidence while at the same time elevating the significance of marginal evidence.

Conspiracy adherents have evidence that they say supports their claim. Obviously, varied hypotheses can be drawn up from inconclusive evidence. Selected evidence can produce many logically consistent pathways through the maze of a complex event, yet only one of these pathways might lead to the truth. The remaining paths, though believable or plausible, lead to wrong conclusions. I want to present more evidence—psychological evidence—that conspiracy theorists have not included in their assessments.

Many of us experienced emotional disorientation and a sense of helplessness as we unwittingly identified with the thousands of victims of the calamity who were trapped in the targeted buildings and in the four airliners used in the attack. To cope with these feelings, some people desperately sought a compensating sense of power or orientation. Based on the proposition that knowledge is power, conspiracy adherents can proclaim: "I know what actually happened! I know the truth! I embrace the truth!" This "knowledge" produces an impression of power and a sense of orientation. It backfires, however, and becomes self-sabotage because it bestows pernicious power on the faceless government officials who allegedly orchestrated 9/11. In locating such horrendous evil in their backyard, conspiracy buffs feel even more at the mercy of powerful malicious forces and hence more "reason" to feel helplessly oppressed.

As one of the larger conspiracy websites indicates, conspiracy adherents continue to protest against "a nightmare scenario" in which they feel oppressed by the fallout effects of 9/11.[87] Indeed, some of those fallouts have an oppressive quality—for instance, the global war on terror, the invasion of Iraq and Afghanistan, the Patriot Act, Homeland Security, warrantless phone tapping, and so on. Yet for emotional reasons, conspiracy adherents are tempted to magnify their sense of oppression and to feel overwhelmed and even impotent in the face of it. This leaves them less likely to engage in vital activities that could help the world get to a better place. Obsessing in this way about 9/11 becomes a form of psychological resistance, a way to avoid becoming truly effective and powerful. According to *Scientific American Mind*, a number of studies "have shown that belief in conspiracy theories is associated with feelings of powerlessness and uncertainty."[88]

---

[87] http://www.911truth.org/

[88] http://www.scientificamerican.com/article/moon-landing-faked-why-people-believe-conspiracy-theories/

Looking deeper still, we uncover the appeal of the uncanny. People enjoy a sense of the uncanny while watching horror movies or reading ghost stories and thrillers. According to classical psychoanalysis, this enjoyment is a tension that stems from the "libidinization" of inner fear. People actually enjoy spine-tingling thrills and the mild shock of fright. Though they feel distress and anxiety on a conscious level, they unconsciously indulge in the titillation of the uncanny. An early sense of the uncanny was encountered in childhood through the mystery of parental sexuality. Our tendency to libidinize fear gives terrorism a certain uncanniness, along with an added jolt of menace and power. (Another version of the uncanny is at play in the zombie craze that has infected popular culture.[89])

The events of 9/11 released repressed instincts of rage in the psyche of many people. Conspiracy theorists often feel, as a countervailing force against their passivity, rage against the government. They also tend to scorn people who challenge their beliefs. Out of a sense of helplessness, people can be quick to feel rage toward others. Anger and rage can feel like power. When children feel helpless or forced to submit to parental authority, they can erupt into temper tantrums and rage toward parents. The government is a pseudo-parent. Some people, particularly those on the Right wing, can feel rage toward the government for allegedly being too powerful and controlling. On the Left Wing, the rage can be directed toward "all-powerful" corporations.

It's possible to go still deeper in this search for psychological understanding of the hidden appeal of the conspiracy position. We're all born with considerable

[89] http://www.bbc.co.uk/news/uk-15418899

self-centeredness. All we know as infants are the sensations of our own existence. It can feel as if everything we see around us is just an extension of us. Classical psychoanalysis says we are born with a primitive megalomania along with a sense of omnipotence. The baby's impression is, "Whatever happens is what I myself wished for." These irrational impressions linger in the psyche of many of us, accounting for much of the egotism and narcissism that exists in the world. Under this unconscious influence, people can project great (even absolute) power and menace on to some faceless entity.

A male child tends to experience his father as a powerful competitor for mother's affections. A few years later, the boy has begun to identify with the father, and projects a sense of absolute power on to the father-figure. As adults, people can easily enough project lingering infantile megalomania on to some allegedly all-powerful entity, particularly when the entity is a father-figure such as the U.S. government. This projection can interpret the entity as either a benevolent or a malicious force, depending on other aspects of the individual's psychology. A nationalist or patriot, for instance, can identify with the government as a powerful, benevolent force.

Conspiracy adherents are engaged in a modern, secular version of the bygone devil fixation: the individual projects lingering megalomania and his unrecognized dark side on to an imagined sinister entity while cultivating, through unresolved inner fear, a feeling of being at the mercy of that entity. A person's tendency to project malice on to others or on to some entity is also influenced by inner dynamics involving the inner critic or superego. In our psyche, we tend to be on the receiving end of malice (criticism, harassment, and mockery) from our inner critic. When we're unaware of this inner dynamic, we can't locate where the sense of oppression or malice is coming from, and we end up identifying false sources.

Our intelligence is much better equipped to discern truth and reality when we become more conscious of psychological dynamics. Now our intelligence weighs the evidence more astutely. Isn't it evident that no government or private entity in the United States could remain undetected after killing thousands of Americans by flying four airliners into skyscrapers and the headquarters of the world's most powerful military force? To do so, such an entity would have to be both evil and all-powerful. Fortunately, there is no such thing on the face of the Earth.

70 . **Curbing Our Appetite for Brutality**

Nelson Mandela's greatness was most visible in his power to overthrow—through his courage, compassion, and peaceful manner—the brutality and murderous ways of the Apartheid regime. He was an ordinary man, he said, as he counseled us to find our own greatness.

How do we acquire greatness? Mandela's power to do good was rooted in his charisma and love. If we are to be liberators like him, we presumably have to shed our negativity, fear, anger, malice, and violent instincts. We have to liberate our self from the darkness within.

From where in human nature does such negativity arise? An article in *The New York Times* tries to comprehend the human capacity for the slaughter of innocent people. Citing examples of horrific bloodletting by terrorists in Kenya and government security forces in Egypt, the article asks: Do we all have the capacity for such wanton murder?[90]

Experts interviewed in the article say *yes*. But they don't get to the core of the question. Instead, they blame the readiness to kill on "a culture of authority and obedience that supplants individual moral responsibility with loyalty to a larger mission …" Also blamed are "a routinization of violence, as well as injustice or economic hardship …" One expert says the most important ingredient in the willingness to murder for a cause is "the dehumanization of the victim."

These explanations are superficial. Mandela, who died in 2013, would have had more to offer. He would want us to ask ourselves: "What is it about *me* that would cause *me* to forgo moral responsibility? Why is it about *me* that wants to see the enemy as less than human? What is it in *me* that is hateful, and what is the source of *my* hidden need to have enemies?" Mandela, it seems, empowered and enlightened himself by taking personal responsibility for humanity's worst instincts. Through courage and sacrifice, he became the embodiment of what he believed we all could be. I don't know, of course, the exact nature of his inner journey to greatness. But I can offer, in the words that follow, vital knowledge that can make us less negative and thereby more loving as well as more powerful.

---

[90] http://www.nytimes.com/2013/10/13/world/europe/behind-flurry-of-killing-potency-of-hate.html?pagewanted=all

We are, of course, admirable and noble in so many ways. But we obviously have a primitive side that, like an ogre or barbarian, comports itself badly on the playing fields of civilization. When upfront self-scrutiny is called for, this underdeveloped part of us kicks up a thick dust cloud of denial and resistance.

Russell Jacoby, author of *Bloodlust: On the Roots of Violence from Cain and Abel to the Present*, writes that the greatest violence has often taken the form of fratricide, where neighbors or blood relations, familiar and similar in so many ways, show greater hatred and murderous intent toward one another than occurs among strangers or outsiders.[91] This counter-intuitive fact makes sense when we consider that such violence and murder have their origins in the "intimacy" of one's own psyche, where the inner clash of chaotic, primitive dynamics impedes our evolving humanity.

When we're not conscious enough, we create conflict and enemies by *projecting* our unconscious negativity on to others. Many people are unaware of both the dynamic of projection and the extent of their negativity (in the form of inner fear, inner aggression, and inner passivity). They're not aware that they're "seeing" and hating in others what they refuse to see of their own naked *in*humanity.

How much is our own unresolved and unrecognized negativity a factor in the huge supply of weaponry throughout the world and in the violence we do to the planet? Much of that negativity arises out of primitive aggression. That aggression is close to home, hiding out

---

[91] Jacoby, Russell. *Bloodlust: On the Roots of Violence from Cain and Abel*. New York, Free Press, 2011.

in our mean-spirited inner critic (superego) which harasses us and holds us accountable to its self-proclaimed authority. Our inner passivity, too, is a part of us that refuses to be fully human and stand up for what's right. Our authentic self, source of our wisdom and courage, is buried under the conflict between inner passivity and inner aggression.

Our inner critic kicks us when we're down and belittles our greatest achievements. For the most part, we manage to hold it in check through the degree of our humanity and mental health. But its self-aggression does constitute an inner tyranny that limits our sense of freedom. Our inner defensiveness and fearfulness are shifted to the external world, prompting us to react to threats in a primitive manner—violently and murderously. In contrast, our inclination when we're more evolved is to respond through the power of diplomacy, rationality, courage, equanimity, and awareness.

When we see the "enemy" as less than human, we're being less than human. How so? Our instinct to engage in warfare mimics the primitive, aggressive instincts of the inner critic. Our inner critic is at war with us. It treats us as less than human, and, through inner passivity, we let it get away with that rough treatment of us. We then transfer on to perceived enemies the expectation that they will treat us with the kind of ruthlessness which we endure from our inner critic.

The transference can activate inner fear along with a heightened sense of the danger that others represent. The more that each side perceives the other from this primitive perspective, the greater the danger of violent conflict. At this point, the instinct to engage in violence arises out of inner passivity rather than from true aggression. As mentioned, warmongers, terrorists, and criminals are driven by inner passivity. Warmongers are under the influence of phony or pseudo-aggression, which is a reaction to the extent to which they are steeped psychologically in a sense of inner weakness. Through this inner passivity, they experience conflict through the prospect of defeat. Such defeat is imagined to be (or associated emotionally with) a kind of annihilation. This sense of annihilation is, in large part, an emotional association with the prospect of how defeat would represent a crushing blow to their ego. Their willingness to go to war now serves as a psychological defense against realization of how fully they are entangled in inner passivity and its accompanying egotism. In other words, their readiness to resort to brutality and murderous aggression is an attempt to cover up the self-doubt and inner fear with which they unconsciously identify. They would sacrifice the lives of others for their personal pretensions.

From the other side, enemies and oppressors can be real and dangerous, and they can indeed treat us in a brutal manner. Nevertheless, the struggle to defeat them must include the effort to raise them to a higher level of consciousness (or the conflict could go on indefinitely). As we raise our own consciousness, we will be, like Nelson Mandela, able to reform the other side.

This depth psychology, as mentioned, is not widely disseminated, even in universities. The media discuss only superficial psychology. So people are not being taught the origins of the deeper impulse toward violence. Why isn't this knowledge widely taught? It's as if we're too titillated by violence and terror, as indeed we are at violent or horror movies, to be truly disposed to eliminate it. The knowledge also offends egotism's idealized self-image. In any case, the time has come to see ourselves more objectively. We can become powerful and enlightened enough to eliminate these horrors of human misconduct. We just have to recognize and subdue the primitive aggression and defensive passivity clashing in our psyche.

As mentioned, we can be remarkably passive when character and resolve are called for. Americans can be passive and indifferent to brutality done to others in the name of national security. This is ultimately because, on an inner level, we're passive to our inner critic and allow ourselves to be bullied by its aggression. In reaction, many people identify in a misleading way with the inner critic, just as they can identify fervently with military might. Meanwhile, in protecting self-image we refuse to believe that we might be silent enablers of both self-abuse (from our inner critic) and the abuse of others (by being passive enablers of violence).

Whatever path of self-knowledge we chose to follow, each of us can become, like Nelson Mandela, a guiding light to the world.

71 . **The Psychology behind Mass Shootings**

While some mass shooters are psychotic or schizophrenic, only about five percent of violence in the United States can be attributed to people with mental illness.[92] The rate of mental illness is higher—an estimated 20 percent—among rampage or serial killers. Most mass murders didn't qualify for any specific psychiatric disorder, according to strict criteria. These individuals—often working-class men who had been jilted, fired, and felt humiliated, or youths who felt rejected and despised—lived next door to neighbors who never imagined them capable of such crimes.

People prefer to believe that the behavior of the shooters is foreign to human nature, not something intrinsic in our makeup. Or we say that a gun-worshipping culture is to blame. Yet might there be another factor, some common element at the heart of human nature, to account in part for these horrendous events?

We all have a dark side. Psychology, literature, and mythology have chronicled this aspect of our nature, yet still we flee from examining it. Carl Jung wrote in his classic, *The Undiscovered Self,* that a true understanding of the inner self recognizes the existence of good and evil within us. In his view, the unconscious was being ignored "out of downright resistance to the mere possibility of there being a second psychic authority besides the ego. It seems a positive menace to the ego that its monarchy can be doubted." Jung also wrote that a lack of insight deprives us of the capacity to deal with evil. Underestimation of the psychological factor, he added, "is likely to take a bitter revenge."[93]

Looking for elements in our psyche that match those of mass shooters is a delicate subject. We prefer to keep

---

[92] http://ajp.psychiatryonline.org/article.aspx?articleid=96905
[93] Jung, C.G. *The Undiscovered Self*. New York: New American Library, 1958. 105. Print.

our distance, as if they belong to a different species. Yet these shootings have been occurring for many years now and could become more frequent and lethal. We have to consider possible answers that lie closer to home.

Let's start by examining a profile that fits many mass shooters. These murderers are often quite intelligent, yet through acute self-centeredness they're likely to be socially awkward or inept. They crave notice and resort to infamy to compensate for how deeply they dismiss their own value and feel like nobodies. They also lack empathy and have little or no affect, a condition that relates to the indifference or disdain they have for their own existence.

Negative emotions accumulate inside them, producing bitterness, anger, despair, and, finally, rage. Their rage, even when hidden from others, produces a third-rate sense of power that covers up their emotional entanglement in hopelessness and passivity. They entertain fantasies in which they engage in wanton violence power because they feel so powerless, yet in their dark negativity they can express only negative, destructive power. They seek death because they feel so powerfully overwhelmed by life.

Because their weak self-regulation compels them to continually recycle negative emotions, they hold on to grudges. These grudges and grievances accumulate in them, giving them a feeling of substance, a place of being to which they cling in the chaos of their inner conflict.

The killer-to-be has also passively allowed himself to plunge so deeply into self-abandonment and self-hatred—meaning his aggressive rejection of all that is good or decent in him—that, like a drowning person, he gasps for the one last "breath" of the only power now available to him, which is to do evil.

An additional factor shapes these menacing time-bombs. These killers-to-be have often acquired a fervent interest in guns. Influenced by others, they passively elevate the gun or the rifle to level of a fetish. In another time and place, they're the kind of people who might have joined a cult. For a troubled individual who is drowning in negativity, to adore guns is to worship death.

From this we can assume that the murderous instincts of rampage shooters originate from profound inner weakness and emotional conflict in their psyche. Their aggression, in part, is based on their reaction to their overflowing negative emotions and their resulting lack of self-regulation.

By way of comparison to everyday people, many of us have considerable deposits of anger, cynicism, and bitterness. People can hold on to this negativity for dear life. Convinced that their bitterness is justified by the alleged cruelty or insensitivity of others, they express various levels of malice toward others. This is the key point: We have to learn and understand that any bitterness we happen to experience is not really due to the malice of others. Rather, *this bitterness and rage is a cover-up for our willingness to indulge in feeling powerless, marginalized, or victimized in some manner or other*. If we don't understand this, then the difference between us and rampage shooters is just a matter of degree.

To heed Jung's warning, we must grow our consciousness. Vital knowledge about human nature can permeate the culture, raising the collective consciousness. When disseminated in the media, the knowledge seeps into the minds of even the least intellectually inclined. This progress would enable parents, teachers, clergy, and others to become more insightful about the emotional state of others and more confident about initiating some form of intervention. Prevention may require that more of us are able to recognize potential killers so that, before meltdowns occur, these individuals make more contact with people who understand them. It's helpful for us to understand, for instance, that during preparations for their assaults, these killers-to-be become fixated on images of their helpless, desperate victims for the purpose of identifying masochistically with the despair of their impending annihilation. This madness is usually visible through expressions of intense bitterness and rage. Astute everyday people, when in contact with such individuals, can sense the danger and warn authorities. As well, potential killers will likely moderate their deadly instincts when they are surrounded by more conscious people, exposed to better psychological knowledge, and made through saner weapons regulation to understand that the death instinct, easily spawned where weapons are sanctified or violent video games promoted, is a social taboo.

What's the most important single psychological fact we need to know? We have to learn, as mentioned, that our negative impressions, impulses, and emotions are *not* caused exclusively by external factors, even when life is difficult and seems unfair. Unconsciously, we prefer to believe that our hurt, anger, and rage are produced by the oversights and malice of others. As long as people go on believing that their suffering is caused by others, they'll be compelled to become angry at others because they're required, through their unconscious defenses, to blame others for allegedly bullying, punishing, oppressing, or persecuting them. This irrational belief stems from the unconscious attempt people make to cover up their participation in their own suffering. In ongoing stubborn denial of this fact, some individuals take their anger to the next level and begin to generate rage and intense desires for revenge toward their alleged victimizers. When people begin to understand how they produce their own suffering, they stop projecting on to others (and stop experiencing from others by way of transference) the negativity churned up by their own unresolved emotions. Now they no longer despise others or see them as the enemy. There is no impulse to destroy the other.

Once we understand this basic concept, we have nowhere to turn for relief but inward toward self-knowledge. When we do so, we can rescue ourselves from our suffering. Parents need to learn this so they represent this truth in their dealings with both normal and troubled children. Liberation from pain and suffering is the next great expansion of our freedoms.

Once we turn our intelligence inward, we come across two great insights. The first involves our understanding of the roles played in our psyche between aggression and passivity. These two aspects of our psyche are in conflict with each other; the more dysfunctional or neurotic we are, the more intense the conflict is likely to be. Typically, people are aware of the painful symptoms of the conflict but not the conflict itself.

Second, we're inclined to recycle and replay, no matter how painful, whatever negative emotions are unresolved in our psyche. Inner passivity, a kind of existential self-doubt with which many of us unconsciously identify, is one of these negative emotions. It causes troubled individuals to feel that aggression, including extravagant displays of it, is their only recourse.

Learning this knowledge makes us wiser and more astute. The troubled people who cross our path are also helped in unseen ways by our evolved nature.

72 . **The Double Barrels of Gun Mania**

We all agree about the need to keep guns out of the hands of the mentally ill. Perhaps we also need to look at some psychological issues influencing staunch defenders of gun rights. Many of these individuals are not paragons of mental health because two of their unrecognized emotional issues are triggering a double-barreled blast of self-defeat.

Before looking down these barrels, let's acknowledge our human temptation to become enthralled by objects such as guns. Collectors certainly love their guns, cars, coins, stamps, antiques, model trains, and so on. This interest or fascination can be harmless enough and a source of considerable enjoyment. Yet psychological development is impeded when we use a possession such as a luxury car or expensive painting to provide status or fill an inner emptiness. Our enthusiasm for possessions can rise to the level of a fixation or obsession, at which point our lack of self-development causes us to lose perspective and sell short the richness of our essential self.

Because guns are relatively inexpensive, they're not usually purchased for status. Instead, they provide two psychological defenses—the double barrels of self-defeat—that make their ownership so desirable. One barrel discharges the illusion of safety and the other the illusion of power. Why do so many gun owners grasp at these illusions or inner defenses?

First, let's acknowledge that some neighborhoods in America are dangerous places. It's possible that some people are safer carrying guns. My point is that unrecognized emotional issues make it more likely that people will be fearful and irrational in ways that are self-defeating. We know that having a gun does not guarantee survival in case of conflict and that expanding gun ownership, to the point where more and more people are packing heat, is socially and morally regressive.

Some Americans have a passion for handguns and assault weapons because these firearms compensate for inner fear. We generate this fear from within our psyche, based on unresolved inner conflicts. A lot of fear is produced, for instance, through our unconscious defensiveness vis-à-vis our inner critic. Much irrational fear is also left over from childhood. But people tend to believe their fear is reality-based, meaning that, in their minds, menace and genuine dangers do indeed lurk outside their door.

Some gun enthusiasts are unconsciously determined to validate their inner fears. Rather than resolve the inner conflict that produces their fears, they make them seem legitimate by emphasizing emotionally the dangers and menace that might exist in their towns, neighborhoods, and workplaces.

Many gun advocates rally around the Second Amendment that protects the right to keep and bear arms, thereby affording protection against home intruders, foreign invasion, and usurpation by rulers. Home "intruders" are often family members or relatives shot by mistake in panic. In the face of government tyranny, guns would likely be self-defeating. Our intelligence and freedom of expression are much stronger weapons. On the domestic front, the heroes of democracy fight with their wits and their written and spoken words.

Weak people, however, do not necessarily feel or practice the power of intelligence and rationality. They can be too deeply enmeshed in impressions of being menaced and overwhelmed by malice or evil to be fully rational. These excessively passive impressions cause them to interpret their safety through brute force.

Let's look down the second barrel of the gun craze, which is the illusion of power that guns conjure up. When we're inwardly weak, meaning filled with self-doubt and inner conflict, we're often desperate to produce an appearance or impression of aggression or power. A man who beats his wife or children is desperate to feel power to cover up or deny his profound inner weakness, namely his abandonment of all that is good and worthy in himself. A woman who constantly berates her husband feels some second-rate sense of power, but underneath she may feel trapped in her relationship and blame her husband when she herself is entangled in a helpless sense of being unable to improve her circumstances. A person failing in life due to neurotic resignation or incompetence can feel that his or her angry complaints and claims of injustice are expressions of strength or aggression. The weaker a person, the more likely he or she can believe in guns as true expressions of power and instruments of justice. Many individuals cling to that illusion to protect their self-image and to avoid recognizing the extent of their neurosis.

Guns don't represent true power. If America were taken over by an immoral force—a financial elite, for instance, that bought off and corrupted our politicians—gun enthusiasts would stand around casually, blithely ignorant of the inner corruption, fondling their weapons only for the defense of their self-image.

This nation's preoccupation with gun-rights is not so much fear-based as passivity-based. We don't connect well enough with our better self and the higher values of integrity, courage, wisdom, and compassion. On an inner level, many people allow their inner critic to be the master of their personality and to pass judgment on their worthiness. Inwardly, they're emotionally weak and defensive, familiar with feeling helpless and overwhelmed, yet desperate to exhibit some pretense of assurance and power.

This is neurosis, not mental illness. A neurotic person is prone to being negative, defensive, fearful, anxious, and reactionary. Too many gun advocates are seeing the world through their neurosis. In many families, it's often the most dysfunctional or neurotic individuals who set the tone for the family and hold sway over it. Only determined intervention by healthier members of the family can save the situation. The American family needs such intervention in many areas of national life, beginning with some lessons about the prevalence and effects of wide-spread neurosis.

73 . Men's Resistance to Women's Empowerment

A lack of fairness and justice still handicap women, and the causes for such discrimination run deep into the recesses of the human psyche. Humanity can only progress to the degree that women do. So we need to root out some of the primitive elements of this inequity.

Injustice surfaces everywhere. "Women are still the majority of the world's poor, the uneducated, the unhealthy, the unfed," Hillary Clinton said in a speech to the United Nations. "Simply put, the world cannot make lasting progress if women and girls in the 21st century are denied their rights and left behind."[94]

For the most part, men are not being overtly malicious. Their discriminating reactions arise from psychological influences that are largely unconscious. The "feminine discount" problem stems in part from an age-old mentality that still perceives social relations in terms of who is superior and who is inferior. This mentality, dating back hundreds or thousands of generations, has been acted out by both sexes through religious affiliation ("my religion is superior to yours"), wealth ("my wealth

[94] http://www.csmonitor.com/USA/Foreign-Policy/2010/0312/Hillary-Clinton-at-UN-Women-s-progress-is-human-progress

puts me in a better class of people"), race ("my race is superior to yours"), intelligence ("I am smarter and therefore obviously better than you"), political power ("my authority makes me a superior person"), and gender ("as a man, I am stronger and therefore better than women.")

This mentality works both ways: while many people of both sexes eagerly believe in their superiority, many others passively accept their alleged inferiority without inner ripples of protest or rebellion. Either way, people are exhibiting a lack of consciousness or evolvement. The missing ingredient is an emotional and mental connection to one's intrinsic value and goodness.

In the West, oppression against women continues to exist in the form, for instance, of low wages, covert discrimination, or limited access to opportunities. Women are up against two forms of oppression: first, the oppression from men and the patriarchal order, and, second, the oppression they inflict upon themselves in the form of self-doubt and self-denial. (The next discussion deals with this second form of oppression.)

The oppression from men is based, in part, in men's fear of femininity and of women. This theme was explored by Freud when he wrote in his essay, "The Taboo of Virginity" (1918), that men have shown over time—through the taboos, customs, and avoidances involving their relations with women—"a generalized dread of women." What is this dread? It's based in the castration anxiety, which is man's fear that women will take away his strength, infect him with their femininity, and reveal him to be a weakling.

It's true that, when it flourishes, man's love for women and our intimacy with them have the effect of making us more tender-hearted and compassionate. So why this continuing fear of femininity and its values? Is it that women, knowing the "baby" in the man, see into the core of our being? Are we still reacting to Mother for challenging our infantile self-centeredness? Or is it the feeling that, in embracing our softer side, we'll lose power and hence be lesser creatures because of the alleged loss?

Psychoanalyst Karen Horney once wrote, "Is it not remarkable (we ask ourselves in amazement) when one considers . . . that so little recognition and attention are paid to the fact of men's secret dread of women?" Actually, it's not so remarkable. Men need a sense of core strength—one not defined by physical strength—in order to be at ease with women. Without that core strength, man is afraid that woman might be his better self. He's afraid because he resonates with (or is emotionally attached to) a profound self-doubt at the heart of his existence. His primitive instinct is to cover up this largely unconscious part of himself by making women out to be the weaker sex and himself the proud agent of mighty exploits. Men are reluctant to share power with women or to encourage women's empowerment to the degree that, on an inner level, we doubt our own value and power.

Men can also feel overpowered by their sexual attraction to women, while at the same time entertaining a sense of insignificance in the face of the natural life-giving power of women. It's common knowledge that many men are afraid of strong women and avoid relationships with them. Some men, skittish about intimacy, run away from acknowledging their inability (stemming from their entanglement in self-doubt) to affirm over time the intrinsic value of their partner. They frequently refuse to address this fear of "losing themselves" (their sense of autonomy, freedom, or independent standing) in a loving union.

For men to feel more at ease with powerful women, it means we have to grow in ourselves. Otherwise, we're uncomfortable with their power. Yet our resistance to inner development is remarkable in its magnitude.

Much progress has been made, of course, since Betty Friedan's *The Feminine Mystique* arrived 50 years ago. Yet men can still project their self-doubt on to women, "seeing" their own weakness in the opposite sex. We can sense instinctively that, should women become stronger, we'll be thrown deep into the horror of profound self-doubt. That means we might, even more frighteningly, become conscious of our emotional entanglement in that primal weakness. Our resistance proclaims, "I'm not a real man if I let women get the upper hand. Therefore, I'll fight and oppose what they stand for and their attempts to assert themselves." Through this pretext, men can manage to avoid the nagging assertion (from the aggressive superego deep in our psyche) that insists, "You're a worthless fraud, and you'll always be one!" Resisting the feminine side and, instead, equating manhood with an acceptance of war, conquest, and economic pillage allows us to escape into forms of denial such as the "glory" and "bravery" of reckless adventurism.

War and violence (in which women are often the greatest victims) become part of the cover-up for humankind's profound self-doubt. Glory in war is the manic thrill of riding the beast that ravishes our better self. Men will feel compelled to destroy as long as they continue, however unconsciously, to project their own weakness on to women and oppose the advance of women.

When men aren't tapping into the power of integrity, truthfulness, goodwill, and evolving consciousness, the only "powers" they can trust are self-aggrandizement, righteous indignation, and weaponry. With this mentality, we also use money, patriotism, and religion to recognize or proclaim our essential value, affirm our collective identity, and swear to our honorable intentions.

As we begin to recognize the fundamental self-doubt deep in our psyche, we expose our emotional entanglement in this negative impression. Even though the self-doubt is unconscious, we still identify with it. Until men get past this weakness, we will remain fearful of women's empowerment. Meanwhile, with greater consciousness, our natural aggression becomes appropriate and much more pleasurable as it's sublimated into healthy competitions, creative activities, and the pursuit of sustainable living.

74 . Aspects of Women's Empowerment

The women's revolution has stalled, in part because of psychological barriers women impose on themselves, writes Facebook executive Sheryl Sandberg in her book, *Lean In: Women, Work, and the Will to Lead.* These psychological barriers "are rarely discussed and often underplayed," Sandberg writes. Instead, many women prefer to blame institutional or external barriers for their lack of progress. But "internal obstacles deserve a lot more attention," she writes.[95]

What are these psychological issues standing in the way of women's progress? Sandberg identifies inner barriers that include fear, self-doubt, guilt, risk-adverse instincts, acceptance of cultural stereotypes, and sensitivity to the feeling of being disliked. The author cites numerous psychological studies and draws on her considerable personal experience to discuss these issues. The women's revolution is a vital aspect of human progress, of course, yet this revolution could conceivably fizzle out if we don't see more deeply into our psychological issues. In the previous discussion, I examined some deeper aspects of patriarchal oppression, and here I consider the deeper elements of women's self-oppression.

Sandberg writes that fear is a major problem for many aspiring women:

> Fear is at the root of so many of the barriers that women face. Fear of not being liked. Fear of making the wrong choice. Fear of drawing negative attention. Fear of overreaching. Fear of being judged. Fear of failure. And the holy trinity of fear: the fear of being a bad mother/wife/daughter.

Both men and women have irrational fears, and these fears are produced out of unresolved conflict in our psyche. We benefit greatly from exposing the inner

---

[95] Sandberg, Sheryl. Lean In: *Women, Work, and the Will to Lead.* New York: Alfred A. Knopf, 2013.

dynamics that produce these fears. Referring back to Sandberg's statement above, let's look more deeply into these dynamics.

Fear of not being liked. Consciously, the individual truly wants to be liked, but unconsciously she's emotionally unresolved with the feeling of being disliked. She lives in some anticipation of being disliked because that negative feeling is a powerful expectation as well as a sense of identity and even an emotional attachment. The fear becomes self-sabotaging because she worries about it and focuses on it, causing the fear to arise even as she thinks, "I'm very fearful of not being liked." In fact, the fear serves as an unconscious psychological defense. We instinctively defend against accusations from our inner critic that we harbor self-defeating wishes or attachments. The defense claims, "I'm not looking to be disliked, I'm not attached to that feeling of being rejected or being seen as a lesser person. Look at how fearful I am of that possibility."

Fear of making the wrong choice. She certainly wants to make good choices, but unconsciously she entertains feelings associated with making a wrong choice. In such an event, she would feel criticized or even condemned by both her inner critic and her coworkers and supervisors. She can feel such criticism in the moment, even when, through her imagination, she associates it with failure that might or might not occur in the future. Even without doing any one particular thing wrong, she can through her imagination absorb the feeling of criticism and aggression being directed at her. This self-critical impulse lives in the psyche of both women and men, and often we don't know ourselves or we can't experience ourselves without this inner limitation and torment. Resolving this conflict produces more inner freedom and sense of autonomy.

Fear of drawing negative attention. It's quite common for people to expect to be seen in a negative light. It part, this is how, through our inner critic, we can see ourselves. Our inner critic can be harsh, mocking, and belittling. This makes us quite sensitive to the feeling that others see us in the same light. Again, this means we're emotionally entangled in this negative impression, often to the degree that it becomes part of our identity. It's an axiom of psychology that whatever is unresolved in our psyche is at times going to be felt intensely by us, even when the experience is quite painful.

Our unconscious defense says: "I'm not looking for the feeling of being seen in a negative light. Look at how much I fear that possibility!" In truth, though, this person does indeed choose unconsciously to feel that she is being seen (or is going to be seen) in a negative light. She might also remember a past incident that was embarrassing or humiliating, and she now feels a need to carefully monitor herself or stifle herself to avoid a repeat occurrence. Another axiom: We fear occurrences of the experience of whatever we're emotionally attached to.

Fear of overreaching. The individual is trying to succeed without overreaching. The implication is that overreaching is a bad thing, allegedly an indication of grandiosity or self-importance. The individual is inwardly sensitive to unfair, demeaning accusations from her inner critic that such behavior is unseemly and arrogant. In contrast, society condones the behaviors of ambitious men who strive aggressively for leadership positions. Our inner critic can attack women more harshly because they don't have the same degree of cultural acceptance for their aggressiveness (although in the West that's changing for the better). As well, their aggressiveness is often mocked and scorned by weak or reactionary men and women. Of course, the unwillingness to "overreach," whatever that might mean to a person, inhibits one's potential and can also produce failure.

Fear of failure. Someone who consciously wants to succeed might unconsciously expect failure. She might have an inner critic that demeans and belittles her. Her inner critic might mock her ability and talent and, like a caricature of a dysfunctional parent, constantly predict the "likelihood" of her failure. As mentioned, we instinctively defend against our inner critic's accusations that we harbor self-defeating wishes or attachments. Her defense claims, "I'm not indulging emotionally in the feeling or the prospect of failure. Look at how much I fear that I might become a failure."

Fear of being judged. She is likely, through the inner critic, to be quite judgmental of herself. She will also be prone to be judgmental of others and sense that others are judging her. Her defense reads, "I'm not looking for the feeling of being judged. Look at how much I fear and hate that feeling!" Another defense claims, "I'm not looking to be judged. In fact, I'm the one who does the judging."

Fear of being a bad mother, wife, or daughter. Again, the inner critic instinctively holds us accountable as it poses as the mistress or master of our personality. It accuses talented women of being selfishly interested only in their own ambitions and not caring enough about others. For social and cultural reasons, women are particularly vulnerable to this accusation. This accusation, for the most part, is false. We're all entitled to pursue self-fulfillment, and we can trust in our inherent goodness and intelligence to avoid being selfish and to remain sensitive to others. But through self-doubt, we unconsciously give credence to the inner critic's accusations. This acceptance of the accusations is facilitated by inner passivity, the enabler of the inner critic. Both women and men are being inwardly passive when we absorb self-aggression from our inner critic. Our guilt is associated with the degree to which we are representing ourselves through inner passivity.

In writing about women's self-doubt, Sandberg also cites "the imposter syndrome." This refers to the sense of feeling fraudulent when presenting oneself as a competent person or professional. This emotional impression is produced largely by a primary conflict in the human psyche, namely the clash between our inner critic and inner passivity. As mentioned, we lose touch with our strength, goodness, and value when entangled in this inner conflict. We feel fraudulent to the degree that we're not in touch with our authentic self. Our authentic self arises out of the resolution of this conflict between inner aggression and inner passivity.

In my view, men tend to be more egotistical than women. That egotism, along with the male's aggressive instinct, can serve as a buttress (though an unstable one) against self-doubt and inner fear. With less egotism, women probably need to connect more deeply with their authentic self to feel their value and power. This is achieved when they clearly understand the nature of inner conflicts.

One technique involves monitoring and witnessing the passive and aggressive voices or feelings inside us, while creating some detachment from them. Sometimes inner voices can express intuitive self-protection, and they can legitimately inform us of something we might be overlooking. It's okay to hear inner voices—whether they're positive, negative, or neutral—as long as they're not governing our emotions and behaviors. We certainly don't want them to be too loud. We want to feel that our authentic self is in charge, that it keeps any inner voices in their place, and that it stands as the true representative of our well-being.

Through their empowerment, women can greatly improve the quality of our institutions. The world desperately needs leaders with true power, meaning people who know how to practice assertiveness and healthy aggression while being able to avoid taking offense, holding grudges, and practicing petty vindictiveness.

Feminine values and skills associated with nurturing, compassion, and social cohesion, along with traditional leadership skills, are needed more than ever in our stressed-out world. Women have to believe in these values and provide leadership to align our institutions with the common good.

75 . Why We Dither on Climate Change

I've been trying for some time to fathom the psychology of educated and supposedly sophisticated people who, in paralysis and resistance, are unwilling to respond rationally to the perils of climate change. We need to look deeply into the heart of this issue.

Why haven't we taken rational or logical steps to shut down our lethal fossil-fuels industry and to replace it with better conservation and renewable-energy technologies? An assortment of psychological reasons for our paralysis present themselves, including denial, greed, fear, passivity, stubbornness, self-centeredness, self-sabotage, and our species' lack of compassion for future generations.

Some concerned citizens see greed as the main problem. They want to break the power of the fossil-fuel industry and force it to keep its trillions of dollars in oil, coal, and gas reserves in the ground. They believe that if the industry is identified as the enemy of humanity, people will rise up to fight a moral battle against it.[96]

This strategy is well and good, yet most of us know the industry can be ruthless and greedy, and still we aren't dashing down the street to join coalitions that oppose it. I believe we have to look deeper into our paralysis. As we do moral battle with the industry, we need to initiate a *psychological* reformation within ourselves in order to become a powerful collective capable of driving social policy and political action. Such inner growth enables us to connect more deeply with our better self. This effort awakens our integrity, courage, and sense of moral responsibility. From this vantage, we're more likely to feel personally responsible for whatever needs to be fixed or reformed in our life and in the world. In this struggle to grow, however, we're all battling against our

---

[96] http://www.rollingstone.com/politics/news/global-warmings-terrifying-new-math-20120719

own resistance. We fight ourselves every step of the way.

Fixing the climate problem means we have to become responsible citizens of the highest order. Reality's imperatives are asking us to step outside our comfort zone and, quite literally, plunge into the metaphysical abyss, that middle passage from the wobbly known to the great unknown, when we die to the old way so as to be reborn into the new. Yet who are we to be so brave, noble, and responsible—so adventuresome and awesome? This is not the *little me* we're so comfortable with. Wouldn't such an undertaking be just as scary as departing Old Europe in a rickety ship to settle an unknown land? Better to hope we'll somehow survive or make-do without the need for lifestyle changes.

We're pinned down by paralysis because we identify, in part, with a limited sense of self that's often fearful, depressed, angry, cynical, and plagued by self-doubt. As one client put it, "It's the only *me* I know." Yet it's also the *me* we put first, above more noble considerations, because our consciousness, pinned down by its lack of evolvement, can't step outside its own self-centeredness and assimilate the bigger picture. Passivity, indecision, and doubt are earmarks identifying this little *me*.

Most people are *not* in denial about climate change. Through our intelligence, we can, of course, see a grim future for our children and their descendants. While we can see our part in causing this catastrophe, we decline to fully imagine the mass suffering and destruction that the climate crisis foretells. Stuck in our psychological limbo, we absolve ourselves of all responsibility for the coming upheaval. We choose to linger at the tomb of non-being rather than shake off our paralysis and become advocates for renewable energy. The interests of future generations—even notions of their being—are erased from the instruction books of our entitlement. Individualism trumps sacrifice.

It's not that we're afraid of Big Oil or Big Coal. Rather, we're fearful of awakening our better self. As author Marianne Williamson has written, "Our deepest fear is not that we are inadequate. Our deepest fear is that we are powerful beyond measure. It is our light, not our darkness, that most frightens us."

Why are we frightened? If we change too much, we won't know the mysterious stranger we're destined to become. Psychologist David Seabury (1885-1960) wrote, "Fear of self is the greatest of all terrors, the deepest of all dread, the commonest of all mistakes. From it grows failure. Because of it, life is a mockery. Out of it comes despair." Psychotherapist Alexander Lowen touched on this theme in his book, *Fear of Life*, as did psychologist Erich Fromm in *The Fear of Freedom*. In our resistance, we cling tightly to our limited sense of self, convinced that letting go will pitch us into the void. Thanks to this denial and resistance, we decline to access the reality that identifies us as menacing creatures, perhaps an invasive species, lacking in self-awareness, unable to regulate the powerful technologies produced by our cunning mind, and unwilling in our pride to bow before Nature or to recognize the humbling truths of human nature.

Resistance is both internal and external. Consider the fierce *external* resistance that suffragists encountered in trying to get the vote, or that black Americans faced during the struggle for civil rights. In world capitals, meanwhile, resistance is politicized: A faction, unwittingly representing the resistance in our psyche, stands firm against the advance of consciousness. In my psychotherapy practice, I see on a regular basis how *inner* resistance pops up in the psyche of my clients as they struggle—two steps forward, one step back—to break free of limited, negative ways of experiencing themselves and the world. I also see how, as their inner work brings forth their integrity and goodness, they embrace the imperative of being responsible for the quality of their experience of life. They're on their way to becoming responsible for the quality of all life.

The collective resistance to action on climate change is an external rendition of the inner resistance we have to self-development. We need to make inner resistance more conscious to avoid the repercussions of collective stupidity and self-sabotage. We've all felt resistance to doing what's right in everyday matters, even if we don't quite understand the dynamic of *inner* resistance. Everyday resistance arises when we're considering whether to do something appropriate or wise, such as taking a walk instead of watching TV or cooking a healthy meal instead of eating junk food. The excuses we use to defeat a noble idea or effort are the weaponry of our resistance. When resistance wins, we lose.

Meditators know all about resistance. In meditation, they practice mental concentration to develop inner strength. The aim is to still the mind and thereby produce inner serenity, along with self-regulation and self-mastery. Resistance invariably kicks in, threatening to sabotage the meditation. The mind intrudes with random, aimless thoughts and speculations that reestablish the old order in which no one is in charge of the inner experience. In meditation, people can observe how this resistance tempts them with swarms of enticing memories, attachments, and validations, all in an effort to abandon the path of inner development. It's become a life-or-death struggle: Does the old mental and emotional chaos prevail or does a wise direction and peaceful bearing calm the storms within?

Now it seems likely that, to save our world, we have to win this great battle between the forces of our resistance and the calling of our destiny.

Maybe it's about saving our souls, as well. If we're prepared to allow life to become a hell on earth for our descendants, what kind of eternity can we expect?

76 . **Eight Ways We Sabotage Physical Health**

This discussion was written by my late wife, Sandra Michaelson, a psychotherapist and author. Her digital and paperback books on relationships and codependency are available at www.WhyWeSuffer.com.

Many studies have shown that stress can cause disease and that suppressed anger or fear can make us sick. Negative thoughts and emotions depress us and affect our immune system. These connections between mind and body are well established in psychosomatic research.

So pain and illness can be seen as manifestations of embedded emotional conflicts. We can use illness either to mobilize us for further psychological growth and enhanced physical health or to mire us more deeply in disease and a victim position.

Health problems often are an indication of a needed change in how we feel about ourselves and our lives. Illness can be a physical representation of forces in all of us that oppose our wholeness, victimize us, stop our progress, and render us powerless.

For example, the disease herpes can become, emotionally, a manifestation of a part of us that's entrenched in feeling defective, contaminated, unwanted, unlovable, and rejected. This disease often represents an expression of unconscious sexual conflicts and feelings of shame and self-rejection pertaining to our sexual conduct and our sexual identity.

All of us in varying degrees have an unconscious resistance to growth. Emotionally, growth can even feel like loss of our old self rather than the gain of a new sense of self. We can feel that if we become healthy we'll have nothing left for which to struggle. Many of us are addicted to struggle or to feeling drained, pressured, or overwhelmed. I knew a lawyer who would always manage to become ill just before an important trial. His courtroom appearance was turned into a major inner trial that was suffused with the prospect of looking bad and being seen as ineffective.

Problems with our physical health can stem from a buried conviction that we really don't deserve health, success, or happiness. Health and happiness feel foreign to us because they don't correspond with our expectations or with our sense of who we are. Loss, deprivation, and feelings of neglect are more familiar to us than prosperity or feeling loved. Even the good in our lives causes anxiety in some of us because we expect it to be lost or taken away. Failing to succeed helps us to avoid the expectation of a painful loss.

Sickness can be a byproduct of the depth and magnitude of our self-hatred and self-negation. It can also be a manifestation of our guilt, regret, shame, and bitterness toward others. Here are eight ways our unresolved negative emotions can be influencing our health:

1) Disease as a way to connect with others. The major attention I received from my mother came in the form of discussions about my problems, particularly my physical problems. I realized that getting sick as a child was a way to get my parents' attention. We can feel closer to others when we get sick. For some, being healthy brings up emotional associations with feeling alone and abandoned.

2) As a way to get back at a parent or spouse. I had a client who exhausted herself to the point of serious illness by overworking and striving for accomplishment in her field. We discovered she was acting out anger towards her husband and her mother. Her motivation was fueled by this hidden feeling: "Okay mother, you insist that I work hard and succeed. I'll do what you want, but I'll kill myself in the process and then you'll see what you've done." Her sickness was an attempt to induce guilt in her mother and husband for how she felt controlled by them. But, in effect, her illness became a way to maintain the feeling of being victimized and enslaved by her mother's and husband's control.

3) As a way to be a victim of neglectful people. Some people, especially codependents or what I call emotional caterers, go out of their way, to the detriment of their own health, to satisfy the needs of others. In turn, they intensify the feeling of being neglected or not supported when they get sick themselves. Their unconscious protest is: "You see how far I go to help you. I'm willing to sacrifice myself, even my health, to show you how much I care. If only you gave me one-tenth of the support I give you!" Illness makes them even more a victim of uncaring people.

They use sickness as a way to feel let down and disappointed when others do not cater to them or take care of them according to expectations. Through illness, they try to put the other person in the role of neglectful parent, recreating their childhood experience of feeling hurt when others (parents) did not respond with sufficient support and acknowledgement.

4) As retaliation against someone close to you. If you feel neglected or hurt by a spouse or partner, you can retaliate by becoming sick and thus unavailable to them. This is particularly common among partners of alcoholics or drug addicts. Getting sick is a common response to feelings of powerlessness against the disagreeable behaviors or attitudes of some family members.

5) As a way to resist the control of others. The person who is sick is able to reverse a situation in which he or she feels controlled or helpless. Now it feels as if the sickness controls the situation. This unconscious maneuver places others at the mercy of the conditions or requirements of the sick person. Developing food disorders is one example.

6) As a way to express dependency. Here individuals shift responsibility for themselves on to others. Such individuals include chronic "dependees," people who often rely on guilt to get others to take care of them and do things for them. Through their illness, they set others up to be caretakers or pseudo-parents.

7) As an expression of one's identity. Some people become emotionally invested in their disease as the primary way in which they know and experience themselves. One of my clients had a mother who was perpetually sick. The mother told her, "Nobody knows what it feels like to be sick like I am." She was invested in having the greatest pain and being the sickest person around, which gave her an unhealthy form of comfort and validation.

8) As a way to avoid commitment. How many of us have used sickness to get out of doing something we really didn't want to do? If we're incapacitated in some way, others won't expect anything much from us. Some people even feel that if they become healthy or successful, others will make more demands on them. We can feel that, if we're healthy, we have more obligations to fulfill and more people to take care of. So illness can be a passive, self-defeating way of saying *no* or a way of isolating.

When we become conscious of these ulterior motives for becoming sick or remaining sick, we can more easily recover our health and move on happily with our life.

VI – STRUGGLES, PROCEDURES AND TECHNIQUES

77 . Overcoming a Type of Resistance to Studying

This topic is addressed as an exchange of e-mails between me and a visitor to my website.

Reader's comment: I have always been a studious person. Grades were important . . . I was also interested in learning and still am. However, now that I'm at university I'm avoiding studying. It's not laziness or not caring. I feel fear. I have studied by myself all my life, so absence of family is not a big factor.

Whenever I do manage to study, I feel depressed afterwards. I feel like I have no energy, am mentally foggy, and at the mercy of my thoughts and criticism. All other life issues come back in full force, and I often cry. I also feel depressed again. I used to be very depressed, but now manage to keep it in check and mostly stand up for myself, except when it comes to studying.

Unfortunately, studying is necessary. I want to understand this reaction. More importantly, I want to feel pleased with myself after having studied for the allotted time. . . With all the inner work I've done, it feels as if this reaction has a strange power to put me right back to the beginning. I find it very painful.

Is it because studying is a "passive" thing to do? I feel much better after physical activity and such. But after studying, I feel robbed of the little inner strength and confidence I try hard to build every day. . . Why would this be? Do you have any ideas?

My reply: I'll suggest one possibility. Let me know whether you think it applies to you. You asked, is "studying a passive thing to do?" It's not passive at all, yet a person can have a passive reaction when doing it or even when just thinking about doing it. It appears that you're having a passive reaction to studying. Through inner passivity, you produce a negative emotional reaction that causes you to experience the challenge of studying through inner weakness. Rather than experiencing the resolve to study and enjoying the acquisition of knowledge, you choose unconsciously to feel that studying is an onerous task that drains and depletes you. Unconsciously, you're opting for that passive experience.

As part of this, you may be approaching studying as something you feel "forced" to do. Of course, in reality you do very likely need to study in order to succeed with your course work. However, you unwittingly add on an emotional component to this requirement: you feel you're being required or forced to do something against your will. Instinctively, you resist this feeling of being forced, and you thereby resist doing the studying. When you do manage to study, you feel as if you were forced to submit or "give in" to that requirement or obligation. This emotional interpretation of your experience leaves you feeling depressed afterwards. Notice that you say, "Unfortunately, studying is necessary." Your use of the word "unfortunately" suggests that you regard studying in a negative sense, as something that's unpleasant and onerous. Unconsciously, you're using studying as a way to experience yourself through the weakness of unresolved inner passivity.

So you interpret the need to study as an obligation that you're forced to comply with. This is an emotional, irrational interpretation of your situation—not a rational one. Nobody is forcing you to do anything. You're the one who has chosen to be a student, and being a student has its challenges and obligations. Meanwhile, you're also passive to your inner critic (as indicated by your statement, "... at the mercy of my thoughts and criticism.") You fear that your inner critic is free to attack you harshly should you, in failing to study, do badly on exams. Your inner critic can also attack you for any procrastination on your part and also for your passive feelings as you struggle to concentrate and to absorb the course material.

Through inner passivity, you're tempted to feel passive to your inner critic. As a result, you allow your inner critic to operate as your inner authority. We all do this to some extent, and then we try to cover up, through unconscious defenses, our propensity to be passive in one way or another. You could be saying in your unconscious defense: "Oh, I don't want to do poorly on exams and suffer from an inner critic attack. Look at how fearful I am that I might fail." This defense covers up inner truth about your unconscious collusion in feeling passive to your inner critic. The defense also contributes to your suffering because you produce stress, anxiety and fear as part of your defense.

Procrastination is also an inevitable painful symptom. It's also a defense. As you're willing, through inner passivity, to feel passive or helpless in the face of the need to study, you can produce this defense: "I don't want to feel helpless. Look at how much I really do want to study. Look at how bad I feel because I'm not studying." When used as a defense, procrastination can become increasingly painful and self-defeating.

If this analysis is correct, you can begin to apply the insight to your daily experiences. You want to stop your inner critic from being so intrusive in your life. That requires you to recognize your inner passivity which is the unconscious part in your psyche that enables and tolerates your inner critic. Deeper insight reveals your emotional attachments to feeling controlled, helpless, and criticized.

As we emerge from inner passivity, we connect with our authentic self. When this sense of self emerges from within, we are empowered and we start to recognize and represent our best interests. Now you can stop interpreting the need to study as something you're forced to submit to. Ultimately, you want studying to be a conscious choice you make to acquire knowledge, empower yourself, and feel the pleasure of fulfillment and accomplishment.

Reader's reply: I think you explained it very well. It has already helped a bit. I think I have a lot of inner passivity. Just doing things to prove the "critic" wrong is often not enough. It pops up in every area of my life. It's very hard to get under control. Seeing through this dynamic takes a lot of energy. When I'm tired or feel ill, passivity is more likely to creep in because it all feels too familiar.

Do you think this evolved consciousness settles in eventually? After such realizations, I sometimes still rebel against my better self and refuse to look deeper again. Or I get lost in the outside world and I forget my own role. It does take energy to keep focusing on yourself.

Your book has been very helpful, but I feel as if both my inner critic and passivity are so strong and familiar... Just wondering, does it get better? Can it become your "first" nature? Would you have any tips to beat passivity when you physically feel low in energy?

It feels difficult for me to stay in control of myself, yet not be rigid or fearful of "forgetting this knowledge and reverting back," especially after wallowing in passivity for so long. Indeed, when I let go and get very submerged in something (like studying), I'm overcome with helplessness and I have difficulty raising my hopes again—even with new knowledge. Overall, I cannot say how much your insights have helped me. It means so much to me to know there is a way out.

My reply: Indeed, it can take a long time—sometimes many years—to work inner passivity out of our system and tame our inner critic. If we practice daily attention to this knowledge, we can observe gradual progress, even from month to month. Even slow progress can leave us feeling deeply gratified and encouraged. It helps to be patient as we allow our destiny to unfold. Remember that if you don't make this effort, the passivity is likely to stay with you throughout your life. As you age, it might get worse, producing more painful symptoms.

The inner critic, too, will continue to "pop up" on a regular basis. Now, though, we see it more clearly for what it is—a primitive aggression in our psyche that will continue to rule us unless we intervene. Each time we expose it, and manage not to take it so seriously or be intimidated by it, we are weakening it.

You say, "It does take energy to keep focusing on yourself." Actually, we waste a lot more energy (producing defenses and acting out painful symptoms) when we're hopelessly caught in inner conflict. Deeper awareness protects us from our harsh inner critic. We no longer need to concoct inner defenses that burn up a lot of energy. That energy can now be used productively and creatively.

You're right that inner passivity can be a bigger problem when you're tired or feeling ill. Yet inner passivity can also be a direct cause of apathy, fatigue, and illness. You'll likely feel better physically as well as emotionally when you're breaking free of it. In conclusion, keep your eye on the ball and don't let inner passivity or the inner critic run your life. See these aspects of yourself in a neutral way, not as something to regret, feel ashamed about, or feel overwhelmed by. Try to respect yourself and believe in yourself even as you might feel you're being swarmed by inner chaos and conflict.

Our authentic self becomes our "first" nature as we resolve the conflict between inner passivity and inner aggression (the inner critic).

78 . **The Futile Dialogue in Our Head**

I've written quite a bit at this point about the conflict between inner aggression and inner passivity. The following discussion is another perspective on this conflict. There's some repetition here, yet there's also a new slant on the subject. As I've been saying, we want to bring the conflict into the best possible focus, and seeing it from different perspectives serves that purpose.

Our mind is the staging ground for the acting out of a recurring dialogue between the two main contributors to the conflict. In people with mental disorders, one of these contributors—inner aggression—can take over or "possess" the consciousness of these individuals and command them to commit dangerous or criminal acts. Yet the rest of us can also experience the conflict in the form of troublesome inner voices. The inner voices of everyday people are more subtle, restrained, and rational than in mentally disturbed individuals. Yet these voices or thoughts can still take control of the consciousness of regular people, producing suffering and self-defeat.

Oppressive inner dialogue consists, on one side, of the point of view of inner aggression. This dynamic or drive is seated in our inner critic or superego. On the other side of the conflict, inner passivity (seated in our defensive subordinate ego) functions as an enabler of our inner critic. Classical psychoanalysis has known about this inner conflict, but the universality of the problem, the self-damage it causes, and its mechanisms of operation are not being well communicated to people.

There's a lot of resistance to seeing this inner conflict because it exposes us, at this deep level, to be quite a bit less informed than we would like to think. There's "a monkey on our back" when we can't self-regulate successfully, and there are "asses in our head" when through inner dialogue we bicker foolishly with our self.

This dialogue proceeds according to a straightforward formula: Inner aggression attacks and inner passivity defends. Our inner critic attacks or belittles us for our slightest mistakes or misdemeanors. Sometimes we're attacked just for what we *think*—we don't even have to do anything bad or wrong to feel the wrath of the inner critic. Meanwhile, on the other side of the conflict, our unconscious subordinate ego jumps up reflexively to defend us, even when the accusations from our inner critic are spurious, cruel, or just plain nonsense. Often our unconscious ego offers up guilt and shame, which is a price we pay in suffering, to placate our relentless, authoritarian inner critic.

We tend to be unaware of the existence of the conflict. Still, our emotions, beliefs, and sense of self are caught in the middle, shifting back and forth from one side to the other, depending on which point of view is most influencing us at any moment. Sometimes we detect the conflict with varying degrees of awareness; we're likely to be more aware of our inner critic than our inner passivity. Like a feeble bystander, though, we're often unable to put a stop to this primitive clash of aggression and passivity.

Below are two examples of this futile inner conflict. Bringing this dialogue into better focus can help us to moderate it (if not eliminate it) when it arises in our psyche.

A businessman reported that, when driving to work, he often got into a debate with himself concerning his investments. On his drive, which took him past the branch offices and retail outlets of major companies, he tried to evaluate their state of commercial activity. This brought up self-doubt concerning the wisdom of his investments. An inner dialogue followed along these lines:

> Inner aggression: *Look at that business and how well it's doing. How come you're not invested in that business!*
>
> Inner passivity: *Yes, it's appears to be doing well, but I can't be invested in everything.*
>
> Inner aggression: *Of course, you can't be invested in everything. But you can still be making better decisions! You're losing money on that last investment you made.*
>
> Inner passivity: *I haven't lost that much. I'm sure it's going to come back. And, anyway, it was my financial adviser that got me into that mess.*
>
> Inner aggression: *You didn't study the market well enough. You should have known what was going to happen. It was a dumb move!*
>
> Inner passivity: *I'm going to talk to a fellow I met the other day. He knows a lot about the market.*
>
> Inner aggression: *Good, talk to him! Maybe he can smarten you up.*

And on it goes. The content of the dialogue, or whether it happens to be rational or relevant, is mostly beside the point. The driving force at play is the compulsion to express or represent either a passive or an aggression viewpoint.

In this next example, a woman caring for her cantankerous ailing mother was feeling exhausted and drained by the experience. This dialogue expressed, in part, her emotional entanglement in the task:

> Inner aggression: *You're not really that kind to her. You should be doing more for her.*
>
> Inner passivity: *What an extraordinarily good person I am for looking after her. I feel like a saint.*
>
> Inner aggression: *That's a joke! You resent every minute of it. You really don't like her that much, do you?*
>
> Inner passivity: *I'm trying my hardest to help her. She takes it all for granted.*
>
> Inner aggression: *Didn't she always take you for granted. That's the way it's always been. What else is new! Now you pretend to be a saint! Why don't you tell her what you really feel!*
>
> Inner passivity: *What's the use now? I can't just abandon her. I have to go through the motions, doing what I can.*
>
> Inner aggression: *Just don't pretend you're some kind of saint.*

And on and on. In these examples, the individuals are identifying with themselves primarily through their unconscious ego, their inner passivity. If, instead, they were experiencing themselves through their authentic self, they would identify with their own trusted inner authority and they wouldn't even be engaged in such dialogue. In this following example, the voice of inner passivity has now been replaced by the voice of our authentic self, representing inner wisdom and strength. This example provides a feeling for how our inner authority can represent our best interests as it neutralizes the inner critic. At some point, there'll be no such dialogue because the inner conflict will be resolved through the emergence of our authentic self:

>Inner aggression: *You made a fool of yourself at the office today. How could you have asked such a stupid question at the meeting?*
>
>Self: *Did I just hear some inner criticism?*
>
>Inner aggression: *Yes, you did! Do I have to repeat myself!*
>
>Self: *Who invited you in? What's this nonsense you're babbling?*
>
>Inner aggression: *Don't think you can brush me aside so easily.*
>
>Self: *You're silly. Go away.*
>
>Inner aggression: *No, I won't!*
>
>Self: *Okay, stay around. I don't care.*
>
>Inner aggression: *Did you hear what I said?*

Self: *I heard you. But I can't take you seriously. I'm no longer in your thrall. I no longer relate to your aggression and negativity. Your power over me has greatly diminished.*

Inner aggression: *Well, you'd better listen. I know what I'm talking about.*

Self: *(Silence)*

Inner aggression: *(Silence)*

When connected to our authentic self, we see our inner aggression (what's left of it) as ridiculous, and we can laugh in the face of it. We now refuse to engage with it because we know it has no interest in being rational and because we no longer give it any credence.

To find that strength, we can say to ourselves, "Oh, that's the voice of inner passivity," or "That's the voice of the inner critic." This ability to identify the voices for what they are helps us to stand outside the conflict and see the situation with a sense of some detachment, objectivity, and separation. We know the voices can't be trusted. They contain no wisdom. They're indifferent to our well-being. They represent opposing sides in our conflicted psyche and simply function accordingly. When we create a sense of separation from them, we're able to bring the conflict into focus and thus become less entangled in it.

Our growing ability to see unhealthy dialogue and to recognize its irrationality means we're establishing wise inner authority. With new consciousness, we can stand back from the conflict and find anchorage in our growing sense of self.

79 . Exterminate Infestations of Negative Thoughts

Recurring negative thoughts are another variation of mental and emotional turmoil. These thoughts are like termites that chew up and spit out our happiness. Many of us are frequently overwhelmed by such worrisome, anxious, fearful, and hateful thoughts. These thoughts gnaw at the fabric of our life, yet we're often oblivious to basic knowledge that can eradicate this intrusive infestation.

These thoughts often seem reality-based. Certainly, it can be easy to believe the content of these thoughts. They seem to capture objectively the nature and extent of our plight. When they overpopulate our mind, they can produce an ugly reality, a self-defeating acting-out of our negative outlook and worst fears. We must understand, though, that they represent a subjective impression rather than any deeper truth about us or our life.

Before getting to the deeper knowledge, let's look at a list of common negative thoughts. (This list is bleak and grim. To introduce a little levity and playfulness, let's read this section as experimental poetry noir.) I've separated this list into three categories that are explained farther on:

A. *Negative thoughts associated with inner passivity:* No one understands me or knows what I feel; I'll never make it; I can't get started; I'm so weak, helpless, and out of control; I can't get things together; I can't finish anything; I don't think I can go on; I feel like I'm alone against the world; I'm sure I'm going to get a serious disease; I'll never be healthy and happy again; I've run out of options; What's the point of trying?

B. *Negative thoughts associated with our inner critic:* I'm no good; My life is a mess; I'm a failure; I'm a loser; I hate myself; I'm also worthless and deserve to suffer; Why can't I ever succeed? How could I have made that stupid mistake?

C. *Negative thoughts associated with inner defenses:* My life's not going the way I want it to; I'm so disappointed in myself; I've let people down; My problem is I'm too lazy; I wish I were somewhere else; I wish I could just disappear; Nothing feels good anymore; I wish I were a better person; My future is bleak; It's just not worth it; Something has to change.

This is just a small selection of what our psyche produces. Hundreds of examples could be provided dealing with inner conflict and emotional attachments concerning rejection, betrayal, loss, abandonment, fear, envy, anger, hatred, and so on.

Studies have shown that "thought suppression" banishes negative thoughts only temporarily. We can't simply make these disagreeable thoughts go away by using willpower to push them out of our mind. Unpleasant thoughts are fueled by hidden dynamics in our emotional life. When we try to use willpower alone, we set up a battle between our mind and our emotions. Our negative emotions often win this battle because our mind, when it fails to access vital knowledge, can't expose the underlying dynamics that produce unwanted thoughts. In this losing battle, we're left feeling our weakness or helplessness even more intensely.

Most mental-health workers don't see the deeper problem. They offer only *advice* on how to stop these intrusive thoughts. Some of this advice, such as a recommendation to postpone the negative thoughts until later, is silly and useless. Other advice, such as encouragement to meditate, does have value. Meditation is the practice of concentration and focus. When done skillfully, it's able to quiet our mind and block unwanted thoughts. Yet the benefits tend to erode when daily practice stops. Meditation, in itself, won't necessarily produce a psychological understanding of the vitally important process by which we generate negative thoughts in the first place.

Negative thoughts are the means by which we mentally register our suffering, unwittingly facilitate it, and, through our psychological defenses, try to explain or rationalize it.

The first category of negative thoughts (the A group from the list above) relates to inner passivity. As mentioned, this inner weakness, dating back to early childhood, is associated with feeling helpless, dominated, controlled, and at the mercy of others or circumstances. In childhood, we were indeed quite helpless and powerless in many ways. As adults, an inner conflict still exists in our psyche between wanting to feel strong versus expecting to be weak or helpless.

So insidious is the temptation to experience life through old, familiar passive feelings that we end up plunging unconsciously into this emotional weakness. In doing so, we generate accompanying thoughts that frame our painful experience.

With more awareness, we can apply insight to our experiences. Whenever we become aware of having one of these negative thoughts in the A category, we can expose the underlying emotional attachment by acknowledging to ourselves that, "I'm choosing to experience myself through unresolved inner passivity, and doing so is producing my painful feelings of being weak, helpless, overwhelmed, and a failure."

As an example, many people who aren't ill nonetheless entertain fearful thoughts to the effect, "I know I have a serious disease." Hypochondriacs, for instance, "buy into" this recurring thought in order to recycle and replay the sense of being at the mercy of an (imagined) illness that will get the best of them. Their suffering is the price they pay for their underlying emotional addiction to the victimhood of helplessness and powerlessness.

With this awareness, we can take responsibility for what's happening in our life. Remember that people resist taking responsibility for their suffering. We deny our complicity in our suffering. Instead, we try to blame it on others or on difficult circumstances.

The second category (B) is associated with negative thoughts generated by our inner critic. As mentioned, this agency in our psyche is harsh and cruel, and it assails us with sarcasm, mockery, and other belittling accusations. When we feel this harassment, we create a corresponding thought that reflects our experience. The more chronic the inner harassment from our inner critic, the more we're plagued by negative thoughts.

Essentially, we feel or we say to ourselves, in the form of negative thoughts and impressions, what our inner critic is saying to us. As we absorb this aggression from our inner critic, we become an unwitting spokesperson for that part of our psyche.

Note that we can also be an unwitting spokesperson for inner passivity, as in category A, as well as an unwitting spokesperson for our defenses, as in category C. For example, inner passivity might generate a thought or feeling to this effect: "Why worry about doing that task today. Let it wait. Go out and relax in the sun." The individual becomes the mouthpiece of this inner impulse, saying to himself or herself: "I'm not going to worry about doing this. I think I'll go out and get some sun." (Our conscious ego, the puppet prince of the mind, hates to see our unwitting compliance to such unconscious dynamics.)

Category C is a list of statements that represent the duplicity of our psychological defenses. Each of these statements can be traced back to show the structure and operation of the underlying defense. As mentioned earlier, one statement on the list—"My problem is I'm too lazy"—is a defense that pleads guilty to what our psyche's accounting system considers "a lesser crime." The defense reads, "I'm not guilty of indulging in feelings of being helpless. The problem is I'm too lazy." The individual, however, pays a big price for employing this unconscious defense. In pleading guilty to being lazy, the person suffers with guilt and tormenting negative thoughts having to do with the alleged laziness.

Eradicating inner negativity is a momentous achievement, and we need good knowledge of our psyche's operating system in order to succeed.

80. Four Steps to Stifle Our Inner Critic

We all have, as I've been saying, an active inner critic. It's a force of human nature that I can, in whimsical moments, visualize as the leader of an outlaw trio that includes the gun-slinging desperado, Yosemite Sam, and his fellow Looney Tunes cartoon character, the ferocious, dim-witted Tasmanian Devil.

There's nothing comic or funny, however, about dealing with this built-in tormentor. It might be more accurately depicted as the leader of a trio that includes Darth Vader and Lord Voldemort. It produces much of humanity's anxiety, fear, and depression. The inner critic can operate inside us like a cruel aggressive tyrant whose intent is to rule our life. Subduing or taming it could be the most heroic thing we ever do.

That process can be accomplished in four steps. First, we must become aware of our inner critic. A lot of people don't even know they have one, though they might be suffering acutely from its influence. We want to notice how and when it intrudes into our life. Second, we begin to understand that our inner critic is a big fat liar. Third, we start to realize how we tend to be passive to it, how we let it get away with harassing, belittling, and punishing us. Fourth, we learn how to stand up to it. Our stronger sense of self and growing inner authority begin to subdue it. Here's how we can make this happen:

Step One – Our inner critic dishes out self-aggression. We all have aggressive energy, and ideally we learn to channel it in creative, constructive ways. But we have to be emotionally strong and healthy to keep our aggressive energy from becoming a negative force, both in terms of how we relate to others and in terms of how, on an inner level, we relate to ourselves.

When our inner critic is acting up and intruding into our mental and emotional life, we want to try to realize that this is occurring. People often don't experience the inner critic in any conscious way. The stream of negativity that emanates from it can do much of its mischief entirely at an unconscious level. Even though our inner critic is a callous bully, it can go unnoticed, like a little ant walking across a carpet. In such instances, we can detect its presence through feelings or thoughts we might be having that are defensive in nature. Examples include, "Nobody is perfect," "I had no choice," and "It wasn't my fault." Such defensive thoughts are produced when our inner critic is in attack mode.

Step Two – Recognize that the inner critic is a blatant liar. It has no interest in our wellbeing. Nor does it care about truth. All it cares about is the expression of its primitive, aggressive energy. It only wants to lord it over us and hold us accountable. It wants us to be passive to it and to feel guilt and shame at its judgments and condemnations.

On occasion, the inner critic comes after us with allegations or accusations that seem to have some basis in fact. For instance, you might have said or done something foolish. Normally, you make note of any apparent foolishness on your part, and you resolve to do better in the future. The inner critic, however, is prepared to berate you mercilessly for the transgression and go on indefinitely doing so. The inner critic declares,

"You were a fool to say that!" or "You should know better!" It gladly makes a felony out of some misdemeanor and blows it out of proportion.

It's important to get a feel for the way our inner critic manipulates the facts. A big part of how we vanquish our inner critic is by seeing clearly just how irrational and cruel it really is. Again, suppose you did something foolish. Now imagine that a good friend talks to you about it. He or she would try to be helpful or supportive, and maybe have advice on how that behavior could be avoided in the future. In contrast, the inner critic lashes out cruelly, holds you accountable, and punishes you. As a general rule, discount anything the inner critic says or implies. It simply can't be trusted to represent truth or to care about your wellbeing.

Step Three –We begin to become aware of how, on an inner level, we're passive and defensive with our inner critic. As a primitive, aggressive part of our psyche, it will rule our inner life if we let it. It whips out aggression like a scorpion snaps its stinger. To empower ourselves, we become conscious of the part of our psyche—inner passivity—that is submissive to it. We need to understand inner passivity in order to get the full scoop on our inner critic.

Not only is our inner passivity an enabler of the inner critic, it is very much ready and willing to play that role. All it knows is the instinct to be passive and defensive. It always operates from a position of weakness because, for one thing, it's intimidated by the inner critic. Much of the fear that people feel has its roots in this inner dynamic.

Many people, in their sense of self, become the voice and experience of inner passivity. They see themselves, others, and the world through the "eyes" of inner passivity. They easily feel victimized and they identify with people who they feel are being victimized. (This identification with the victim is not an experience of compassion. Compassion involves being heart-felt and loving, so it's not a painful feeling. Compassion is likely to inspire people to respond effectively to help reform situations. In contrast, experiences that are influenced by inner passivity tend to be painful and are more likely to produce apathy or paralysis.)

Step Four – As we bring inner passivity into focus, we become aware of how we have been far too accommodating to our inner critic. We start to feel how we can now stand up to it. We do this *not* by enlisting inner passivity as an ally but by experiencing our authentic self as it emerges out of the conflict between the inner critic and inner passivity.

We identify with inner passivity one moment, the inner critic the next. Our weak sense of self is buffeted back and forth between the polarities. We're weakened when trapped in that conflict because too much of our sense of self is smothered or consumed by the influences of those two parties to the conflict. The conflict, as mentioned, also binds up considerable energy that would otherwise be employed for useful, creative, and pleasurable pursuits.

When we see the conflict, we can manage through our intelligence not to participate in it. We're no longer inwardly defensive. We demote the inner critic to being just a minor nuisance, saying in effect: "Go away! I don't take you seriously anymore!" In this process of liberating ourselves from the negative inner critic, we see more clearly the irrationality of both the aggressive and the passive sides of the inner conflict.

We now evolve away from conflict toward greater harmony. With the inner critic no longer able to get away with its belittling harassment, we acquire a fuller sense of our integrity and goodness. We begin to feel our sense of authority. We stop second-guessing ourselves. Self-doubt evaporates. We trust ourselves more. We believe in ourselves and in our value.

81 . Ease Tension and Stress at Family Gatherings

Lingering emotional wounds from our family of origin are like riptides in our psyche. Most of us in childhood experienced, to some degree, feelings of being refused, controlled, betrayed, or rejected. As adults, many of us, swept along by old emotional undercurrents, are unable to enjoy our time together at family gatherings. Here are some principles of depth psychology to help us foster better relationships with family members.

Most of us, of course, do want to feel affection and love for parents, brothers, sisters, and other relatives and in-laws. But time we spend with close or extended family can challenge us emotionally, producing shades of anxiety, shame, embarrassment, anger, and envy. Such gatherings bring to the surface any unresolved issues we have from childhood.

In the emotional world of our psyche, time and place are compressed. An old hurt we feel now as an adult on the West Coast can be as painful as when we first experienced it 50 years earlier on the East Coast. As we're becoming more psychologically astute, we're able to observe how, through our emotional imagination, we surreptitiously return to the scene of the "crime" to conjure afresh the old hurts of yesteryear. Without that astuteness, people have no clear idea how their emotional pain is being produced.

Our discomfort can be traced, in part, to childhood experiences involving broken promises, misplaced trust, willful neglect, unexplained absences, verbal and physical abuse, and the playing of favorites. Impressions of being overlooked and undervalued, and the tribulations of competing for affection, also leave visible or hidden emotional scars. Even when people aren't aware of harboring grudges or feeling hurt, they might still unconsciously maintain an emotional and physical separation that cuts them off from the pleasures available in old, abiding relationships.

The following example shows such dynamics at play. A client in his forties attended a memorial service for a family member and left after a few hours feeling anxious and depressed. Later, he felt guilty and discouraged for not having connected in a closer way with any of his relatives in attendance. He had spent about twenty minutes talking to his mother, during which time she had made remarks to him that were critical of people in attendance at the service.

Based on what I knew of his family dynamics, I offered him this analysis for his consideration: "In childhood, you often felt judged and criticized by your mother. You also heard and observed her being judgmental and critical of others, often relatives. It's now tempting for you to identify with anyone who is being negatively evaluated. You resonate emotionally with that feeling. You unconsciously absorb, either directly or through identification with others, the feeling of being criticized. When this happens, you soak up a lot of negativity. You're bound to have an unpleasant emotional reaction. When you're around relatives, the feeling of criticism and its emotional associations are activated in your psyche. You see your relatives—and you feel yourself being seen by them—through this issue. That makes it difficult for you to connect with them in a way that's comfortable or pleasurable."

I continued by saying, "Your mother's emphatic righteousness is another influence on your emotions. It feels to you, as it did in childhood, that her perceptions and points-of-view are dominant and must prevail, and that she's shoving her opinions down your throat. You become passive to her influence as you allow her critical opinions to intrude so forcefully into your emotional life. Unconsciously, you're open and receptive to her influence, even though, on a conscious level, you might reject what she's saying. You'll be more relaxed and comfortable at family gatherings when you keep a clear eye on these weaknesses of yours. You must recognize how you have been willing unconsciously to recycle them. In other words, you begin now to recognize your attachment to these negative emotions, meaning that you become conscious of how you're making an inner choice to fall back into them. And remember, this weakness is not your fault—you don't have to feel bad about yourself because of it. We're all dealing with the vagaries of human nature."

Resentment for our parents' flaws and imperfections serves no good purpose. At this stage of evolvement, human nature is imperfect, period. Just about everyone is exposed to some insensitivity and injustice in childhood. We might not like it—but it is reality. Our challenge, if we want to be happy, is to liberate ourselves from our compulsion to go on feeling victimized and hurt by reality's sharp edges. That's how we become stronger and then capable ourselves of good parenting.

In the attempt to understand our negative reactions to family members, it's important to keep in mind that much of childhood is experienced subjectively. The resentments we hold toward others aren't always based on a fair or just assessment of what occurred. Our impressions as children are often an irrational extrapolation based on our acute sensitivity to feeling deprived, refused, controlled, rejected, criticized, abandoned, and betrayed. Our childish mind is simply unable to be objective concerning the complex dynamics and interplays of family life.

We make unconscious choices to keep the hurt alive. If we can recognize this self-defeating manipulation of our memories and expose the unconscious dynamics that hold painful interpretations in place, we see the solution in our deepening awareness.

In understanding ourselves more deeply, we can begin by appreciating the extent or magnitude of our negative instincts. Much of the writing in this book addresses our unconscious inclination or temptation to experience displeasure instead of pleasure. While *consciously* we almost always pursue opportunities to feel pleasure, *unconsciously* we're willing and ready to recycle negative emotions that are unresolved in our psyche.

Many psychologists offer only lame advice on how to avoid conflict with family members. Such advice recommends avoiding any discussion of unresolved issues, focusing on memories of the good times, and grinning-and-bearing one's way through the ordeal of a get-together, knowing it will soon be over. In order to offer more value, psychologists have to stick their own toes in the cold deeper waters of self-knowledge. Insight and self-knowledge, not superficial advice, resolve our emotional hang-ups and makes us truly smarter.

82 . Deliverance from Low-Level Anxiety

Many people suffer from low-level anxiety, which produces, as one sufferer said, "a frequent feeling of dread, a sense that I'm not up to the challenges that face me, a fear that I won't make it, that everything will crumble."

I had this distress and tension in my mind and body for many years, starting in my early teens. The feeling ebbed and flowed through my twenties and thirties, and often it was painfully intense, particularly when I felt blocked in my efforts to be creative. I tried one "expert's" advice, but it didn't help: "Don't worry about the future: Take each day one anxiety-attack at a time."

Kidding aside, I now live for the most part in a state of considerable inner peacefulness. Though my anxiety lingered on until I was well into my forties, I was rescued by depth psychology. It provided me with insight into the source of this distress and immense relief from it.

An undercurrent of tension, stress, and anxiety can occur for no apparent reason. Sufferers often can't pinpoint a cause. Some scientists believe the problem is a dysfunctional amygdala in the brain, which they say needs to be "reset." This grouping of neurons behind our brow is a kind of processing center for our emotions. It can become overstimulated, producing anxiety from non-threatening everyday events. I believe, however, that our amygdala, for the most part, is only reacting to unresolved emotional issues in our psyche. In my view, these emotional disturbances or inner conflicts cause the overstimulation in the amygdala. We "reset" it when we resolve the inner conflicts.

Mainstream psychologists sometimes advise people to combat low-level anxiety with positive thoughts. People are told to apply logic and rational thinking to convince themselves that their anxieties, worries, and fears are ill-founded and that everything will work out fine. Sometimes this approach is helpful temporarily. People can also get an emotional booster-shot by leaning on the "ego strength" of the therapist. They might feel better for a few days. But they're now operating like a battery that needs to be plugged into some outside source. They won't likely establish their own inner power if their therapist is not helping them to recognize the nature of the conflicts churning in their psyche.

Let's try to trace the anxiety back to its source. Very often the source is that primary conflict in our psyche between inner aggression and inner passivity. These two parts clash when they become activated, drawing us into some experience of distress, anxiety, or suffering. The clash, as mentioned, produces painful symptoms such as fear, worry, anxiety, insomnia, depression, muscle tension, nervousness, irritability, and lack of concentration. Anxiety is just one of the many symptoms (including addictions and compulsions) that are produced by this inner conflict.

Anxiety sufferers frequently look for some cause in the world around them to account for their anxiety. Frequently, they blame others (a spouse, boss, or friend) who they claim is neglecting or mistreating them. Or they place the blame on, say, their working conditions or problems with where they live. As a consequence, they're likely to begin to react negatively and with self-defeating behaviors toward the individuals or the situations that are being blamed. This following technique or practice gives us a chance to lessen and eventually to liberate ourselves from chronic low-grade anxiety:

Stop for a few minutes when you feel the anxiety (when it is possible throughout the day to do so.) Close your eyes, and try to connect with yourself. This can be difficult to do if your mind is churning and you're unable to calm down. A churning mind, in itself, denotes some inner passivity, some weakness on your part in regulating your mind and stopping it from gallivanting out of control, producing random, often negative and pointless thoughts and feelings. It also can mean that you're identifying with your mind instead of, ideally, identifying with your authentic self. (Some meditation practice might be necessary.)

Do your best, in any case, to connect with what seems like a center within yourself. This is, in fact, your authentic self, which is quite different from your mind. To feel your authentic self is to feel your goodness, value, inner peacefulness, inner authority, and oneness with life. You might have to spend some time just trying patiently to believe that this center of peacefulness is there inside you, awaiting liberation through your efforts. Even experienced meditators often have to focus and concentrate for several minutes before they're able to establish that inner connection.

You want to bring inner conflict into focus. Your anxiety could be a symptom of the clash between inner aggression and inner passivity. You may be able to detect inner voices that represent the thoughts or feelings being expressed by your inner aggression and your inner passivity. (Examples of such inner dialogue appear in "The Futile Dialogue in Our Head").

In this practice, you're trying to produce more awareness of your inner passivity. You're trying to get a feeling for its existence. Even when inner aggression is active, remember that you are allowing, through your inner passivity, that criticism and harassment to occur.

Again, try to sense the inner passivity lurking behind your anxiety. Note any tendency to feel overwhelmed, to experience self-doubt or self-blame, or to anticipate your failure or collapse. Look at it as if you're a scientist peering through a microscope. You've tumbled into this inner weakness because it's an emotional default position. It's familiar to you. In fact, you don't quite know who you are without it. You hold on to it (or you're unconsciously drawn to it) because, while painful, it's part of your old identity and your emotional memories of childhood. As you look at it objectively, you might feel some ability to create a sense of separation from it.

Now, of course, you know that consciously you want to let go of it. Imagine that, in the process of seeing your inner passivity with such clarity, you're acknowledging how familiar it is to you and how resistant you have been to moving into this no-man's land in your psyche to claim that space in the name of your authentic self. (Note that your anxiety can be produced by attachments other than inner passivity, such as refusal, rejection, criticism, betrayal, and so on. Do this exercise on the basis of your best determination, in that moment, of your emotional attachment.)

Just quietly see your inner passivity (your attachment to inner weakness). Don't judge it. Don't even dislike it. It's part of you, somewhat like a weak inner child who's been cooped up in the dark. Seeing it is an act of power, an expression of consciousness. In seeing it, you're infusing your inner space with the power of intention and the quality of integrity. Now the anxiety can fall away because your determination to reveal inner truth and connect with yourself is itself an act of noble aspiration and great power. Do this repeatedly, and monitor whether or not it's easing your anxiety. Be patient. Try to feel that you are doing your best. Watch to see if the inner critic is mocking your efforts. If so, feel that you can laugh in its face.

An extension of this technique involves "checking in" with yourself throughout the day. Ask yourself, "How am I feeling right now?" Then answer the question, and do so honestly. Don't just quickly say, "Oh, I'm fine." Instead, really feel what you're feeling. Whether the feeling is good or not so good or even awful, say so honestly. Be true to yourself. You're trying, in this technique, to be true to yourself and supportive of yourself. You want to accept yourself, whatever it is that you happen to be feeling. You're trying to become your own best friend. You won't be so anxious when you have a sense that you can fall back on this inner self that is accepting of you, whatever you're going through, and won't judge you critically.

83. Hidden Dynamics of Marital Strife

When marital conflict leads to divorce, conflict in the human psyche is the culprit, not the institution of marriage. Many people are too conflicted and divided in their psyche to maintain the union of a loving relationship.

Rather than examine ourselves, many of us elect to betray love and skip town. We forsake our partner because we can't stomach our own bile. We simply refuse to approach the unconscious part of us that harbors and cultivates the negative emotions that feed marital unhappiness. Through resistance and denial, we prefer to avoid the disturbing idea that we're the architects of our own suffering. It's just so easy to blame our tribulations on the annoying characteristics of our partner—or on faulty genes, biochemical imbalances, the malice of others, or the cold, cruel world.

In some cases, getting a divorce is the sensible thing to do. For various reasons, some feuding couples are unlikely to re-establish harmony and love. Of course, many other marriages can be saved. Intimacy and love can be restored—and even greatly enhanced—if we look deeper into our personal issues.

For starters, try approaching marital conflict as a no-fault situation. Recognize that the pain you're feeling is not your fault or your partner's. Both of you need to become more conscious. You can agree to have a partnership that's intent on helping each other discover and resolve the dynamics of one another's inner conflict.

What are these hidden dynamics? The essentials can be found in *Divorce Won't Help*, a psychoanalytic classic written more than 50 years ago. This book by Edmund Bergler is available at used-book websites. Bergler writes:

> There are four parties involved in every marriage. In addition to the two people who took out the marriage license, there is for each of them an invisible unconscious partner. This unconscious partner is really the deepest part of the person himself, but works so silently that the person is unaware even of its existence. Yet so powerful are the unconscious partners, and so efficient in their work, that they determine the whole course of the marriage and every other important aspect of the lives of these people.
>
> It is a curious situation. The man and woman think they make their own decisions about their marriage and that its fate lies in their own hands. But the truth is that the conscious life of each of them is only the outer expression of a huge network of deep-lying motives and complexes of

which they are quite unaware. In comparison with the total structure of their personalities, the conscious aspect is of no more importance than an underling who carries out orders but has no part in making decisions ... The person who consciously carries out the orders ... fancies that he himself determines his own acts; he does not realize for a moment that he is acting on orders from the forces within. (1-2)

What Bergler writes is essentially true, though I am inclined, at least for the sake of softening the blow to self-image, to describe the unconscious partners as being somewhat subordinate to the conscious partners. Love is the saving grace, and it abides in the hearts of even the most neurotic among us.

Bergler says that the "orders from forces within" arrive as impulses or compulsions to act out in present time those old negative emotions we acquired long before we even met our partner. These emotions, as described in "Vital Knowledge for Marriage Intimacy," are often acted out with our spouse through 1) projection, 2) transference, and 3) identification.

Though Freud introduced those three clinical terms 100 years ago, we still fail to monitor or regulate these processes as they pertain to our suffering and self-defeat. Many divorces and other acts of self-sabotage—with their accompanying suffering—wouldn't occur if people were psychologically more astute. I believe the failure of mainstream psychology to teach and disseminate this depth psychology is a terrible disservice, comparable to denying educational opportunities to women in centuries past and in some present-day societies.

While divorce might be the best option in some cases, that doesn't mean it's a solution. Divorced individuals typically haven't resolved the inner conflicts that led to divorce in the first place. These inner conflicts can cause them to repeat the pattern of disharmony in their next romantic endeavor, or else they avoid subsequent relationships for fear of failure.

As an example of transference in marital disharmony, I cite at length a passage from *LoveSmart: Transforming the Emotional Patterns That Sabotage Relationships*, written by my late wife, Sandra Michaelson. Here she describes a complication of our early marriage:

> It was another of those ho-hum nights. I'm on the couch and my husband Peter is relaxed in his easy chair, glued to the TV. I initiate small talk about the events of the day, and he responds with unintelligible grunts. I conclude from his meager display of communication that he doesn't want to be with me or that he isn't interested in me or what I feel. Consequently, I take it as license to indulge in feeling deprived and rejected, much in the same way that I felt with my father who rarely talked to me except to order me around or scold me. Since my husband is revealing little about himself and his feelings, I'm unable to resist the temptation to feel deprived, denied, and left out of his life.
>
> When I attempt to talk about this arid state of affairs, he gets up from his chair, claims he's tired, and goes to bed. "I might as well be living alone at the South Pole," I moan to myself. However, the resolution of my feelings doesn't depend on

getting him to change, but in understanding the emotional underpinnings of my reaction to him.

The emotional freeze I experienced was almost identical to what I'd endured with my father. From my perspective, my father had shown no enthusiasm for me as a person, not for my homework, grades, or other accomplishments. He communicated to me and to my brothers and sisters in the form of orders and lectures. I felt like a burden, required to make up for being a nuisance by always helping around the house...

This emotional deprivation I'd felt with my father allowed me to relive with Peter the familiar feelings of being ignored and neglected [transference]. Fortunately, with therapeutic intervention I was able to see the deprivation and disappointment I was secretly willing to maintain. I learned not to take my husband's lack of responsiveness personally, as a deliberate attempt to deprive or reject me. He was simply acting out what he learned in his family where no one talked about their underlying emotions.

Peter told me that revealing his deepest feelings felt like trying to speak a strange language. "It's very hard to put feelings into words," he said. "In my family, weakness and shame were associated with any unsettling or disturbing feelings. I would be seen as weak and experience my feelings being discounted, dismissed, even scorned. There was also the feeling that family members not only would be embarrassed by any such disclosures but that they weren't interested in knowing me in this way."

Once Peter and I began to discover our past patterning and its influence over us, we began to open up to each other and talk more intimately about our personal feelings. I no longer have those old feelings of being ignored and deprived.

Marriage is a spiritual and emotional investment that can grow at a high rate of interest. Sandra and I were together for twenty-two years. We worked hard to resolve our issues and deepen our relationship. It's a constant source of fulfillment and happiness to me now that, when she died of breast cancer in 1999, we were deeply in love.

84 . When Eyes Are Blinders of the Soul

One way to diminish our suffering is to become conscious of when our eyes go looking for something that upsets us. Another way is to be watchful of what our imagination is up to.

Just as sponges can soak up dirty water as easily as clean water, our eyes can also take in impressions from the world around us that leak misery into our soul. We like to think we use our visual faculty in pursuit of pleasure, but we also use it to entertain old hurts, grievances, and longings. Our eyes go looking for pleasure and stimulation—but also needlessly for ways to suffer.

Groucho Marx famously asked, "Who are you going to believe, me or your own eyes?" The drollery is delightful, yet our eyes are suspect nonetheless. Our eyes, along with our imagination, quite readily go searching for things to see that we can, for emotional purposes, misinterpret. Through our eyes and imagination, we can be tempted to look for sights or impressions that stir up within us negative emotions relating to deprivation, refusal, helplessness, rejection, and unworthiness.

The writer Johann Wolfgang von Goethe once said, "The hardest thing to see is what is in front of your eyes." He meant, of course, that we're emotionally blocked from seeing objectively, that we're determined to see what we want to believe rather than what's real or true. We're willing to believe what's irrational or false when doing so safeguards our resistance, denial, projections, and illusions. While we unwittingly block out gleanings of truth and reality, we also allow, unimpeded into our minds, subjective perceptions that stir up negative emotions that have remained unresolved in our psyche.

Meanwhile, we also possess an imagination that, in our mind's eye, can conjure up images and visualizations that dress up our inner life with speculative fears, negative propositions, and gruesome considerations.

To avoid unnecessary suffering, we can become more conscious of our visual capacity (termed the *visual drive* in psychoanalysis) in order to regulate it. We want to be able to monitor ourselves so that we can correlate our negative feelings at any given moment with the related visual impressions we're absorbing or the imaginative musings we're producing. In this way, we catch ourselves dipping into negative emotions for no other purpose than to generate unresolved sorrows and hurts. Once we see what we're doing, we're in a stronger position to say, "No thanks, I'm not interested in engaging in such painful considerations, especially now that I have the inner resources to avoid doing so."

When we look at a beautiful object, we naturally want to feel some pleasure. Instead, we could in that moment be feeling deprived of the object and envious of those who own it. Or we could be creating reasons in our mind to belittle the object. In doing this, we're using our eyes to deepen the hurt of feeling deprived or to wallow in the feeling of being a lesser person because we don't possess the object.

Orlando says in Shakespeare's *As You Like It*: "But O, how bitter a thing it is to look into happiness through another man's eyes." Indeed, the negative feeling of envy is a bitter one. However, an emotion that's deeper than envy is at play. This is our emotional entanglement in deprivation, a leftover effect from the oral stage of childhood and a driving force behind consumerism. Deep memories of deprivation—and unresolved resonance with that feeling—make us frantic consumers at the SuperMart of materialism, loading our shopping-carts with what we're determined to believe are the basic essentials of the happy life.

We imagine, as a way of unconsciously choosing to belittle ourselves, that others are happier than us because of their wealth or possessions. The resulting feeling of envy is both a symptom and a defense. The defense contends, "I don't want to feel deprived. Look at how envious I am of that rich person with all his possessions. I want to be like him and have an abundance of things."

We move about our environment with famished eyes, pawns of our psyche's determination to feel marginalized, disrespected, unfairly treated, and deprived. We don't do this all the time, of course. The tendency comes and goes, but it can be excruciating painful when it does come upon us.

There's a quaint, rather comic term from psychoanalysis—*negative peeping*—that identifies our tendency to absorb visually that which induces a negative reaction within us. When people look into the world, they're often "peeping" to see how others are indifferent to their existence. Or they're looking around to see how they can feel superior to others. Racists do this for the unconscious purpose of cozying up to unresolved feelings of inferiority within themselves. A hoarder creates mounds of clutter and then peeps at it in dismay, stirring up unresolved feeling of being helpless and overwhelmed by it all. A youngster can be peeping when she watches closely to see whether her brothers or sisters are getting more attention and love than she believes she gets from mom and dad.

The other related misuse of the visual drive involves our imagination, and here the same principles apply. Now we're seeing images and visualizations with our inner eye. Writers, artists, scientists, entertainers, and others use their imagination to create dramatic effects, useful products, or beautiful objects. We can all use our imagination wisely to produce pleasant thoughts and feelings. But many of us (worriers, for instance) produce images of bad things happening because of our unresolved affinity for feeling overwhelmed and helpless in the face of challenges or calamity. As well, painful feelings of fear, along with unresolved emotional attachments to feeling dominated or overpowered, are often behind the misuse of the imagination.

French novelist Marcel Proust was right when he wrote, "The real voyage of discovery consists not in seeking new landscapes, but in having new eyes." New eyes refer to the consciousness behind the eyes. English poet William Blake immortalized this point when he wrote, "This life's dim windows of the soul / Distorts the heavens from pole to pole / And leads you to believe a lie / When you see with, not through, the eye." In other words, we're unlikely to perceive our world with wisdom and insight unless we're developing an interior life, a growing consciousness, which sees from the depths *behind* our eyes. When we see in such a manner—from behind our eyes—we're more conscious of how to resist being lured visually into the arms of negative emotions such as deprivation, helplessness, and feelings of unworthiness.

85 . Avoidable Miseries of the Workplace

Work, paradoxically, is a blessing and a curse. It can torture us when we have it and depress us when we don't. What's worse, loading "Sixteen Tons" of manure from "9 to 5"on "Maggie's Farm" after "A Hard Day's Night," or having to beg, "Brother, Can You Spare a Dime" in "Allentown" because the "Unemployment Blues" means "I Ain't Got No Home in this World Anymore"?

Work satisfies basic physical, psychological, and emotional needs, yet people can find ways to suffer even when they hold excellent jobs. Psychological insight can help workers find greater enjoyment and creativity in their labor. Once we manage to avoid unnecessary emotional suffering, we're much more capable of appreciating our work and being successful at it. In other words, take away the negative and the positive will take its place.

How do we sabotage the satisfaction and joy that work can produce? One way is to feel controlled and dominated by supervisors or bosses. Often people can feel this kind of tension even when their boss is being appropriate and just doing his or her job. Many of us carry an unresolved conflict in our psyche: We hate feeling controlled, yet the feeling is familiar from our past. We're emotionally inclined to interpret different situations through that impression of being controlled or dominated. Actually, the feeling is not so much about actually being controlled as it is about feeling that we're being forced to submit to the person with the power. In other words, because of our attachment to feeling controlled, we produce an aversion to that feeling, partly as a defense and partly because that's simply the price in suffering we pay whenever that attachment is triggered. The big hurt, meanwhile, is in feeling that we're somehow a lesser person because of our "required" submission.

Your boss might not actually be controlling or dominating you. However, if you have an unresolved issue with feeling controlled, you're programmed, in a sense, to feel that you're being controlled, dominated, and forced to submit. Your impression of reality becomes subjective, not objective. You slip into an old, familiar feeling of submission that you believe your boss is causing you to feel. In experiencing your boss in this way, you're choosing unconsciously to cozy up to that disagreeable feeling. The feeling originates from old memories of childhood "submission," particularly to the necessary requirements of the process of socialization (whereby we become civilized creatures). The rage of the child during the "terrible twos" is the loud protest against the feeling of being "forced" to comply with (submit to) the authority of parents. In their self-centeredness, children simply feel offended, then enraged, that others are daring to impose their will upon them and to require their compliance. As adults, we fail to see this part in us that's willing to relive those old affronts or emotional associations. Instead, we blame the boss for trying to control us, and we might even suspect that he or she is taking pleasure in having this power over us.

Sometimes, of course, the boss is actually a controlling personality. This can make it even easier for us to feel controlled. If we don't have an issue with feeling controlled, we won't suffer even if our boss is actually being a jerk and assuming a controlling, dominant posture. When our own inner conflict with control issues is being resolved, we don't easily get triggered by a controlling personality. We don't feel dominated by the boss, whether he or she is a petty tyrant or not. If the boss is neurotic or dysfunctional, we don't take personally his or her directives or tactics. We're able to do our work, even enjoy it, without feeling like a slave or some lesser person. However, we're only able to be cool and detached in this way when we have resolved or at least recognized our emotional attachment to the feeling of being controlled or manipulated.

We can also muffle or stifle the satisfaction of work when we're prone to feeling devalued and unappreciated. It's the sense that both our work and our own person are not appreciated. With bosses and coworkers, we can feel we're not respected and valued. This introduces other emotional issues. Unconsciously, we may be inclined to lug along our expectations of rejection, criticism, or disapproval wherever we go. Such expectations, like the expectation of being forced to submit, are mostly unconscious. *Consciously*, we hate the rejection or the criticism; *unconsciously*, we expect it, are compelled to replay experiences of the negative emotions, and then get upset when it all happens.

Other psychological issues can produce agony in the workplace, and these also originate from within us. They include expectations concerning failure, along with problems of procrastination, blocked creativity, and personality clashes.

Many people feel like failures, even when they're relatively successful. Our inner critic can rule our personality with unreasonable demands and unfair accusations. We can be particularly vulnerable to inner critic attacks because we carry in our psyche an *ego-ideal*. This is an unconscious self-concept that derives from the self-centeredness with which we are born. Children are speaking under the influence of their ego-ideal when they boast about or think about the great accomplishments they will achieve in the future: "I'm going to be president when I grow up," or "I'm going to be the greatest artist in the world." Freud discovered the existence of the ego-ideal, and in 1914 he wrote that what a person "projects before him as his ideal is the substitute for the lost narcissism of his childhood in which he was his own ideal."

This means that, while acute self-centeredness usually fades as the child ages, the child and later the adult still maintain remnants of grandiosity in the ego-ideal. This inner agency can become a serious liability for adults. That's because our inner critic will unjustly torment us for not living up to the illusions of our ego-ideal. Our inner critic lashes out at us with any discrepancies found to exist between the grandiose presumptions of our ego-ideal ("I am great; I will do great things") and the hard-nosed reality of our less-than-glamorous circumstances in the world ("I'm just the editor of a small-town newspaper"). Many people feel guilt, anxiety, and intense dissatisfaction when reminded inwardly that they're not living up to their ego-ideal, even though its expectations are childish and naïve. We take a verbal beating on the psychic battlefield. Our inner critic doesn't care that its accusations have no basis in reality. It attacks us wherever we're weak. Our ego-ideal constitutes a weakness when its presence remains unconscious. It makes us sitting ducks for the inner critic. We can escape from this suffering by becoming conscious of our ego-ideal and how, through it, our inner critic is able to belittle us and our achievements.

Another misery of the workplace involves showing up unprepared for important meetings. The unpreparedness could represent, for instance, an acting-out of one's attachment to being seen in a negative light or an expression of one's willingness to experience oneself as a disappointment to others and to oneself. Sure enough, the unpreparedness produces those outcomes, though the individual typically doesn't see or understand what he's acting out. This person might rationalize that extenuating circumstances kept him from finding time to adequately prepare. But "not finding time" is itself part of the acting-out and the self-sabotage. Understanding this, the healthy individual makes sure he or she is prepared, knowing the pleasure and fulfillment that await those who function at their best.

86 . Taming the "Little Monsters" of Insomnia

"I've always envied people who sleep easily," one insomniac wrote. "Their brains must be cleaner, the floorboards of their skull well-swept, and all the little monsters closed up in a steamer truck at the foot of their bed."

People can have trouble sleeping for lots of different reasons, and perhaps chief among them are those "little monsters" that cavort in our mind like gremlins at a hip-hop concert. "Crash the night," the sleep deniers shout, "time to break out, dance the wipeout, swing and freak out!" These little monsters (better known as random, unwanted thoughts, feelings, and fears) gambol to the music of worrisome speculations, dire considerations, nightmarish scenarios, and plain old chitter-chatter.

Blake Butler, who once endured an epic 129-hour bout of insomnia, describes very well the grueling experience of insomnia in his book, *Nothing: A Portrait of Insomnia*. Below is an excerpt from his book. I quote Butler here at some length because his experience of insomnia, detailed with literary moxie, relates to what I say further on in this discussion.

> This act of 'sleep catastrophizing' is ten times as commonly reported as other disruption stimuli,

centered in our tendency to dwell on the worst possible outcomes of a given situation ... And so the frame shakes. And the self shakes. And in the self, so shakes the blood, the mood, the night, disturbing, in the system, further waking, further wanting, if for the smallest things, the days of junk, reinforced on both sides ... Some nights the self seems to flood so thick it might never turn off—no clear center, overflowed—a sudden nod turning to surging—small juts of adrenaline, like a grenade of sun against the chest upon the cusp of X-ing out, eyes spinning in the black meat of the head—*I am not asleep now. I am not asleep now.*—looking somewhere heavy in there for some traction, a truer blank inside the blank. ... And even further out, over weeks or months or years, or into packs of years, in decades, the condition might unfurl, become quiet, massive at once, sudden, returning in the wake of its seeming disregard, a flooding flood of flux and flux of flux, unto any inch of self becoming questioned, blurry, some faceless lock without a key.[97]

Butler immerses us in the agony of his insomnia and writes about being caught in a cerebral loop: "Such kind of aimless mental spin—all without answer—is the kind so many nights that keeps me up long after I lay down, stuck in inevitable fixation over nothing, pointless thinking—the day again once come and gone and nothing new—each day passed the ways the days do." While the author describes the nature of the suffering associated with insomnia, his book doesn't really get to the heart of matter. What causes this "aimless mental

---

[97] Butler, Blake. *Nothing: A Portrait of Insomnia*. New York: Harper Perennial, 2011. Print.

spin" he writes about? While insomnia has a variety of causes, it's one of the many symptoms of inner passivity. When our psyche is saturated by inner passivity, we have trouble, among other things, in standing up for ourselves, believing in ourselves, or practicing self-regulation. Keeping those nighttime relentless, random thoughts at bay is a matter of self-regulation.

A person lying awake at night has none of the daytime distractions that keeps one busy and occupied with *doing*. The insomniac is stuck with the experience of *being*. At such times, inner passivity can easily infiltrate our sense of being with self-doubt, along with impressions of being overwhelmed, at risk, and helpless to cope with some future challenge or to still or quiet the mind right in the present moment. The insomniac often becomes agonizingly focused on the consequences of *not* sleeping: "I'll be exhausted tomorrow"; or "I won't get my work done and I'll get in trouble with my boss"; or "I'll be overwhelmed by a backlog of work." Thoughts and feelings like these embellish upon the sense of being weak and unable to deal with challenging situations. This is the "helplessness trap" into which inner passivity can pull us.

Let's continue to follow this thread of passivity into our psyche in order to see more clearly its relationship to insomnia. Many people, of course, are quite aware of their passivity, as when they recognize, as one example, a painful inability to express themselves confidently in everyday situations with family and friends. The passivity I'm talking about—*inner* passivity—is more subtle and insidious. It prevents us from standing up for ourselves and representing our best interests *on an inner level*. At this deeper level, most of us are more passive than we realize. We can be entangled emotionally in this inner condition when experiencing the helplessness of being unable to fall asleep. The "aimless mental spin" that Butler writes about is often the defensive musing or ranting of inner passivity when it answers defensively and compulsively to the inner critic. At such times, the person is experiencing himself or herself through defensiveness, self-doubt, helplessness, fear, and even panic. When trying to sleep, he or she is overwhelmed with foreboding content or with random, aimless speculations and considerations. The feeling of being overwhelmed is, in itself, the experience of inner passivity in action. When we expose our inner passivity clearly enough, we're seeing in that moment exactly what's keeping us awake. In other words, we're lying there helplessly unable to fall asleep because we're choosing instead—unconsciously—to experience our attachment to inner passivity. We're thrown into a helplessness loop: the longer we stay awake unable to fall asleep, the more deeply and painfully we feel our attachment to inner passivity.

Sleeplessness can be caused by abuse of substances such as psychoactive drugs and stimulants. While these drugs can certainly produce undesirable side-effects in the brain, it's also true that such drug abusers, to begin with, are lacking in self-regulation and likely entangled in profound experiences of passivity. They'll be even more passive and unable to quiet their mind when it's time to fall asleep.

Awareness of one's inner passivity helps to overcome insomnia. A person lying in bed unable to sleep can repeat to himself or herself the refrain, "This helplessness is what I want to feel. This helplessness is what I'm choosing to feel. I'm the one who's tempted to feel this helplessness in this moment." This acknowledges our emotional attachment to the helpless feeling, making the attachment more conscious. When we can hold on to this awareness for ten, fifteen minutes or more as we lay in bed, we have a decent chance to drift into sleep. Mysteriously, our resistance doesn't want us to be conscious at this level. It doesn't want us to know or to expose our emotional attachment to helplessness. And so our resistance, on these occasions, does us a favor by helping us to drift off into unconsciousness (sleep).

We can understand this process from another perspective. When we hold on at any given moment to an awareness of our attachment to helplessness, particularly when we're feeling the cost of being entangled in it, we're practicing inner strength and acquiring self-knowledge. This pulls us out of agonizing passivity, producing relief and, ideally, a pleasing sense of self and the peace of mind to fall asleep with ease.

Meditation can also help with sleeplessness. As mentioned, it's the practice of concentration and focus. On an inner level, it's a way to counteract the effects of inner passivity. Through meditation, the person is practicing self-regulation of mental and even emotional processes. When done skillfully, it's able to quiet our mind and tame unwanted thoughts. Practice meditation for twenty minutes or more before bedtime and you'll improve your chances of overcoming insomnia. It also helps to take slow deep breaths for a minute or two once you've climbed into bed. Still, awareness of inner passivity and its self-defeating effects may help more than anything.

87. **Deliverance from the Lonesome Blues**

More people are living alone than ever. In America, forty percent or more of all households contain a single occupant.[98] Many people happily live alone—but others are tormented by the wail of the Lonesome Blues. That oldie can echo in our ears even when we're surrounded by friends and family.

Loneliness is a common brand of human suffering. Many believe that loneliness is an inescapable fact of human existence, a curse we're fated to endure from birth to death. The novelist Thomas Wolfe spoke to this idea: "The whole conviction of my life now rests upon the belief that loneliness, far from being a rare and curious phenomenon, is the central and inevitable fact of human existence."

Wolfe was famous and admired during his lifetime, which apparently offered little solace or good company for his loneliness. Even "super-famous" Albert Einstein succumbed to the misery. "It is strange to be known so universally and yet to be so lonely," he candidly commented. Being a rich celebrity doesn't appear to help: "Hollywood is loneliness beside the swimming pool," observed the actress Liv Ullmann.

Loneliness appears to have infiltrated if not occupied human nature. Impervious to the exhilarations of fame, wealth, and power, it produces assorted misery, ill health, and increased risk of heart disease.[99] Maybe we

---

[98] http://www.nytimes.com/2012/02/05/opinion/sunday/living-alone-means-being-social.html?pagewanted=all

can't exterminate it, but we can see and understand the emotional conflict that make loneliness more painful than it would otherwise be. Being human is challenging enough. We don't have to endure unnecessary suffering.

Most people who suffer with chronic loneliness are entangled in unresolved emotional attachments. Unwittingly, they chose to recycle unresolved emotions from their past. Usually these are associated with feeling unloved, rejected, betrayed, and abandoned. The conflict behind loneliness is often our wish to feel loved and connected to life *versus* our unconscious willingness to go on feeling the old familiar abandonment and sense of being unloved and unworthy.

When we feel connected to our authentic self, we don't suffer from loneliness. We might feel pangs of loneliness once in a while, but loneliness as a chronic condition is simply not present. Our connection to self and the world is too rich and fulfilling to allow loneliness to gain any traction.

It's difficult to stop the suffering and self-defeat produced by inner conflict when we don't see clearly enough the nature of the conflict. Unconsciously, we deny that a conflict even exists: We offer up our loneliness as "proof" that we're not colluding in our suffering. Our unconscious defense maintains: "Are you nuts! I don't want to feel unloved or unworthy! I'm not clinging to old hurts! Can't you see, in my loneliness, how desperately I want to feel love, connection, and value in my life!"

---

[99] http://www.health.com/health/condition-article/0,,20286170,00.html

Who would have thought that loneliness could be part of a psychological defense? The loneliness defends us from the inner truth we hate to acknowledge because that truth is so amazing and humbling. In other words, we produce loneliness in order to cover up our willingness to experience again and again what's unresolved in our psyche. The defense is offered up to our inner critic which protests against our indulgence in our suffering. Here's another rendition of the unconscious defense: "How can you suggest that I'm secretly invested in feeling unloved and abandoned! My loneliness proves how much I want to be loved. Look how much I suffer from the feeling of *not* being loved! Look at how much I hate being alone! Surely that proves that I'm not still clinging to the opposite feeling."

The individual can make this defense more convincing by feeling more intensely the pain of loneliness. As with most of our psychological defenses, we often have to increase the level of suffering and self-defeat in order for the defense to continue over time to be effective (in the sense of deluding us). This produces (when loneliness or some other symptom such as anger is used as a defense) a stubborn determination to hold on to the misery of it.

Other factors can be at play on the field of loneliness. We can be fearful of not being accepted by others and fearful of being a disappointment to them. This means we're emotionally attached to feelings of not having value and not being worthy. In a sense, we're abandoning our own self by not believing in our self. "It's so lonely when you don't even know yourself," one sufferer noted. However, it's more to the point to say, "It's so lonely *because* you don't know yourself."

A harsh inner critic, one that mocks and harasses us at the slightest provocation, can also create more feelings of isolation and loneliness. So can inner passivity, which can paralyze us in a helpless conviction that there's no escape from loneliness and no way to connect with the richness of the self.

A remedy was proposed by Hermann Hesse, the Nobel Laureate who wrote *Siddhartha*, a novel about the spiritual journey of an Indian man at the time of Buddha. Hesse said, "We must become so alone, so utterly alone, that we withdraw into our innermost self. It is a way of bitter suffering. But then our solitude is overcome, we are no longer alone, for we find that our innermost self is the spirit, that it is God, the indivisible. And suddenly we find ourselves in the midst of the world, yet undisturbed by its multiplicity, for our innermost soul we know ourselves to be one with all being." Key words in this passage are, "But then our solitude is overcome …" The pain of our solitude is overcome when we're sincerely interested in escaping this suffering (rather than indulging in it) and have the insight to do so. It helps to stay conscious of our resistance to letting go of suffering.

Once we see and begin to undo our attachments to feeling passive, rejected, unloved, and abandoned, we do, as Hesse said, connect with our innermost self and the whole of existence. Loneliness no longer fits like a ragged shawl across our shoulders. It falls by the wayside, a worn-out cloak that fades in the distance along with the wail of the Lonesome Blues, as we go forward with a lighter heart.

88. The Helplessness Trap in Cravings and Addictions

When a powerful craving strikes, we often react with a sense of inner helplessness. Will our intense desire to engage in a self-defeating behavior prevail? Do we even have a chance to successfully resist, knowing our history of being overwhelmed by our cravings? (For another perspective on this topic, see also, "The Human Weakness Behind Alcoholism.")

Addictive individuals become slaves to their cravings. Cravings arise for substances such as food, alcohol, drugs, or cigarettes, or for behaviors such as gambling, shopping, or promiscuity. As cravings intensify, so do feelings of helplessness. Why are the cravings so powerful?

When an addiction is serious enough to be life-threatening, the craving can represent a death-wish, an unconscious desire to sink into the utter passivity of oblivion. The short-lived pleasure or altered state of consciousness that derives from a drug high can serve as a defense that denies the underlying death-wish. This wish to lose or minimize one's consciousness is a common phenomenon, and it can be practiced—minus the cravings and addictions—through denial, resistance, and willful ignorance. Substance addictions, when less self-destructive, can still be renditions of a desire to escape from existential anxiety or what is felt to be the overwhelming magnitude of being fully awake in an awe-inspiring world. It's as if we prefer at such times to settle for being a simpler life form with less challenge, less complexity, and less fear.

Let's back off from such grim considerations and look at the problem of addictions at the "ice-cream level." One overweight client describes his cravings for ice-cream: "I don't want to eat it, it's not good for me and has too much sugar. But I eat it anyway because the carvings are so strong. I yield to the cravings, the cravings win out, but it all feels like a defeat." In depth psychology, as previously mentioned, an addiction with its accompanying cravings is understood to be, at least in part, a self-defeating symptom of one or more inner conflicts. This perspective—compared with the disease model for understanding addictions—gives us more opportunity to intervene on our behalf: We can rescue ourselves with insight and self-knowledge. We're not at the mercy of experts or an expensive medical system.

As mentioned, inner conflicts are expressions of unresolved negative emotions in our psyche. An example of a common inner conflict that contributes to addictive behaviors involves wanting to feel loved when entangled in self-rejection. This conflict can produce cravings for sweet compensation such as ice-cream. The cravings serve as an unconscious defense: "I don't want to feel empty inside, bereft of love, and disconnected from my loved one or myself. On the contrary, I want to feel connection, and so, with this ice-cream, I give comfort, support, and nourishment to myself."

Other conflicts also can fuel cravings. Someone who is seeking success when encumbered by expectations of being seen in a negative light can, as a result of this conflict, have less self-regulation with alcohol. A person who yearns to be praised and respected when entangled in self-criticism can crave the ego-boost of certain drugs. An individual who is emotionally attached to betrayal and unworthiness can crave fame and riches.

Addictive individuals who learn about their inner conflict, and then manage to maintain that understanding and mental focus during their struggles for self-regulation, are taking a giant step toward becoming addiction-free.

Let's look at this idea of a "helplessness trap," and then we'll attempt to understand it through inner passivity, its primary source in the psyche. In the minutes or hours leading up to their self-defeating behavior, addicts typically slip into this helpless feeling. It's a profound, painful sense of mounting passivity and loss of self-control. Cravings soon arise. In themselves, the cravings are expressions of the intense feelings of helplessness and loss of control. The individual believes that the cravings are directed toward some desired object or behavior, yet, paradoxically, what he desires is not so much the object or behavior as it is his addiction to the feeling of becoming helpless or powerless to resist. This means, in one sense, that his powerlessness is something he's familiar and even identified with. He's obliged to experience this powerless at times because, psychologically, it's a large component of who he feels he is. Why does the powerlessness feel so all-embracing? The emotion is, in part, a lingering effect of the helplessness that all us experienced in early childhood when we were totally dependent on parents and caregivers for our survival. Unlike other animals which become independent within months or a few years, we humans experience helplessness in varying degree for many years until we grow old enough to live and survive on our own. This feeling is often unpleasant (as it often is with teenagers, for instance, who are yearning to be more independent), and the feeling becomes a default position deep in our psyche. It can cling to our feeble self like an inherent, practically hard-wired weakness.

To repeat this vital point, unresolved negative emotions from childhood (having to do with feeling helpless, deprived, refused, controlled, rejected, betrayed, abandoned, and criticized) produce inner conflict. This conflict in turn produces suffering, self-defeat, cravings, and out-of-control emotions and behaviors. We can overcome the disruptive influence of inner conflict, and thereby enhance our capacity for self-regulation, when we see our psyche's inner dynamics clearly enough.

To benefit from depth psychology, people who are addicted to substances or behaviors benefit from identifying their unresolved negative emotions and from understanding how their addictive behaviors are symptoms of that inner conflict. These unconscious dynamics are not being calibrated by the mainstream addiction-prevention community which can understand being addicted to a substance or behavior but not to a negative emotion.

Inner passivity is in conflict with our inner critic, and until the conflict is resolved we're going to experience the fallout. We compulsively replay the conflict, and then we act out the symptoms. As mentioned, people with addictions to substances and behaviors are just like the rest of us in that we all have hidden emotional addictions. For those addicted to certain substances and behaviors, the challenge can be more acute and the self-damage more severe.

Let's keep looking into the nature of the cravings. They often produce the sensation of one's inability to resist them. When cravings arise, addicts often know, consciously or unconsciously, that it's only a matter of time before they succumb to them. Even on the occasions when they don't succumb to the cravings, their feelings of self-doubt and inner weakness during their struggle to resist can be intense. As cravings intensify, addicts can experience a growing, more profound experience of their helplessness and faltering powers of self-regulation. When they do finally succumb, they can collapse even deeper into helplessness, experiencing a certain degree of dissociation in which they mindlessly carry out the imperatives of their cravings.

This profound helplessness creates an inner vacuum into which the inner critic inserts itself. The more passive we are, the more vicious the inner critic is likely to be. The conflict between inner passivity and inner aggression now becomes more intense. The addictive person, at this point, is often besieged with vile aggression that extends beyond self-criticism into self-condemnation and self-hatred.

As mentioned, addicts collapse into helplessness (in this case, the loss of self-regulation) because the helplessness itself is the addiction. Consciously, addicts are focused on the object of their desire (drugs, alcohol, gambling), which creates the illusion that they're addicted to the substance or to the behavior. Unconsciously, however, they're entangled emotionally in the helplessness itself, that old emotional complication from the past that they never succeeded in fully outgrowing. The more intensely they feel the cravings, the more deeply they feel the helplessness. This is the nature of unresolved emotions and the conflicts they produce: On and off, we feel them deeply and painfully unless they are resolved.

Addicts produce defenses that try to save face and cover up their emotional entanglement in passivity. One such defense proclaims, "I am choosing, of my own free will, to have this drink." This defense produces the illusion of power, though later on it will create more guilt for having "chosen" such unwise behavior.

Once the emotional addiction is identified precisely, the individual becomes aware of how determined he or she has been to continue to experience this unresolved negative emotion. (Read "Stop Smoking through Psychological Insight" for a perspective on another emotional addiction.) People who are not addicts can, through the same inner dynamics, also experience helplessness and passivity in everyday situations, as well as other unresolved emotions, though the self-defeat may be less obvious or painful.

Our entanglement in unresolved negative emotions is mostly unconscious. These emotions produce inner conflict that can profoundly influence—often in undesirable ways, though also in satisfactory sublimations—our behaviors and decisions. Because these deep negative emotions are unresolved, they act as attachments or addictions. If we don't have deep enough self-knowledge, we can keep experiencing them painfully, especially in life's challenging moments, and end up turning these emotional addictions into substance and behavioral ones.

89 . Prose to Shatter Writer's Block

There's nothing more painful than having writing talent—yet being blocked from expressing it. A lifeless imagination withers the spirit of the aspiring scribe. The problem is called writer's block.

Writer's block and other creativity blocks are symptoms or consequences of one or more unresolved psychological issues. Such issues hinder many varieties of self-expression and satisfying achievement, whether in the arts, sciences, mass media, or other endeavors. The challenge is (1) to solve the mystery of whatever is blocking you, and (2) to have the will to move forward against the resistance you will feel in working through the issue or issues.

In the case of literary fiction, writers produce their content by way of their intelligence, knowledge, and unconscious mind. Often the richest and most original content emerges from the unconscious mind. The flow and quality of this content is influenced by the writer's shifting psychological dynamics. The work of art itself becomes, in part, a dramatization and sublimation of the writer's unresolved inner conflict. In other words, the writer's creative powers are somewhat at the mercy of unconscious defenses and counter-defenses. The writer is trying to settle an inner conflict, and the quality of the story or the book hangs in the balance.

When writers successfully sublimate the inner conflict, they're able to produce artful, entertaining, and even illuminating content. Blocked writers, in contrast, succumb to the unconscious determination to be overtaken by what is unresolved in their psyche, often an emotional attachment to feeling refused. They end up experiencing, in an especially painful way, the refusal of their imagination to produce lovely words and interesting plots. Often they're able to produce a steady stream of prose but the material is inferior to what they would be able to create if not for the inner conflict.

Writers feel pleasure and egotistical satisfaction in producing clever, interesting prose. The feeling is, "I, myself, am the originator of this brilliance." But lurking in their psyche is a lingering emotional attachment to refusal that goes back to the oral stage of childhood development. Their defense is, "I'm not attached to feeling refused; see how much pleasure I feel when I give these clever words to myself." The writer's psychological conflict, in this case, is between wanting consciously to produce lovely words and thoughts but anticipating unconsciously that his or her imagination will refuse to give or provide that material. This is why many writers live in fear of losing their creative powers.

Along with refusal, writers can also suffer from a related emotional attachment, namely feelings of helplessness. Consequently, they become powerless to act on their own behalf. They can't feel the ability or power to exhibit their intelligence and to fulfill themselves. As they agonize that the words aren't flowing or the material is mediocre, they're cozying up to the emotional attachment to helplessness. Being a blocked writer—and feeling sterile and impotent—is the fulfillment of the attachment.

When defenses are stable, many writers can produce successful sublimations in the form of high-quality writing. Over time, however, defenses can become unstable as unresolved inner issues intensify, exacerbated perhaps by challenging events in a writer's life. Now the writer's output no longer resolves the inner conflict. As well, his or her creative energy is drained in the production of ineffective defenses. The flow of words now dries up, and the writer becomes, in terms of literary output, sterile or impotent.

Is there evidence for the truth of this psychoanalytic contention? The best works of fiction portray a protagonist who attains some measure of inner growth and self-development, if not moral or spiritual triumph. However, many novelists, including ones who are highly regarded by critics, present flawed characters who fail to rise above their circumstances or predicaments. Often the hero or protagonist is presented as a likeable (or at least sympathetic) rascal, fool, loser, or degenerate. These books are often portraits of family dysfunction. Often the main characters experience their situations through helplessness and hopelessness, and walk away at the end feeling empty and disappointed. Little or no inner growth is achieved.

This is Norman Mailer's assessment of American literary novels:

> Writers aren't taken seriously anymore, and a large part of the blame must go to the writers of my generation, most certainly including myself. We haven't written the books that should have been written ... We haven't done the imaginative work that could have helped define America, and as a result, our average citizen does not grow in self-understanding. We just expand all over the place, and this spread is about as attractive as collapsed and flabby dough on a stainless steel table. (*The Spooky Art: Thoughts on Writing.* Random House, New York, 2004. 163)

Unconsciously, the writer of such mediocre books is trying to convince his inner critic (along with his readers) to support his defense, to the effect that suffering in the forms of refusal, emptiness, disappointment, helplessness, failure, and moral weakness is the way of the world. "This is how it is," the writer's defense contends through his description of his characters, "this is the way people are. I'm not the only one who is hopelessly attached to these forms of suffering." Many readers of these books, who don't want to feel challenged by a protagonist's heroic struggle for inner growth, buy into the author's defense. Sometimes people just read the books because more inspiring ones are hard to find.

Good fiction is tremendously important to young readers. It helps them to experience challenging situations through the eyes of others and to identify with characters who are noble and who achieve some degree of victory in their struggles. I remember reading *The Adventures of Tom Sawyer* when I was about eight years old. The book helped to undo my egocentricity and ignite within a little shooting star of consciousness.

Lesser writers are skillful at covering their psychological tracks. Norwegian crime-writer Jo Nesbo, for instance, writes in an essay, "Revenge, My Lovely," that the fantasies of violence and torture that he frequently produces in his mind are exercises in "man's sublime capacity for abstract thought."[100] His essay is, in fact, a rationalization and defense for his unconscious wish to identify, through the inner passivity behind his fantasies, with the torment and helplessness of victims of crime. Nesbo's novels, as Wikipedia says, are "violent and often feature women in peril …" His tough detective, Harry

---

[100] http://www.nytimes.com/2014/05/04/opinion/sunday/revenge-my-lovely.html

Hole, battles alcoholism. It appears that Nesbo uses his writing to sublimate his inner conflict between the wish to be aggressive (in the character of his tough detective) and his wish to experience the feeling of being at the mercy of evil criminals or at the mercy of an addiction (his detective's inner passivity). He's entitled to do that, of course, but his writing is likely to suffer if he's not more conscious of the inner story line. The blockage in consciousness manifests as mediocrity in writing.

Still, fiction writers do often produce glimpses of inner truth, as when best-selling novelist Jonathan Franzen writes in his novel, *Freedom*: "There is, after all, a kind of happiness in unhappiness, if it's the right unhappiness."

Here are some issues, defenses, and symptoms—many of which are interconnected—that can produce (or be a factor in) writer's block and other forms of creative inhibition:

1. Fear of exposure as a failure, with issues of shame and humiliation.
2. Expectation of being rejected, as well as self-rejection or even self-hatred.
3. Feeling inadequate, flawed, and defective.
4. Issues of passivity, powerlessness, and helplessness.
5. Lingering effects of parental messages.
6. Self-doubt, self-criticism, and self-condemnation.
7. Perfectionism.
8. Negative exhibitionism and the claim-to-power defense.
9. Self-defeating use of the imagination.
10. Feeling drained by the effort required to succeed.
11. Fear of missing the boat. Feeling refused and deprived.

12. Unspecified guilt.
13. Negative inner voices.
14. Injustice collecting.
15. Excessive self-centeredness, producing lack of purpose other than ego satisfaction.
16. Intellectual impairment (as differing from impairment of the imagination) caused by neurosis or emotional dysfunction.

Writer's block can be very painful for the writer, to say nothing of the unpleasantness of lost income. However, the writer can undo the blockage when he or she makes conscious the underlying issue and understands the nature of the defenses.

Even talented, successful writers can bring their work to a higher level of accomplishment by recognizing and dealing with hidden emotional issues that are at play in their psyche.

90 . **Stop Smoking through Psychological Insight**

I started smoking cigarettes when I was 17 years old. Luckily, I stopped within six years. I had become one of the "nicotine slaves" Willie Nelson sings about in his anti-smoking song, "Smoke Smoke Smoke that Cigarette," who at the Golden Gate make St. Peter wait while they puff another cigarette.

I started because I thought it was cool and would give me status among my peers. So low self-esteem—a psychological issue—got me started. We can also have psychological reasons why we can't stop.

Deep psychological insight reveals a fascinating aspect of the smoking problem. The nicotine in cigarettes does indeed create a strong physical addiction, yet a psychological addiction coexists along with the physical one. Insight into this psychological component can also help people to stop drinking, smoking marijuana, and taking hard drugs.

Smokers often appear to enjoy their addiction, and many of them claim the activity gives them considerable satisfaction But the satisfaction is somewhat of an illusion. What possible satisfaction is available from engaging in an activity that typically produces less pleasure as the risks and symptoms of ill health increase? The satisfaction is at best second-rate if not third-rate.

Smokers settle for this low-grade pleasure or illusion of satisfaction because they have started using smoking as a psychological defense. As such, the need for the inner defense trumps the issue of one's health or the fact that the smoking itself is a fading pleasure. What does this all mean?

Unconsciously, smokers are trying to "prove" that they want satisfaction. Smokers do this to cover up their inner determination to go on experiencing dissatisfaction and inner emptiness through unresolved emotions involving deprivation, refusal, and passivity that go back to the oral stage of childhood development.

Because of such unresolved emotions, most of us can feel at times that something essential or vital is missing from our life. The feeling is, "There is no richness in the moment. The moment is unsatisfactory." To fill the missing something, we often acquire material objects and pursue pleasure through food, sex, money, and drugs. Of course, most of us are able to pursue fun and pleasure in healthy ways. People encounter problems when in daily life they chronically encounter this painful emptiness. This sense of emptiness means that, at a deeper level, they're conflicted and thereby not appreciating their uniqueness, goodness, and value.

Smokers who are trying to quit the habit can experience this emptiness more acutely or consciously. As they try to resist smoking, the physical addiction closely corresponds with the emotional addiction which is to that empty feeling, the sense that their very being is inadequate and incomplete. Only a cigarette, they feel, can rectify their plight. But, as I said, their smoking addiction is only a symptom of the deeper issue—that sense that something vital is missing from their life.

In our psyche, we have an instinct to cover up or deny (or to defend against) the inner choices we make to recycle unresolved emotions such as deprivation, refusal and the feeling that we're missing out on something of vital importance. These emotions are orally-based, and they're first experienced in the oral stage during the first 18 months of childhood (see, "A Chaos Theory of the Mind"). In their cover-up, smokers produce an inner defense that is largely unconscious. The defense proclaims, "I'm not interested in feeling deprived, passive, or emotionally empty. Look how much I want and crave the physical (oral) satisfaction I get from smoking."

Hence, as a psychological defense, the individual embraces the illusion that smoking is satisfactory or pleasant. Through the illusion, smokers fool themselves into believing that the craving for the cigarette represents a determination to get satisfaction. Again, this is a defense that attempts to cover up one's determination to continue to experience and recycle the attachments to deprival and refusal. Typically, many smokers do experience an increasing sense of dissatisfaction from the habit, showing that their defense is wearing thin. Smokers need to understand that they're not craving cigarettes as much as the underlying emotional addiction to deprivation and to the feeling that life itself is refusing to provide the energy, pleasure, or sustenance they require.

Smoking is also a passive way, as is alcohol or drug abuse, to commit aggression against oneself. Self-aggression is a drive in our psyche that consists of harsh and relentless inner attacks that demean our value and undermine our decisions. The individual who goes on smoking despite the increasing danger to health and life is weak and passive in the area of self-protection. The U.S. government reports that people with psychiatric disorders consume 44.3 percent of all the cigarettes smoked in this country and that depression increases the risk of smoking.[101] This shows a correlation between smoking and emotional weakness.

Smoking becomes an acting out of the inner critic's determination to extract punishment for underlying passivity. The smoker, in absorbing aggression from the

---

[101] http://www.nimh.nih.gov/news/science-news/2009/expert-panel-addresses-high-rates-of-smoking-in-people-with-psychiatric-disorders.shtml

inner critic, inflicts his own brand of self-punishment in the process. His or her psychological defense proclaims, "No, I am not passively willing to absorb pain and harm in the form of self-aggression (cigarette smoking). The problem is that I am addicted to these cigarettes. I just can't stop smoking because the addiction is so strong." At some terminal stage the smoking can become an acting out of a death wish, and the smoker becomes another casualty of the death drive and unconscious masochism that haunts the psyche of humankind.

91 . A Remedy for Feeling Trapped

Millions of people know the feeling of hopelessly trying to wiggle out of a vise. We can feel trapped by our jobs, relationships, and financial circumstances. We can feel trapped in an elevator or an airplane, or in our house, neighborhood, or the state where we live. Some people even feel trapped in their mind or their body.

"Here we are," novelist Kurt Vonnegut noted bleakly, "trapped in the amber of the moment. There is no why." Playwright Tennessee Williams was no less grisly: "We all live in a house on fire, no fire department to call; no way out, just the upstairs window to look out of while the fire burns the house down with us trapped, locked in it." Poor literary writers! Is this the sense of desolation that results from doing daily battle with a balky imagination?

It's true, of course, that people can be trapped somewhat in unpleasant situations or predicaments. We might not have enough money, for instance, to just pick up and leave our job, relationship, or the town where we live. But often we embellish upon the feeling of being trapped, accentuating the misery of it all. At its worst, the feeling produces claustrophobia.

At a conscious level, people prone to feeling trapped want to feel free and unrestricted. But unconsciously, meaning outside their awareness, they have an affinity for (or resonance with) the feeling of being trapped. The feeling stems from lingering emotions and memories having to do with childhood helplessness and passivity.

So while we like to think we want to feel free, we might not quite know how to live without our old familiar sense of isolation, restriction, and boring routine. Hence, instead of confidently navigating our way into better situations, we remain stuck in the old pain of feeling trapped. Right from the start, we're also quite capable of trapping ourselves in a difficult situation for the unconscious purpose of living our life through that familiar, painful experience.

A daydreamer of adventuresome escapades and uninhibited freedom is apt to be attached emotionally to feeling trapped. Those flights of fancy are defenses against the unconscious willingness to feel isolated, controlled, or trapped. Avid motorcyclists are often people who are trying to flee from their tendency to interpret situations through that trapped feeling.

British researchers recently presented findings that link feelings of being entrapped and defeated to anxiety and depression.[102] Those findings are no surprise. Feeling

---

[102] http://www.sciencedaily.com/releases/2013/12/131205220031.htm

trapped is a negative emotion that certainly doesn't invite happiness and joy. The emotion can produce a downward spiral: Feeling trapped produces anxiety and depression, and now people can feel, through the anxiety and depression, even more trapped.

A higher incidence of happiness is experienced by people who are passionate about their work (I'll exclude workaholics which falls into another category). This means, of course, that they *don't* feel trapped. Why does enthusiasm for work tend to make us happier? While there's an assortment of explanations, one consideration recognizes that we're more likely when passionately engaged to be less under the influence of inner passivity. As well, we're obviously less likely when making money to sink into the feeling of being financially strapped in a money-driven economy.

Inner passivity, an aspect of human nature that hides out in our psyche like an ancient isle shrouded in mist, is a direct cause of feeling trapped. Usually, we can only begin to identify our inner passivity through its many painful and self-defeating symptoms such as self-doubt and feeling trapped.

Here's the most important thing to understand about inner passivity: We're determined unconsciously to experience it, no matter how painful. In large measure, we know ourselves through inner passivity as we struggle in our psyche to hold our ground against inner aggression (inner critic). As I've said (granted, repeatedly), the clash between our inner critic and inner passivity constitutes the major conflict in the human psyche.

Feeling trapped is a direct experience and symptom of inner passivity. Take a moment and go into that feeling of being trapped. It's a feeling of helplessness and powerlessness. You're entangled in a spider web and can't wiggle free. This feeling, while unpleasant if not painful, has an enticing allure at an unconscious level when it's experienced through inner passivity. It resonates with emotional memories from childhood that are repressed but not resolved. This feeling, fueled by unconscious masochism, wants to be felt. What does that mean? It means that, at least metaphorically, your inner passivity wants you to be trapped in the clutches of a particular weakness. Inner passivity is very much interested in its own survival. Even though it's an emotional weakness, it wants to thrive within you, and it will fight for its life. It can hold on and survive as long as you're willing to go on experiencing yourself through it, which you likely are doing with some masochistic elaboration when you find yourself feeling painfully, helplessly trapped. Like the inner critic, inner passivity does not want you to come into your own power. Both inner passivity and the inner critic are afraid of the emergence of one's authentic self because they'll be vanquished and vaporized by it.

Inner passivity, when acute and excruciatingly painful, can lead not only to feeling trapped, but also to anxiety, depression, and suicidal thoughts. This quote, written by Pulitzer-Prize winning poet Annie Sexton, appeared in a newspaper column on suicide. Sexton committed suicide in 1974 at the age of 45. Her words convey feelings of being overwhelmed, isolated, and trapped. The agony behind her words can help us to recognize inner passivity in ourselves, even when we have less intense experiences of it.

> Now listen, life is lovely, but I Can't Live It ... To be alive, yes, alive, but not be able to live it. Ay,

that's the rub. I am like a stone that lives ... locked outside of all that's real ... I wish, or think I wish, that I were dying or something, for then I could be brave, but to be not dying and yet ... and yet to [be] behind a wall, watching everyone fit in where I can't, to talk behind a gray foggy wall, to live but ... to do it all wrong ... I'm not a part. I'm not a member. I'm frozen.[103]

Suicide is an extreme passive-aggressive action that follows upon excruciatingly painful feelings of being paralyzed in helplessness and trapped in despair.

People might hesitate to break out of their sense of entrapment because of fear of the unknown. They fear dire consequences for taking bold action and changing course. But this fear tends to be irrational. For one thing, the future is always a big unknown, whether one is passive or bold. Fear of the unknown is an expression of self-doubt which itself is a symptom of inner passivity. This fear is a product of the individual's inability to believe in his or her own authority, strength, and value. The person feels that he or she won't be able to cope with what the future brings. The fearful feeling, in revealing our inner passivity, provides a learning experience. We benefit by exposing our inner passivity and bringing it into focus. We have to bring it into focus in order to overcome it. Without this clarity, we remain emotionally entangled in the experience of it. We won't be able to separate who we really are from our identity in passivity.

Sometimes people who feel trapped in a relationship or job will claim they have a commitment to others to stay

[103] http://www.nytimes.com/2013/12/06/opinion/brooks-the-irony-of-despair.html?_r=1&

put. This sense of commitment, however, can be self-defeating. It can easily be used as a rationalization or excuse for the unconscious determination to continue feeling trapped and passive. It's usually the case that we have to produce some plausible explanation to ourselves (which in fact amounts to self-deception) for why we're continuing to remain passive and why we're prepared to go on feeling trapped.

Yet walking away from a situation that produces trapped feelings isn't the answer in itself. People feeling trapped are often advised, even by mental-health experts, to be brave and walk away from the disagreeable situation. However, we can't just walk away from inner passivity. If we try that, we're likely to wander into another situation in which we're again soon feeling trapped (or feeling other symptoms of inner passivity). People often feel trapped in situations in which they would normally be flourishing if not for their inner passivity. So the remedy involves recognizing our inner passivity and overcoming it.

92 . **Stung by Ingratitude**

Neglecting to say "Thank you" can infuriate the best of men. Did someone deny that courtesy to Shakespeare? If so, he let his characters do the talking. Viola proclaims in *Twelfth Night*, "I hate ingratitude more in a man / Than lying, vainness, babbling, drunkenness, / Or any taint of vie whose strong corruption / Inhabits our frail blood."

Shakespeare wasn't finished. His King Lear thundered, "Ingratitude! thou marble-hearted fiend, / More hideous when thy show'st thee in a child / Than the sea-monster."

Not all of us, fortunately, are so painfully stung by ingratitude. Benjamin Franklin apparently took it more in stride, observing that, "Most people return small favors, acknowledge medium ones and repay greater ones—with ingratitude."

Yes, most of us have felt some sting from the ingratitude of others. Often the hurt is remembered and experienced anew many years after the offense. For the sake of our equanimity and peace of mind, what ought we to understand about ingratitude?

King Lear's "hideous" disgust for a child's ingratitude is misplaced. Young children quite naturally have little sense of gratitude. They tend to take for granted the benefits of food, clothes, toys, and loving kindness. Seeing this ingratitude, parents sometimes wonder if they're spoiling their children. Children are often prodded: "Say thank you now!" They say the words but don't necessarily register the feelings.

Their inability to feel gratitude is based in the nature of childhood consciousness. Young children take for granted the "good" that they receive because, in their acute self-centeredness, they tend to believe the benefits are self-bestowed. The benefits are also experienced as an entitlement or even a right. At the same time, young children are quick to feel that any refusals from others, or experiences of deprivation, are offenses against them and even acts of malice. In the still undeveloped mind of a child, everything that's good is self-bestowed, while everything bad comes from the outside.

Adults who are chronically ungrateful are still operating, at least in part, through this childish irrational point of view. Neurosis develops when we emerge out of childhood still largely under the influence of irrational, negative perceptions and emotional associations. In varying degrees, neurosis is widespread through the adult population, and it accounts for much of the dysfunction, malice, and stupidity—along with extremist beliefs and self-defeating behaviors—that burden our political, economic, and cultural life. Neurosis is overcome through a process of acquiring self-knowledge and thereby seeing ourselves more objectively.

Ingratitude can be seen in a person's inability or unwillingness to be generous with words and feelings. One problem is that we're inwardly conflicted and ambivalent about so many things. We can feel, for instance, that we're supposed to be grateful to our parents for all they did to support our existence. Yet we also can have decidedly mixed feelings about how, in our view, they failed to do right by us.

There are many ways to feel ungrateful, and often they're unconscious. Many people feel they can't be happy unless they get more benefits or money. They never feel they have enough. It's common to feel ungrateful to teachers, policemen, and doctors. Often it never occurs to us to remember kindly our forebears who struggled mightily to gain our prosperity and freedoms.

One particular class of ingrates—neurotic adult dependents—live passively with others (often their parents) in the expectation of being taken care of. These dependents, rather than being grateful to their providers, frequently experience bitter disappointment and complain incessantly for what they see as the lack of generosity and support bestowed upon them by others. Not only do they return kindness with passive ingratitude, they return it with accusatory discontent. In their view, the world owes them a living. They can be quick to spread the pain of their neurosis around to others.

Adult dependents, or "dependees," can't accept or appreciate kindness because, unconsciously, they're determined to continue to live through the feeling of not being adequately taken care of. In childhood, they often felt neglected and unappreciated. Consciously, they live in painful disappointment, while unconsciously they cling stubbornly to the old hurt of feeling refused and neglected. This inner conflict creates an acute form of self-sabotage: They're determined unconsciously to display to others and to the world just how badly, in their subjective assessment, the world has treated them.

It's vitally important to understand (and so I'm repeating it once more) that, even with decent parents, children can experience refusal, control, and rejection through their subjective assessments of family dynamics. Of course, many of us do experience rough childhoods and poor parenting. Our challenge as adults is to refrain from succumbing to the unconscious readiness, even compulsion, to go on experiencing life through these painful memories and negative emotions. To escape this fate, we have to begin to understand the inner process whereby we go about maintaining and recreating our old hurts and grievances.

Adult dependents are in a painful predicament, yet they can overcome their neurosis with psychological insight. While they constitute only a small minority, the problem of ingratitude is widespread, and all of us at times can feel it within ourselves.

Many people, through their self-centeredness or egotism, can feel reduced in stature at the idea of being dependent on the goodness and protection of others. They resist feeling gratitude because feeling it acknowledges their dependence on a circle of life beyond their self-centeredness. They often cling to an illusion of self-sufficiency. To acknowledge the other and to express gratitude can feel to them like a further weakening of their fragile sense of self. They feel obligated or beholding to the benefactor. It can feel as if the benefactor now has the upper hand and is taking satisfaction in feeling superior. Ingratitude becomes a passive-aggressive withholding, a kind of retaliation, and a way of saying, "I am self-sufficient! I don't need you!"

People can often feel gratitude in a religious way as they "commune" with a higher power, while at the same time they're unwilling to feel or express gratitude to another human being. They're using religion to justify if not exalt themselves ("the higher power recognizes and loves me"), but they can't bear to "lower themselves" to acknowledge their fundamental, terrestrial dependence on the goodwill of everyday people.

Many religions consider ingratitude to be sinful. It's perceived this way because, in part, the unconscious willingness of many people to identify with the alleged lack of value in others and in life itself produces inner guilt (the impression that one is doing a bad thing and deserves to be punished). Rather than see ingratitude as a sin, it's more helpful to see it as a blind spot in self-awareness or as a "sin" against oneself. Ingratitude is a measure of how little we feel the wonder of our own existence.

Finally, let's look at how, like King Lear or Viola, we can manage to get triggered so much by the ingratitude of others. There's no need, of course, to get triggered by the behavior of ingrates, because, as we've seen above, their behaviors have nothing to do with us personally. When we do get triggered, it's because it feels to us that they aren't recognizing our value or appreciating us. The sense is that what we have given to them or what we might mean to them is not valued, and we take that personally. Our painful reaction means that we ourselves are resonating with the feeling of lacking in value. We're making an unconscious choice to go there and feel that negative impression, even though it's not true that we are, in any intrinsic way, lacking in value. If we wish to overcome this emotional weakness, and thereby refrain from needless suffering, we only need to recognize and work out our emotional attachment to feelings of unworthiness. Common the world over, it's an old impression that lingers from childhood, and our consciousness can dispel it.

Gratitude is felt, in its most sincere rendition, when we connect with our goodness and sense of intrinsic value. We're grateful for the pleasure of this consciousness, and we're grateful to anyone or anything that has helped us to enhance it. Gratitude becomes, instead of an obligation to others or an effort that seems to detract from one's self, an integral part of our pleasure in life.

93 . Does Inner Growth Require Practical Steps?

Is insight into our personal issues enough to speed inner growth? Or do we need to follow a comprehensive program that includes practical steps or strategies?

A visitor to my website asked, "Once we understand some of the principles of depth psychology, are there practical steps we can take to overcome the loathsome condition some of us find ourselves in?" He went on to write, "Just having deeper insight doesn't seem enough to me. It sounds kind of a vague notion."

Many people do wonder about this. Let me respond by saying, firstly, that strategies (or practical steps) can't really be separated from insight. Acquiring insight is the best strategy of all. And the best strategy calls for more insight. They operate as one. Moreover, life itself offers structure and practical steps. What we learn in the way of insight flows and circulates through the moment-by-moment experiences that make up daily routine.

If there's any one good strategy, it's to keep the insight in focus. Learn it and remember it. Insight can dissolve if we don't capture it. We can do this by writing it down on notes or in a journal and referring back to it regularly. We then have to begin to apply it to our everyday experiences. Acquiring the insight in itself is a grand achievement. Depth psychology has a certain vagueness or obscurity about it, especially when we apply it to ourselves. It's a complex subject, ideally fitting the complex creatures we are. We need to apply all our intelligence to bring it into focus.

Some important insights involve better understanding of our defenses and resistance. For instance, resistance produces its own rationalizations. Even someone asking about "practical steps or strategies," while appearing to make a reasonable request for information, could be hiding behind unconscious resistance. The person's unconscious intention might be to use the pretext of needing "steps and strategies" in order to avoid absorbing the deeper, powerful insight and thereby remain emotionally attached to, say, inner passivity. As a defense, this person could be saying, "I'm not willing or prepared to experience my passivity. The problem is I don't have practical steps by which to proceed. If I had those steps, I would go forward."

The knowledge of depth psychology also seems vague because our unconscious mind operates according to its own rules of logic and procedure. It's as if we have two brains operating simultaneously, one that guides us through everyday life and the other that processes inner dynamics. At the inner level, as mentioned, our mental and emotional processes operate counterintuitively. They defy the laws of logic and protocols of common sense. For instance, while it does make sense that we want to be loved, it doesn't make sense that we can also want to feel rejected, abandoned, and devalued. How could we possibly want to experience these negative emotions? We begin to make sense of this question as we experience the contradiction within ourselves. We acquire the self-knowledge that uncovers how we suffer and how we keep stumbling into self-defeat. Our intelligence begins to comprehend what had previously seemed nonsensical.

In other words, our intelligence seizes hold of inner truth and uses it to transform our life for the better. This is why I don't pay a lot of attention to practical steps or strategies. When assimilated, the knowledge by itself and the insight it produces operate in a mysterious Zen-like way to transform our lives. The real challenge is to assimilate the self-knowledge, namely the insights that reveal how we produce our unhappiness and self-defeat.

We don't want to be running around trying to be happy. Nor do we want to scramble about trying not to be unhappy. Instead, we're simply acquiring self-knowledge. What we learn knocks out the pillars that prop up our attachments and our old self-image. Yet, of course, the knowledge can seem quite vague when we're early on in the process of assimilating it. We can feel stuck in no-man's-land, where our old attachments and identifications are being discarded but where our new sense of self is yet to be sighted. A lot of people, at this point, turn around and run back into the arms of their old self. They're not quite ready to leave that suffering waif behind.

The learning process can proceed more quickly when a person is in therapy with someone who is trained in this method. When I work with clients, I put the emphasis on teaching them knowledge concerning unconscious self-defeating dynamics. The teaching involves discussions with my clients about how these dynamics appear to be operating in their psyche. In other words, the emphasis is in helping them to acquire self-knowledge and making it possible for them to access inner truth.

Typically, my clients begin to notice after a while that their emotional and behavioral symptoms are becoming less painful and problematic. They see how much better they're handling a given situation than they would have three months, six months, or a year earlier. Many people, I've come to believe, don't have to do therapy with a professional in order to make progress. They can study the material on their own and learn how it applies to them. Still, it's a tricky business doing it this way. It's like learning a new language without having a tutor. You've got to be pretty determined to succeed. It will be more difficult if not impossible on your own if you have severe behavioral and emotional problems.

The challenge is to bring into conscious awareness what previously had been unconscious. In the process, people strengthen their intelligence. They gain "intelligence" (in the sense in which the CIA would use that word) about what were previously secret (unconscious) operations. They also gain intelligence (in the sense of elevating their wisdom and discernment) because they uncover the ways in which they had been deceiving themselves through their psychological defenses. Finally, they gain intelligence (in the sense of having more creative energy) because now the energy that went into denial, repression, and defenses is freed up for constructive and pleasurable pursuits.

Because I work at a deep level, I don't have much to say in the way of advice. My advice is not going to liberate you from misery and self-defeat. You liberate yourself through *your* insight. Someone in my position, meanwhile, can help lead you in the direction of that insight.

Okay, despite what I just said, here's some advice. I don't recommend that anyone set goals. Life is open-ended. Let it all unfold. Your goals might be short-changing you. Just point yourself in a good direction, stroll along with a keen alertness, and be sure to check in with yourself to make sure you're enjoying the walk. You know what, I take that back. That advice about not setting goals isn't worth a whole lot. Go ahead and set goals if you want. Either way, it doesn't really matter. My point is that, compared with insight, advice is of marginal value.

Okay, here's some more advice. Write down what you're learning. We have, as I've said, thick skulls that seem particularly well adapted to deflecting self-knowledge. Write down the insights that you're fortunate enough to acquire and read them over several times every day. Now, guess what happens when I give you structure or homework like this? You'll likely resist doing it. I don't want to add more resistance to your already considerable deposits of it.

That said, there are practical procedures that are part of the knowledge base. In the following discussion, I'll provide a method (an exercise) for acquiring and assimilating important self-knowledge.

94 . How to Be Your Own Inner Guide

Some people can begin to overcome their emotional and behavioral problems without needing to see a psychotherapist. Still, by all means find one if you have the time and money to get personalized psychological help. If you have a diagnosable mental disorder, you should definitely be under the care of a psychotherapist or psychiatrist or both.

Professional help can certainly speed up the process of overcoming painful difficulties with career, relationships, and daily living. However, most therapists will not address your deeper conflicts, defenses, and attachments. It grieves me to say it, but many therapists only succeed in comforting you in your pain. They don't help you to vanquish it.

Many people can, on their own, make inner progress with the method and knowledge that I describe in my books. People acquire knowledge by studying the material and learning how it applies to them directly. In the discussion here, I offer the essentials of how this can be done.

I've written earlier about this essential knowledge, and it bears repeating in this new context. Two distinct levels of negative emotions need to be recognized. One level consists of the symptoms. These symptoms are the result of inner conflict that's occurring at a deeper level in our psyche. The symptoms tend to be more conscious, while the deeper level of emotions is mostly unconscious. The challenge is to go deeper and become more conscious of the source of the symptoms. This is how the problems can be fixed once and for all.

Let's start by listing some of these symptoms. The symptoms consist of negative experiences as well as self-defeating behaviors. *They include anger, worry, anxiety, stress, depression, loneliness, self-pity, boredom, insomnia, cynicism, addictive behaviors, chronic patterns of failure, feelings of being overwhelmed and trapped, psychosomatic ills, and so on* (list 1).

The source of these symptoms, as mentioned, resides at a deeper level in our psyche. *These are unresolved negative emotions, and they include feelings of being deprived, refused, controlled, rendered helpless, criticized, rejected, betrayed, abandoned, and unloved* (list 2).

At this deeper level, the negative emotions of list 2 tend to remain unresolved from our childhood biology and experiences. Unconsciously, we tend to hold on to these emotions, in part because we aren't recognizing our attachment to them. We're not seeing how identified we still are with those old painful ways of experiencing ourselves. Unconsciously, we're determined to recycle and replay these negative emotions in situations that develop in our present life.

Look closely at list 2. You'll see that these emotions are common to toddlers and young children. Even when we have good and decent parents, we can, in part, experience the world around us through these emotions because our childish interpretation of what's occurring is so self-centered and subjective. As we age, these emotions can become addictive. In other words, we're unconsciously determined to continue to experience them.

If emotional and behavioral problems weigh you down, you likely remain entangled in (or attached to) these deeper negative emotions. You need to determine which of them reside in your psyche. A typical person is attached to three or four of the negative emotions in list 2. Usually, one or two of these will be more problematic. I believe that two of these—feelings of being helpless and being controlled—are universally the most problematic. Throughout this book I have described these attachments as inner passivity. However, the other attachments in list 2 also have elements of inner passivity. For instance, the attachment to feeling rejected also incorporates a feeling of being unworthy and lacking in value, which are symptoms of inner passivity. The attachment to feeling betrayed, as another example, incorporates a feeling of being isolated and victimized, which are symptoms of inner passivity.

Life is often a struggle between negative and positive experiences. In our psyche, this struggle is reflected in our tendency, even willingness, to continue to recycle and replay those negative emotions (list 2) that remain unresolved from childhood. We use a variety of psychological defenses (unconscious expressions of our refusal to recognize inner truth) to cover up our readiness to feel these old attachments in various new contexts.

Anger is one of the most common defenses. As an example, someone who is attached to feeling rejected, criticized, or controlled is easily triggered, and he or she might get angry at the person who's doing (or who appears to be doing) the rejecting, criticizing, or controlling. The unconscious defense contends: "I'm not looking for the feeling of rejection (or criticism or control). Look at how angry I get at him for rejecting (or criticizing or controlling) me." Self-pity also serves as a defense: "I'm not looking for rejection (or criticism or control). Look at how bad I feel, how much it hurts, when I am rejected (criticized or controlled)." Notice in these two examples how the painful symptoms (from list 1) are also simultaneously being employed unconsciously as defenses.

There are hundreds of ways we use defenses to cover up inner truth. You have to expose your defenses if you want to make progress in this method of depth psychology. It's a tricky business doing so when you don't have a skilled therapist to assist you. If you keep studying yourself in this light, however, the insights should eventually come to you. (Meanwhile, I would be pleased to train as many therapists as possible in this method.)

Here's a procedure whereby you can identify and work through an emotional attachment, and thereby resolve an inner conflict.

1 – Describe a situation in which you became upset. Did you feel that someone refused you, or tried to control you, or criticized you? Get beneath your surface reaction such as anger or self-pity (or other symptoms in list 1). Recognize that you're reacting to a deeper emotion. It will be one of the negative emotions in list 2.

2 – Let's say you suspect that you're reacting to the feeling of being criticized. Produce memories from your past in which you felt criticized. Was your mother or father critical? Did they appear to be inwardly critical of themselves? Did they disapprove of you? Did you feel you were a disappointment to them?

3 – Where else in your life have you experienced feelings of being criticized? Did it happen in your relationships? Think about, or write down, the different ways you have felt hurt by the criticism (or what you took for criticism) of others.

4 – Ask yourself, "Am I a critical person?" "Do others experience me as being critical?" "Am I critical of myself?" The more we're sensitive to feeling criticized, the more likely we're self-critical as well as critical of others. Whenever you're having painful, critical feelings toward others or yourself, recognize that your impulse to be critical comes from how you resonate with criticism (are attached to the feeling of it), whether you're on the receiving end of it or whether you're dishing it out.

5 – Look closely at your past relationships. Have you had a tendency to become involved with critical people? Have you felt hurt and passive when criticized, or have you lashed out in a tit-for-tat manner with criticism of your own? Have there been times when you might have provoked others, through careless mistakes or insensitive oversight, to be critical of you? Did they experience you being critical of them?

6 – Are you something of a perfectionist? This would mean that you try desperately to do things perfectly, likely out of fear of being criticized by others or by your inner critic. We usually have some fear of feeling whatever we're attached to. The fear serves as a defense: "I'm not looking to feel criticized. Look at how perfectly I try to do things. Look at how much I try to avoid being criticized, and how fearful I am that it might happen."

If you have an attachment to criticism, this procedure will help you to identify it. (This procedure can also be used to help us to detect in ourselves any one of the other deeper negative emotions in list 2 to which we can become attached.) It's so helpful to recognize our attachments, because then we can begin to untangle ourselves from them.

7 - Now when you start to feel some form of distress, anger, or anxiety, go looking in your mind (or knowledge base) for an explanation. Try to see which of the negative emotions from list 2 you're reacting to. Once you recognize the negative emotion, you expose the fact that you were making a choice (albeit an unconscious one) to slip into an experience of that emotion. This is important—you need to take "ownership" of the fact that, unwittingly, you are choosing to gravitate toward that negative emotion. You

know from past experiences how painful it is to do that. Your intelligence and good intentions now will be able to help you "back out" of that negative experience. Now that you recognize exactly where you were going emotionally, you can say, "No thanks, I'm not going there."

It might be helpful, at this point, to ask yourself, "Do I have the power to possess this knowledge? Or do I feel it's beyond my grasp?" If in serious doubt, you might be grappling with inner passivity and thereby feeling your tendency to experience yourself through weakness. Many of my discussions in this book deal with the subject of inner passivity, and rereading sections of the book can help you to ease your way out of this attachment.

Our tendency to drift into the negative side can happen very subtly. We can be drawn into a painful experience without seeing how it's happening. One client kept expressing his sense of hopelessness about ever being able to establish a healthy relationship. Right in that moment, as he felt that hopelessness, he was making an unconscious choice to feel passive and helpless. Up until that moment, he had believed that his sense of hopelessness was a rational assessment of his dire prospects. Suddenly flooded with insight, he saw that his feelings of hopelessness were a result of his choice, *in that moment*, to experience himself through the sense that he didn't have what it took to make himself happy and fulfilled. In that moment, he saw his emotional addiction to inner passivity. This was a vital step in his process of liberating himself from it.

Another client, a business executive in a high-paying position, kept ruminating painfully on whether he should be involved in "a more dynamic business" where he would presumably fulfill his dreams and aspirations. His unconscious intention was *not* to clearly see his way forward but to remain stuck in confusion, self-doubt, and disappointment in himself. He was emotionally attached to this weak sense of himself, and he would not likely have become aware of this attachment without the therapy that he did with me.

Many people can achieve this kind of insight without personal therapy, but they really have to want to uncover inner truth.

VII – REFLECTIONS ON CONSCIOUSNESS

95 . Achieving Inner Freedom

We're not as free as we think, even if we do live in a democratic country. People who have achieved substantial political freedom can still be sorely lacking in psychological freedom. We're likely to feel like prisoners of fate when emotional conflicts limit our creativity and potential.

How can we be free if we don't even have free will? Neuroscientists say humans are just puppets dancing to the brain's unconscious tunes. Philosopher-neuroscientist Sam Harris writes in his recent book, *Free Will*:

> Free will *is* an illusion. Our wills are simply not of our own making. Thoughts and intentions emerge from background causes of which we are unaware and over which we exert no conscious control. We do not have the freedom we think we have.[104]

Harris is right when he says we don't have as much freedom as we like to think. But he's wrong in other ways, notably his implication that the "background causes" of our thoughts and feelings are beyond our conscious influence. He says at one point, "No one has ever described a way in which mental and physical processes could arise that would attest to the existence

---

[104] Harris, Sam. *Free Will*. New York: Free Press, 2012.

of such freedom [of will]." With this statement, Harris apparently dismisses depth psychology. A discussion of that subject goes missing in his book.

Depth psychology, which dredges up unconscious content from our psyche and makes it conscious, becomes our means to acquire a higher range of free will and inner freedom. We become more conscious as we uncover the ways that our unresolved negative emotions have been producing our suffering and self-defeat. We're indeed lacking in inner freedom until we're able, at a deeper level, to break free of our compulsion to recycle and replay these negative emotions that are unresolved from our past.

The quality of our consciousness is the foundation of inner freedom. Many neuroscientists claim that our consciousness, meaning in this context our capacity to reflect on our existence and discern reality, consists of "working memory" stored in our brain. But it's much more than this. Consciousness cannot be constrained by the boundaries of the brain or the borders of science. It is the essence of our humanity, a luminosity that acquires greater power and objectivity as it consumes the nutrition of experience and self-knowledge. Consciousness is best understood metaphorically, as the fingerprint of our individual existence, the poetry of the universe, and, hopefully, our ticket to the next dimension.

Lacking the consciousness produced by self-knowledge, we can indeed be at the mercy of inner dynamics. As David Eagleman, author of *Incognito: The Secret Lives of the Brain,* says, we are "not of one mind. Everyone is of many minds all the time." Depth psychology tells us, though, that we can establish one dominant mind, a mind that reigns as our true inner authority and can be trusted for its wisdom and virtue.

We start by understanding the concept of *self-responsibility*, which means that we begin to see and understand how we can be our own worst enemy. The traditional sense of responsibility involves respecting others, obeying laws, taking care of our health, and contributing to the well-being of family, community, and nation. In comparison, a deeper sense of responsibility, as described here, requires that we learn to become responsible not only for our obvious daily duties and moral obligations but also for our negative emotions and impulses toward self-defeat. When weighed down by unresolved negative emotions, we lack inner freedom and free will because we're inwardly compelled to recycle those negative emotions that are not only painful but produce self-defeat and self-sabotage.

Depth psychology offers a way to see more precisely how we produce anger, greed, fear, envy, paranoia, hatred, the lust for revenge, and weak self-regulation. Blaming others or difficult circumstances is no longer acceptable. Our attention turns to ourselves, not to blame ourselves, of course, but to see objectively into the inner processes that prompt us to react negatively to everyday events or challenging circumstances. We begin to see that we have been making unconscious choices to interpret ourselves, events, and circumstances from negative perspectives. We see how our suffering is based on our unconscious determination to plunge into a negative way of experiencing a particular situation, based on emotional memories and attachments going back to childhood.

Now we're able to see how and why free will is not so free. It has been hijacked by inner conflict. Our free will is impaired to the degree that we unwittingly make choices that contravene our best interests. We possess in our psyche an unconscious intention to limit our potential and to do ourselves harm. This is the dark secret of human nature that mainstream psychology is reluctant to approach.

The concept of free will needs to incorporate *healthy* choice and *wise* authority, or else it's not a will that's truly free at all. Instead, it's imprisoned by unresolved emotional conflict. Much of our behavior in our daily life is predicated on how we wiggle and squirm in avoidance, denial, and defensiveness from an awareness of the specific dynamics of our inner conflict. In order to avoid honest self-reckoning, we're required to act out negative or self-defeating *reactions* to our inner conflict. Such reactions have then become instinctive, marked by a lack of inner freedom and a dearth of conscious choice.

Closely related to self-responsibility is the concept of co-creation. We *co-create* the life we experience. Most of us are not innocent victims suffering at the cruel hands of fate. Rather, we participate in the circumstances of our lives according to how we experience given situations. The notion of co-creation enables us to see, for instance, the existence and the nature of our inner passivity. Through this passivity, we indulge in negative emotions that rob us of initiative as we remain inwardly defensive and self-centered, resisting the development of a more evolved self.

Most times we want to feel that our suffering is a bona fide experience, meaning it's just what any normal person would feel in our shoes. We go around looking for evidence that we're entitled to suffer, that we have no choice in the matter, while we try to enlist sympathizers to justify our distress. This is the default position of the unevolved person. Before we realize what's happening, we've become chronic complainers, injustice collectors, and jailers of our own free spirit. Obviously, inner freedom is curtailed when we're tangled in such conflicts and feeling oppressed by their negative reverberations.

A rising level of consciousness fortifies our intelligence, enabling us to see ourselves and all life more objectively, while making us more capable of producing pleasure from life's everyday experiences. With such inner freedom, human nature matures and free will comes along for the ride.

96 . **The Golden Rule Needs Depth Psychology**

The Golden Rule, which invokes us to treat others as we would like to be treated, is the cornerstone of social order and the foundation of civilization. Fortunately, we usually make some effort to abide by it. Unfortunately, though, the Golden Rule gets broken on a regular basis. A hidden conflict in human nature explains, in part, why this is so.

We do indeed, on a conscious level, want to be treated kindly, yet we often expect unconsciously to be refused, controlled, or dominated—or to be criticized, rejected, disrespected, betrayed, and abandoned. Not only do we expect such treatment, we often go about provoking it.

Note that children sometimes provoke their parents to punish them. In subtle ways, adults can also provoke others, often through unconscious passive-aggressive behaviors and tit-for-tat emotional reactions. Addictive personalities, codependents, people with guilt and shame issues, and people prone to career and relationship failure are likely to induce criticism, disapproval, and punishment from others. They act out with others what is unresolved in themselves.

Our negative emotions and self-defeating behaviors, which derive from inner conflict, make it more difficult for us to feel compassion. In light of these conflicts, the Golden Rule might need an addendum: "Best applied under the supervision of depth psychology." We usually need some degree of resolution of our inner conflicts in order to become truly open-hearted.

Compassion and love are the mainstays of the Golden Rule. But often people don't know what it means to be compassionate. Codependents or enablers, for instance, feel "compassion" for the dysfunctional person who is being enabled, and they allow this misguided sense of caring to lead them into painful experiences and self-defeat. Pro-life individuals can claim to feel compassion for the fetus, but it may be that they're mostly feeling emotions aroused by their projection on to the fetus of their own issues with feeling rejected or devalued; a person can feel sorry for others because he or she is resonating with their self-pity; a person's "compassion" for stray animals or homeless people might be partly aroused by his or her own unresolved issues with rejection, abandonment, and feelings of unworthiness.

Karen Armstrong, author of books on comparative religion, says compassion is the single attribute common to all religions. (See her TED talk, "Let's Revive the

Golden Rule.")[105] The Golden Rule requires self-knowledge, and "it is not easy to love ourselves," she says in her book, *Twelve Steps to a Compassionate Life* (Knopf Doubleday, New York. 2010).

In *Twelve Steps*, Armstrong writes that, "We are so often the cause of our own misery." She notes the phenomenon of projection through which we dislike or detest in others a character flaw that we unconsciously decline to address in ourselves. Indeed, many people, as one example of this, despise the poor because they project their own unconscious self-doubt and shame upon the poor, rather than see in their own psyche their emotional attachment to these negative emotions. This judgmental attitude obviously impinges upon compassion.

Armstrong also writes, "Instead of reviling ourselves for our chronic pettiness and selfishness, it is better to accept calmly the fact that the cause of such behavior is our old brain." The problem, as I see it, is not the brain in itself but the level of our consciousness. We can't replace our reptilian brain, but we can become more conscious of how our perceptions and feelings are influenced by unresolved negative emotions that we first experienced in childhood. This deeper insight activates a healing process as we reveal (instead of trying to cover up or defend against) our unconscious determination to know and experience ourselves through unresolved negative emotions such as self-doubt and passivity.

Genuine compassion is a manifestation of strength and power. To be compassionate toward all life requires not

[105] http://www.ted.com/talks/karen_armstrong_let_s_revive_the_golden_rule

only that we have a solid foundation in a sense of our goodness and worthiness but that we also feel the power and magnanimity, through the quality of our consciousness, to share spontaneously that inner wealth with others.

Imagine strolling through a mall and encountering a little girl who, while standing beside an adult, looks forlorn and dejected. If you identify with what you think she's feeling, you're more likely to feel pity for her than to feel compassion. She might feel scorn toward you if you look at her with pity. But if you look at her with compassion, she will more likely accept it and be strengthened by it.

When compassion is activated, you're able to look at that girl and really see her for the precious little being that she is. You're not projecting your own issues on to her. If the child at that moment is looking back at you, she can, in seeing how you observe her so kindly, feel comforted and strengthened by your generous attention, indeed your moment of loving her. This compassion or love is real and can be felt like a current of energy. It has no agenda and it's not influenced by unconscious issues. It's the ability in a fleeting moment to experience and to convey connection and oneness, and as an attribute it's unlikely to arise out of one's self-doubt or low self-esteem. Impeded by self-doubt, we're unlikely to make any connection with this girl in the first place. Or, if we do, we're more likely to identify with what we imagine to be the girl's sense of helplessness, rejection, or unworthiness. Such negativity, as mentioned, will squash all compassion.

A refined sense of self is the foundation for compassion. Our self (or Self) makes us understand as it emerges in our consciousness that we're part of a greater whole, that we're no better or worse than anyone else. Armstrong recommends Buddhist knowledge and practices throughout her book as a way to develop compassion through our sense of oneness with all life. This is all commendable, yet the Buddhist concept of no-self may be too esoteric to be useful to most Westerners. It refers, in part, to the ability to experience the quiet inner space of nothingness or emptiness, to discard all attachments and reference points, and to find solace and connection through one's consciousness and simple existence. In my opinion, Westerners need, in contrast, an emerging Self, the refinement of our being that transcends ego, if we're going to find the power to make compassion the guiding principle for ourselves and the world. We need in these complex, turbulent times to believe in our self as a tangible agent of destiny. This self is an energetic and perhaps spiritual manifestation of the quality and imperishability of our consciousness (just as ego identification is a manifestation of a less-refined consciousness). The self represents our transcendence into compassionate beings.

Armstrong says that our greedy, needy selfishness was inherited from our ancient ancestors. She quotes Buddha saying, as a way to detach from our negativity, "This [negativity] is not what I really am; this is not my real self." Again, to apply the tenets of depth psychology, this negativity, while not intrinsic to our essential Self, is nonetheless a part of our psychological self. The negativity can't simply be wished away. The healing process, from the perspective of depth psychology, involves "owning" these negative emotions, meaning we recognize them and take responsibility for generating them from within ourselves. We might say, "This negativity is a component of my psychological self. I can see that more clearly. I now understand how, through my lack of self-knowledge, that negativity has been able to maintain itself. Now I can see how to transcend this negativity." This knowledge reveals, in psychological terms, what has been causing us to lack compassion.

Armstrong writes that through mindfulness practice, we learn over time "how often the real cause of our suffering is the anger that resides within us." This statement is imprecise. Many other negative emotions—our entanglement in helplessness, for instance, along with a sense of deprivation and unworthiness—can cause our suffering. Moreover, the anger is not the problem in itself. The anger is a symptom of deeper conflict. The anger is also a defense that's used to blame others and to hide from our awareness our interest in maintaining, rather than resolving, the inner conflict that produces suffering.

No one is to blame for our lack of compassion or our inability to master the Golden Rule. Human nature is a work in progress. We're trying to evolve toward greater wisdom, integrity, and compassion. We'll get there faster when we muster the courage to see ourselves more objectively. The Golden Rule can guide us even better when it incorporates more understanding of the critical dynamics that govern human nature.

97 . **The Need to Believe in Yourself**

This discussion is based on an email a visitor (I'll call him Tony) sent to me. Tony presents some details of his life and his struggle to find happiness, and he asks for my thoughts and suggestions. This exchange is set up in the form of a dialogue between us.

Tony: I am a 22-year-old student with hopes of studying psychology in a graduate program one day. I am enjoying reading *Why We Suffer* and I've found your words to be very insightful as I come to terms with my own psychological issues.

As briefly as I can, I'd like to attempt to explain to you a dilemma that I've stumbled upon during my recovery. I understand you have no obligation to respond, but if you have any ideas for me or know of any writings that could be helpful I would really appreciate it.

I have a deep self-worth void that was created in childhood as a result of my father's emotional abuse toward me. I have experienced problems with addiction, codependency, and chronic emptiness my whole life, and I believe these are the symptoms of deep issues at the core. I understand that in order to overcome this problem I must validate the inner child that was taught to feel worthless and miserable.

Me: It's best not to emphasize the idea that you "must" validate the "inner child," as you refer to this part of yourself. Rather, you want to become an observer of how you are inclined to reject, criticize, and disrespect yourself. It's alright, of course, to experience that part of you as an inner child, yet you could also recognize that part as an "inner adult" that's carrying unresolved negative emotions from childhood. All of us, in varying degrees, can be disrespectful of ourselves through the agency of our inner critic. Try throughout the day to observe your tendency to belittle yourself with various thoughts, feelings, or inner voices. As you recognize this happening, you become aware that this emotional abuse is being produced through your inner critic. Your inner passivity allows the abuse to continue. This means you aren't standing up for yourself on an inner level. Such inner conflict occurs in all of us, to one degree or another. When we understand it, we can overcome it as we acquire insight, emotional strength, and self-respect.

Tony: On with the dilemma. I am an atheist and therefore do not believe in the existence of any absolutes. I have gone back and tried to validate myself at the core with affirming messages. The problem is, without a belief in an absolute and intrinsic value in every human, I am struggling to come up with any "truths" to counter the negative messages I received as a child.

Me: You have a basic responsibility in life to make every attempt to believe in yourself. My impression is that you're making a point or an issue of your lack of belief in a god because that corresponds with your lack of belief in yourself. What's important is that you believe in yourself. Your own worthiness is the truth that gives you standing in the world. Without it, you will be lost, having rejected or abandoned yourself. Since you have a life on this planet, doesn't it make sense that you have a responsibility to respect that life and be supportive of it? Now that you're an adult, you're the one who has to provide emotional support for your existence if you want to thrive. You might be lucky enough to get some support from others, but ultimately it also has to come from you.

You may be having a difficult time providing that support because you appear to be emotionally attached to the feelings of self-criticism and self-rejection. An emotional attachment to those negative feelings can be powerful. If you keep seeing the irrational, emotional nature of this negativity, and you refrain from giving credence to the inner accusations of being flawed and unworthy, you're likely over time to weaken the hold these attachments have over you.

Tony: I try telling myself that I was/am a beautiful, whole, intelligent, loving, perfect human being just as I am—but this message always leads me to believe that my worth is contingent upon those qualities, which does not allow me to fill myself with an unconditional self-worth at the core. How do I establish my self-worth unconditionally if I don't believe that we're endowed with intrinsic worth by a creator/god?

Me: Don't try to establish your self-worth unconditionally. That's too difficult. You'll only feel frustrated. You've framed your situation in such a way that you create a sense of helplessness, which means you're likely entangled in an unresolved attachment to helplessness (inner passivity). Just live your life with the growing awareness of the nature of your inner conflicts and the negative emotions to which you're attached. In your case, it appears that you're also attached to feeling that you have little worth or value. You may be using a defense, called a "negative pseudo-moral," to cover up awareness of this. The defense would make the case, bitterly and unconsciously: "You see, father, I'm just being what you said I was—some useless person with no value." If you don't see through the defense, you can become stuck at this painful inner level.

Tony: Where does a human's worth come from, and is there a way to love yourself unconditionally without assuming the existence of a deity?

Me: A sense of worth and self-love comes when we clear away our entanglement in unresolved negative emotions. Feeling your value and worth is your birthright, but it's not handed to you on a silver platter. You have to do the inner work of clearing out the dregs and debris in the psyche. Many people believe in God largely because, through inner weakness, they're dependent on feeling validated and loved by God. As we're becoming stronger, we're not as emotionally dependent on feeling love from outside sources. Our growing connection with our authentic self infuses us with love. We become naturally loving and compassionate, and the more we spread these feelings around the more they grow in us.

I believe in the importance of our evolving consciousness which grows as we acquire self-knowledge. It's through evolving consciousness that we know the truth of our goodness and value. As we feel our own intrinsic value more deeply, we can feel the intrinsic value in others and in all life. This awareness leads us deeper into truth and reality. At this point, you're on your own, psychologically-speaking. You decide what's true with respect to God, and you live at peace with your truth.

Again, when you say "love yourself unconditionally," you might be setting yourself up for failure. It's such a difficult goal that you might never live up to it, and that could translate for you into an impression of being weak, helpless, and flawed. In this way, you might be making an unconscious choice to continue experiencing yourself through self-doubt and an inner sense of nonbeing.

Tony: What messages can I feed myself to combat a feeling of chronic emptiness and inadequacy?

Me: Don't feed yourself messages. Just look for awareness and self-knowledge through an understanding of how you're holding on to old painful impressions of yourself. These painful impressions are false readings of your true nature. Once you see and understand how, through inner conflict, you produce negative experiences, good feelings will follow automatically as your birthright.

Tony: Thank you for your thoughts or suggestions.

Me: You're welcome. I'm sorry that your father was emotionally abusive toward you. If he couldn't respect you, it means he was unable to respect himself. Now you can do for yourself what he was unable to do for you (and also for himself.) Even though your father was abusive, you can have a great and happy life. Your challenge is to learn how to let go of the ways in which you continue to live with (and are emotionally identified with) the negative feelings that your father had for you and for himself.

98 . **Enjoy the Quality of Your Consciousness**

Why don't we feel more simple pleasure from being alive and conscious in a fascinating world? That has to be one of life's great enigmas. We can feel pleasure easily enough when we're stimulated by art, literature, movies, sports events, relationships, sex, food, alcohol, and racy cars. We have a hard time, though, feeling pleasure from everyday, moment-to-moment experience.

These plain, old everyday moments are often taken for granted. Or they're overrun by worries and considerations, regrets and fears, toils and troubles, and desires and cravings. We chase after stimulation, jumping on life's speedy twirling roller-coaster rides while missing the magical-mystery train that chugs out of our station every morning.

Basically, we block access to everyday pleasure because, unconsciously, we're producing too much displeasure. I've been writing about this all along, and here I'll try to frame it with some different words and perspective.

We automatically start to feel more pleasure from daily life as soon as we stop producing displeasure. The displeasure is produced when, unconsciously, we recycle and replay old unresolved emotions. Once we turn off this inner misery-machine, we enhance the quality of our consciousness and we can feel a higher degree of moment-to-moment pleasure. We also stop taking life for granted because the quality of our consciousness attunes us to the richness of the here-and-now.

We can bring the pleasure to a higher level by fine-tuning our consciousness and aligning ourselves with a sense of purpose. Stephen Pinker, Harvard psychology professor and author, put it this way: "I would argue that nothing gives life more purpose than the realization that every moment of consciousness is a precious and fragile gift." In his statement, replace the word *purpose* with the word *pleasure*. Purpose and pleasure, in my mind go together. I have purpose behind my writing, and the act of writing with purpose brings me great pleasure. I'm doing the best I can in this moment, for myself and for others, and the feeling is exhilarating. Great satisfaction and inner peace abide long after the exhilaration has passed.

We don't need, though, to have a particular purpose in order to feel fulfilled. We can experience pleasure when we see a tree or when we look at an apple or a bird. Such pleasure can sometimes be quite intense, and it's more dependably available to us through the quality of our consciousness. We monitor or record the moment through attention and appreciation. The being that does the monitoring and the recording is awake, alert, and hungry for pleasure. We possess in this moment the power to feel the thrill of wonderment in a grain of sand. This capacity is enhanced by the beneficial effect of insight that frees us from the old attachments to negative emotions. Rising consciousness produces pleasure in the form of inner peacefulness, enhanced self-regulation, freedom from negativity, discernment and compassion, appreciation of beauty, and knowing of oneness. What is it we're most grateful for in this moment? What is bringing us all this pleasure? The quality of our consciousness.

We can link pleasure to all our qualities—integrity, goodness, sincerity, honesty, generosity, and capacity for self-regulation—by registering the pleasure, meaning that we consciously note it and make an intention to continue feeling it. Pleasure is obviously also available through our health, wonder, and joy.

To raise our consciousness, we have to keep coming back to how we produce *dis*pleasure. We produce displeasure in thousands of ways. Consider, as one example, our feelings on walking or driving past a homeless man. We would be suffering needlessly if we were to identify with the pain he might be feeling: unworthy, rejected, betrayed, or abandoned. When we identify in this way, we're not producing true empathy. What we're producing is self-centered; we're connecting through someone else with what's unresolved in us. This will produce confusion, anxiety, and guilt. As a society, we're less capable of dealing with the problem of homelessness when we operate at this level.

We could also unconsciously refuse to register the existence of the homeless person, as if he were invisible. Such blindness would mirror some degree of disconnect with our self, meaning the extent to which we aren't fully registered with our own existence.

Compassion, like love, is associated more with pleasure than with emotional pain. Through compassion, we can experience the homeless man in our heart without any suffering on our part. We may or may not decide to be generous and give him some money or later donate funds to a homeless shelter. Yet our fullest compassion and generosity derive from seeing the man's humanity and feeling comfortable enough in ourselves to share a moment of connection with him. We see him as a fellow creature rather than as a negative projection that's based on some unresolved issue in our psyche.

The nature of our consciousness may be the most important subject facing humanity. Here is how neuroscientist Daniel Bor, author of *The Ravenous Brain*," explains it:

> On a personal level, consciousness is where the meaning to life resides. All the moments that matter to us, from falling in love to seeing our child's first smile . . . are obviously conscious

events. If none of these events were conscious, if we weren't conscious to experience them, we'd hardly consider ourselves alive—at least not in any way that matters. . . Our consciousness is the essence of who we perceive ourselves to be. It is the citadel for our senses, the melting pot of thoughts, the welcoming home for every emotion that pricks or placates us. For us, consciousness simply is the currency of life.[106]

Despite his eloquence, Bor skims around on the surface of the subject. Like Richard Friedman,[107] he believes[108] that the role of the *unconscious* mind has been overestimated. Yet is it not perhaps egotistic—or at least biased in favor of humankind's "supreme" mental prowess—to state so emphatically that this is so, especially when the world is awash in misery, folly, and self-defeat? The influence of our unconscious mind is, in fact, much more appreciated when, in courage and humility, we expose the vital self-knowledge that we have so strenuously refused to acknowledge.

In the above excerpt, Bor says, "Our consciousness is the essence of who we perceive ourselves to be." I believe it's more helpful and insightful to say, "Our lack

---

[106]

http://www.slate.com/articles/health_and_science/science/2012/09/consciousness_science_and_ethics_abortion_animal_rights_and_vegetative_state_debates_.single.html

[107]

http://www.nytimes.com/2011/01/18/health/views/18mind.html?_r=3&n=Top%2fNews%2fScience%2fColumns%2fMind&

[108]

http://www.slate.com/articles/health_and_science/science/2012/09/consciousness_science_and_ethics_abortion_animal_rights_and_vegetative_state_debates_.single.html of consciousness produces a false or limited perception of who we are." With limited consciousness, we experience ourselves through narcissism, vanity, victimhood, and entitlement. Such consciousness is not the *essence* of who we are. It's more like the *illusion* of who we are.

We need to become smarter and wiser to deal with the world's increasingly complex challenges. History at its best tells the story of us getting to know ourselves more fully, art at its best captures the joy of creativity, life at its best produces adventures in growing consciousness, and psychology at its best challenges us to become truly great through humility and inner freedom.

Consciousness, rather than power or wealth, also produces the pleasure of being ourselves and living free in ourselves. When we're more conscious, when our openness to life has been enhanced by vital self-knowledge, we're less egotistical, less likely to abuse power or hoard wealth, and more likely to care about the well-being of others. Typically, people who are not working on becoming wiser and more evolved do not pay any heed to consciousness, and they miss seeing its vital role in helping them evolve and in aiding us all to fashion a better world.

Albert Einstein a century ago ushered in a new consciousness of physical space. Now we need to acquire a new consciousness of inner space to help us journey onward successfully.

99 . Teach Your Children Well

America's future is at risk if schools do not improve, says a report published by the Council on Foreign Relations, a research and policy organization.[109] This warning, in my opinion, ought to make note of the dangers to the nation and the world if psychological education does not improve.

Superior education teaches self-knowledge. Such teaching penetrates into the psyche or unconscious mind, making conscious what has previously been unconscious. This self-knowledge is needed to break through the thick clouds of unknowing and self-doubt that trouble so many children. It's also what adults need to navigate through complex, perilous times.

Higher learning is fundamentally developmental, write Richard P. Keeling and Richard H. Hersh in *We're Losing Our Minds: Rethinking American Higher Education*. Such learning, say the authors, "inspires, reinforces, and reflects the growth and maturation of the learner as a whole human being."[110] This learning is not limited to the acquisition of new information. Rather, "it is centered in the potential for change in the learner as a result of engagement with new knowledge and experiences."

Keeling and Hersh are writing about education at the college and university levels. Yet, of course, children at

---

[109] http://www.nytimes.com/2012/03/20/education/panel-says-schools-failings-could-threaten-economy-and-national-security.html
[110] Keeling, Richard P; Hersh, Richard H. *We're Losing Our Minds: Rethinking American Higher Education*. New York: Palgrave Macmillan, 2011.

elementary levels can also experience learning as a transformative process. That will certainly be true if they are taught the basics of how emotional suffering and self-sabotage are created and held in place in our psyche.

If we could put our psyche under a high-powered microscope, we would be stunned by the extent of the inner cognitive and emotional processing that our naked eye (common sense) knows nothing about. Our psyche is a reservoir of positive and negative emotions, and from it arises mental and emotional processing that's contaminated by inner conflict, irrationality, egotism, passivity, and aggression.

What is it that needs to be taught? Let's look at examples from everyday life. For instance, how many jealous people know that they're strongly tempted to indulge in the unresolved negative emotions of rejection and betrayal? How many compulsive gamblers know that they're unconsciously addicted to the feeling of losing? How many envious people are aware that they're emotionally attached to the feeling of being deprived or refused? How many greedy people know their greed covers up their entanglement in feelings of having little intrinsic value? How many angry people are conscious of the fact that they use their anger to cover up their readiness to indulge in feelings of being victimized, oppressed, or insulted? How many fearful people know that their fear is usually not based on reality factors in their environment, but instead is based, in large measure, on their fear of their inner critic and their lingering emotional memories of childhood helplessness and powerlessness? How many addictive personalities can see that their emotional attachment to unresolved inner passivity is stonewalling self-regulation? This list could go on and on.

This is not rocket science. Young people can acquire this knowledge when it is presented with sufficient clarity. Here are examples of simple clarity: the jealous person wants love but expects betrayal—sure enough, she provokes her partner into betraying her; a compulsive gambler wants to win but expects to lose—soon he's mortgaging his house to pay his gambling debts; the envious person wants to get some cherished object, yet inwardly she circulates the pain of not having it—and often she chooses an object that's beyond reach; a greedy person wants riches in order to feel more important, substantial, and valuable—yet the riches produce a deeper emptiness in him; an angry person demands justice, yet goes on feeling victimized through impressions of injustice; a fearful person buys a gun for personal protection—yet still his inner fear remains fixated on prospects of being a victim of crime, terrorist attacks, or Armageddon.

I remember being taught a few basics of psychoanalysis when in high-school in the late 1950s. I distinctly remember being intrigued even while somewhat befuddled by the subject. I was somehow comforted and reassured by this knowledge about the ego, id, and superego. The knowledge helped me to demystify my mind, and it gave me a comforting sense of having some regulation over my frail emotions, along with a passing, nodding acquaintance of my elusive self. Unfortunately, the subject was taught to us only for a few days and then left behind.

Educators do try to produce awareness and self-esteem in young people, but not by teaching them the basic principles of depth psychology. Instead, they often offer unearned praise that gives kids an inflated sense of their abilities and misrepresents their knowledge and skill level. Psychologists are part of the problem. They have stubbornly refused, individually and collectively, to agree upon the basic psychological truths that could be presented to children as a course of study beginning in early grades. (See "Three Great Truths from Psychology.") Psychologists as a group have also been too passive in not insisting that psychological insight be taught effectively in our schools. Without top-notch psychological education, how can our children raise the level of human consciousness and help us to avoid ongoing self-sabotage and impending calamity?

Voices of resistance will arise to oppose any educational initiatives that threaten narrow belief systems. The psychological community, by uniting in common purpose, can counteract this resistance by speaking with power and wise authority, while communicating the value and necessity of acquiring essential self-knowledge.

Such a project could produce a textbook of the finest insight and wisdom, written with great skill to communicate the knowledge that, because of psychological resistance, can be challenging to learn. What is this vital knowledge that needs to be taught in our schools? Some of that wisdom might include the following precepts from depth psychology.

Lesson 1: Much of what goes on in our emotional life is unconscious. We react to events and situations based on our conscious or unconscious memories and associations. We repeat and recycle painful emotions that are unresolved from our past, no matter how painful or self-defeating they may be. Hence, it's vitally important to become more conscious of the issues, motivations, and intentions behind our impulses, thoughts, actions, and feelings.

Lesson 2: Strength can manifest as physical power and athletic ability. It can also manifest as mental prowess that can solve complex problems. Yet it may be that the greater strength is emotional. This is the strength to avoid, with some degree of success, becoming upset, frightened, stubborn, or angry when someone is being inconsiderate, mean, or rejecting toward us. We learn about our emotional weaknesses—particularly our sensitivities to feeling deprived, refused, controlled, rejected, criticized, and devalued—with the aim of overcoming them.

Lesson 3: Often we treat others the way we treat our own self. We can be mean to ourselves through our inner critic, the part in us that's habitually insensitive, demeaning, and aggressive. We're capable of tormenting ourselves for the tiniest mistakes through this agency or drive that operates in our psyche. Meanwhile, if we're also mean to others, we likely have someone in our life who is (or has been) mean or insensitive to us.

Lesson 4: Feeling like a victim can lead to a self-defeating state of mind. True, there are some genuine victims of unfortunate circumstances. But often we embellish or exaggerate the feeling, partly because we make an emotional association with the helplessness and vulnerability we felt as young children. We tend to identify with people who might feel helpless, criticized, rejected, and unworthy, because these are negative emotions we're prepared to stir up in ourselves.

Thinking like a victim has its source in our emotional attachments to these negative emotions. Feeling like a victim, we're more likely to draw bad things our way.

Lesson 5: Meanness, malice, and bullying are aspects of an unevolved human nature. These behaviors exist because people haven't learned how to control or regulate their own negativity and aggression. The perpetrators of unkindness and abuse are responsible for curbing that behavior, while those who feel themselves to be recipients of such negativity also are encouraged to acquire the emotional strength, in the form of verbal skills and other resources, to avoid making themselves easy targets.

Lesson 6: Growing in wisdom means we no longer identify with our mind, body, personality, possessions, skills, and athletic prowess. While we should feel good, of course, about our qualities and abilities, we want to understand that our essential being—the consciousness at the core of our existence—is the source of our greatest happiness, fulfillment, and wisdom. That core value already exists inside us. Our task is to help that light become brighter and brighter.

Other important precepts can be taught to children. Knowing ourselves more deeply and profoundly, we access wisdom, emotional strength, and the power of self-regulation. We'll be planting the seeds for peace and harmony in coming generations.

100 . Our Global Strategy for Self-Defeat

Through depth psychology, we can see a connection between future decline and the inner landscape of the mind. As such, it's possible we're acting out a Global Strategy for self-defeat, creating a world of such complexity that we're finally—in homage to inner passivity—overwhelmed and destroyed by it.

Science fiction has certainly explored the theme of artificially created life-forms acquiring power over us, either through hostile takeovers (cybernetic revolts) or through our passive corroboration with artificial intelligence.

Instead of losing our autonomy to androids and robots, we're talking here about being defeated by the complexity of global operating systems such as the ones that govern economics and finance. Such self-defeat may already be upon us. The global economic system is dependent on energy sources that produce climate change. It's a system that's contaminated by arcane financial derivatives that make up galaxies of debt. We're also economically dependent on jobs and profits from the production and proliferation of high-tech weapons, which makes the road to world peace increasingly complicated. Complexity is growing exponentially. Even in health care, the prescribing of drugs has become a complex calculation and guessing-game involving potential side-effects, contraindications, and questions of efficacy. As physicist and author Stephen Hawking says, we have entered "the century of complexity."

What agency representing our common well-being has the power and resources to oversee and understand, let alone regulate, all the offshoots of this labyrinthine activity? Is the U.S. government, as a central intelligence constitutionally charged with practicing wise oversight, the last bastion of national and global protection? The U.S. government, however, has been discouraged from prosecuting possible wrongdoers in the 2008 financial collapse because of the complexity involved, which includes political and economic fallout. Such paralysis not only fails to reform the system but can obviously be damaging to the values and morale of society.

We get little guidance from our brightest people. Highly specialized experts are breaking down our knowledge-base into smaller and smaller units. They become experts in tiny slivers of information, and we start to lose focus on the bigger picture. "You can see this retreat into specialized, impenetrable verbal enclaves in every academic department across the country," writes author and activist Chris Hedges.[111] "People learn to bluff their way through, day to day," writes columnist David Brooks. "Experts don't really understand the complex things going on in their own companies. Traders don't understand how their technological tools really work. Programmers may know their little piece of code, but they don't have a broader knowledge of what their work is being used for."[112]

---

[111] http://www.truthdig.com/report/item/20081208_hedges_best_brightest/P100c

[112] http://www.nytimes.com/2014/04/11/opinion/brooks-the-moral-power-of-curiosity.html?_r=0

A deep menace hovers over this question of how we appear to be creating unmanageable complexity. All of us, not just the managers of our social and economic operating systems, contribute to the self-defeat. We all possess a psyche that's familiar and comfortable with feeling passive. We can, for instance, quickly become passive to any new technology, meaning we become enthralled or enchanted with it to the point that the new systems or devices intrude to a pronounced extent into our consciousness in a manner that is potentially self-defeating. This behavior is identified in the book, *iDisorder: Understanding Our Obsession with Technology and Overcoming its Hold on Us* (Palgrave Macmillan, New York, 2012). Ideally, we want to keep such objects or systems in perspective. They're just curiosities, delights, and tools to ease our way along destiny's path. We need to know that egotism, narcissism, and a sense of entitlement encourage us to create operating systems that mirror a grandiose self-image.

In *Willful Blindness: Why We Ignore the Obvious at Our Peril*, Margaret Heffernan ponders the perils of complexity:

> As I've watched BP [British Petroleum] wrestle with its operational issues, I've begun to wonder whether we now have organizations that are simply too complex to manage. There's a whole army of complexity consultants who seem to revel in the sheer difficulty we have created for ourselves. After John Browne left BP and the company sat down to try to analyze what had gone so horribly wrong, a kind of intellectual hubris that, incredible as it may seem, saw the ability to manage internal complexity as a source of

competitive advantage. This is Daedalus gone mad. Instead of worshipping complexity, we need to challenge it.[113]

BP is not the only company in love with complexity, Heffernan writes. "Many organizations view their own impenetrability as a feat of fantastic intellectual curiosity. In reality, it's a huge cause of blindness and explains why, when such companies get into trouble, they can't find their way out of it."

Such complexity produces an impression of being overwhelmed. We're induced to replay and recycle this old feeling because of our unevolved human nature. Because we act out whatever is unresolved within us, we would be unconsciously tempted to produce that effect of feeling overwhelmed. Behind an idealized self-image, we may be acting out, in the name of progress, an elaborate cover-up for self-sabotage.

As long as we're managing "to ride the wave" of a complex system, we can feel intoxication and grandiosity. We're identifying with the alleged magnificence of the complex system. Our inner weakness, particularly inner passivity and its accompanying self-doubt, makes the intoxication so appealing. This arrangement is unstable. Since we act out what's unresolved, we're fated to dip back into a state of helplessness that produces fear, panic, and painful self-defeat.

The existential psychologist Rollo May warned decades ago that we have "overrationalized" our society,

---

[113] Heffernan, Margaret. *Willful Blindness: Why We Ignore the Obvious at Our Peril.* New York: Walker and Company, 2011. 243.

extracted the mystery, and left ourselves with only a small part of our imagination and intelligence to deal with life. "Humanity will become so lacking in inner resources that we might as well die anyway, May wrote. "It's a kind of mass suicide." Our expanded imagination and integrity inform us that the quality of our consciousness far surpasses in satisfaction and value the playthings of the world. Just as an intelligence agency needs good information from its sources, we need to drink from the cool depths of our psyche.

Living unconsciously is like living in a totalitarian state. When we live with insufficient interest in what makes us tick, we're accepting some degree of inner tyranny and are susceptible to the propaganda of self-deception. Self-knowledge, our chronometer of inner navigation, can help us as a species to find our way forward. With self-knowledge, we refuse to crash on the shoals of fate. Instead, we set course for the distant shores of destiny.

101. **Welcome Aboard the Voyage of Self-Discovery**

Centuries ago, explorers launched the Age of Discovery. Now it's time to launch the Age of Self-Discovery. Our vessel is in need of favorable winds. Storm clouds of worldwide calamity are gathering on the horizon.

Climate change and nuclear weapons proliferation are two thunderheads of approaching destruction. Humanity's response to these dangers has amounted to "the social psychosis of denial," as one social reformer calls it.[114] Psychologists have other names—learned helplessness, normalcy bias, and motivated blindness—for our tendency to deny approaching or existing danger. We're likely to deny reality to the degree that we're in denial of important aspects of our human nature. As columnist David Brooks puts it, ". . . the most seductive evasion is the one that leads us to deny the underside of our own nature."[115]

If we deny our own nature, how can we expect to save Nature? If we fail to appreciate our own nature, how will we even want to protect Nature? If we don't care to know ourselves, we won't care enough about saving our planet.

Our better nature, our courageous self, is entangled in the conflict between inner aggression (the superego or inner critic) and inner passivity (the unconscious or subordinate ego). Humanity hasn't broken out of widespread neurosis because we're trapped in this inner conflict. We're afraid to make many kinds of decisions, especially ones requiring courage and inner fortitude, because our authoritarian superego challenges us and sends us scuttling back into inner passivity. Bullied by inner aggression and enfeebled by inner passivity, we absorb the bile of the superego: disapproval, harassment, disgust, and mockery.

In this conflict between inner aggression and inner passivity, we unwittingly end up representing one side or the other. We feel that we're locating our true north

---

[114] http://www.commondreams.org/view/2011/11/10-8
[115] http://www.nytimes.com/2011/11/15/opinion/brooks-lets-all-feel-superior.html?hp

with our own thoughts, words, or feelings, when instead we're drifting south, expressing only the defensiveness of inner passivity or the aggressiveness of the inner critic. Meanwhile, through our ego (the limited self that serves as our mental operating system), it feels to us that our thoughts and feelings are our own true voice rather than the voices of inner conflict.

We can feel that our inner critic is a legitimate conscience, a true system of navigation, when in fact it's mostly a demanding, demeaning inner tyrant. Through inner passivity, we allow the inner critic to be captain of our ship. Meanwhile, the voice of inner passivity talks us out of being brave or assertive. Now we're inauthentic. Our moral compass oscillates aimlessly. If we can't captain our own little vessel, we'll be excess baggage on the voyage of life, easily and quickly jettisoned when the storms come.

When not being passive, we swing over to the other side and become inappropriately aggressive. Much of the time, as mentioned, our consciousness is entangled in a conflict-ridden dialogue in which inner aggression *accuses* and inner passivity *defends*. When our intelligence penetrates into the core of this conflict, we discover our authentic self, our legitimate inner authority, awaiting its release. As our self emerges and grows, the conflict itself dies away because our awareness nullifies those dynamics.

Through self-discovery we realize that we're not just our own captain but, collectively, all crew-mates in the same boat. We find our greatest pleasure in travelling together, pulling together, seeking our destiny on safer shores.

Our authentic self is more highly refined than either our ego or our personality. Like democracy, it represents a higher form of government (self-government) that requires our participation in its evolvement. Ages ago, power was vested in monarchs, and their "divine right" to rule was considered a branch of the divine rule of God. Now we're trying through democracy to invest the power in the people. But people have to be evolving. We have to feel our right to rule. That *right* is legitimized through the expansion of our inner freedom. That freedom is acquired as we calm the storms of inner conflict and establish our authentic self in the pilot-house.

EPILOGUE

102. The Love Song of the Self

The character Prufrock in T.S. Eliot's ironically titled great poem, "The Love Song of J. Alfred Prufrock," personifies the painful plight of people who are unable to connect with their authentic self. Contemplating "a hundred indecisions," Prufrock saw the moment of his greatness flicker: he "lingered in the chambers of the sea" and drowned in his self-doubt.

Prufrock lived in the shadow of his self, measuring out his life "with coffee spoons." What then is this self—or Self—that supposedly rescues us from a life half-lived? We catch glimpses of it when our mind clears and life feels like silk upon our skin. Yet it's not always easy to describe this core or essence that makes us feel at home in our body and in the world. So let's heed Prufrock's summons (though not his fate): "Oh, do not ask, 'What is it?' Let us go and make our visit."

We can note, for starters, that the role of the self tends to be overlooked in mental health treatments. Writing in *The New York Times Magazine*, Linda Logan describes her treatments when hospitalized several times over a period of many years for a debilitating mood disorder: "Everything was scrutinized except the transformation of my self and my experience of its loss." If anything, she writes, "it seems that psychiatry is moving away from a model in which the self could be discussed. For many psychiatrists, mental disorders are medical problems to be treated with medications, and a patient's crisis of self is not very likely to come up in a 15-minute session with a psychopharmacologist."[116]

The self is, as literary critic Allan Bloom put it, "the mysterious, free, unlimited center of our being." For science, the self is mysterious indeed, an annoying phantom that won't sit still under a microscope. Neuroscience sees the self, like the mind, as a mental neurological map comprising substance, function, and activity through which we identify ourselves as a single organism. Yet no single brain structure embodies the self. From the perspective of neuroscience, the self is the ghost in the machine.

Science tends to be "into" the frustration of not knowing, while the self is "into" the joy of the mystery.

Someone asked me, "Can the self be buried alive in the unconscious?" That's an interesting way to put it. As I see it, the self is like a seed buried under inner conflict, and that seed can more easily grow when we till the soil with insight and water it with self-knowledge.

For our purposes, the precise nature of the self is not the main concern. What really matters is our experience of being that self. Is there a sense that we're growing and making progress with our self-development? Is the experience of our self pleasant or unpleasant? To what degree does that experience help us in regulating our emotions and behaviors? Does it feel that we've finally found what we've been searching for? As we connect

---

[116] http://www.nytimes.com/2013/04/28/magazine/the-problem-with-how-we-treat-bipolar-disorder.html?pagewanted=all&_r=0

more with this self, we feel more pleasure in (and gratitude for) the simple fact of our existence.

How can we establish a good relationship with our self? Many methods are known to be helpful, including techniques for stress reduction and relaxation as well as yoga, meditation, mindfulness, self-study, and psychotherapy. When we learn this depth psychology, we can embark on a rescue mission to liberate our self from the underworld of the psyche. Our self has been buried there, something of a seedling, under painful emotional attachments and inner conflict that go back to childhood.

The self is not self-centeredness, of course. Many of us, like children who are naturally self-centered, put our own existence at the center of the world. The world spins, it feels, around us. We smuggle our "I" into just about every experience and situation, and take our subjective impressions as the sole yardstick of reality. The unconscious feeling is, "Only by putting the accent on myself can I protect myself from being a lesser or a worthless person or even a non-entity." We put this accent on ourselves because, deeper down, our connection with our self is weak. In this weakness, we feel the need to produce an artificial sense of self, a false self that's often dependent on external validation and materialistic trappings for its sense of being.

Through the self, we experience a deep trust in our goodness and value. We manage to avoid being triggered by situations that in the past would have sent us tumbling painfully into withdrawal, bitterness, anger, and self-defeating behaviors. Our self, rich in emotional connection to our intrinsic value and goodness, banishes loneliness and depression. Rid of self-centeredness, we experience empathy and compassion.

We can now see others in their own light, without judgment, without projecting our issues on to them. We're less likely to misinterpret the intentions of others. We don't identify with the neurotic suffering of others. Guilt, shame, and fearfulness have largely departed. Even when the world seems to be having a panic attack, our self maintains our courage and upholds our integrity. In the search for meaning, the self is itself the meaning.

In this process of self-development, we also create an abode of privacy and inner freedom that can't be compromised by government spying and the marketing intrusions of advanced surveillance and tracking technologies. We're not afraid of this paranoid scrutiny or radical data-collecting. We've already leaped beyond it, and the stragglers will follow along behind. The self establishes an inner democracy of peace and harmony, and it's thereby the great champion of democracy everywhere.

Through the self, we can experience the joy of doing our best, even though we might not succeed. The self can handle the present moment. It embraces the present moment and isn't overwhelmed by it. It's strong enough to seize the moment. Discover your self, and all else that matters to you will be known.

At a more advanced stage of our development, we can move beyond our mental landscape. Our consciousness acquires a vaporous softness, and we're not afraid to drift like fog in and out of emptiness and nothingness. Existence just is, independent of me, yet counting on me. Consciousness is our home, and hence we're at home with the known and the unknown. Our one desire is to preserve the consciousness that our precious self illuminates.

J. Alfred Prufrock, archetype of suffering humankind, asked anxiously, "When I am pinned and wriggling on the wall . . . how should I begin . . . how should I presume?" This representative man, despite poetic flair, allowed life to defeat him. We know better. Through inner knowledge that liberates the self, life becomes the victory that was our birthright all along.

Printed in Great Britain
by Amazon